iChoose2
Love My Life®

a one-year journey toward living a life you love

Written by the iBloom Team:

Kelly Thorne Gore, Lori Burrell, Leigh Ann Napier,

Betsy Ringer, Gena Sorenson, and Jane Thorne

www.ibloom.us

iChoose2 Love My Life®: a one-year journey toward living a life you love

Copyright © 2011 by iBloom

Published by iBloom, LLC
Lexington, KY 40555
www.ibloom.us

Requests for information should be addressed to:
iBloom, PO Box 55131, Lexington, KY 40555

Cover by Sarah Erdmann

ISBN: 978-0-9826626-3-2

In Loving Memory of Bill Thorne

Bill Thorne was the father of Kelly Thorne Gore, iBloom's Founder & President. After a courageous battle with cancer, Bill met Jesus face-to-face on Saturday, April 16, 2011.

Bill started the iChoose2 Love My Life journey while he was in the midst of chemotherapy and radiation treatments. The iChoose2 Love My Life journey radically changed Bill's perspective and ultimately how he lived his final days.

Acknowledgements

Lord, thank you for entrusting this gift to us and guiding us along this journey. Thank you for the life experiences and lessons that made this book possible. May you use this book to inspire and equip every woman in the world to live a life she truly loves!

Thank you to our family and friends for their continual support and encouragement. Without them the work we do would not be possible.

Thank you to our incredible support team Jon Gore, Sherry Shumate, Sarah Erdmann, and Kathy Hadzibajric for their diligent work behind the scenes to make this book a reality.

Contents

Go to http://ibloom.co/ichoose2 to join a community of women from around the world on this life-changing iChoose2 Love My Life Journey.

Meet the iBloom Team

Kelly Thorne Gore, iBloom Founder & President
kelly@ibloom.us

Kelly and the iBloom team are on a mission to inspire and empower every woman on the planet to live a life she LOVES (and ultimately live a life that honors God)! Kelly is passionate about living life intentionally and making each day count. Kelly enjoys spending quality time with her husband Jon, daughter Sophie, family, and friends. She's a girly girl, loves bright cheery colors, gerbera daisies, University of Kentucky Basketball, and Tyler Perry Movies!

Lori Burrell, iBloom Associate
lori@ibloom.us

Lori's favorite word is "joy" and she loves to help others seek and find it in their own lives. She is grateful that God is allowing her to pursue her passion of coaching women to live a life of no regret! Lori loves spending time with her 2 daughters, family, and friends. She also enjoys sunsets, reading, walking, and volunteering.

Leigh Ann Napier, iBloom Associate
leighann@ibloom.us

Leigh Ann is the Happy Marriage Planner on a mission to inspire every couple on the planet to have a happy, life-long marriage. She helps couples create a game plan to love each other for a lifetime, rather than just wing it after the honeymoon, and then cheers them on each step of the way. She and her husband Mike live in Lexington, KY where they are continually entertained by their two daughters Halle Kate and Kenley Jane.

Betsy Ringer, iBloom Associate
betsy@ibloom.us

Betsy is a Certified Personality Specialist, Speaker and Life Coach. She has been sharing her expertise with a wide variety of audiences for over 25 years. Through humorous and action-oriented messages you discover your design and how to shift from surviving to thriving. Her authored resources serve as a personal guide to help you flourish in your everyday living. She helps entrepreneurs establish themselves as the expert in their business or ministry by teaching them how to create their one powerful talk in a way that truly makes a difference. Her adventuresome spirit is contagious and you will certainly catch her zest for life.

Gena Sorenson
gena@ibloom.us

Gena is energetic, full of life, compassionate, peaceful and goal oriented. She is passionate about engaging in authentic relationships and serving others. She loves spending time with her husband, Justin and their dog, Lucy. In her spare time you can find her gardening, reading, and building relationships with friends. She is also very active in church ministry.

Jane Thorne
jane@ibloom.us

Jane loves working behind the scenes encouraging the iBloom team to have ripple effects that inspire women around the world. She handles the finances for iBloom, ships products, and is most fulfilled by the honor and privilege of praying for the needs of our iBloom community. Jane enjoys spending time with her family and friends and LOVES having "Sophie-time" with her new granddaughter.

iChoose2 Love My Life

For years you've longed for something that would jumpstart your journey toward living a life you *really* love. Finally, here's the motivation you need! This is a book written by a dedicated team of women who have a heart for helping others shift from surviving to thriving. Through this one-year journey, we want you to experience a life:

- Without regrets

- Where you intentionally invest in yourself

- Full of joy, purpose, and love

- Where you aren't just existing, but instead, living your legacy

Throughout the year as you make small changes at a determined and steady pace, you will be transformed. Our iBloom team of life coaches will be here to inspire and motivate you through each step of your journey. There is power in this little book and a whole lot of potential in you that is just waiting to get out!

This book will be your adventure guide for the next year. There are 52 entries- one entry per week for an entire year. You might be tempted to skip ahead, but don't do it! Our iBloom team has intentionally designed this journey as a one-year experience, so that you have a full week to make small, steady changes that will lead to true transformation. Be sure to write the answers to your coaching assignments in your book, so that you will be able to track your progress throughout the journey.

This is your opportunity to focus on yourself and become the woman you long to be. As your life coaches for this journey, we give you permission to really spend time investing in yourself over this next year.

This is your opportunity to move from ordinary to extraordinary and begin living a life you *truly* love!

This Week's Challenge:

The first step on your iChoose2 Love My Life journey is to take an honest look at your life today and then determine where you hope to be in the future.

My iChoose2 Love My Life journey begins on: _March 20, 2017_
_9:15 pm_

What is going well?

Eating healthy
Purposely not trying to be critical.

What is not going well?

I don't feel the joy as I used to. ....
Longing for a man, and to feel worthy -
yet knowing I am enough for God.
I feel I am negative all the time.
Worry so much
Feeling inadequate
things need to be my way or I get
angry.

13

What needs to change?

"Whoa is me" attitude!

One-year from today, when you complete this iChoose2 Love My Life journey, what do you hope will be different?

- Be Joyful again.
- Discerning + not just negative
- Other focused in a Godly way (not to prove I am good).
- Have a growing coaching business.
- Have a healthy inadequacy in God, not in every day life.
- Believe in my worth as a human.

#2:

iChoose2 Live Intentionally

Choosing to live intentionally is a conscious decision. It doesn't happen by chance. It means that you choose to live each of your days with intention and purpose. Living intentionally means having a vision and setting a course for your life. It implies that you have a sense of the direction.

Living intentionally is taking your priorities (those things you value most) and creating a plan that is flexible; it's like a road map showing you how to get from point A to Z. When you don't have a clear, pointed vision you tend to just drift through life - moving from one thing to another. It's like wanting to go to a state that you've never visited, but with no map. You may arrive there eventually but it will take much longer and the journey will be more difficult. But when you have a map, it makes the journey much easier and more comfortable and you can even stop whenever you want and enjoy the path along the way. Intentional Living is the map that you create for your life.

This Week's Challenge:

What 5 things do you value most?

1. _____

2. _____

3. _____

4. _____

5. _____

Journal:

Take a moment to look over your list. Are these 5 things currently incorporated into your daily life? Look at your schedule and spending habits from the past 30 days, is it obvious that these are the 5 things that you value most? If not, how can you begin to incorporate these values into your daily life?

_____

_____

_____

_____

_____

_____

_____

_____

_____

_____

_____

_____

_____

_____

_____

_____

_____

#3:

iChoose2 Have a Theme

Instead of making a new year's resolution, how about setting a THEME for your year? Choose a theme that reflects your assignment for this particular time of your life. Your THEME can be applied to many areas of your life and will allow some freedom for failure and the excitement of surprise.

Your THEME is not random. It may be balancing out your previous year or it may be something you see God leading you toward, or you might see a new direction emerging. For example, maybe last year was hectic and frazzled, so your THEME for this year might be Rest or Quiet. By focusing on Rest, you allow yourself to sit, to say "no" to a request, or go to bed earlier. Your health and spirit will be renewed and your life will be more fulfilled.

Maybe there is a need in your life for friends, better health or de-cluttering. Be positive and use words that will help you take action. For example, instead of having a theme of Making Friends, choose Be a Friend. That implies taking action that will most likely lead to connection with others. Some THEME ideas to get you thinking - Simplify, Adventure, Health, Move my Body, Write, Surrender, Laughter, Paint, Savor the Moments, or Discover my Passion.

This Week's Challenge:

Create a theme for this season of your life.

Coaching Assignment:

Take the following steps to identify a THEME for the year ahead:

Step #1: Picture your life being richer because of your attention to your theme. At the end of this year, what will make you smile as you look back over the year? What is your assignment for this particular time of your life? Ask God to give you direction in selecting a theme.

_____

_____

_____

_____

_____

_____

_____

_____

_____

_____

_____

_____

_____

_____

_____

Step #2: Write out several themes that seem to emerge from within. Give some thought to how they might be carried out in your day to day living. Is it a theme that can be realized in your ordinary routine as well as jump start you to try something new?

_____

_____

_____

_____

_____

_____

_____

Step #3: Select your theme. Embrace it. Be excited about it. Write it on several cards and place them in strategic places to remind yourself about your THEME. For example, place THEME cards on your bathroom mirror, over your kitchen sink, on your computer, hanging from the rear view mirror in your car, and wherever else you look frequently.

My Theme for this year is: _____

_____

Step #4: Give yourself permission to evaluate your theme quarterly. Is it still a good path for you? If not, change it. Or, recast the vision - how will it make your life better having allowed this theme to be carried out in your life?

#4:

iChoose2 Manage My Time

"Better three hours early than one minute too late"

William Shakespeare

You probably know someone who seems to be able to have all of their work done with plenty of time to spare. How do they do it? Many times, people assume that they must be smarter or more talented at the task, but it's probably more likely that the person has developed a skill of creating a schedule that allows them to work, to relax, to fix unpredictable problems, and still allow for some wiggle room to be available to others.

The first step to effective time management is to commit to a disciplined work ethic and have a "STOP" time each day. Yes, you need to work and do chores, but you also need to allow time to eat, sleep, exercise, decompress, talk with God, and serve others. It seems obvious that each day should have all of these, but you rarely find someone who can do it effectively. So, you need to say to yourself, "I promise to only work during my work time, and stop working at ____ o'clock."

The second step is to determine how long your daily tasks take to complete. People can create very detailed to-do lists, but rarely assign a time frame to that task. If you know that you have daily chores (ex. laundry) or activities (ex. exercise) to do, time how long they take to complete. If these are necessary chores and activities, then you know that you must set aside the total amount of time each day to do them.

The next step is to break-up large, abstract goals into short-term, concrete ones. If you know you need to complete a big project today, how long do you think that will take? One hour? Two hours? Five hours? If you don't know how long it will take, how will you know if you will have time to do anything else? People's to-do lists often include an abstract goal that has no real time frame (ex. "work on my project") rather than a smaller sub goal that chips away at the bigger one (ex. "brainstorm solutions," or "gather supplies"). The sub goals allow you to get the job done and to feel a sense of accomplishment that abstract goals cannot provide.

A trick to effective time management is to always **overestimate** how long the task will take until you can determine a realistic time frame. This increases the chances that you will finish early and be able to either reward yourself or begin on the work that needs to be done the next day.

If you are consistently finishing early, you will also find that your weekends can be spent enjoying your family and friends rather than catching up on what you couldn't finish. You will find that this strategy not only reduces the items on your to-do list, but that you actually get more done by the end of the week.

Finally, it is important to leave "wiggle room" between activities. Obstacles WILL get in the way of your planned schedule. By overestimating how long projects will take, and purposefully scheduling 1-2 hours of wiggle room into your schedule, you will have time to attend to unforeseeable problems rather than get frustrated that your schedule failed. Also, purposefully scheduling time to attend to unpredictable events makes you more inclined to have time to serve others and be available when they really need you.

This Week's Challenge:

Set your "STOP" time.

I promise to stop working every day this week at _____ o'clock, even if I have not completely finished everything on my list.

List your daily chores and activities and time how long they take this week. Use the table below to help you keep track:

Chore/Activity	It Takes This Long to Complete

Pick one, big project you have and break it into five smaller sub goals. Assign a time frame (in hours) to each piece. If you are tempted to state the time frame in days, it is too big and needs to be further reduced. Remember to overestimate how long you think it will take!

Project = _____

Sub goal #1 _____
This sub goal will take me _____ hours to finish.

Sub goal #2 _____
This sub goal will take me _____ hours to finish.

Sub goal #3 _____
This sub goal will take me _____ hours to finish.

Sub goal #4 _____
This sub goal will take me _____ hours to finish.

Sub goal #5 _____
This sub goal will take me _____ hours to finish.

Try creating a detailed schedule for ONE day this week. Assign a task for each hour of the day, include sleeping, eating, working, chores, exercising, family/friend time, and "wiggle room."

12:00-1:00   _____

1:00-2:00   _____

2:00-3:00   _____

3:00-4:00   _____

4:00-5:00   _____

5:00-6:00   _____

6:00-7:00   _____

7:00-8:00   _____

8:00-9:00   _____

9:00-10:00   _____

10:00-11:00   _____

11:00-12:00   _____

12:00-1:00   _____

1:00-2:00   _____

2:00-3:00   _____

3:00-4:00   _____

4:00-5:00   _____

5:00-6:00   _____

6:00-7:00   _____

7:00-8:00   _____

8:00-9:00   _____

9:00-10:00   _____

10:00-11:00   _____

11:00-12:00   _____

No one will do this completely right at first, but you may have done better than expected. Journal about the issues that came up with this schedule, the wins you had, and strategies you have for the next time you do this. You may also realize that you are taking on more than you should, and that some of these activities need to be eliminated, or the time working on them needs to be reduced.

_____

_____

_____

_____

_____

_____

_____

_____

_____

_____

_____

_____

_____

_____

_____

_____

_____

_____

#5:

iChoose2 Stop Procrastinating

Are you a procrastinator? Do you know what needs to be done, but instead of getting to work, you find yourself doing everything except what is most important? If this describes you, then you're not alone. However, this is your week to stop procrastinating.

There are three common reasons many people procrastinate: overanalyzing the task, feeling overwhelmed, or wanting it to be perfect.

Suggestions for overcoming procrastination:

- Each morning, assess your to-do list. What are the 2 most important things that need to be done that day? Then, get to work completing those tasks first. Once they are done, be sure to reward yourself.

- For big projects, do a brain dump by creating a list of all the components to your project. Prioritize your list by tasks that need to be completed first, even if they are the more difficult ones. Estimate how much time each task will take and then assign dates for when you'll have each task completed.

- Do a 60-minute blitz! Remove all the things that distract you (television, email, Facebook, phones, etc.) and focus 60-minutes of uninterrupted time working on your project.

- Have a deadline. You'll be amazed at how focused you'll be when you know your tasks have to be completed by a specific deadline.

This Week's Challenge:

In the table below, create a procrastination list - include things that you want (or need to do), but just haven't marked off your to do list. Then, choose to tackle at least 2 or 3 projects this week.

My Procrastination List:

Task	Goal Date	Finished!!

Before You Move Forward

Date: _____

Identify at least one thing that you accomplished this month as a result of doing the iChoose2 Love My Life journey.

_____

_____

_____

What went well this past month?

_____

_____

_____

What didn't you do, but intended to?

_____

_____

_____

What 3 things would you like to continue to implement?

1. _____

2. _____

3. _____

#6:

iChoose2 Be Grateful

"God gave you a gift of 86,400 seconds today.
Have you used one to say "thank you?"

William A. Ward

Being grateful begins with realizing how "full" your life is with "great" things! Gratitude begins with what's right in front of you and ripples out to your health, relationships, opportunities, material possessions, etc.

Even in the midst of challenges and trials, there is always room to be grateful. So, instead of focusing on what you don't have or on what is going wrong this week, choose to be grateful for God's abundant blessings in your life. Let this week be the beginning to developing a heart of gratitude.

This Week's Challenge:

Start a gratitude journal. Find a time each day (starting today!) to list at least 5 things you are grateful for- list more if you can! Your gratitude journal will become a great resource, especially for those days when "life happens" and you're feeling less than grateful. On those days, instead of creating your list, read back through your previous entries and be reminded of God's abundant blessings in your life.

#7:

iChoose2 Forgive

"To forgive is to set a prisoner free
and discover that the prisoner was you."

Louis B. Smedes

Have you been deeply hurt by the words or actions of someone? Perhaps you have an alcoholic parent, your spouse had an affair, or you felt abandoned by a friend when you needed her most. These wounds hurt and can often leave us feeling angry, resentful, and bitter.

Forgiveness doesn't mean that you forget how you were wronged. Instead it is a *decision* to release the anger, resentment, and bitterness you feel as a result of the wound. Forgiveness is more about you than the person who wronged you. By choosing to move beyond the negative feelings, you'll be able to release the control the person and the situation have over your life.

Just because you forgive someone doesn't mean they will change. Forgiveness isn't about trying to change the person who has wronged you. Instead forgiveness is your opportunity to replace those negative feelings that have controlled you for God's love, peace, and joy.

"Forgive, and you will be forgiven."
Luke 6:37

Journal:

Who do you have feelings of anger, resentment, or bitterness toward someone or a situation? If so, who do you need to forgive?

_____

_____

_____

_____

_____

_____

_____

This Week's Challenge:

Choose to forgive. Decide that you will no longer be controlled by the words or actions of someone else. Ask God to replace your feelings of anger, resentment, and bitterness with love, peace, and compassion.

Write a Forgiveness Letter to the person who has wronged you. This letter is your opportunity to work through the healing process. How has this person wronged you? What specifically are you forgiving them for right now? How will you move forward with your life as a result of releasing the control this person and/or situation has had over your life? Forgiveness is about you, so there is no need to send the letter to the person who has wronged you, instead slowly tear up the letter as a tangible way of releasing control and embracing forgiveness.

#8:

iChoose2 Be Optimistic

"A **pessimist** sees the difficulty in every opportunity;
an **optimist** sees the opportunity is every difficulty."

Winston Churchill

The dictionary defines optimism as "a disposition or tendency to look on the more favorable side of events or conditions and to expect the most favorable outcome." Whereas, pessimism is defined as, "the tendency to see, anticipate, or emphasize only bad or undesirable outcomes, results, conditions, problems, etc."

Philippians 2:14-16 (God's Word Translation) tells us to, "Do everything without complaining or arguing. Then you will be blameless and innocent. You will be God's children without any faults among people who are crooked and corrupt. You will shine like stars among them in the world as you hold firmly to the word of life."

This Week's Challenge:

Choose to be optimistic. Do everything without complaining, arguing, or criticizing. Refuse to be negative all week. Be the positive voice among your co-workers, family, and friends. Choose to see the good in each situation you encounter.

Choosing to be optimistic can be difficult, so tie a string around your finger as a visual reminder of your commitment to doing everything without complaining, arguing, or criticizing this week.

Meditate on this verse.

Philippians 4:8 (God's Word Translation) says, "Finally, brothers and sisters, keep your thoughts on whatever is right or deserves praise: things that are true, honorable, fair, pure, acceptable, or commendable."

Journal:

After you've completed your "refuse to be negative" week, come back and journal about your experience. How did you do? Did you find this challenge difficult?

_____

_____

_____

_____

_____

_____

_____

How can you replace pessimism with optimism on a daily basis?

_____

_____

_____

_____

_____

#9:

iChoose2 Be Joyful

"When you wish someone joy, you wish them peace, love, prosperity, happiness... all the good things."

Maya Angelou

"Joy is the feeling of grinning on the inside."

Melba Colgrove

Choosing to be joyful is pretty easy when everything is going well. But, choosing to be joyful during those difficult seasons of life can be quite challenging.

Unlike happiness, joy is not based on our circumstances. Happiness is something we feel. Joy is something we intentionally do. Happiness is fleeting. Joy is recognizing the depth of God's abundant blessings in your life, even through those most difficult seasons of life.

Choosing to be joyful doesn't mean being fake or acting like everything is perfect. Choosing joy is being able to see God's goodness, even when life is hard and messy.

Before your feet hit the ground each morning, choose joy. Then, continue to choose joy throughout your day. Being joy-filled or joyful is to live above your circumstances and to tap into the love and peace that can come only from God.

This Week's Challenge:

Create a Joy Board. Get a piece of poster board and some markers. Hang your joy board in a prominent place in your home (or office). Throughout the week, as you choose to be joyful, fill your poster board with quotes, scriptures, song lyrics, praises, pictures, etc. that remind you of God's goodness in your life. If you have a family at home or co-workers, invite them to participate with you.

Journal:

After you've spent the week filling up your Joy Board, come back and journal about your experience.

_____

_____

_____

_____

_____

_____

Use the space below, to duplicate your completed Joy Board, so that you're able to remember this experience when you re-read your book!

Before You Move Forward

Date: _____

Identify at least one thing that you accomplished this month as a result of doing the iChoose2 Love My Life journey.

_____

_____

_____

What went well this past month?

_____

_____

_____

What didn't you do, but intended to?

_____

_____

_____

What 3 things would you like to continue to implement?

1. _____

2. _____

3. _____

#10:

iChoose2 Embrace My Personality

Isn't it amazing how your friends, family members and co-workers are similar, but at the same time think and act so differently than you? Your personality is part of your design, your internal make-up. Over 2000 years ago, a physician named Hippocrates observed four distinct personality styles in people. Since then, many people have explored this interesting topic and found the information valuable in relating to others. (Littauer, 2006)

See if you can identify yourself:

- **Popular Sanguine** - "Let's do it the fun way!"
- **Perfect Melancholy** - "Let's do it the right way."
- **Powerful Choleric** - "Let's do it MY way."
- **Peaceful Phlegmatic** - "Let's do it the easy way."

You are designed in a specific way. Take some time to get to know your own personality. Sanguines are playful, make friends easily, and laugh a lot! Melancholies are generally organized, like having things done a certain way, and attend to details. A Choleric is usually dynamic, "in charge," and doesn't shy away from a good challenge. A person with a Phlegmatic personality can "go with the flow," is reliable and often has a dry sense of humor.

You see we all view life from a slightly different perspective. One is not right or wrong nor better than any other. Just different. This perspective is formed by the personality we were born with as well as where we were born, our family dynamics, education, birth order, and other influences. Many times people try to be like someone else rather than embracing their own personality. Of course it's okay to aspire to acquire good qualities we see in others, but we are most effective when we choose to nurture the valuable features of our own distinct personality.

Remember, one personality style is not better than another. We need all the styles. So get to know the people you interact with on a daily basis. Learn to appreciate their particular personality style. How can you adjust your own personality when you are communicating with them to make your interaction more effective? Do you need to talk less and listen more? Are they the kind of person who gets impatient with details and needs just the basic facts? Do they need you to be sensitive to their feelings? How can you show you value them for who they are?

Each personality style has strengths and weaknesses. The goal is NOT to be perfect but to know yourself well enough to cultivate your strengths. Know your strengths and let them shine through. Be aware of your weaknesses that tend to appear when you are stressed. Watch for them and choose to take care of your stress so your weaknesses will retreat. Be intentional about managing your strengths and weaknesses – it's a choice!

The table below lists common strengths and weaknesses for each personality type. Your goal is to embrace your own personality and to learn how to get along better with others!

Sanguine		Choleric	
Strengths	Weaknesses	Strengths	Weaknesses
Enjoys life	Dislikes routine	Leads confidently	Can't relax
Makes friends easily	Calendar too full	Decisive	Impatient
Optimistic	Gets distracted	Dynamic	Seizes authority
Expressive	Can talk too much	Accepts challenges	Misses details
Inspiring	Interrupts others	Sees big picture	Intimidating
Phlegmatic		Melancholy	
Strengths	Weaknesses	Strengths	Weaknesses
Steady, reliable	Procrastinates	Likes charts and graphs	Hard to please
Dry sense of humor	Stubborn	Conscientious	Overly sensitive
Considerate	Indecisive	Detail-oriented	Can be critical
Listens to others	Resists change	Follows the rules	Unforgiving
Relational	Not goal-oriented	Precise/Proper	Skeptical

This Week's Challenge:

Make a list of five of your strengths. You can use the table on the previous page to help you.

1. _____

2. _____

3. _____

4. _____

5. _____

How can you use your strengths in your:

Personal life?

_____

_____

Business?

_____

_____

Make a list of three weaknesses that you have noticed in yourself:

1. _____

2. _____

3. _____

Select one of your weaknesses and brainstorm how you can turn that into a strength.

#11:

iChoose2 Discover My Passions

What do you daydream about when you're stuck in traffic? What would you love to do even if you never got paid to do it? In other words, what makes you come alive? God placed passions in you and wants you to live life to the fullest!

Discover your passions so you can plan ways to live them out. You may be able to find an occupation that involves your passion(s), but this is not always the case. You may be one of the fortunate people who can incorporate your passion into your job. However, if you can't, you can still fulfill your passions with hobbies and volunteer opportunities. The important thing is to enjoy and include your passions in your life.

Be aware that certain seasons of your life may seem to neglect your passions. You may have a new baby, have a health situation, or other obligation that is taking up your time. While this can be frustrating, be assured a true passion will still be there when you can begin living it again!

Don't try to squelch a passion! You may have a deep longing to do an activity or serve a group that none of your family members or friends have the desire to do. Remember that you are unique; God created you to be you.

Coaching Assignment:

As a child:

What is something you dreamed of doing as an adult?

In your neighborhood, you were the kid who was known as the one who...

Now as an Adult:

What concern, cause or issue preoccupies your mind?

What do you LOVE doing for others?

Is there a group of people you're most drawn to (i.e. cancer patients, homeless, immigrants, women, kids, teens, etc.)

Someday, when things calm down, my house is clean and I'm relaxed I'm going to.....

If time, talent or resources were not an issue, what would you like to do?

This Week's Challenge:

Write a simple statement describing an area of passion:

_____

_____

_____

_____

What are 3 ways you can incorporate your passion into your life in the next month?

1. _____

_____

_____

_____

_____

2. _____

_____

_____

_____

_____

3. _____

_____

_____

_____

_____

#12:

iChoose2 Identify My Spiritual Gifts

Have you ever felt that you are serving or volunteering out of your comfort zone? Or maybe you felt that someone else could do a better job at a particular task? That's why it is so important to take the time to identify your Spiritual Gifts.

What is a spiritual gift? A spiritual gift is a particular competence that the Holy Spirit grants Christians so they can attend to the needs of others and support God's plan. Every Christian has at least one Spiritual Gift. Typical Gifts include: administration, evangelism, encouragement, faith, giving, helping, hospitality, knowledge, mercy, leadership, service, teaching, and wisdom. You can find more information about the Spiritual Gifts in the following Bible passages: 1 Corinthians 12, 13, 14; Romans 8; Ephesians 4; 1 Peter 4.

No one is meant to have all the Spiritual Gifts. Christians need to use the Gifts they have been given and work together to care for others. The Gifts you possess are unique to you.

This Week's Challenge:

Discover your unique Gifts by taking an online assessment. Recommended assessments can be found at http://ibloom.co/ichoose2resources.

Based on the assessment, what are your top 2 to 4 Spiritual Gifts?

1. _____

2. _____

3. _____

4. _____

How can you use these gifts to serve God? If you are already using these gifts, reflect on how you are using them and if there is another way you'd like to serve.

_____

_____

_____

_____

_____

_____

_____

_____

_____

_____

_____

_____

_____

_____

_____

_____

#13:

iChoose2 Operate In My Strengths

"Always be a first-rate version of yourself, instead of a second-rate version of somebody else."

Judy Garland

You have probably been frustrated many times when what you *don't* do well is pointed out to you. Maybe your boss focuses much more on imperfections rather than on your strengths. Parents and teachers zoom right in on a student's lower grades rather than applauding the student's achievements. A coach concentrates on improving weak areas in their players rather than identifying their strengths and helping players fully develop those.

The truth is you simply aren't good at everything. If you identify your strengths and focus on using them in work, learning, personal interests, and even sports, you are much more likely to succeed.

God created you with different abilities and talents. You are intended to be interdependent. Our society operates much more efficiently when you identify your strengths and use them to work for you, as well as for the benefit of others.

Use these tips to enrich your life. Successful people and those who experience life satisfaction:

- Know their strengths and use them in daily work and activity

- Develop and apply their strengths and 'manage' their weak areas
- Use their strengths to triumph in difficult situations

This Week's Challenge:

What are your top 5 strengths?

1. _____
2. _____
3. _____
4. _____
5. _____

Are you utilizing these strengths in your life? If not, what can you change? How can you use your strengths to become a better person, parent, employee, volunteer, etc.?

_____
_____
_____
_____
_____
_____
_____
_____
_____
_____

Before You Move Forward

Date: _____

Identify at least one thing that you accomplished this month as a result of doing the iChoose2 Love My Life journey.

_____

_____

_____

What went well this past month?

_____

_____

_____

What didn't you do, but intended to?

_____

_____

_____

What 3 things would you like to continue to implement?

1. _____

2. _____

3. _____

#14:
iChoose2 Eat Healthy

Food is plentiful and all around you. It's easy to eat without being mindful of what you are putting into your body. Try to stop and think about what you're *really* eating. Food is the fuel meant to keep you strong and allow your body to operate properly. When you eat haphazardly, you rob your body of its disease-fighting strength for a healthy future.

Eating healthy is one of those annoying things always lingering somewhere in the back of our minds! Why is that? And why is it so hard? One thing that makes it difficult is that most of us are the "all or nothing" types; if we eat one bad thing, we figure we've blown it for the day. We tend to put so much pressure on ourselves to do everything "right" and when we fail at that, we're discouraged and give up.

So what about taking a new approach? Start small – if you don't eat breakfast, start by having a piece of fruit or toast. Or if you are a big fried/fast food eater, maybe you could eat one fresh meal per day. Try drinking some nutrients by way of a healthy shake or juice. If you begin making small changes every day, you'll soon find yourself eating healthier and feeling better!

If you eat out a lot, be sure to make wise choices. Check the restaurant's nutritional chart – you'll be surprised how much fat and salt are contained in what you thought was a healthy choice. Be informed.

Limit foods with refined sugar and simple carbohydrates. Think ahead. Plan out your menu for the week. Take a well thought out list to the grocery store. Remember, in a weak moment at home, you will want to reach for something easy! Make sure you have nutritional food around the house instead, such as apples, bananas, carrots, nuts, yogurt, and berries.

Keep a food journal. Be honest – write down EVERY bite you take. It is revealing. You will be able to see areas where you can improve your eating and it will help you be accountable to yourself.

See the sample food diary on the next page. You can use it, or you can design your own that better suits your needs. To download the sample, go to http://ibloom.co/ichoose2resources.

Food Diary

Date:			
Food and **How it was prepared**	**Carbs**	**Calories**	**Fat**
Breakfast: Time:			
Snacks: Time:			
Lunch: Time:			
Snacks: Time:			
Dinner: Time:			
Snacks: Time:			
Total			

#15:

iChoose2 Move

Movement can give you more energy, help you feel stronger, and improve your overall quality of life! Exercise has been proven to reduce stress, improve your mood, strengthen muscles and bones, increase brainpower, reduce weight, alleviate pain, and improve your immune system.

So, why wouldn't you move? Three common reasons many fail to incorporate movement into their daily lives is too little time, lack of knowledge, or they simply don't enjoy doing it.

Let's take a quick self-assessment of your current level of exercise:

_____ **Level 1**: My exercise amounts to housework, maybe pushing a stroller, and walking from my car to the store.

_____ **Level 2**: I do some intentional exercise when I think of it... walk, ride a bike, stretch. Maybe once a week.

_____ **Level 3**: I exercise about 3 times per week. I go to the gym, walk, or play a sport.

_____ **Level 4**: I exercise about 5 times per week. I workout vigorously at least 30 minutes. I do a combination of weight training, aerobic, and recreational exercise.

Now that you've assessed your current level, think of ways that you can move to the next level. If you are at Level 4, what are some ways you can change up your routine or add a new form of exercise?

As you choose to add movement to your life, think about these 3 things:

- **Plan:** Plan a family outing such as bike riding or swimming. Find a walking buddy. Schedule exercise and activities on your personal and family calendar- write them in ink.

- **Play:** How can you walk more? What recreational activity would be fun to try (Frisbee Golf, Tennis, Basketball League, Walking Club, etc.)? How can you stretch your muscles?

- **Profit:** When you choose to incorporate movement into your everyday life you will benefit in overall better health and wellbeing. Find what works best for you.

Once you start feeling better and experience results, you'll find time (and energy) for more movement.

This Week's Challenge:

Even if you have to start small, choose to move more this week. No matter how busy you are, commit to moving at least ten minutes in the morning and before bedtime.

Here are some ideas:
- Walk the dog
- Do a few trips up and down the stairs
- Play with the kids
- Stretch while you watch TV
- Park the car farther away from the store

When you are on the computer, stop every 30 minutes and sprint up your stairs, do push-ups or crunches, stretch.

#16:

iChoose2 Live Stress Free

"Lord, grant me the serenity to accept what I cannot change, the
courage to change the things I can,
and the wisdom to know the difference"

Reinhold Niebuhr's "Serenity Prayer"

Countless studies have shown a link between stress and physical health. People who say they experience high levels of stress are more likely than others to catch a cold, have a heart attack, and develop cancer. It may seem difficult to rid your life of stress, but there is an important fact about stress that allows you to manage it: the effects of stress depend entirely on your perception of what happens to you, rather than on your life experiences.

There are two ways you can deal with stress. The first way is to examine how you interpret your experiences. Numerous psychological studies have shown that people are more likely to be stressed out when they interpret negative events as internal ("it's all my fault"), stable ("this kind of thing always happens to me"), and global ("this is going to ruin my entire week/life"). People who experience less stress are able to see the temporary nature of stressful events, or they think of the big picture, meaning they are able to see how challenging times strengthen them in the long-term. In other words, they see negative events as external ("this is a challenging situation"), unstable ("this will eventually go away"), and specific ("this problem is only occurring in one area of my life, so I can contain it").

OK, so you may be experiencing things that are difficult to reframe. After all, if you live or work with a difficult person, if you suffer from a chronic illness, or you live in a threatening environment, it may seem impossible to think of it differently than it really is. That is when you should consider the second way to deal with stress, which is managing your response.

The important thing to remember is that stress uses up your body's energy, a resource that could instead be used to fight disease. All of the ways to manage stress involve saving energy, or making your body a more energy efficient machine.

There are several ways you can manage your response. The following is a list of simple, and often FREE, ways to do it:

- Exercise regularly. Your body uses energy more efficiently when you are in good shape.
- Eat healthy foods that provide long-term energy. This does NOT include energy drinks or caffeine! Instead, use the tried-and-true rules of nutrition to provide the best fuel for your body.
- Learn how to relax. Managed breathing and focusing on muscle relaxation is key. Even five minutes of this can feel like a power nap!
- Talk about it with a trusted friend. Expressing how these stressful events make you feel to someone you know and trust can not only make you feel relief, but it can also strengthen the bond you have with that person. Note: This is not the same as venting your frustrations!

This Week's Challenge:

Write down ALL of the things in your life that make you feel stressed (use a second piece of paper if you have to!):

_____

_____

_____

_____

_____

_____

Now, give each of those stressors a time frame. How long does that stressor exist before it typically goes away? Be realistic here.

_____

_____

_____

_____

For the stressors that you've identified as temporary, start brainstorming things you can tell yourself when you are "in the moment" that will remind you to reframe your perceptions:

_____

_____

_____

_____

_____

For the stressors that you've identified as long-term, try the following when they are brought to mind:

- Find a room where you can get some privacy (the bathroom is a great candidate, especially if you're a parent). Sit down, lock the door, and turn off the lights.
- Breathe in through your nose and out through your mouth. Inhale for 2 seconds, exhale for 2 seconds.
- Try increasing by 1 second the air you inhale. Breathe out.
- Now, try increasing by 1 second the air you exhale.
- Continue increasing the time it takes you to breathe in and out until you are up to 10 seconds each.
- Once you've reached your 10 second breathing, focus on your muscles at the top of your head and work on relaxing them.
- Now, move your focus to your facial muscles and relax them.
- Move down to your neck, relax. Move down to your shoulders, relax. Continue working through your whole body until you have relaxed all of the muscles all the way down to your toes. This is called progressive muscle relaxation, or a "body scan."
- Take in one more deep breath, and blow it out. Open your eyes, stand up, and re-enter your life.

You will find that doing this may not "fix" all of your problems, but it has the power to make you feel energetic and relaxed. It will allow your body to keep the energy it needs.

#17:

iChoose2 Sleep

Adequate sleep is a vital part of healthy living. Your body needs sleep to perform at its best. During sleep, your body and organs rest and rejuvenate for the upcoming day's activities.

When our bodies are routinely deprived of sleep, cellular damage can occur. You need sleep to produce enzymes and hormones your body needs to keep cells working optimally. Sleep deprivation can actually cause premature aging. Your emotional health is more vibrant when you are rested and renewed. Adequate rest promotes a bright outlook on life and helps you handle day-to-day stressors!

Think about your sleeping habits. What is your sleeping style at this time in your life?

_____ I love to sleep and sleep well.

_____ I love to sleep but sleep lightly and wake up often.

_____ I toss and turn much of the night.

_____ I wish I could just skip sleeping- I'd get so much done!

_____ I tend to go to bed too late and get up too early.

Sleep isn't just for enjoyment; it has a purpose. Your body repairs and rejuvenates the various organs and systems during sleep.

This Week's Challenge

Choose from the list below what steps you could add to promote peaceful sleep in your life:

- Plan for your sleep. What time do you need to get up? How much sleep do you require each night? Count backwards and make that your bedtime. Aim for 15 minutes before that!
- Begin to unwind one hour before bedtime. Listen to soft music or read to relax.
- Stop using your computer at least one hour prior to bedtime.
- Stop eating at least two hours before bedtime.
- Get some exercise and fresh air during the day.
- Make sure your mattress and pillow are clean and comfortable.
- Clear out the clutter in your bedroom. Make it inviting for rest and sleep.
- Turn down the temperature a few degrees and nestle under a cozy quilt.
- Keep a gratitude journal. Before going to bed, reflect by writing down things you are grateful for that day.

#18:

iChoose2 Get a Medical Check-Up

"If I knew I was going to live this long,
I'd have taken better care of myself."

Mickey Mantle

According to the Centers for Disease Control and Prevention, "Chronic diseases – such as heart disease, stroke, cancer, diabetes, and arthritis – are among the most common, costly, and preventable of all health problems in the United States."

According to the Journal of Chronic Diseases and Health Promotions (2005), 133 million Americans – almost 1 out of every 2 adults – had at least one chronic illness. And, 7 out of 10 deaths among Americans each year are from chronic diseases. Heart disease, cancer and stroke account for more than 50% of all deaths each year. This alone is reason enough to get regular medical check- ups. Most of these diseases are preventable and very treatable if caught early. Unfortunately, many people wait until a crisis occurs, and by then permanent damage may already be done.

Having a regular medical check-up will allow your doctor to see critical numbers like blood pressure, blood sugar, cholesterol, and heart rate. These routine checks will often indicate immediate abnormalities. By having a conversation with your medical professional you'll have the opportunity to discuss how you are feeling. Plus, they can assess for other warning signs.

You only get one body. Choose today that you'll begin caring for yourself in a way that will promote great health and overall well-being.

Vital Signs: Know Your Numbers

Get to know the important things about your body, by knowing your vital signs.

Cholesterol: Total _____ HDL _____ LDL _____	
Blood Pressure: _____/_____ Goal: _____/_____	
Mammogram: Date _____ Result:_____	**Pap Smear:** Date _____ Result: _____
Other:	

This Week's Challenge:

Do you need a physical, pap smear, mammogram, eye exam, or dental cleaning? What have you been avoiding? Where have you been procrastinating? Make it a priority this week to schedule appointments with your health care providers.

Before You Move Forward

Date: _____

Identify at least one thing that you accomplished this month as a result of doing the iChoose2 Love My Life journey.

_____

_____

_____

What went well this past month?

_____

_____

_____

What didn't you do, but intended to?

_____

_____

_____

What 3 things would you like to continue to implement?

1. _____

2. _____

3. _____

#19:
iChoose2 Cultivate My Relationship with Christ

You spend a lot of time cultivating and investing in your relationships. You would never expect a friendship or love relationship to flourish if you went weeks without talking or spending time together. So, how can you expect your relationship with Christ to grow and flourish if you never spend time with Him?

Cultivating an intimate relationship with Christ isn't about following a bunch of rules or just going to church on Sunday mornings. Many Christians subconsciously have their "Good Christian Checklist" that looks a little like this:

- ✓ Go to Church
- ✓ Read my Bible
- ✓ Journal
- ✓ Pray
- ✓ Tell a friend about Jesus
- ✓ Go to Bible Study
- ✓ Listen to Christian Music

Did you know that more than these things, God is far more concerned with your personal, daily relationship with Him rather than just checking items off a list? God wants all of you. Are you willing to entrust every facet of your life to Him? He has your best interest in mind. His plans are perfect. He loves you unconditionally. And He longs for a personal relationship with you.

There is nothing wrong with the things on the "Good Christian Checklist," but instead of doing them out of obligation; you can now do them because you want to cultivate a more intimate relationship with Christ.

Make it a priority every day to spend time deepening your relationship with God. There is no task or activity more important than being in God's presence. During this sacred time with God, you could listen to worship music, praise Him, read the Bible, pray, listen, or just be still.

Journal:

Have you been viewing your relationship with God as an obligation or an intimate relationship?

_____

How can you begin cultivating a more intimate daily relationship with Christ?

_____
_____
_____
_____
_____

Here are a few things you might want to incorporate into your life. Remember, you aren't doing these as obligations, but instead because you desire a more intimate relationship with Christ.

- Read a daily devotional.
- Set aside time each day to pray.
- Join a Bible Study that allows you to delve into scripture and learn more about Him.

Write out a scripture (maybe a favorite or one that speaks to you in this season). Post it around your home/office/car. Carry it with you. Memorize it. Journal about anything God reveals to you.

_____

_____

_____

_____

_____

_____

_____

_____

_____

_____

_____

_____

_____

#20:

iChoose2 Trust

"Trust the Lord with all your heart,
and don't depend on your own understanding."

Proverbs 3:5 (NCV)

You put your trust in people and things every day. You trust your husband to pick up dinner, your children to come home on time, and your car to get you to work. However, people and cars will fail you at some point. You may not want to believe that, but it's true.

Did you know that there is someone who you can trust with everything? Someone who will walk alongside you even when things get tough or don't seem fair? That someone is God; His ways are perfect and He will never fail you. Is it hard for you to place your trust fully in God's hands? Are there things you are holding onto because you don't want to be hurt or disappointed again?

You can put your complete trust in the One who loves you. It is safe to give everything to Him! You just need to release and surrender every person and situation to God; nothing is too big or too difficult for Him to handle. You will be filled with a unimaginable peace when you finally let go of trying to control every detail of your life. Choose to trust God today with every part of your life.

This Week's Challenge:

Create a list of concerns you are currently experiencing.

_____

_____

_____

_____

_____

_____

_____

_____

_____

_____

_____

_____

_____

_____

_____

_____

_____

_____

_____

Intentionally give each concern to God.

- Trust Him to care and provide for you.
- Thank Him that He is trustworthy and will never disappoint you!

#21:

iChoose2 Be Still and Listen

"Be still, and know that I am God."

Psalm 46:10 NIV

What a fabulous verse! This verse is a reminder of our deepest desire in life - to connect with God -to *really* connect with Him. The normal pace of life makes that very difficult, unless you are willing to STOP and LISTEN.

Only when you're silent are you able to hear God's still small voice. How can you expect to hear His still *small* voice with the volume of everyday life? He wants you're undivided attention. He wants you to seek Him each day. He wants you to need Him. When you're still, you have the assurance that God is with you. It is then that He speaks to the deepest part of your soul.

This Week's Challenge:

Set aside a devoted amount of time each day this week to be still and listen. As you spend this quality time with God, journal in the space below how you sense God speaking to you.

Day 1

_____

_____

_____

Day 2

_____

_____

_____

Day 3

_____

_____

_____

Day 4

_____

_____

_____

Day 5

_____

_____

_____

Day 6

_____

_____

_____

Day 7

_____

_____

_____

#22:

iChoose2 Surrender

"Take your everyday, ordinary life
your sleeping, eating, going-to-work, and walking-around life
and place it before God as an offering."

Romans 12:1, MSG

Surrender is the willingness to give something to God and entrust it to His care. Surrender is releasing control and believing that God will do a better job. It is an acknowledgement that you are simply the steward of all He has asked you to manage for Him on earth.

This Week's Challenge:

Think through all of the different aspects of your life (finances, relationships, physical health, emotions, family, church, career, flaws, purpose, future, home, daily decisions). Are you willing to surrender everything to God?

Coaching Assignment:

Which areas of your life are the most difficult to surrender?
Spend a few moments praying and journaling about these things.
Why are they more difficult?

_____

_____

_____

_____

_____

_____

_____

_____

_____

_____

_____

_____

_____

_____

_____

_____

_____

_____

_____

_____

Before You Move Forward

Date: _____

Identify at least one thing that you accomplished this month as a result of doing the iChoose2 Love My Life journey.

_____

_____

_____

What went well this past month?

_____

_____

_____

What didn't you do, but intended to?

_____

_____

_____

What 3 things would you like to continue to implement?

1. _____

2. _____

3. _____

#23:
iChoose2 Live in this Moment

Have you heard the saying, "Participate, don't anticipate?" That's great advice for all of us. We often fill in our day planners with meetings, family activities, and upcoming holidays. We can be so planned that we don't make time to enjoy the moment.

Every day is God's gift to us, thus the name "the present". Wake up ready to embrace the here and now- to enjoy the people and events placed in our paths. We certainly need plans to guide us through our days, but don't let those plans rule your life!

Stop and smell the roses...an old saying, but wise words.

Are you living a life that doesn't include the present? Make the decision right now that you'll be in the moment this week. What will that look like for you?

Do you need to...
- Turn off your phone during dinner (and yes, even the text messages and email!)?
- Let the dishes sit and take a walk with your children, husband, or friend?

STOP and just take in a deep breath?

This Week's Challenge:

Choose to live in the present moment! Each day this week intentionally find an opportunity to truly live in the moment. Journal about your experience. How did you feel? How did your perspective change?

Day 1

_____

_____

_____

_____

_____

Day 2

_____

_____

_____

_____

_____

Day 3

_____

_____

_____

_____

_____

Day 4

Day 5

Day 6

Day 7

#24:

iChoose2 Connect

Making time for connections with your family is vital. This is when memories are made and relationships grow. It's where lessons are taught and learned; and laughter, talking, and tears are encouraged. It's how family history is passed down and love is strengthened.

The dinner table is a natural place for connections to happen. Families are busy, so be proactive and schedule at least one family meal per week! Before, during, and after the meal is the perfect time to have prayer and family devotion time. You might go around and tell your "sads and glads" or tell things for which you are grateful. Maybe you purchase or write your own conversation starters for each person to select to encourage discussion.

Family traditions are also ways to connect throughout the years and across the miles. Begin holiday traditions along the way such as pumpkin carving, serving a Thanksgiving meal, looking at Christmas lights, or watching the Super Bowl together. Why not schedule Friday night pizza and game night or Sunday brunch after worship?

Find activities you can do together such as bike riding, walking the dog, and or playing cards. Look online or in the newspaper each week for festivals, concerts, and sporting events in your area that the family will enjoy! Be creative and enjoy your time together!

This Week's Challenge:

Be intentional about connecting as a family this week. Schedule a fun family gathering where you can discuss ways that you can connect more as a family. Create a list of activities that you would enjoy doing together. Be sure to schedule a few of the activities into your family calendar.

Activities?	When?

Journal:

How can you intentionally carve out more time for your family to connect throughout the week?

_____

_____

_____

_____

#25:

iChoose2 Encourage

Everyone needs to have people in their life that lift them up, who are their biggest fans and cheerleaders! It's important to let the members of your family and your friends know how much you love them and how special they are!

This is especially true for parents. The world bombards our children with negative talk and images, and they need adults who counter that with unconditional love and acceptance. Be the first and last person to impact your children each day. Don't allow a busy schedule to keep you from tucking them into bed at night or having meals together. Use these times to tell them how great they are and how much you believe in them.

Each day is a new opportunity to encourage the people in your life. Leave notes for your spouse by the coffee pot or in their car saying how much you love them. Put a note in your child's lunchbox or backpack wishing them a great day. Create family traditions like the "special plate." The "special plate" is given to a family member at mealtime to celebrate their birthday, accomplishment, or "just because" we love you!

Remember to be present and attentive with your family and friends. We often discourage our loved ones by checking our phones or emails during meals or time spent together; most of the time we aren't even aware of this!

A little encouragement goes a long way in the lives of our family and friends! Be a relationship adder, not a relationship taker!

This Week's Challenge:

Be intentional about encouraging your family and close friends this week. In the table below, write the names of family members and close friends along with ideas for how you can specifically encourage each person this week.

Suggested Encouragement Ideas:

- Send a DaySpring ecard- http://ecards.dayspring.com/
- Give a "just because" gift
- Send a handwritten note

Who?	How?

#26:

iChoose2 Create a Routine

Most of us thrive best with a routine. Life flows better when people have a plan and are prepared for the unexpected. This doesn't mean that every minute of every day is scheduled, but that most days have an order to them that allows for more productivity and less stress!

At night, lay out your clothes and have your children do the same. This takes a huge amount of stress (and tears) out of the morning routine! Go on and pack lunches and backpacks, sign all permission slips and find money for what you need. Look over your day planner and take a mental "walk through" of the next day and try to think of anything out of the ordinary you need to pack. Preparing the night before will help you begin your day with a plan.

Bedtime is an important time to stick to a routine. Children need time to unwind with books and music; time with their parents to snuggle and talk. Children and adults need adequate sleep each night, so don't let distractions keep you up past bedtime.

During the day it's helpful to keep meals, naps, exercise, and work as consistent as possible. This is especially true for children, but adults benefit from a routine, too. You cannot expect your children to behave when they haven't had their daily nap or lunch is an hour late. A routine doesn't mean life is boring, it means you have looked at the big picture and found ways to keep it moving smoothly.

Journal:

Look at your day and, if applicable, your family's schedule. Are things hectic in the morning? Evening? Trips? What could you do in advance to make these times flow better?

_____

_____

_____

_____

_____

_____

This Week's Challenge:

1. Have a family meeting and discuss the family routine.
2. What is working? What is not? How can it be improved?

Coaching Assignment:

What would an ideal routine/schedule look like for your family? List each day and schedule your family activities. Keep in mind that having a routine makes life so much easier!

Go to http://ibloom.co/ichoose2resources to download a template that can be used to create your ideal schedule.

Before You Move Forward

Date: _____

Identify at least one thing that you accomplished this month as a result of doing the iChoose2 Love My Life journey.

_____

_____

_____

What went well this past month?

_____

_____

_____

What didn't you do, but intended to?

_____

_____

_____

What 3 things would you like to continue to implement?

1. _____

2. _____

3. _____

#27:

iChoose2 Create and Live by a Budget

Do you want to live in financial freedom and have the peace that comes with that? Do you want to know exactly where your hard-earned money is going? If so, then it is essential that you create and live by a budget.

The purpose of a budget is to plan how you'll spend your money before you actually spend it. You'll want your budget to be realistic and livable. For instance, for most people it would be very unrealistic to say that you're never going to eat out, so you don't allot any money to that category of your budget.

A budget is essential for maintaining a debt-free life. It's simply a plan you use to decide where your dollars will go. You control your money instead of your money controlling you!

To create a budget, you'll want to do the following things:
- Estimate current income and expenses
- Track actual income and expenses
- Review your actual versus budgeted income and expenses each month (This is a *MUST*!)
- Make adjustments as needed

Creating and living on a budget is a shift in your mindset and can give you more peace and freedom than you ever imagined possible.

This Week's Challenge:

Make the decision that you will take control of your financial life. A great way to get started is by tracking your spending for the next month. To do this, keep a log each day of your expenses and categorize each purchase. At the end of the month, you will be ready to create a *realistic* budget that works for you.

Go to http://ibloom.co/ichoose2resources to access several great resources that will help you create your budget.

#28:

iChoose2 Eliminate Debt

Last week, you began the process of creating and living with a budget. During that process, you categorized your payments and the expenses that you owed. Your next step is to tackle your debt!

Debt is a word that can bring fear to some. Fear that can paralyze, making you incapable of facing the mound of debt that might be engulfing you. Debt can be so overwhelming that you don't even know where to begin. It can take on a life of its own, steal your peace and joy, destroy marriages, and become your all-consuming thought.

There is such freedom in eliminating debt from your life. Living a life that you love requires that you take control of your debt. Refuse to let it have any power over you!

Are you experiencing the paralysis of debt? If so, this is the week you get to face your fears! Eliminating your debt will not happen overnight, but with slow and steady commitment you can be debt free!

This Week's Challenge:

The first step toward becoming debt-free is to face the reality of your current situation. Evaluate your current debt by compiling a list with balances and interest rates.

Name of Debt (ex. Visa Card #1)	Amount Owed	Interest Rate	Minimum Monthly Payment

Follow a Debt Snowball Plan

Create an action plan for becoming debt-free. Make a commitment to yourself that you WILL do this! The following is a plan for eliminating debt proposed by Dave Ramsey:

1. Figure out how much money you can budget toward paying off your debt. This may require cutting some unnecessary spending from your budget.

2. Rank-order your debts based on the amount owed, from lowest to highest, not counting your mortgage.

3. Pay the minimum monthly payments on all balances EXCEPT the debt with the LEAST amount owed. Whatever is left in your budgeted amount for paying off debt after paying the minimum on the others goes toward this one source of debt.

4. When you have paid off the first source of debt, move on to the next source of debt on your list that has the least amount owed. That source will now receive payments from whatever is left in your budgeted amount for paying off debt. All others will still get the minimum payment.

5. Continue this process until you are able to put the entire budgeted amount for paying off debt toward the debt source with the MOST amount owed. This is your trophy. When you pay this one off, you are officially done!

When you are done, plan on only using credit cards for purchases you have already budgeted.

#29:
iChoose2 Be Content

The world teaches us that bigger is better and more is what we are working hard to attain. Commercials and advertisements tell you that you deserve to have the newest and best products. You should want more and more stuff (money, new job, designer purses & shoes, jewelry, bigger house, better car, iPad; etc.). These things aren't bad, but have you ever stopped to focus on being truly content with what you already have?

Without contentment you are running a race you will never win. Your new phone or laptop is out of date three months after the purchase. You can usually find a boss that will pay more than your current boss. But the feeling of having the latest and greatest item is short lived. You often buy these items or take that new job to fill a void in your life, however, you soon discover that no purchase or job position fills the void for long. You may think you can overcome loneliness or boredom with "things," but "things" break, get old, and lose their luster.

Contentment is choosing to thank God for everything. It is realizing how much better off you are than many others in the world. It is being grateful for your life exactly as it is today, not how it could be tomorrow. It takes discipline and practice to be content in your present situation and circumstances. Ask God to give you this new mindset. Ask Him to help you be content with all you have and not be consumed with what you don't have.

Choose to be content and experience a newfound freedom as you are released from the "gotta haves and gotta dos." Enjoy this place of peace and contentment!

This Week's Challenge:

In what area of your life do you find it is hardest to be content?

_____

_____

Are you willing to surrender this area to God?

Spend time this week reflecting on why you enjoy obtaining more things or titles? What void in your life are these things filling? (loneliness, boredom, insecurity, etc.) What positive way can you fill this void? (volunteering, going out with friends, helping your elderly neighbor, etc.)

_____

_____

Be conscious about how you spend money this week. Before making a purchase, ask yourself, "Is this something I *really* need or just want?" Learn to pause and ask yourself this question all through the day.

Remind yourself of God's abundant blessings in your life by referring back to your gratitude list in Section #6.

#30:
iChoose2 Save

Having a saving system is the key to controlling your finances. We must break the cycle that so many have of using credit cards for emergency expenditures and large purchases.

It is important to have an emergency fund of $1,000 even *before* you are debt free, so that you avoid the cycle of continually going further in debt every time an emergency happens. An emergency fund is for a true emergency only and is not to be used for items you see and want.

Emergencies are a part of life. Don't fool yourself into believing they won't happen to you. Emergencies do happen—the car will need to go to the repair shop, the refrigerator dies, the furnace stops working, and so on. Decide today that you will be prepared!

To be successful, open a savings account that is exclusively for your Emergency Fund. By having a separate account you won't be tempted to use these funds for non-emergency purchases. Having this fund is vital to stopping the new debt cycle that happens each time you have an emergency for which you are not prepared. Make it a priority to establish your $1,000 emergency fund as soon as possible. To make this happen, you may need to have a yard sale, sell things on Craigs List or Ebay, or diligently put money aside from each paycheck.

After establishing your minimum $1,000 emergency fund and eliminating your debt (everything but your home), your next step is to save 6-12 months worth of expenses—again, these are expenses, *not* your salary. This financial cushion will allow you to be prepared for the unexpected, like losing your job or being unable to work because of an illness. This is true financial freedom!

Saving for large purchases is also essential to avoiding debt. For instance, if you know you'll need a new car within the next 4 years, start saving now. Let's say you want to purchase a $15,000 used car in 48 months. Setup a separate account and begin setting aside at least $312.50 per month to save toward this purchase. Then, once you've saved your $15,000, you'll be ready to pay cash for your next vehicle.

Decide today that YOU will be in control of your finances. Choose to save, so that you are prepared for those unplanned financial emergencies.

This Weeks's Challenge:

- Open a savings account devoted exclusively to your Emergency Fund.

- What are some creative ways that you could earn $1,000 to establish your Emergency Fund quickly?

  _____

  _____

  _____

Now, get started! What is your goal? Fill in the blank below.

I will have $1,000 in my Emergency Fund account by _____.

- What are your monthly expenses? How much money will you need to have 6-12 months' worth of expenses? Remember, before you start saving toward your 6-12 months of expenses, you'll want to have paid off all of your debt (except your home).

- Think about the next 5 years, what large purchases will you need to make?

  _____

  _____

  _____

  _____

#31:
iChoose2 Give

Other than people, what is most valuable to you? Many would say time and money. Are these things you are willing to give up or give to another person? That is exactly what God is asking you to do. He commands you to "love your neighbor as yourself." What does that look like? Does it mean you throw a couple dollars in the offering plate on Sundays or volunteer once a year at your office service project? Or does it mean you give out of love and sacrifice?

One of the hardest areas to give is your time. It sounds easy until you are asked to help a single Mom pack and move on a Saturday when you already have plans. Or your church asks for volunteers in the youth program on the night of your favorite television program. Another area that may be difficult for you to give is your money. You probably have plans on how you want to spend your money and that doesn't always involve helping other people and organizations.

So, how do you go from holding on tightly to your resources of time and money to being a generous person? First, it is important to remember that everything you have belongs to God; money and time are His resources. He places resources in your hands to allow you the opportunity to serve and bless others. God doesn't need your time or money to accomplish His plans; He allows you the opportunity to give so that you will receive the true blessing. When you give with a heart that desires for others to have more and expect nothing in return, you will be filled with joy!

Journal:

Spend time praying and reflecting on how you can begin to give by sharing your time and money with others.

How can you adjust your spending habits, so that you can give more financially?

_____

_____

_____

_____

_____

_____

_____

_____

How can you create margin in your schedule, so that you're available to serve others?

_____

_____

_____

_____

_____

_____

Before You Move Forward

Date: _____

Identify at least one thing that you accomplished this month as a result of doing the iChoose2 Love My Life journey.

_____

_____

_____

What went well this past month?

_____

_____

_____

What didn't you do, but intended to?

_____

_____

_____

What 3 things would you like to continue to implement?

1. _____

2. _____

3. _____

#32:

iChoose2 Be a Friend

"Friends are those rare people who ask how you are
and then wait for the answer."

Author Unknown

"A friend knows the song in my heart
and sings it to me when my memory fails."

Donna Roberts

When you think about the word friend, what characteristics come to mind? There are many adjectives you could use to describe a friend such as gentle, loving, honest, trustworthy, giving, exuberant or selfless. Remember, the things you desire out of a friendship are the same things your friend desires.

Being a friend means being willing to ask questions and truly listen. Encouraging them, laughing with them and most importantly, finding time for them is key.

Friendships aren't easy and should not be taken lightly. They require work just like any other relationship. Sometimes you may feel like you are giving more to the friendship than the other person. That's okay! Focus on being the friend you'd love to have. There might be a time when you get so bogged down with life that you need your friend to just be your friend, and not expect anything in return. That's what true friendships are all about.

This Week's Challenge:

What qualities do you admire in a friend?

_____

_____

_____

_____

_____

_____

_____

How can you be that type of friend?

_____

_____

_____

_____

_____

_____

_____

_____

#33:

iChoose2 be Authentic

In a world that seems to love reality TV, it seems odd that we still have a difficult time being real with each other. Granted, reality TV is probably anything but reality. There are production crews, editing, and the cast is trying to stay on the show more than be real with us.

Is your life more like a reality show than you would like to admit?

Are you more concerned about what others think of you than you are in having meaningful friendships? Do you edit what is really happening...just to try to "stay on the show" a little longer with your friends, family, work, even God? If you are doing your best to not let others see what your reality is, you are not being real. You are missing out on real community with others and you are cheating yourself of your best life.

It's hard to be more than who God created you to be. Acting like one person at home, another at work, and another at church isn't easy. Choose to be authentic in all areas of your life – even when it's not pretty. Let those who are closest to you see the real you.

This Week's Challenge:

Be authentic with someone. Do you need to let your spouse or a close friend know something you are struggling with or that you are hoping for in the future? Is there a habit you want (or *really* need) to break? Is there a dream you need to share? Be intentional about choosing to be authentic with someone this week.

Journal:

Does being authentic come natural to you or is it a challenge?

_____

Who in your life *really* knows the real you?

_____

_____

Who are you going to be authentic with this week?

_____

_____

_____

How do you plan to be authentic with this person?

_____

_____

_____

_____

#34:

iChoose2 Invest in a Deep, Meaningful Relationship

"Invest in the human soul.
Who knows, it might be a diamond in the rough."

Mary McLeod Bethune

Social Networking allows you to connect and reconnect with friends. You may have lots of "friends" on Facebook or "followers" on Twitter, but do you have any close relationships? Do you have relationships that go beyond texting and e-mail? Real friends are those people who would rearrange their day, give up watching a TV program, or take your midnight call because they care about you. They are the types of people you can talk to on the phone for extended periods of time.

In order to have friends, you need to invest in them. Has your life become too busy or self-focused to invest in meaningful relationships? There is something wonderful that happens in your heart when you start giving of yourself to others. You feel happy, fulfilled, and needed. You see lives change and blossom (including yours!).

Deep friendships are like quilts. First, you must cut out the pieces, arrange, stitch together, and then start to quilt. By the time it's done, you've spent hours with your project. There were great moments when the colors and fabrics came seamlessly together. There were also moments of knotted threads and needle-pricked fingers. Relationships take time, good and bad, but the end result is a beautiful tapestry of love!

This Week's Challenge:

Be intentional about being a friend. Choose ONE friend to invest in this week. How will you invest in that person? Here are a few ideas to get you thinking:

- Write a letter that tells that person why you value and appreciate her or him
- Take that person out for coffee or lunch
- Get a manicure or pedicure together
- Send that person "just because" flowers or a card
- Go on a hike or to a local park together

_____

_____

_____

_____

_____

_____

_____

_____

_____

_____

#35:
iChoose2 Make a New Friend

In this day of job transfers, divorces, and moving to take care of aging parents, many people find themselves looking for friends. Some are empty nesters, retirees, or just in a season with more time and desire to invest in others.

So, how do you go about making friends? First of all, you need to be a friend, to make a friend. Be the one who asks the other person to meet for lunch or a movie. You may have to ask several times before the other person responds; don't get your feelings hurt, keep asking!

Do random acts of kindness for those around you. Surprise a neighbor, someone at church, or the gym with a "just because" gift- perhaps a gift card to your favorite restaurant or bookstore. And don't forget the lost art of sending notes to people. Everyone loves receiving them!

If you find yourself lonely, bored, or missing long distance friends, remember that you aren't alone. There are others feeling the same way. In fact, they are probably hoping to make a new friend, too. Have you considered joining a group to pursue an interest or maybe attending a class at church or Community College? Be intentional about cultivating new friendships- they often last a lifetime!

This Week's Challenge:

Are you in a season of life where you desire a new friendship? If so, identify someone that you'd like to get to know better. How can you be intentional about connecting with that person this week?

_____

_____

_____

_____

_____

_____

Journal:

What qualities are you looking for in a friend?

_____

_____

_____

How can you intentionally cultivate new friendships? Is there a specific group or activity that you would like to investigate?

_____

_____

_____

_____

_____

_____

_____

Before You Move Forward

Date: _____

Identify at least one thing that you accomplished this month as a result of doing the iChoose2 Love My Life journey.

_____

_____

_____

What went well this past month?

_____

_____

_____

What didn't you do, but intended to?

_____

_____

_____

What 3 things would you like to continue to implement?

1. _____

2. _____

3. _____

#36:

iChoose2 Invest in Myself

"It takes courage to grow up and become who we really are."

e.e. cummings

Do you often feel guilty for taking time to sit down and read or even exercise?

Why do you jump at the chance to help others, but often neglect your basic needs? Are you being a "slacker" when you meet a friend with a problem for coffee instead of attending your Pilates class? Well, sometimes, yes. But most of the time your desire to care for others overshadows your desire to care yourself.

Put yourself at the top of the list. You are worth the time and effort! Eating right, exercising, learning new skills, and allowing time for fun, are vital to your happiness, and growth as a person.

Look at your life as a personal bank account. Do you have a healthy "balance"? Is enough coming into your account to cover what's going out? If there is a deficit, what needs to happen? You might ask a family member or a friend to help you evaluate your life. An outsider often has great insight. Take the time - make the investment in yourself - reap great returns!

This Week's Challenge:

Set aside at least one hour this week to begin dreaming about ways you can invest in yourself. Are there things that you have always wanted to do or to accomplish?

Perhaps it's visiting all of the states in the United States, getting an advanced degree, going on a mission trip, getting in shape, bungee jumping, eating something new, or going to a spa.

Make a list of all of the things you would like to do or accomplish in your lifetime. You can use the table on the next page.

Can you think of 50 things?

Your list can be comprised of big things, but also of small everyday things that you just haven't had a chance to do.

When you are done with your list, circle the FIRST thing you'd like to do. Put it on your calendar and make it happen. Have fun as you start doing the things you've always dreamed of doing!

My Bucket List

#37:

iChoose2 Laugh

"Laughter gives us distance. It allows us to step back from an event, deal with it and then move on."

Bob Newhart

We all need laughter in our lives. In fact, when was the last time you had a good belly laugh? You know the kind, the laugh that brings tears to your eyes and makes your stomach hurt. The laughter is so loud others want to know what's so funny. If you can't think of a time that this happened within the past few weeks, then find something to make you laugh.

Laughter is good for your mental state and there's nothing better to put a smile on your face even on a bad day. To have laughter, you must stop taking everything so seriously. Each day we have a choice to get upset about a situation or choose to laugh.

When you choose to laugh, it becomes a great story to tell in the future. It also defuses the situation so you can take the needed action. The next time you begin to get upset or angry, catch yourself and choose to laugh!

This Week's Challenge:

Generate a list of all of the things that make you laugh, whether it's a movie, a song, a TV show, a CD of your favorite comedian, a YouTube clip, a goofy picture, or a funny friend.

Make a plan to have these at your disposal for when you are feeling down or upset. This could include:

- Making a library of funny YouTube clips
- Creating a compilation of silly songs that you love
- Creating a photo album of silly pictures
- Buying a season of your favorite funny TV show on DVD
- Scheduling a regular time to spend with your funny friends

_____

_____

_____

_____

_____

_____

_____

_____

_____

_____

_____

_____

_____

_____

_____

#38:

iChoose2 Get a Hobby

"Today is life-the only life you are sure of. Make the most of today. Get interested in something. Shake yourself awake. Develop a hobby. Let the winds of enthusiasm sweep through you. Live today with gusto."

Dale Carnagie

What is a hobby? According to the dictionary, a hobby is "an activity or interest pursued for pleasure or relaxation and not a main occupation."

Why is it important for you to have a hobby? A hobby is something to look forward to. It's something you enjoy doing even if others think it seems like a daunting task. It may take a special effort to plan.

An example of this is gardening . You have to tend and care for a garden – planting, pruning and weeding. It's a hobby for some that reaps a bounty of beauty and joy.

You can reward yourself after a hard day, week or month by planning something you enjoy doing. A hobby may also challenge you and keep your brain working. Ask most men about their golf game and they'll tell you it's a hobby for a lifetime- you'll never master it.

This Week's Challenge:

Take an honest look at your life- are you having fun? Is there something you've always wanted to try but didn't have the time or money? Have you become dull because life is work, work, and more work?

What are a few things you enjoy doing?

_____

_____

_____

_____

Look over this list of popular hobbies, and circle the hobbies that you would like to pursue.

Basketball	Gardening	Pottery
Biking	Golf	Quilting
Book Club	Hiking	Rock Climbing
Camping	Hockey	Running
Canning	Home Improvement	Scrapbooking
Cooking	Horseback Riding	Snorkeling
Couponing	Ice Skating	Soccer
Crocheting	Knitting	Softball
Cross Stitch	Music	Swimming
Drawing	Painting	Tennis
Fishing	Photography	Wine Tasting

What is a hobby that you could try out this week? Schedule some time to do it and get started!

#39:

iChoose2 Pamper Myself

What does it mean to pamper yourself? The definition of pamper from AudioEnglish.net is: "Treat with excessive indulgence." What exactly is an indulgence to you? This will be different for different people. For you, it may be a bubble bath, while for someone else it's an invigorating hike. The key is identifying what makes you feel relaxed and special.

Take time out to decompress and care for yourself as part of your health and well-being. When you feel relaxed and stress free you are happier; and happier around your family, friends, and coworkers. You will be more productive when you take time to give back to yourself.

Decide that pampering yourself is a necessary part of your lifestyle. Don't feel guilty for taking time out to do things for yourself! If you have children, you are being a good role model when you take care of yourself. It's okay to have someone else care for your children while you work out or enjoy a vacation day shopping with girlfriends. Just make sure that you incorporate these expenses into your budget and keep track of what you spend.

Ask for help with your young children or trade "child-watching time" with your spouse, other family member, or close friend so you can have some uninterrupted time to be pampered.

This Week's Challenge:

Create a list of things that make you feel special. What did you do before life happened? Create a list of books you want to read, movies you would like to see, friends you want to visit, or other ways you could pamper yourself. Dream big- don't think about time or money- just write it down! Keep the list in your wallet; you never know when you'll have a spare hour or two just to yourself.

Makes me feel special...	Books to Read	Movies to See	Friends to Visit

1. What does pampering look like to you?

_____

_____

_____

2. How will you intentionally include pampering into your lifestyle?

_____

_____

_____

_____

3. What needs to happen to make your pampering dreams a reality?

_____

_____

_____

_____

Pampering Suggestions:
- Taking a bubble bath
- Pedicure/Manicure
- Massage
- Walking or other form of exercise
- Going out to lunch by yourself or with friends
- A trip to a beauty salon or spa
- Sitting in the library looking at magazines
- Playing golf, tennis, or other sport
- Add your own items...

Before You Move Forward

Date: _____

Identify at least one thing that you accomplished this month as a result of doing the iChoose2 Love My Life journey.

_____

_____

_____

What went well this past month?

_____

_____

_____

What didn't you do, but intended to?

_____

_____

_____

What 3 things would you like to continue to implement?

1. _____

2. _____

3. _____

#40:
iChoose2 Make My Home a Haven

Home is where you belong- "where your story begins." Home is your safe haven. It's where memories are made, where you sleep peacefully, where you sort through struggles, and where you partner with others through life.

A house is something you build, while a home is something you create. You have many choices when deciding how you would like your home to look and feel, and what takes place within those walls. Spend time thinking about what is most important to you before creating a haven for you and your family. Whether you live alone or with a dozen other people, you want a place where everyone feels comfortable and safe. You want your home to be a place where family members and guests want to gather and spend time together. And remember, no matter the size, style, or location of your home, it's the love and joy that "live" there that matters!

1. What kind of home environment do you want?
   Circle what applies to you:

Meals together	Kindness	Safe Haven
Sharing Chores	Encouraging	Supportive
A Place to Belong	Faith-based	Laughter

Other:

2. A place for family members to learn:

Relationship skills	How to adjust to different personalities
Conflict Resolution	To develop happy memories

Other:

3. Physical atmosphere:

Orderly	Uncluttered	Lived-in Look
Clean	Casual	Kid-friendly
Stylish	Relaxed	Better Homes & Gardens
Inviting	Peaceful	Prepared for Guests

Other:

4. Look back over your answers and create a short summary that describes the kind of place you want your home to be.

_____

_____

_____

_____

Much of what makes a house a home includes the memories that are created there. Identify some of the ways you build memories in your home. Put a check next to the statements below that you already do in your home.

— Traditions (holiday, birthday, etc.)

— Simplify (less "stuff," limit activities, less technology, etc.)

— Family activities (game night, serve together, eat meals together, home projects, etc.)

— Invite friends and relatives to your home

— Take pictures and display them

— Home is organized but not "fussy"

— Décor reflects your personality or family values (i.e. colorful, spiritual sayings, pictures from trips, books, piano, etc.)

— Spiritual atmosphere (Bible study, praying, encouragement, etc.)

— Peace (even if you have high activity much of the time there are times of peace whether it's a bedtime ritual, meal time conversation, reading time, sitting on porch, watching a movie, etc.)

— Atmosphere of health (exercise, healthy foods, rest is valued, kindness prevails, etc.)

Now go back over the list and put a + next to each statement that describes something <u>you would like to incorporate</u> into your life to enhance your home.

Below, write out how and when you will do that:

_____

_____

_____

_____

_____

_____

_____

_____

_____

_____

_____

_____

_____

_____

_____

_____

_____

_____

#41:

iChoose2 Manage My Home

Decades ago, managing a home was clear. There were everyday chores that needed to be done. At the end of the day the reward was sitting down as a family, eating a meal together, and then reading or listening to music together. Times have changed and managing a home has become a challenge.

You are the cook, the maid, the chauffer, the accountant, the organizer, the peace-maker, and the list goes on. Being all of these things can be overwhelming, especially if you work outside the home. Your "work" day doesn't end when you leave the office because you still have a household to manage.

How can you lighten your load? Can you enlist the help of your family? We are all wired differently and there are probably things that your husband and children can do to help around the house so that managing the household is easier.

Suggestions/Ideas for Managing your Home:
- Maintain a family calendar
- Plan your meals out for the entire week
- Set aside one night to pay bills
- Create a cleaning to do list and schedule
- Make it a priority to have dinner as a family
- Create systems that allow you to use your time efficiently

This Week's Challenge:

In an average week, what needs to be done around your home, so that it's managed well?

Are there things on your list that can be delegated? To whom?

What are 3 things you could do this week to manage your home more effectively?

1. _____

_____

2. _____

_____

3. _____

_____

#42:

iChoose2 Declutter

"Life is really simple, but we insist on making it complicated."

Confucius

We all have some clutter in our lives. Those things or thoughts that make life way too complicated. Maybe it shows up as:

- Mental clutter: double-mindedness, confusion, wrong thinking that is stumping you and keeping you stuck.
- Physical clutter: paper, too many knick-knacks, clothes that you haven't worn in years, and project clutter (all of those unfinished projects that make you feel guilty when you look at them whether it is photos, furniture you want to re-finish, or a hem that needs repairing).
- Financial clutter: debt, confusion around your investments, or simply bad habits of spending too much and saving too little.

Physical clutter is a good starting point. Whether your tendency is to be naturally organized or "messy," excess clutter in your living or work environment saps your energy, wastes your time, and increases your stress. The goal is not to generate more stress by demanding a sterile environment but to create systems that help you maintain your surroundings with ease.

What is the motivation for decluttering? Simply stated, less chaos allows more time for the people and activities that are most valuable to you. You can delight in the sense of well-being you experience when you eliminate the excess clutter around you.

This Week's Challenge:

Decide that you are going to take steps to declutter your surroundings and set up some systems that work for you.

Coaching Assignment:

Select one of the following decluttering techniques to focus on this week:

1. Develop a simple habit of decluttering daily.
   - Set the alarm on your phone or watch to remind yourself to practice this decluttering method twice a day, every day.
   - Twice a day, every day, set the timer for 15 minutes and for just that short time declutter one area as quickly as possible. When the time is up, you are finished – until the next 15 minute time slot.
   - Before you set the timer decide what area you will declutter: a drawer, the family room, the piles on the kitchen table, your bathroom counter, etc.
   - Once you set the timer, move quickly to get as much done in the short period of time as possible.
   - The goal is to get in the habit of doing this twice a day, every day. You will be amazed at how much you can accomplish in just 15 minutes on a regular basis.

- Record your progress in the table below. Write in the day of the week. Then fill in the time of the first 15 minute decluttering period and the second 15 minute decluttering period. Remember to continue twice a day every day, after the week of recording your progress is completed.

Day of the Week	1st 15 minute period	2nd 15 minute period

2. Set up one system that will help you keep the areas you use clutter-free. Choose just one for now. Later you can set up more.

- Make sure the things you use all the time have a "home." What drawer do the scissors go in? Put your keys in the same place after each use. Have a place where the batteries and flashlights are kept. Teach family members to put things back after each use. It is best to handle each piece of paper once – put it where it belongs or throw it away.

- There will always be items that need attention later or we need to think about. Put them in a designated folder. Once a month go through that folder and either handle the need or throw it away.

- Have one "clutter" drawer. Put the "clutter" that you don't know what to do with in that drawer. During one of your 15 minute declutter sessions, clean out that drawer.

- Develop your own system according to the needs that you have.

#43:

iChoose2 Get Organized

"Don't agonize. Organize"

Florence Kennedy.

"I just don't have time!"

"It will get worse before it gets better."

"Some people are naturally organized. I can *get* organized but I can't *stay* organized."

"Truthfully, I'd rather catch up with my DVR and eat ice cream."

You may have reasons for your chaos. Your excuses for the piles of paper around you, being late for appointments, or not being able to find something have been practiced over and over again. They seem natural to you now and you even believe them. Imagine "the BEST you" is looking at how you run your life. What do you see? Do you see someone who is wasting time looking for things? Do you see someone whose frustration level is climbing because the details of life seem to be spinning out of control? Is that chaos and disorder allowing "the BEST you" to shine through?

Each day your choices determine which direction you will go. Is *this* the week you will finally take that important next step to get organized? Is *this* the week you will choose one area you can conquer so that in the long run you will have more time and less frustration?

Don't try to catch up with your super organized friends in one day. Know that it will take time and that it will happen...slow and steady wins the race. Choose just *one* area to devote time to this week toward getting organized. Then take some time to celebrate your accomplishment and resolve to stay organized in this one area!

This Week's Challenge:

Choose to get organized in one area. Set up a system that will help you get and stay organized. Realize it takes time to form a new habit so work on just one area until it is a natural part of you. Celebrate that you have conquered this one area.

Coaching Assignment:

Examples of areas to organize and steps to take:

1. Create a Bill Paying System
    *   Make a list of all bills that need paying each month.
    *   Put that list in a folder and place each bill in that folder as it comes in.
    *   Decide two dates each month that you will pay the bills.
    *   Put a check mark and date beside the bill on the list as you pay it.

2. Calendar

   • Select your calendar of choice: the one on your phone, your computer, a paper calendar at your desk, a family calendar on your refrigerator.

   • Choose one calendar to use this week for all of your appointments and important things.

   • Choose a time each morning and each evening you will update it. For example, 8 AM and 8 PM; or right after breakfast and right after dinner.

3. Identify the area that tends to collect the most piles of paper: your desk, kitchen counter, dining room table, etc. Set up a system that will help you keep that area more organized.

   • Examine the categories of papers that collect and make a list.

   • Decide where each category needs to go. For example, can you make file folders for each category? Would desk trays labeled a certain way help you place the papers where they can be handled?

   • Once you get that area organized, practice keeping it organized. Put the papers in the proper file or tray. Don't forget the most important "file" of all – the trash can!

Your Turn – Get Organized in ONE Area:

1. Area you have chosen to get organized:

   _____

2. Steps you will take to organize that area:

   a.

   b.

   c.

   d.

3. How will you celebrate?

   _____
   _____
   _____
   _____
   _____
   _____
   _____

Doesn't it feel great? Now work at staying organized in that one area until it is a habit for you!

#44:

iChoose2 Go Green

"Unless someone like you cares a whole awful lot,
Nothing is going to get better. It's not."

Dr. Seuss, from The Lorax

"Use it up, wear it out, make it do, or do without."

Proverb

According to the United States Census Bureau, the present world population is 7 billion people (Kung HC, 2008). By 2050 it is expected to be 10 billion. We all use the same resources, collect an incredible amount of garbage, and use way too many products that end up in the landfills. Consider your neighborhood and how much garbage you see each week on the curb, ready to be picked up. Now consider that on a worldwide scale. The habits of each country affect other countries around the world.

Remember the slogan, "Reduce, Reuse, Recycle"? You may be involved in a family or community that encourages one another to put the promptings of this slogan into action. Or maybe you know the saying and have become negligent in using it.

How can you can follow the "Reduce, Reuse, Recycle" slogan? REDUCE the amount of waste material you leave behind. How can you purchase less? REUSE items or fix things rather than tossing them out. RECYCLE what can be recycled in creative ways.

Read through the following Go Green Ideas and select a few that you could try for yourself. Act as a model for your family and your neighbors and show them how easy it can be.

Go Green Ideas:

1. **Try a CSA.**

    Community Supported Agriculture is a way to purchase a share of vegetables from a local farming community. During the growing season in your area you will pick up your products at a designated area every week or every other week. Your share most likely will include 6 – 10 vegetables and fruits for 2-4 people. It's fun to see what you receive and to try new vegetables and recipes. Do an internet search to find CSAs in your area.

2. **Host a Private Exchange**

    Have a party! Have each person bring gently used clothes, jewelry, kitchen items, or toys. Have fun trading with each other. Take the "extras" to a local charity.

3. **Unplug Electronics When Not Using**

    Appliances and electronics still consume energy as long as they are plugged in. So get in the habit of unplugging your toaster, coffee maker, cell phone chargers, and laptop chargers. When you go on vacation, unplug your TVs, computers, and other appliances and electronics.

4. Choose to Make Paperless Payments

Many credit card bills, utilities, and even tithing can be paid online. This option saves all the excess paper and expense of envelopes, postage, checks, and clutter. Create folders in your email to keep records of payments and receipts that are necessary for your taxes.

5. Make your own Non-Toxic All-Purpose Cleaner

Yes, you want to maintain a clean home environment. But most people have too many types of cleaners. Most of these cleaners come in packaging that can't be recycled. Try making your own all-purpose cleaning solution. One "recipe" is to mix 1/2 cup vinegar and 1/4 cup baking soda and ½ gallon of water. Buy glass spray bottles to keep it in. Divide it into several spray bottles to keep in each bathroom and in the kitchen. Use on sinks, counters, windows, mirrors, and chrome fixtures.

6. Use Your Phone to Store your Lists

Most cell phones have a great feature where you can make your grocery list, errand list, or any other list you can think of. It takes getting in the habit of using this feature, but once you do, you will see how convenient it is. You no longer have to keep track of paper lists, you use less paper, and you simply delete it when you are finished.

7. **Borrow it from the Library**

   Libraries are a great way a community can come together to reduce over consumption of products. Borrow books and movies from the library rather then spending money and then having them take up room in your house. Give or sell used books, movies, and CDs to a local used bookshop. Go to the library to read newspapers and magazines. Many are available online now as well. While you're at it, share power tools and other items with neighbors to cut down on everyone owning tools that are only used every once in a while.

8. **Use Reusable Bags**

   Keep several reusable bags in your car. Yes, you may have to go back out to the car when you realize you forgot to bring them into the store. But, once it becomes a habit, you will feel much better about how you are contributing.

These are ideas to get you started.
Now it's time to make a plan!

This Week's Challenge:

Engage your family and friends and to select some new ways you will Go Green.

Coaching Assignment:

Choose three ways you are going to take responsibility for Going Green this week. Choose from the ideas above or choose your own. Ask a young person – especially elementary school children – and they can give you many ideas. They learn about going green in school!

Write out the 3 areas you will focus on this week.

1. _____

How well did you do?

_____

_____

_____

2. _____

How well did you do?

_____

_____

_____

3. _____

How well did you do?

_____

_____

_____

Before You Move Forward

Date: _____

Identify at least one thing that you accomplished this month as a result of doing the iChoose2 Love My Life journey.

_____

_____

_____

What went well this past month?

_____

_____

_____

What didn't you do, but intended to?

_____

_____

_____

What 3 things would you like to continue to implement?

1. _____

2. _____

3. _____

#45:
iChoose2 Invest In Others

"Love and kindness are never wasted.
They always make a difference."

Barbara De Angelis

Stop. Sit down with someone. Listen. Those are three things we don't do often enough. When spending time with others, most of the time we feel the need to engage in an activity – dinner, movie, shopping, etc. What happened to just going to someone's house and chatting?

However you spend time with someone, the important point is to treat it as a long-term investment, not a short-term one. Make the choice to be intentional about that relationship. Give that person your undivided attention – no texting, emails, Facebook or Twitter. Put your phone on silent. Stop and listen to the needs, desires, and struggles of that person.

Too often, serving others is perceived as attending to a short-term need. Many would rather invest for 20 minutes than a long-term commitment. What would happen if, instead of dispersing your energy to serve the short-term problems of many people, you made a long-term commitment to just a few people? Are you ready to make that type of commitment to someone in need?

When you have determined who would benefit from a long-term commitment, consider these five ways you can invest in that person:

1. **Rejoice in one Another.** Look for their strengths and tell them. Celebrate a job promotion, a birthday, or an A on a test. Send a funny or thoughtful card.

2. **Respect Boundaries.** Plan ahead, but leave room for spontaneity. Talk through issues without being offended. Connect with this person often, but be sensitive to their other responsibilities.

3. **Relax and chat.** Invite that person over and spend time each week catching up with each other. Enjoy just being together.

4. **Relate personally.** People are relational. You can encourage and stretch each other in a loving way. Share about childhood experiences, hopes and dreams, and future plans. Share ideas and suggestions. Brainstorm ways to solve problems. It is not your responsibility to "fix" this person's situation, but you can certainly walk alongside them and help them make their own decisions. While there are times you and this person may caution one another, it's important most of the time to encourage each other to stretch and grow, pointing out strengths.

5. **Remember to Laugh and Be Silly.** There's just something about a good hearty belly laugh with someone. Create "silly" memories. Sometimes these belly laughs happen automatically and sometimes you have to shift perspective to view something in a funny way. These laughter experiences become times of bonding and deep connection.

This Week's Challenge:

Choose to invest in one person who you believe could really use you in the long-term. Challenge yourself to provide this person with loving attention, guidance, and/or assistance for as long as you are able.

Coaching Assignment:

Reflect on what you have just read about choosing to invest in another person. Journal about the following questions:

1. What are some ways another person could invest in you?

_____

_____

_____

_____

2. How could you use some of these ideas for investing in someone else?

_____

_____

3. Choose someone you would like to invest in. Write their name here and list several ways you plan on investing in them.

_____

_____

_____

_____

_____

_____

_____

_____

_____

_____

_____

_____

_____

_____

_____

_____

_____

_____

_____

_____

_____

#46:

iChoose2 Take a Risk

"Too often we underestimate the power of a touch, a smile,
a kind word, a listening ear, an honest accomplishment,
or the smallest act of caring, all of which
have the potential to turn a life around."

Leo Buscaglia

What is a risk that you feel God is asking you to do? Most Americans are raised to play it safe, follow the rules, and to be comfortable. However, if you were to share your greatest accomplishment or an exhilarating experience, you would probably be describing a time when you were out of your comfort zone – you took a risk.

You may need a fresh perspective about taking a risk. You might think it's doing something irresponsible, or highly dangerous, or will result in poor consequences. Instead, think about taking a risk as a step that will get you out of a rut, stretch you beyond your comfort zone, and give you a memorable experience. When you live your life so that you are always safe and comfortable, you can become numb to being the most you can be.

Without noticing it, fear can creep in – fear of failure, fear of looking silly or stupid, fear of getting hurt, fear of making a mistake, and fear of the unknown. Fear has a way of creeping in without you realizing it. So take steps to squelch fear by regularly trying something that is out of your comfort zone.

This Week's Challenge:

Taking a risk to serve others requires you to step outside of your normal comfort zone. For this week, volunteer someplace that normally would make you feel uncomfortable. Think about a group of people that you think you might feel uneasy around and seek a group who serves them. There are several groups who desperately need your help because many people are afraid to approach them. These groups may include:

- Homeless
- Unwed mothers
- People in nursing homes
- People in prison
- Orphans in the U.S. and overseas
- Children and adults with special needs
- People with debilitating physical and mental challenges

Most of the time you will find your fear disappearing when you realize how much all people have in common. Try doing some things to get yourself out of your comfort zone on a regular basis. You'll be surprised at the fear that has been holding you back. You will be delighted in the sense of freedom you will feel when you take a risk and experience the richness of life.

Journal:

Journal about what fears you think influence you and keep you from taking risks.

_____

_____

_____

_____

_____

_____

_____

_____

Coaching Assignment:

List some "risks" you are going to challenge yourself to take. Remember, taking a risk means doing something out of your comfort zone.

1. _____

_____

2. _____

_____

3. _____

_____

#47:

iChoose2 Be the Church

"Do not be interested only in your own life,
but be interested in the lives of others."

Philippians 2:4 (NCV)

There is so much to do in a day. The needs of your family, job, and simple daily living can be exhausting. Yet you can't help but acknowledge that people all around you have great needs. There is the homeless person digging in the trash can on the city street, the child of a friend who desperately needs medical care they can't afford, or the elderly widow next door who can't keep up with her house repairs. You may hurry by, turn your eyes away, or mumble, "I can't save the world."

But what if you considered taking some time each day to attend to the needs of others? What impact would that have in your community? What if you chose to *be the church* by reaching out to someone in your area who is having a hard time? One person won't "save the world." However, if we each choose to serve just one person and the people around you help another person, then together we can make a big impact.

Think about all of the superheroes that have been created in comic books and movies. Despite having a variety of supernatural powers, they all have one thing in common: they set aside time every day to attend to the people around them and to their needs. You'll find that allowing a small margin of unscheduled time in your day to serve will allow you to have a significant impact, and you don't need superpowers to do it!

What is the one thing you sense God nudging you to pay attention to? When you focus on one person's needs or on a group of people, you can see the difference you are making. As you build relationships with these people, you realize they are ministering to you as much as you are ministering to them!

This Week's Challenge:

Choose to be the Church – be aware of how is God nudging you to help someone else.

Choose an hour each day this week to look for ways to help others around you. Make sure you pay attention to what they need rather than using the time to tell them what you think they need.

Look for opportunities to serve others this week. You could...

- Pay for someone's coffee/meal behind you in the drive-through lane or give your waitress an extra tip.
- Be aware of needs around you. Does a neighbor need help with yard work? Does a mother need a break from her children? Is someone collecting clothing for a group of people?
- What group or person can you invest in? Is God nudging you to help fulfill a certain need regularly?

Journal:

How did it feel to have margin in your schedule, so that you were available to see the needs of others?

_____

_____

_____

_____

_____

_____

_____

How were you able to serve others this week?

_____

_____

_____

_____

_____

_____

_____

_____

_____

_____

_____

_____

#48:

iChoose2 Make a Difference

"I will give thanks to You, for I am fearfully and wonderfully
made; Wonderful are Your works,
And my soul knows it very well."

Psalm 139:14 NASB

You want your life to count. You want to make a difference. You
DO make a difference everyday by being who God created you to
be. You have learned that you have been magnificently designed
by the Creator of the Universe! Yes! God gave you a unique mix
of personality, passion, Spiritual Gifts, strengths, and interests.
There is only one YOU and YOU will make a difference when you
live into your design.

You have heard the expression "baked with love." Think of God
selecting just the right "ingredients" in you so you could make a
difference according to His plan. He puts together special
ingredients to make each of us slightly different and to
contribute to the health of His precious creation. Your
ingredients will be slightly different from someone else's.

God uses varying amounts of compassion, yearnings, and
abilities; He uses different flavors of personalities, strengths, and
Spiritual Gifts in each of us. You have a part to play; a difference
to make; a way to leave the world a better place. You accomplish
that by being the person God created you to be.

Choose to be who God created you to be in your own sphere of influence. Your ordinary life can be lived in extraordinary ways simply by intentionally carrying out the design God gave you. Focus each day on using your personality, strengths, Spiritual Gifts, passion, abilities, and interests. Choosing to make a difference through being who God created you to be will contribute to the well—being of the people God places in your path.

This Week's Challenge:

iChoose2 Make a Difference in ordinary, everyday ways by sharing the unique design that God has given me.

Coaching Assignment:

1. Write out a description of how God designed you. What are some of the ingredients He used? You might think about your personality, Spiritual Gifts, interests, strengths, and abilities. What are the qualities in yourself you would like to rise to the surface?

   _____

   _____

   _____

   _____

   _____

   _____

   _____

   _____

2. How would others describe you? Ask five people who are close to you to list five words that describe you. Combine the words on those lists below.

3. List three simple ways you can make a difference in your sphere of influence. For example: listen to your friend, spouse, children; write notes of encouragement; volunteer to take meals to someone who is sick; write a "how-to" blog or article; share a good belly laugh with someone; teach; lead; sing; read to someone; organize; invite; give; take pictures; build; love; show mercy, etc.

1. _____
   _____

2. _____
   _____

3. _____
   _____

Before You Move Forward

Date: _____

Identify at least one thing that you accomplished this month as a result of doing the iChoose2 Love My Life journey.

_____

_____

_____

What went well this past month?

_____

_____

_____

What didn't you do, but intended to?

_____

_____

_____

What 3 things would you like to continue to implement?

1. _____

2. _____

3. _____

#49:
iChoose2 Appreciate My Past

When you think about your past, your mind may land on wonderful memories, simple accomplishments, tough challenges, surprise twists and turns, or people who influenced your life. It's important to recognize that everything that has happened in your life has a purpose. Good or bad, God can use it all!

This week is a time to reflect on your past. Imagine you are looking at your life's journey in photos. Identify some of your experiences that have been defining moments: a book you read, a disease you had to adjust to, the loss of a job that may have led to a job you liked better, being treated unfairly that resulted in greater compassion, a loss, a kindness shown, going on a mission trip, getting a degree, moving; etc.

Your life experiences have made you the person you are today. You may have accomplishments that you are pleased with and challenges you have conquered. On the other hand, you may have some regrets from your past, decisions that you wish you had made differently. You now get to decide how to use those decisions that were not always so wise. Like it or not, your past experiences have molded you into the person you are today. You can choose to dwell in the past or move forward to the future.

The reality is that the past can't be changed no matter how much you wish it could. Let your past decisions—good and bad— guide your present life and you will leave a legacy that will make you proud. Appreciate the lessons you learned and let your past shape and form you into a person that honors God and others. Choose to appreciate your past. God can use each circumstance for His glory. It's the foundation for the legacy you are leaving.

This Week's Challenge:

Identify the 12 defining moments that have significantly shaped your life.

Coaching Assignment:

In the space below, begin brainstorming the experiences that have greatly influenced your life or contributed to who you have become (i.e. conversation, career change, birth of a child, marriage, illness, loss, advanced degree, etc.).

_____

_____

_____

_____

_____

_____

_____

_____

_____

_____

Based on your brainstorming, identify which 12 defining moments have had the greatest impact on your life. In the table below, list each of your defining moments in chronological order (with 1 being your earliest defining moment and 12 being the most recent).

My Defining Moments:

1		7	
2		8	
3		9	
4		10	
5		11	
6		12	

Look back over your list. Which moments were positive and which were negative? Reflect on each of your defining moments. What did you learn? How is your life different? How are you different?

_____

_____

_____

_____

_____

_____

_____

_____

If you could remove anything from your past, what would you choose to remove? Why?

_____

_____

_____

_____

_____

_____

Based on your defining moments, identify 3 lessons or themes that God has been teaching you throughout your life.

Lesson/Theme #1:

_____

_____

_____

_____

_____

Lesson/Theme #2:

_____

_____

_____

_____

_____

Lesson/Theme #3:

_____

_____

_____

_____

_____

"Trust in the LORD with all your heart and
lean not on your own understanding;
in all your ways submit to Him,
and He will make your paths straight."

Proverbs 3:5-6 (NIV)

#50:
iChoose2 Take Responsibility

You have ONE beautiful life. ONE life. It's YOURS. No one else is living it. It had an exact beginning – the day and time you were born. And it will have an exact ending. What are YOU going to do with the time in-between? Actually, what are you going to do with the time you have left?

It's YOUR choice. YOU are the CEO of your life. Of course, God guides and directs you, but He trusts you with the responsibility of making the most out of the ONE life He has given you. As Chief Executive Officer of your life, you have many decisions and choices to make. It won't do any good to blame someone else for the condition of your life. YOU are the one who can start fresh today.

What "story" have you been telling yourself for years that is keeping you from being all you can be? Do you attribute being overweight to your family genes or having babies? Do you blame the "mean girls" in school for your low self-esteem? Listen to how you talk to yourself. Do you think life would be better if you were smarter, prettier, richer, or lived someplace else? Are you being kind and encouraging to yourself or are your words harsh and degrading?

You can change your "story" and you can adjust how you talk to yourself. As you shift your thinking and your actions, you experience freedom and hope for a brighter future. Instead of waiting for "something" to happen so you can live a life you love, be the CEO and decide that you are going to love your life. Change your negative story into positive action and overcome the challenge. Turn your self-talk into words you would use with someone you loved dearly.

Instead of waiting for your circumstances to change, change your circumstances. Sometimes that simply means changing how you think about your circumstances. View them as stepping-stones to something better. Look for the "door" that will move you closer to the life you really want. Watch expectantly for a blessing. Ask yourself what God wants you to do with these situations. A fresh perspective helps you climb out of a rut.

A CEO addresses problems, looks for solutions, and takes responsibility. Step into your role. Choose to take responsibility for your life.

This Week's Challenge:

Choose to take responsibility and view your life with a fresh perspective.

Coaching Assignment:

1. The "stories" we tell over and over seem like truth to us. When in fact, they may simply be excuses for not overcoming a challenging situation. Sometimes we "excuse" ourselves from taking responsibility by telling a story that seems logical and reasonable. What "stories" have you been telling that keep you from overcoming obstacles?

    _____

    _____

    _____

    _____

    _____

2. What ten adjectives best describe you when you are at your best (joyful; content; clear-thinking; creative; energetic; peaceful; understanding; problem-solver; etc.)?

10 Adjectives that Describe Me:

Now, write these adjectives on separate index cards and place them where you will see them. (i.e. on your computer, bathroom mirror, Bible, favorite chair, over sink, microwave, etc.). Write your new story using these words.

#51:
iChoose2 Live with Meaning

Ask anyone over 50 and they will tell you, "Life goes by so quickly. I just don't know how that happened."

Life zooms by. It is so easy to fill your days with lots of things to do but not actually CHOOSE to live in a meaningful and intentional way. When you live intentionally, you identify what is truly important to you and then set boundaries so your life doesn't spin out of control. When you don't identify how you want to live your life, you end up skimming your life instead of actually living it.

Choose how you live your everyday life. It may seem to you that you have an infinite number of days ahead but learn from the wisdom of those who have gone before you – looking back, the years are very short.

In the movie, "Love Happens," the main character gives workshops to help others overcome grief. In one scene he takes his class outside the downtown building and asks them to identify what they hear. They reply, "jack-hammers, sirens, car horns, and squealing tires."

He takes them back inside, up the elevator to the roof of the many storied building. Again he asks what they hear and they reply, "wind blowing – and quiet."

He says, "What's the difference? We are in the same location but we hear different things?" One participant says, "It's the same location but a different perspective" (Camp, 2000).

That's what choosing to live intentionally is all about for you: a shift of perspective. You can choose to live in the screaming noise of everyday life or you can choose boundaries that will allow you to live intentionally and meaningfully. Craft today – each day - so that it is well lived. Choose NOT to let your life slip away, but embrace it and truly live your moments, days, and years.

This Week's Challenge:

1. Think about what is truly important in your life. What do you really want to be intentional about?

   _____

   _____

   _____

   _____

   _____

2. List the people who are the most important to you. Then make a list of the people who are clamoring for your attention. How can you rearrange your life activities so you give the people who are important to you the most attention? (it's really okay to disengage from some of the people in your life – we can only have effective relationships with a few people – choose).

People who are most important to me:

_____

_____

_____

_____

_____

People who want my attention, but must come AFTER
my MOST IMPORTANT list:

_____

_____

_____

_____

_____

3. Reflect on your answers and write down three steps you
   can take to live more intentionally.

_____

_____

_____

_____

_____

#52:

iChoose2 Leave a Legacy

What a treasure it is to leave the world a better place because you were here. That's what it means to leave a legacy. Perhaps you've been to a funeral that was actually called "A Celebration of Life," where the service was all about how that person had influenced the people around them and was committed to a cause that made a difference. Sometimes scholarship funds are established in honor of a person's contributions. Other times, the people they influenced continue to live in a way that honors that person.

Ultimately, everyone leaves a legacy - some small, some large and some good, others not. Whatever the legacy, it can have a ripple effect for generations to come. In what way will others' lives be better because you were here? What kind of legacy do you intend to leave - and for whom? It is better to think about the legacy you will leave and to influence what that legacy will be rather than to *hope* those you love will find something in you they want carried on.

As you think about the legacy you would like to leave, make it true to who you are, what you are passionate about, or how you want to be remembered. Perhaps it is how you take on each day, or a character trait God has refined in you, or a cause that you care deeply about. Most of the time a legacy is left through ordinary living with extraordinary influence.

Remember, even when you don't realize it, you are having an impact on others by what you say and do. Do you have a hearty laugh, a merciful heart, a thirst for learning, courage to take on tough issues, or maybe a love for the beauty of God's creation?

What "fragrance" do you leave through your words and actions? Does delight spill out of you into the lives of others or does your negativity smother the joy within a 50 foot radius? Would you call yourself an Encourager? A Problem-Solver? Someone others can count on during rough times? Or do you drain others of their time, energy, and resources? How is someone's life better having walked across your path? How are they better because they have been in contact with you?

Think about what others might remember about you and what they might say at an event that honors you – or at your "Celebration of Life." Choose to live each day to leave a legacy. Whether it is big or small to you, it leaves our world a better place.

This Week's Challenge:

Create a To-Be List

It's important to be real and be YOU. Think about how you want to BE. What qualities and actions do you want to be remembered for? When you make your To-Be list, write it out as if you already show those qualities and actions. You might incorporate a To-Be list right along with your to-do list each day.

Your perception of yourself affects how you carry out your To-Be list. For example, if you have a child who is difficult to listen to and you find yourself always wanting to correct rather than to listen, write on your To-Be list, "I am a good listener." This will remind you to listen and help your child feel like you really hear him.

Or if you write "I am generous," then when a friend says she is collecting for a certain charity, it will be easier for you to give unselfishly.

You might try to add your To-Be list to your To-Do list

My To-Be List	
My To-Do List	

Conclusion: iChoose2 Love My Life

Congratulations, you have just completed the iChoose2 Love My Life one-year journey toward living a life you love!

At the beginning of this journey, you completed a self-assessment where you took an honest look at your life and then determined where you hoped you would be in one year. It has now been a year since you took that initial assessment. Go to page 11 and 12 to review your answers, but be sure to mark this page, so you can come back.

After reviewing your initial assessment, how have you changed? What is different about your life? Are you living a life you truly love?

_____

_____

_____

_____

_____

_____

_____

_____

_____

_____

Now, take a few moments to look at your response throughout your book. What have been your biggest ah-ha moments throughout this journey?

_____

_____

_____

_____

_____

_____

_____

_____

_____

Each day you will be faced with an array of choices. Our hope is that through this journey you've discovered how to make intentional choices that will help you live a life of passion, purpose, fulfillment, and significance. So, ultimately you are living a life that YOU truly love!

Your journey doesn't end here. Our iBloom team will continue to be available to inspire, empower, and equip you as you strive to live a life you truly love. Find us at http://ibloom.us!

References

Camp, B. (Director). (2000). *Love Happens* [Motion Picture].

Chronic Diseases and Health Promotion. (n.d.). Retrieved November 18, 2011

Kung HC, H. D. (2008). Deaths: final data for 2005. *National Vital Statistics Reports*, 56(10).

Littauer, D. M. (2006). *Wired that Way: The Comprehensive Personality Plan*. Ventura, CA: Regal Books.

INSPIRINGwomen

iBloom is your go-to place for Christian Life Coaching for Women! We exist to inspire and empower every woman on the planet to live a life she loves!

iBloom offers the following for women:

iBloom Membership

Individual & Group Life & Business Coaching

Motivational Speakers

Special Events

Resources to equip YOU

Plus, much more!

For more information, visit us at www.ibloom.us.

Other Ways to Connect with iBloom:

Email – info@ibloom.us

Facebook – www.ibloom.us/facebook

Twitter – www.twitter.com/ibloom

Become an iBloom Member

Join a community of women who are investing in themselves. This is your first step toward having ongoing access to the iBloom Life Coaches and a supportive community all at a very affordable rate! For just the cost of a lunch out, you can begin living a life of passion, balance, and purpose.

Privileges of the iBloom Membership include:

- **Monthly group coaching calls with the iBloom Team & Experts**. And, there is no need to worry about scheduling conflicts because you'll have access to digital recordings of each call. These MP3's can easily be downloaded to your computer or iPod.

- **iBloom Membership Community**: Members have access to an exclusive online gathering place just for fellow iBloom members and the iBloom team. This is a great place to cultivate friendships and get ongoing encouragement throughout the month without ever leaving your home. The journey toward living a life you love happens best in a supportive environment- which is why this iBloom Community exists!

- **iBloom Discounts:** As an iBloom member, you are a part of our inner circle and we want to pass on FABULOUS discounts to you! So, you'll always save at least 10% on any additional iBloom resources!

To join women from around the world on this life-changing journey, go to http://ibloom.co/member and sign-up today!

Creation's Kaleidoscope

Embracing Light Devotional

Deborah A. Goshorn-Stenger

*Our mission is to share the love of Jesus through His Word,
nature, and creativity. We believe that God's beauty is all around us,
if we'll pause to see it, and give Him honor and praise.*

2 Pause and Praise Creations

Creation's Kaleidoscope: Embracing Light Devotional (Volume I)

Copyright 2021 © by 2 Pause and Praise Creations

Requests for information should be directed to:
2 Pause and Praise Creations
5315 Long Street, Suite 518
McFarland, WI 53558

ISBN: 978-1-954690-004

Deborah Goshorn-Stenger, and her husband, Douglas

Creation's Kaleidoscope:
Embracing Light Devotional

Table of Contents

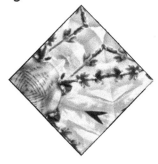

With Dedication

Dear Jesus,
This is our offering of love, gratitude, and praise. May every line, be like a song unto Your throne.

Dear Douglas,
I offer you a heartfelt "thank you" for being my right-hand—to hold as we walk, daily—to pray with, work with, to live and love with, in every step of this project. You're my best friend, and my earthly and heavenly treasure! I love you, and cherish every day of our journey.

Dear Family and Friends, to those who "*believed*" in me, and the talent given by God's Spirit—to bring His creations to life—I appreciate your support, and notes of encouragement.

A very special thank you, to my early readers/reviewers. I treasure your kindness and insights for this endeavor!

In loving memory of my Mom, *Pauline Rubeck Goshorn*, I'm thankful because you were my cheerleader and sharer of poems (as you've dubbed them "spiritual blessings") for many years. May God reward you for your part in this ministry on earth, and for His kingdom. We love you and appreciate every life you've helped touch with God's love.

I am grateful to each of you, and my readers, and pray that this Volume of *Creation's Kaleidoscope*, will bring you blessing, joy, and God's grace, nearly and dearly, to your hearts.

In His Love,

deborah goshorn-stenger

Preface

Do you remember the wonder that you felt as a child, when you discovered, the kaleidoscope? At first, you may have thought, "What is this?" After all, from the outside it looks ordinary enough. Some of them are void of design, while others are printed or wrapped in bright colors and designs. Yet, it isn't until you pick up this tube and peer inside, that you discover a magical world, an intricate place of imagination, that this "toy" seems to come to life.

Well, one day I was pondering (you might say daydreaming), as part of my meditation with the Lord, when I began to wonder what God sees from heaven. In my mind, I began to form myriad kaleidoscopes. Just envision the earth's colors from subtle to vivid, from an arial view.

Imagine every source of light from the heavenlies, touching earth. Imagine the varied angles, textures, colors and designs, and all living things that God has made, as they form facets, prisms, and fragmented designs. Then, pause to behold Him.

All of creation seemed to come alive, as if I was viewing it, for the first time. These, seemed to dance in the circle of my mind, as if forming a crown. And perhaps, that is exactly what all of creation is/does, before our Creator.

6

Then I began to think how our Creator's heart must have skipped a beat, as He formed every living thing in the Genesis Account: light, the sun, moon, stars, came—out of nothing—into perfection, to display from the inside, out, the facets of God's love.

I can imagine His delight, as He brought all things to life. Then, He wanted fellowship, and created man (men, women and children) in His own image, so that we could share in this world of beauty and miracles. Thus, *Creation's Kaleidoscope*, joined these images and ideas, to bring Him praise.

So come, journey into a place of childlike wonder. Come, you're invited to explore God's Word, His majestic world, and some moments in His company. After all, many of us first heard about our Lord as children, right at the beginning of our lives, with this vivid story of how God made the earth and heavens. So that is where we'll begin. Come, pause, like the turning of a kaleidoscope's wand, to behold His imaginative, and interesting marvels. Come, discover the many facets of His character and loving-kindness.

The *Creation's Kaleidoscope: Embracing Light Devotional,* gives you a multi-faceted, multi-dimensional view of the Creator, His love and grace. It's meant for you to pick up, and peer into. It's a place where God's Word, photography, prose, poetry, and prayers unite, to guide you to reflect upon Your Maker as Artist, Sculptor, Painter, and Architect, etc. And it's a place where He welcomes you like a child, to delight in His presence.

Out of void, Genesis tells us that God created all things. From galaxies to the starry hosts, from sunrises and sunsets ... light embraces us to display God's love. What most intrigues you about this holy account? Why?

How to use this Devotional

This work has been designed to be structured but not formulaic, and to have a creative, free-flowing narrative. It is intended for you to read as you wish. What do I mean? Read one entry a day or several at a time. Read and absorb, at your own pace. But please, allow time to meditate—upon each picture, entry, Scripture, and concept. Use this as an enhancement of your personal time with God—when you have time—to delve into its insights and truths, to pick up and peer into, as you would a kaleidoscope.

As to its parts? You'll notice some entries are poems, some are more prose in style, and still others are prayers. The prayers, are entitled "Spectrum of the Heart." They came directly from my personal journals. They were based upon, my "Thank You's to God." This is a style or method of meditation that the Lord taught me to display my gratitude for all that He does, on a daily basis. They are intended for you to learn and grow closer to the Lord, in a personal way.

There are also spaces included for you, to explore your own "Thank You's to God." At the end of each section are entries entitled the Soul's Introspection. These, are a combination of Scripture references relating to each topic or facet of God's character, love and grace, and devotional questions. They are provided for your study and reflection, and would be appropriate for small-group fellowship.

As you read page by page, I hope you will see and feel the Master's touch, not only in creation, but reflected within your own life.

Prayer of Meditation

I might suggest that you begin each reading with this prayer ...

Dear Lord,

*I'm pushing "pause" in my activities and coming to meet
with You. I'm setting aside this time to seek Your presence.*

*Let Your Word soak into my mind and come alive,
in my senses. Let Your truths be applied, to change
and mold me into Your likeness.*

*Help me to come with a humble, teachable spirit,
so that I grow in the knowledge of Who You are. And may
everything in all of creation, bring me a greater
awareness of Your nature, so that I can praise Your name.*

*May I be like a prism—reflecting these promises
as rays of hope, love, and grace, I pray. Amen.*

So let's begin where it all began ... Genesis 1, 2:2 VOICE (Excerpts)

"In the beginning, God created everything: the heavens above and the earth below. Here's what happened: At first the earth lacked shape and was totally empty, and a dark fog draped over the deep while God's spirit-wind hovered over the surface of the empty waters. Then there was the voice of God.

God: Let there be light.

And light flashed into being. God saw that the light was beautiful and good, and He separated the light from the darkness. God named the light 'day' and the darkness 'night.' Evening gave way to morning. That was day one.

God: Let there be a vast expanse in the middle of the waters. Let the waters above part from the waters below.

So God parted the waters and formed this expanse, separating the waters above from the waters below. It happened just as God said. And God called the vast expanse 'sky.' Evening gave way to morning. That was day two.

God: Let the waters below the heavens be collected into one place and congregate into one vast sea, so that dry land may appear.

It happened just as God said. God called the dry land 'earth' and the waters congregated below 'seas.' And God saw that His new creation was beautiful and good.

God: Earth, sprout green vegetation! Grow all varieties of seed-bearing plants and all sorts of fruit-bearing trees.

It happened just as God said. The earth produced vegetation—seed-bearing plants of all varieties and fruit-bearing trees of all sorts. And God saw that His new creation was beautiful and good. Evening gave way to morning. That was day three.

God: Lights, come out! Shine in the vast expanse of heavens' sky dividing day from night to mark the seasons, days, and years. Lights, warm the earth with your light.

So God created huge sea creatures, all the swarm of life in the waters, and every kind and species of flying birds—each able to reproduce its own kind. And God saw that His new creation was beautiful and good. And God spoke this blessing over them. ...

... **God**: Be fruitful and multiply. Let creatures fill the seas. Let birds reproduce and cover the earth.

Evening gave way to morning. That was day five.

God: Earth, generate life! Produce a vast variety of living creatures —domesticated animals, small creeping creatures, and wild animals that roam the earth.

It happened just as God said. God made earth-creatures in a vast variety of species: wild animals, domesticated animals of all sizes, and small creeping creatures, each able to reproduce its own kind. God saw that His new creation was beautiful and good. And God paused.

God: Now let Us conceive a new creation—humanity—made in Our image, fashioned according to Our likeness. And let Us grant them authority over all the earth—the fish in the sea and the birds in the sky, the domesticated animals and the small creeping creatures on the earth.

So God did just that. He created humanity in His image, created them male and female. Then God blessed them and gave them this directive: 'Be fruitful and multiply. Populate the earth. I make you trustees of My estate, so care for My creation and rule over the fish of the sea, the birds of the sky, and every creature that roams across the earth.'

God (to humanity): Look! I have given you every seed-bearing plant that grows on the earth and every fruit-bearing tree. They will be your food and nourishment. As for all the wild animals, the birds in the sky, and every small creeping creature—everything that breathes the breath of life—I have given them every green plant for food.

And it happened just as God said. Then God surveyed everything He had made, savoring its beauty and appreciating its goodness. Evening gave way to morning. That was day six. ...

... On the seventh day—with the canvas of the cosmos completed— God paused from His labor and rested."

God created all things, by the sound of His voice. What is He saying to you, through creation, at this present time in your life? Have you been listening and observing His signs?

Out of Darkness

Focusing-In

The kaleidoscope's interior lies dormant—until it's lifted up to a source of light. Then, it reveals miracles of color, design, facets, and wonders to behold. From a veiled interior that gave you only a dim view, now radiate images that encourage your imagination to run free.

Did you ever think of dawn as a treasure, that dispels every shadow and illuminates all the amazing things that our Creator has made from the beginning of time? Have you ever seen light, as a form of God's embrace to all mankind? Have you ever wondered where God is, during times of difficulty in your life?

Darkness—it's a physical state, meaning a lack of light. It can also mean an emotional state, as well— of illness, depression, sadness, or when circumstances weigh heavily on one's mind and spirit.

Light came to earth, as a babe; His name is Jesus. He rules and reigns, on high. He is the same yesterday, today and forever. This Light will never fade.

Let the Lord shine His light into every corner of your mind, heart, and life. He's the One you can trust—always. He is the One Who is the Light of the World and heaven. He is the glow within the soul of every child of God.

Section 1

Out of Darkness

Out of void, out of nothingness, came Creation.

When I found this fullest moon reflected in a simple puddle, it was like the passage below, had come to life. Even in the darkness, God is listening—to our prayers, to our pleas. Because He is Lord, Creator, Maker—visible and invisible—He shines forth at all times, and is available at all hours. He is the light within our hearts, to illuminate every soul that calls upon His name.

Colossians 1:9-17 NASB

" ... We have not ceased to pray for you and to ask that you may be filled with the knowledge of His will in all spiritual wisdom and understanding, so that you will walk in a manner worthy of the Lord, to please Him in all respects, bearing fruit in every good work and increasing in the knowledge of God; strengthened with all power, according to His glorious might, for the attaining of all steadfastness and patience; joyously giving thanks to the Father, who has qualified us to share in the inheritance of the saints in Light. For He rescued us from the domain of darkness, and transferred us to the kingdom of His beloved Son, in whom we have redemption, the forgiveness of sins. He is the image of the invisible God, the firstborn of all creation. For by Him all things were created, both in the heavens and on earth, visible and invisible, whether thrones or dominions or rulers or authorities—all things have been created through Him and for Him. He is before all things, and in Him all things hold together."

God gave us a sun for the daytime and the moon for nighttime. They are lanterns to demonstrate that He is our guide and source of light and hope. Out of darkness, everything was created. Out of it, He rises, to embrace us with His loving-kindness. May you feel the blessing of God's banner of love, every moment of your life!

Earth was void

Out of void,
    Out of utter nothingness,
        Out of silence,
            Out of shapeless, fathomless darkness,
God created heaven and earth.

It was in the beginning, that God made all of the wonders that we see. He made galaxies and starry hosts, calling them each by name. He formed land and the seas, sea-life, all vegetation, flora and fauna, animals, livestock, birds, and insects—each in their own types and varieties. Then He breathed life, out of dust, to create mankind.

In six days, the Lord made all things, then He declared everything to be beautiful and "good." Then, He rested. Imagine it. All of heaven's majesty was in place. All of earth's miracles and delights were on display. Out of the void, came life, from the Creator, Life-Giver, Artist, Architect, Painter, Potter, and Sculptor, to show us the existence of nature and to demonstrate His own, so that no one is without excuse: to see Him, know Him, experience Him.

"Before the mountains were formed, before the hills, I was born—before he had made the earth and fields and the first handfuls of soil. I was there when he established the heavens, when he drew the horizon on the oceans. I was there when he set the clouds above, when he established springs deep in the earth. I was there when he set the limits of the seas, so they would not spread beyond their boundaries. And when he marked off the earth's foundations, I was the architect at his side. I was his constant delight, rejoicing always in his presence. And how happy I was with the world he created; how I rejoiced with the human family!" Proverbs 8:25-31 NLT

Creation, has been placed within the heart of every human and every created thing. Like a heartbeat, every color, angle, landscape, starry host, and person, has been made in order to declare Him to be Lord, and to give Him glory. And so from the void, Jesus comes with His Spirit, with His love and grace—to fill us, as He has the whole earth and heaven—with His presence and majesty.

Earth was void, until He began to fill every space with His very being. As we journey through the story of creation, we'll see how He longs to do the same in our hearts. For as He was in the beginning, He is still today, everlasting.

Unto the Hills

We were out on a drive one late summer's night, to escape the evening's still hot temperatures. Into a quiet, desolate area we traveled, when across the way, twinkling lights lit the hillside. In our modern-day world, it is as close to complete darkness as we usually come, unless we have a power outage that occurs in the wee hours.

Think of it, without light, we search for a flashlight, a candle, anything to keep us from stumbling around in the dark. But even on the gloomiest of nights, the moon usually makes an appearance, or stars peep through the stratosphere. Rarely, do we feel the complete void, that was present at the beginning of creation. But what occurred to me on our late night journey, was that even these tiny spots of illumination, brought a feeling of comfort. They brought a sense of peace—of knowing—that we were not alone.

When darkness seems to surround us, we too, can know that our Eternal God is aware of us. He knows our name; He knows our rising, resting, times of working and slumber. There is nothing, no circumstance, no trial, that we experience on our own—because He is the source of all light and truth. His presence, His Spirit, is as near as our first whisper.

On this night, it was as if Jesus said to us: "Lift your eyes to the hills, that's where the light is." It's where our hope lies, our peace rests. It's where we come to pause and bring our praise, requests, concerns, and the things on our heart. It's where our focus shifts from an earthly perspective, onto our heavenly Father and His glory. It's where the void of doubt, emptiness, loneliness, grief or fear, are met with the Warrior's weapon of piercing Light.

> *"I look to the hills! Where will I find help? It will come from the Lord, who created the heavens and the earth. The Lord is your protector, and he won't go to sleep or let you stumble." Psalm 121:1-3 CEV*

Unto the hills, raises our awareness of God's nearness. For any present darkness, is only momentary in the light of God's Spirit that resides in our hearts. Here, we whisper His name and come into personal communion. Here, we enter holy ground that is lit with His love. Here, we discover that darkness has no power over us, because the Light has come for all mankind.

Even the Darkness …

Dusk, was falling quickly. In fact, it was descending so rapidly that we were rushing toward the park's gate, so that we were not shut-in for the night. Yet as I snapped photo after photo of this purple twilight, my mind could not help but remember this verse: "If I say, 'Surely the darkness will cover me, and the night will be the only light around me, even the darkness is not dark to You and conceals nothing from You, but the night shines as bright as the day; Darkness and light are alike to You.'" Psalm 139:11-12 AMP

Imagine it, though this beautiful sense of hush was lowering over the trees, and the first stars were on the rise in this location—in another area of the world, dawn was beginning to break; light was beginning to shine forth. What a solace to our minds when we feel troubled, lonely, or are hurting. Right?

Darkness, is not so, to our Father. He is awake at all hours, available in every circumstance, in any space of void, time of grief, difficulty, or when we find our hearts racing with anxiety. And to me, it brings comfort, that nothing can separate us from His love. No shadow. No sin. No lack on our part. Nothing that we do or don't do.

Even on the darkest night, God is present; His light is dawning. So may your heart, rest tonight, knowing that He is at watch, because you are safely held in the Guardian's care, faithfully. Light and dark are the same to our Sovereign Lord. Let that truth settle your soul and let you dream in shades of purple twilight, until the break of dawn.

Father, when we feel darkness, void, or loneliness settle around our shoulders, or enter our minds and hearts, may Your light pierce every space, to disarm the shadows. For in You, is peace. In You, I find rest. In You, I am held from dusk to dawn, because I am loved by the One Who has written in the stars, His love for all mankind. Shine upon me Lord, right where I am, for I trust in You. Amen.

Darkness is not so, to the Lord. Since He is the Light of the World, there is no space in which shadows cannot be illuminated. Name a time as a child, when a parent or adult gave you assurance that darkness was not as scary as you perceived it to be. Name a time when Jesus shed some light on a situation, to do the same.

Oh, the storm clouds have gathered,
Heavy, they are laden with rain;
They shift in the sky,
Looking, like veins.
As they rolled like a wave,
They looked ready to pour down a tide.
Pale to dark, white to slate,
They are engraved,
With the power of Your name.
Now there begins,
The anthem—
A thunderous chorus can be heard.
It echoes with the movement overhead,
And as it nears,
I see a flash,
And Your might is displayed.
It is engraving,
The awesomeness of Your fame.
Oh, the rain begins its song,
A shower like a symphony,
Now the drums,
And the strings are added in.
In the distance,
The whistle of the train,
Blends like a note of harmony;
It's engraving Your majesty,
On the morning.
Out of darkness,
The wonder of Your name,
Is being proclaimed.

"I create light and darkness, happiness and sorrow. I, the Lord, do all of this. Tell the heavens to send down justice like showers of rain. Prepare the earth for my saving power to sprout and produce justice that I, the Lord, create."
Isaiah 45:7-8 (CEV)

There is nothing like a storm to proclaim the name of Jesus. The wind was moving the clouds, and each shape, made visible the rain, the thunder and lightning. All, came together to display the power and might of our Creator, as God and King of the universe. As He engraved each image upon the sky on this particular morning—it was like seeing His hand, shaping our lives.

Sometimes storm clouds gather and rain comes, thunder resounds and lightning appears ... but I am finding, that often, they are drawing me to Him—to display His power in my life, so that His promises become fully etched upon my heart.

Lord, may Your majesty be written in every crevice. May Your love, run through my veins. And may I always, forever, proclaim the wonder of Your name. Amen.

Don't be afraid of the darkness, only fear if God is not your Companion. Today, is the time to make Him your Lord, your Friend, your Shepherd, Let the storm proclaim that God reigns, in any shadow and in every light.

The Storm Ahead

Sometimes we can see the storm ahead of us. Sometimes, we can see the clouds gather on the horizon. We can feel the wind heighten, and billow around us. And though we walk on a winding path, we know that God will lead us safely, into His peace.

Storm clouds offer a version of darkness. Emotionally, this is true as well. Think about a situation that left you feeling like clouds surrounded you. How did you come-into the light?

19

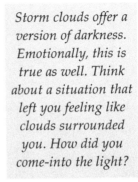

I feel clouds surrounding me daily. My son — causes extreme

There was a winding path,
Lined with weaving grass,
Overhung with clouds,
With a storm about to pass.
It was formed with a veil of blue-gray,
Laden with a burden of rain.
Light and shadow held a beauty,
That was majestically plain.
It had a perfect simplicity,
Although just a country scene;
It displayed a form of peace,
Before the storm, earth was calm, serene.

Our lives are like a winding path,
Lined with things that weave in and out;
Joy and sorrow intermingle,
Rainbows and storms, fear and doubt.
We can be clouded by a lack of faith,
Shadows can cover our thoughts.
We have moments of perfect trust,
Times we seek, times we are sought.
Following Jesus isn't always simple;
It doesn't always lead to the popular scene.
Yet we can be wrapped in His peace,
In His hope, supreme.

When there is a storm on the horizon,
And clouds are gathering before your eyes,
Look for any ray of sunshine,
For God, the Savior, to arise.
If you can just feel His presence,
In the wind, in the rain,
Lean into His shelter,
Seek His embrace in times of pain.
You will find Him in the good times,
See His provision and care …
It is in these moments,
That we learn to trust Him, there.

Whether we can see life's storms coming, or whether they are a
surprise, if we are following Jesus, we learn to know that He walks
beside us. We learn to trust Him. We learn to see the evidence of His
care and provision for us, and that gives us the faith to persevere
when we are faced with difficulties.

He is available in the good times, the tough times, the stormy times,
the sorrow-filled times. He is the One you can trust and turn to, on
the winding path, or along any road that you face. He will gather you
close, shelter you and protect you. He is Lord of the weather,
Guardian of the storms, and He loves you with a constant, abiding,
protective embrace for all time.

He doesn't listen to my parents or me. Somehow, I get the blame since my parents will not blame Ian.

Darkness and Light

Light, poured through this forested area. Darkness had met its match, as purity seemed to stream through the branches. In fact, the sun itself was cradled in the curve of a limb—as if the very beams were framed—held there, majestically, in mid-air. One half of the picture is in shadows; the other half, shines, highlighting each leaf in great detail. So it is in our lives.

I can't even go for a 30 minute walk in the AM, without hearing my mom complain that she does more than me when it comes to taking care of him.

Darkness and light, fight, compete—at every turn—in nature, in our emotions, in the spiritual realm (Ephesians 6:12). Yet darkness is not so, to the Lord. (Psalm 139:12) He rules above it, beneath it, over it, through it, in it. In fact, we enter into the world, enveloped in spiritual darkness, having a sinful nature from the moment of our birth. (Romans 3:23) Yet Jesus made a way for us to be pure—by being our sacrificial Lamb.(1 Peter 1:17-19) This is His invitation of love to us. It's His grace shining down, into the heart, as illumination to draw near to us.

Each of us must choose where we want to live, in the light or in the darkness. So too, we must choose whether we wish to invite Jesus into our hearts, to follow His Will and obey His directives, or not. And also, we must choose where we want to spend eternity. (Romans 6:23, Revelation 3:20)

Light came into the forest, on this early morning to illuminate one side, while the other remained in shadows. Jesus, offers to come into every heart, but He also gives us choice—light or darkness. Now's the time to choose grace. Now is the time, to let His hope illuminate every decision, dream, and emotion.

I mostly do everything except my dad does take him out once a day →

May the Light of Christ dwell in you, above you, beneath you, over you, through you—until your soul is illuminated—from within and from without. Because when He's Your Savior, Shepherd and Lord—darkness, has met its match. It's already been defeated on your behalf.

Darkness and light will always be at war. But peace comes in knowing, the Light of the World.

Dark to Light

One very early morning, I traced a wee hour from its darkest moment, to dawn. In the first image, only a street light illuminated our small front porch. In the next, a hint of brightness began to become evident, and even the first hues of blue sky lit the atmosphere. In the third, the light was almost milky, translucent. And in the final one, subtle shades of gold filled in the space, making it inviting, drawing us out to explore the new day.

Some mornings are subtle in their shading, like this one. Some, are filled with vivid shades of rose, lavender, and peach, or they are strikingly set against various backdrops of white billowy cloud formations that fill our imaginations, like when we were children. Yet others, are laden with coming rain.

Isn't this transition, that happens everyday, amazing? How often do you stop to enjoy it? Do you get up in time to observe it? Are you filled with wonder at the changes? Are you drawn to the Creator Who controls the darkness and the light? Do you seek Him whether He is visible or invisible?

> *"Dear friends, it's not as though I'm writing to give you a new commandment. Rather, I'm giving you an old commandment that you've had from the beginning. It's the old commandment you've already heard. On the other hand, I'm writing to give you a new commandment. It's a truth that exists in Christ and in you: The darkness is fading, and the true light is already shining."*
> 1 John 2:7-8 GW

From dark to light—whether night or morning, or times of the soul—always remember that God is near.

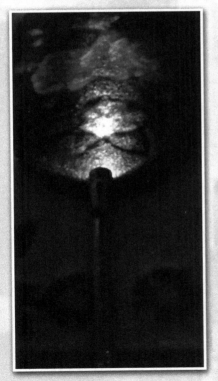

The Safety of …

Do you remember as a kid, having a nightmare? Remember calling out, from a dream or from waking, and one of your parents appeared by your side? Perhaps they even wielded a flashlight to alleviate your fears by searching under the bed, or in the closet, or in the darkest corners of your room?

Somehow, safety came from the simple source of light and brought peace. Right? Yet now as adults, we know it was not the flashlight at all, but our parent, that brought that sense of security. It was their presence and nearness, and being willing to shed light into the darkness, that helped our hearts quiet their rapidly beating pace.

Jesus, knows something about darkness. He entered into it at Gethsemane, at Calvary, and at the grave. Yet, He conquered each of these, to rule and reign over the gloom, over the night of the soul. And He is available to us, as Abba Daddy, the most compassionate Papa, to shed light on any situation that we find ourselves in.

Do you find yourself in the midst of a nightmare, though you're fully awake? Come into the safety of His arms. Come into the security of His company. Come discover the One Who knows you intimately. For He shines His light into every corner of our hearts, minds and circumstances, so that we know that we are never alone.

God gave man the skill to create a flashlight. But it is only a small beam of light created from a battery. If you want to be free of earth's darkness—come into the Light. Come and dwell, in the safety of His faithful, endless, care.

"The Eternal is my light amidst my darkness and my rescue in times of trouble. So whom shall I fear? He surrounds me with a fortress of protection. So nothing should cause me alarm." Psalm 27:1 VOICE

Abba Daddy, I feel a void in the area of _____. But I am coming before You, as a child. I am laying it down at Your feet. Please remove this darkness. Shine Your light of love and hope into my heart, I pray. And bring healing to this space. For I want to trust You, with even, this. Show me how, Jesus. Amen.

Spectrum of the Heart:
The Ballad of Earth

In the stillness, even before the sun came up, the birds began to sing. Then light began to shine into the room. We got up and visited a local garden for a walk; everything that we saw, appeared as if a great composer was writing a song line by line, note by note.

It was how I saw the morning, come to life.
It is how God comes alive, in us.

The ballad of earth, is His love song to every heart. He does not want anyone to miss the lyrics, the measures of His grace.

At the sound of Your voice …
Darkness became light,
The sun, moon and stars,
Began to record our days.
The birdsong began,
Creating lyrics,
As a ballad.
The rivers and waves,
Pour out a symphony,
Of Your power, mercy and grace.
The flowers, plants and gardens,
Perform measure upon measure,
Of Your glory and creativity.
The trees, fields, and mountains,
Display Your heart of love.
All, combine as music,
To invite us to know You,
And to sing Your praise.

Lord, may every heart see the bounty, the variety, the wonders, the simple, the complex, of all that You have made. May every man, woman and child, be drawn to You, by something specific that Your hand has created. May birds, animals, flowers, the atmosphere, landscapes, something in nature, pull their heart toward You so powerfully, that they cannot help but be in awe. And then, may You fill each mind with words, and their lips with a song of praise, as never before. Amen.

"I will praise the Lord at all times; His praise will always be on my lips." Psalm 34:1 HCSB

We must be aware of God, if we are to praise Him. We must praise Him, if we are to proclaim Him in all the earth. For the ballad of earth is never silent. So, may our hearts and lips, never be!

The Gift of Creation

May all, come to know God,
Through the things that He has made.
For out of darkness,
Light was first arrayed.
As He created all things,
In heaven and on the earth,
They are the signs and wonders,
That show His omnipotent worth.
They are the proof of His existence,
Written out like a scroll.
Sunrise and moonbeams,
Are the sketches of His soul.
Birds and bees and butterflies,
Were all given wings with which to soar;
The deer, squirrel and bunny,
Live upon the woodland floor.
The starry sky is a canopy—
He named them one by one,
Then filled the universe with plant-life,
He was not nearly done.
There are mountain peaks, and foamy seas,
Rivers and valleys to hold the snow.

All of this majesty,
Was His gift of creation, to show …
That He is Lord,
He is King,
Over everything,
So that no one would have excuse,
Or be able to proclaim,
That they were obtuse.
For how can you not see His hand,
In the intricate?
How can you not behold His heart,
In the beauty that He's made?
For this alone is a witness,
Each, alone, has the power to save!

> *"For the truth about God is known to them instinctively; God has put this knowledge in their hearts. Since earliest times men have seen the earth and sky and all God made, and have known of his existence and great eternal power. So they will have no excuse when they stand before God at Judgment Day. Yes, they knew about him all right, but they wouldn't admit it or worship him or even thank him for all his daily care. And after a while they began to think up silly ideas of what God was like and what he wanted them to do. The result was that their foolish minds became dark and confused." Romans 1:19-21 TLB*

I love this passage in Romans, for it tells us that God made creation, to lead us to Himself. This alone can bring us to our knees. The beauty that He has surrounded us with, is to show us and teach us His character, His nature. The external things that we can see, hear, and experience, are here, to make Him real within us! So do you know, the Creator?

We are not to worship the creation, but the One Who made these things. But these verses are clear … by His creations, we can know Who He is. We can have a reverent-spirit by simply noticing God's majesty. We can give Him glory, through reading the scroll that is rolled out before us, day by day, as a gift.

> *Romans 1:20 tells us that God gave us the gift of nature, all manner of creation, so that no one has any excuse in not knowing, seeing, or believing upon His name. Do you worship Him willingly or is your heart stubborn to His existence, love, and offer of grace?*

It is evening,
It is very early morning,
All is quiet, all is still;
Only creation sounds can be heard.
And each of these,
Is muted, floating upon the breeze.
There seems to be a holy hush o're all the earth.
It is the space of time when twinkling stars begin to shine,
—Until, before the sun doth rise.
Calm descends.
Love transcends.
All else fades away.
There is only God and us,
And a holy hush,
Where His Spirit whispers, calls.
It communicates more than a shout or a proclamation.
In this stillness, our soul unfurls like dawn.
Awakening,
To shine.

Has God's holy hush enveloped your heart, to draw His Spirit, near? For these are the prayer hours. These are the moments when tranquility breathes within us, to awaken His Will, fresh as the coming dawn.

Holy hush, invade my heart, until … Your Spirit
Lord, is all I know, feel, and hear. Amen.

God speaks to us in many ways. But creation, more than any other method, seems to bring His attributes, to life. Perhaps it's because nature is all around us. Maybe it's because we are witnesses to everyday miracles—in the seasons, in earth's daily changes, or as light and darkness sweep across our hours, like the tide. Or maybe it's the way we connect to certain colors, textures, smells, or sounds. I believe God tells us we have no excuse for not seeing His existence, because His very presence is so difficult to miss.

His attributes and character are visible from the moment we wake in the morning, until we close our eyes in sleep at night. He has fashioned all creatures, from bold and strong, to fragile and delicate, so that we would be drawn to His workmanship and artistry. And in the telling of His own story, we are given glimpses of Who He is. And if earth is His voice piece; Heaven is His megaphone. But the wise, hear both within the soul, calling, to know Him as Lord.

- God's hope, rises from the void of darkness, lifting as night yields to day.
- His faithfulness is like the dawn, new each morning.
- His mercy moves, like a quiet, flowing stream.
- His gentleness, opens like the newest leaf and tender bud, that arrive in Spring.
- His joy, lifts our hearts with the sweetest anthem of worship, as the birds sing His praise.
- His Spirit can be as subtle as the wind's whisper, or can crash as powerfully as a raging ocean.
- His Living Water, is like a gushing waterfall that never runs dry.
- His grace sweeps over us, like a covering of freshly fallen snow.
- His strength is like a mighty mountain, steadfast and sure.
- His love is endless, as the grains of sand on the seashore.
- His peace, is like the calmest lake after a storm has passed.
- His loving-kindness cannot be measured; it's like the starry canopy that fills the velvet sky.
- He is infinite, like the landscape of earth stretched from end to end.

- He is omnipotent and omnipresent.
- He is perfect in wisdom and authority.
- He is gracious, and just.
- He is holy, righteous, and deserving of all glory and honor.

With every creation, or created being that has or ever will be born, God is speaking of His love. He is moving, shaping, designing, refining. His character is visible, displaying His invisible Spirit to us, through all that He has made. And we are blessed, if we will pause to behold Him—in all of these myriad facets. Because to miss Him, would be tragic. And who would want to? When He has so much to say!

Revelation 4:11, Isaiah 45:8, Psalm 136:26, James 1:17, Psalm 84:11-12

Spectrum of the Heart:
Creation's Gift of Prayer

Dear Lord, creation is like a prayer from Your heart, to my soul. Every new sunrise, is a promise that You are with me. Every night, the moon and stars, are reminders of Your care—of Your presence throughout the night.

The mountains speak of Your majesty. Flowers, show the intricacy of Your hand. The birds display Your love of music. The wind, Your Spirit's movement, within me and upon the earth.

Thank You, for these tender, peaceful, healing moments. When I achieve stillness, I see You, feel You, and have the fragrance of Your love enfold me. Your invitations through creation are blessing me, and help me commune with You on a spiritual level. They reach me; and teach me that You are always near.

And with each beautiful thing that You display, I in turn, give You praise and prayer—my heart is lifted as an offering to Your soul. This is the dance of love between us. It is to be one with You, united as creation with Creator, and as Your child with my Abba Daddy. Amen.

"Honor and majesty surround Him; strength and beauty fill His sanctuary." Psalm 96:6 NLT

To Glimpse Creation

We had gotten up in the predawn hours to capture this sunrise. It was fairly early in our marriage, and was at the beginning of my husband's career. In fact, it was to be our first assignment, Biloxi, MS. As I gathered precious memories and photos for this project, this one stuck out for a few reasons.

First of all, the sun and moon and star's rotation all over the globe, gives us a glimpse of God's original creation, daily. Second, as dawn comes to life right before our eyes, it unfolds, to change with each passing hour. Third, God is surely an Artist with His panorama of delightfully painted scenes.

Think of it ... out of darkness, comes light. Lamentations 3:22-23 tells us, that God's faithfulness is new every morning. And as I began to see dawn's breaking—as coming out of the void of nighttime's veil—it was a fresh reminder of this truth. Even on the cloudiest day, there is a brightness that rises at the horizon. It's as if God is giving us insights into His nature, if we will but take the time to observe them.

Just pause and behold the colors of this special morning. This is not photoshop, this is God's grandeur. The play of light and shadow and reflection, are His version of prisms, rainbows and refractions of His majesty. And while we got to be there firsthand, everyday that we wakeup, open our eyes, take a breath, is a gift to us.

Out of darkness, we wake from our slumber. Out of darkness, we rise, to see light shine through our rooms and upon the earth. And every day, we get to experience the Light of the World in some new faceted way, as He lives and moves and breathes upon all creation.

"The faithful love of the Lord never ends! His mercies never cease. Great is his faithfulness; his mercies begin afresh each morning." Lamentations 3:22-23 NLT

To catch a glimpse of creation, is to hold a little child-like wonder in our hearts, no matter our age. Great is Your faithfulness, indeed, O God. Each morning, I will pause to behold You and give You my praise. Amen.

Internal Light Shining

The interior of the sanctuary had been darkened completely. Then, the auditorium was lit, only enough for the ushers to safely begin the procession of the candle's glow. From one single flame, the room came alive. Each person touched their wick to the next, until these simple white candles seemed to radiate, as one internal light, shining. As we rose to our feet and began to praise, it was surely a lovely demonstration of—out of darkness—comes hope, comes light, comes the Son.

Internal light was created,
From a single candle's flame.
Within these walls,
—Darkness,
Fought, but could not remain.
The shadows were lifted,
As each wick was shared.
And the presence of His Spirit,
Was soon visible, there.

Internal light is created,
From a single whisper to the soul.
Within the heart, God speaks,
Offering grace,
To make us whole.
The shadows are lifted,
And Jesus removes our scarlet stain.
In His eyes, we're made righteous,
Illuminated, born-again.

*"For God, who said, 'Light shall shine out of darkness,' is the One
who has shone in our hearts to give the Light of the knowledge of the
glory of God in the face of Christ." 2 Corinthians 4:6 NASB*

Internal light, shone within this room, from the space of a veil of
shadows. With just one spark, a holy glow filled every corner.
Internal light, shines from our soul, when we invite Jesus to be our
Lord and the Light within us. He becomes our source of hope, peace,
and joy. Like a flame, He is alive, to shine, as we simply share His
love with our neighbor, with our world.

*Have you ever
participated in a
candle-light service?
What did you notice?
Did you have an
emotional response
as your candle was
met by the
adjoining flame?*

Joy

This metal plaque, lay on a stack of new merchandise in the holiday season a couple of years ago, in a store that has since gone out of business. I was drawn to its brushed and cut metal design, that displays a form of artistry. Doug couldn't quite see its potential, even as I explained that while it was "empty"—I had a plan.

He told me that he trusted me, since he's seen me take objects before and transform them, so we made the purchase. I added light to the back, turned it on, and hung it up. Then, Douglas could see my vision, come to life.

We're made with room for God's Spirit to indwell us at our conception. We're empty (born with a sinful nature until we invite the Light of the World to come and make His home in our hearts). Then we shine—to become who God envisioned, all along.

Empty, was the plaque till I gave it light. Now, it glows to make our room a little brighter, cozier. Empty, is the soul, till God's Spirit enters and communes, to illuminate it, change and renew it. God made you perfectly—to indwell you— eternally, with His Light.

I've decided to keep my plaque on the wall all year long, as a reminder that God can work in every space—out of darkness— to shed forth hope and peace. May each child of the King, bring a little joy to the world, indeed!

The Gem of Meditation

The Pause:

Darkness yields to dawn. The shadows are replaced with shades of gold, rose, lavender, pearl, and azure. The simple formation of the day displays God's holy creation to my heart. Lord, empty my spirit of any doubt, fear, failure, past mistake or hurt, so that Your light is reflected in and through my life. Amen.

How does the demonstration of night turning to day, illustrate to your heart God's faithful care and love?

Pause here, and take notice of a few ways:

....

....

....

....

....

....

The Praise:

Lord, I gain great peace from the verse in Psalms that tells me darkness is not so, to You. Thank You for being available at all times, for my every need. Please make this truth real to my heart. I praise You, as You teach me that Your light transcends every shadow. I draw upon your strength, and hope, as I meditate upon You.

....

....

....

....

....

....

This is a freeform space, designed for you to write a few "Thank You's" to the Lord. It's a place for you to express some praise, or some need, or simply "speak your heart" to the One Who loves you and knows you, completely.

Has God delivered you from darkness? Physically, perhaps from illness, an accident, or a particularly difficult time in your life? Emotionally, from a time of pain or grief? Or spiritually, to make you His child? Expressing gratitude, brings God joy.

From darkness, we are delivered into the light of His love. If nothing comes immediately to mind … take a few moments to meditate upon the miracle that is, darkness into dawn. Or thank Him for this new day and the breath that fills your lungs.

....

....

....

....

....

....

Soul's Introspection — Out of Darkness

Father, thank You, that darkness is not daunting to You. I am thankful that I am known and loved. These truths encourage me ...
1)
2)
3)

"The Lord merely spoke, and the heavens were created. He breathed the word, and all the stars were born. He assigned the sea its boundaries and locked the oceans in vast reservoirs. Let the whole world fear the Lord, and let everyone stand in awe of him. For when he spoke, the world began! It appeared at his command." Psalm 33:6-9 (NLT)

Have you ever gotten up before dawn, in order to arrive at a beach or a special location to watch the sun rise, out of complete darkness? What did you observe that may have surprised you? What emotions did you experience in this space of time?

"The voice of the Eternal echoes over the great waters; God's magnificence roars like thunder. The Eternal's presence hovers over all the waters." Psalm 29:3 (VOICE)

Jesus knows a lot about "void." He died and rose from the grave. How does this help you see Him as an empathetic Father and Abba Daddy when you experience pain or illness or go through times of trial or grief?

"I have come as a light into the world, in order that everyone who believes in me will not remain in the darkness." John 12:46 (LEB)

What "void" are you currently feeling, that only God can fill?

"But you are a chosen people, a royal priesthood, a holy nation, God's special possession, that you may declare the praises of him who called you out of darkness into his wonderful light." 1 Peter 2:9 (NIV)

How can a period of darkness (physical, emotional or spiritual) teach us to trust God?

All of us feel—alone, unworthy, not enough—at some time or another. How does knowing that God loves you unconditionally, keep you from falling into a pit of darkness?

"I will lead the blind by a way they do not know; I will guide them in paths that they do not know. I will make darkness into light before them and rugged places into plains. These things I will do [for them], and I will not leave them abandoned or undone." Isaiah 42:16 (AMP)

Light Within

It's lying among the treasures of the storekeeper's shelves. It may be tucked in a bin with other trinkets. But you spy it ... perhaps for the first time, perhaps with a childhood memory, firmly fixed. You pick it up—put it to your eye and lift it toward the light. Suddenly, radiant colors, patterns, and 3-D images, come to life. Angles and geometric designs begin to form and change, to dance, inside a simple tube. And your imagination is brought to the fore.

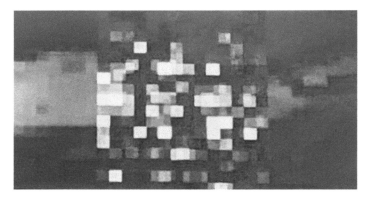

The earth was void. Darkness hovered over the water, over the atmosphere, to surround the expanse of nothingness. God spoke—quietly? Loudly? But make no mistake—at His voice—light, dawn, the sun, moon and stars—all the heavenly hosts came into being. Everything that He fashioned next, came into focus with beauty, majesty, and with His glory. His very divinity, sovereignty and presence, became visible—to touch every created thing, every blooming and growing thing, person, and creature.

The Light of the World, seeks to do the same, in every soul. We were born with the darkness of a natural, sinful nature. Yet His Spirit is the illumination within every heart that surrenders to His call. Like a kaleidoscope, God wants to take every life, and give us the facets of His love and character traits.

You may feel like you are behind a closed door, unnoticed. You may feel like your color is running a little dull. You may feel drained by life's present uncertainties—but God's touch, His light and love are upon You, dear one. He is near. He is the Master of having His eye upon every creation, every heart—all at once. That's why He's called omnipotent. He knows you. He sees you. He cares about you. No angle of your life, no moment, no present need—is without His knowledge and attention.

The kaleidoscope must be picked up and held to the light, in order to be appreciated. Have you allowed the Lord, to do the same with your mind, heart and soul? For if you have, if you do, you will find that your life—comes to life—with completely new dimensions. He may even fill your heart with so much joy and peace and love and contentment ... that you shine ... when you would have formerly identified, with being the kaleidoscope's simple exterior tube.

Light, makes all the difference to what we see in this fascinating "toy." It makes all the difference to our viewing and appreciating God's miracles and wondrous creations—even our own countenance. And it makes all the difference to our world, if His Spirit's glow is radiated outward, by how we love and serve our Master.

Have you ever owned a kaleidoscope? What images drew your eye and caused you to dream?

....

What in creation reminds you of a kaleidoscope? Why? How does that image touch your heart?

....

How has the Light of the World shown you the facets of His love?

....

Embracing Light

Focusing-In

Do you remember as a child the
sparkle that lit your eyes when you saw
twinkly Christmas lights, for the first time?

Have you ever shone a flashlight on a wall, to
watch your kitten, dance?

Have you ever gotten up at 4 am to savor the nuances
of a sunrise, from complete darkness to its zenith—at a
beach, or from your favorite tranquil spot?

Light embraces us in many forms.

Earth and heaven are filled with it and glow with light. It
shines from our eyes, from our souls. And the kaleidoscope
can teach us a few lessons.

There's something about this object that draws young and
old alike, because ...
- Light transforms it.
- We participate in forming the art.
- It's different every time we pick it up.

Perhaps God uses every source of light, and the
dance of light and shadow, to embrace us 24
hours a day—with His love.

Will you look for the warmth of the Son
in every light source that
surrounds you?

Section II

Embracing Light

Light was separated from darkness, and the sun was formed.

"Praise the Lord, my soul.
Lord my God, you are very great;
you are clothed with splendor and majesty.

The Lord wraps himself in light as with a garment;
he stretches out the heavens like a tent
and lays the beams of his upper chambers on their waters.

He makes the clouds his chariot
and rides on the wings of the wind.

He set the earth on its foundations;
it can never be moved.

He made the moon to mark the seasons,
and the sun knows when to go down.
You bring darkness, it becomes night, …

May the glory of the Lord endure forever;
may the Lord rejoice in his works—
he who looks at the earth, and it trembles,
who touches the mountains, and they smoke.

I will sing to the Lord all my life;
I will sing praise to my God as long as I live.

May my meditation be pleasing to him,
as I rejoice in the Lord. …
Praise the Lord, my soul.
Praise the Lord."

Psalm 104: 1-3, 5, 19-20a, 31-34 and 35b (NIV)

Light embraces us, from our rising, into our sleeping hours. But it is the Lord, Himself, that gives warmth and illumination to the heart, mind and soul.

Tranquility

Before the first rays of the sun appeared, this was the setting upon the beach. Translucent light and pastel colors, lit the morning with the softest glow. If you could paint a room in your home with peace, you may choose these same shades. Doesn't it evoke a sense of tranquility in your soul?

From the purest white,
Of the softly ebbing surf,
To the billowy clouds, above…
From the golden tones,
That are rising in the east,
To the rosy mist at the horizon's line …
From the bluest sky,
To the sea-foam green of the sea …
The entirety of the scene,
Was tranquility.
This predawn moment,
Was like a promise,
A rainbow's covenant,
That the Prince of Peace,
Had made it,
For anyone who would pause,
To behold it.
For to do so,
Was to behold, Him.

"And he will be called Wonderful Counselor, Mighty God, Everlasting Father, Prince of Peace. Of the greatness of his government and peace there will be no end. He will reign on David's throne and over his kingdom, establishing and upholding it with justice and righteousness from that time on and forever." Isaiah 9:6b-7 NIV

"He who made the [cluster of stars called] Pleiades and [the constellation] Orion, Who turns deep darkness into the morning and darkens the day into night, Who calls for the waters of the sea and pours them out on the surface of the earth, the Lord is His name." Amos 5:8 AMP

Tranquility, is an emotion that we can experience in any place. It was experienced here. Not simply because of the beautiful imagery, but because the Creator invited us to pause, and we beheld something of His grandeur. In these moments of predawn, the shades of His grace surely fell upon the earth, and upon our hearts.

If you need to experience tranquility, turn toward the Prince of Peace.

The Solace of Light

- Do you long for a place of solace?
- A place to pause and rest, not just your body, but your heart and mind, as well?
- Do you seek a place of joy, peace, a perfect communion?

That's what I was thinking of, when I captioned this piece, "the solace of light."

There's something magical about light. From the first rays of dawn to the way it reflects, to how it shimmers and dances and changes over the landscape, to the way it illuminates every shadow, to the way it embraces our hearts … We are drawn to it, enveloped by it, and given warmth, comfort, hope and peace, from its ethereal glow. We can even experience the feeling of God's love through its existence.

Jesus is called the Light of the World, and in Him is the radiance of the Father. Come discover His faithfulness, that is endless, eternal. For in the space of His light, you'll be embraced by His love, hope, guidance, assurance, and loving-kindness. Every source of light that surrounds us, that shines upon us, has the ability to fill us with God's Spirit.

> Dawn unfolds upon the horizon.
> Pastel shades of jewel-like tones explode like Iolite,
> Pale Ruby and tranquil Amethyst, to illumine the coming day.
> Upwardly, cool Topaz moves in the sky toward its zenith.
> And whether you have noticed the beauty or not,
> Light has embraced you.
> It has touched you, your home, and your environment.

The love of Jesus is like this. It is always near, just as the sun—gracing, moving, dancing, shaping, shadowing, reflecting, hovering, embracing—holding us in its fathomlessness. But we must embrace God and His light, if we are to see and know Him, personally, intimately, and experientially.

When you hear the word "light," what do you think of? Perhaps you picture a flickering candle in a window? Or the first rays of dawn creating rainbow colors in the sky? What about prisms that dance, reflect in a window, or as light graces the sea or a calm lake? How about the way light dispels the darkest shadows? Perhaps you envision the twinkling of many strings of lights on a tree, wreath, or somewhere in your home? Or even the flipping of a light-switch to read a book, or work (or play) on your computer?

Light, touches us, surrounds us, embraces us, everyday. And to me, it has the power to evoke hope, warmth, love, and joy. To my heart, it symbolizes the very presence of our Creator, the Lord of the universe, personally and profoundly.

"Bless the Lord, O my soul! O Lord my God, You are very great: You are clothed with honor and majesty, who cover Yourself with light as with a garment, who stretch out the heavens like a curtain."
Psalm 104:1-2 (NKJV)

Spectrum of the Heart:

Early Morning Light

In the palest light of morning,
Before the sun even appears,
I call out to You, Jesus,
And feel every shadow disappear.
Though the sky,
Still bears its last remnant,
A cloak of misty gray,
Soon a glow of rose and golden tones,
Will shine forth as the clouds part,
As nighttime, yields to day.
There's a promise on the horizon,
It's the hope that comes,
Simply, because it's dawn.
It's the flame that keeps my faith alive,
Because the Light of the World,
Is always on.
Within my heart,
You are illuminated,
Ignited, by my first words,
Of prayer.

Dear Lord, I love beginning conversations with You even before dawn breaks. For in these moments where darkness meets light, I seem to sense Your nearness, so nearly and dearly. The shadows are being dispelled, even as the hope of a new day, shines forth. And I am reminded each morning, that You are faithful and true. If that isn't a message of faith, I don't know what is. So I will whisper and shout of Your loving-kindness, for You are the light within my soul. And I praise. Within a prayer, rises oneness with Your Spirit. Within this quiet conversation, I know I am loved and known and held in light for all time. Amen.

Psalm 57:7-10 (TLB), just seems to echo my soul's refrain: "O God, my heart is quiet and confident. No wonder I can sing your praises! Rouse yourself, my soul! Arise, O harp and lyre! Let us greet the dawn with song! I will thank you publicly throughout the land. I will sing your praises among the nations. Your kindness and love are as vast as the heavens. Your faithfulness is higher than the skies."

Early morning's light, is the perfect time to meet with the Lord. For the hush of darkness and first light, are as the Spirit and soul, meeting to kiss. Here, is the embrace of God's heart with ours.

45

You give a light,
Each new morning.
It comes from darkness,
To stand above us.
It forms shadows to remind us,
That we are ever,
'Neath Your sheltering care.
One falls,
As another rises.
Twice daily, You give this cycle,
To demonstrate—
Death, resurrection,
Life, light and love.

Dawn—unfolds, stands, creates shadows, then falls, to lift the moon. Highest heaven, is God's canvas to display His love for us. It is no accident that we can see His death, burial, resurrection, and the shadow of His ever-present care, in nature. All of His weavings reflect Him. Dawn, is His love in motion, the cycle of His heart, reaching out to ours, daily.

How does the sun, with its rays of warmth and hope, wash across a room or the ocean—and create not only rainbow colors, but a sense of peace? How does the moon, do likewise?

The Lantern

Upon the wall,
Hangs a scroll-work lantern.
Inside it,
Stands a candle,
With a wick,
Of wax-coated thread.
With a single match,
A spark,
Explodes,
Into a moment of light.
The two join,
To create a flame.
And inside,
The interior of the globe,
Is lit,
To shine,
To reflect its radiance,
Throughout the room.

Dear Jesus, may this process be likewise, duplicated, within my soul. For as I surrender, not only my heart, but my every dream and hope and goal, may You transform each, into the spark of faith. And may this flame send light, beyond the scope of my days, turning my life into a testimony for Your kingdom. For though I will likely never travel the globe, help me to illuminate the tiny places in which I dwell, with Your love, joy, hope and grace, I pray. Amen.

Every child of God, should be as a lantern (glowing, showing, shining) the Light of the World, into the sphere of every space that we occupy.

"And you, beloved, are the light of the world. A city built on a hilltop cannot be hidden. Similarly it would be silly to light a lamp and then hide it under a bowl. When someone lights a lamp, she puts it on a table or a desk or a chair, and the light illumines the entire house. You are like that illuminating light. Let your light shine everywhere you go, that you may illumine creation, so men and women everywhere may see your good actions, may see creation at its fullest, may see your devotion to Me, and may turn and praise your Father in heaven because of it." Matthew 5:14-16 VOICE

Let Love Arise

Let love arise,
Like the first rays,
Of dawn, unfolding.
As light moves upon the horizon,
May Your Spirit open within me.

Let it shine,
With radiant, rainbow colors,
Moving upward, moving outward,
Until it dances,
As if upon a crystal sea.

For as You become alive in Me,
Your love fills my soul.
It explodes like a flame,
To glitter and illumine everything,
Everyone,
Even bringing darkness,
Out of the shadows,
Into Your glorious covering.

Let love arise,
Like the beacon of Your heart, O God,
Unfolding freshly each new morning,
As You paint it, newly.
Be the light of this temple,
Until Your Spirit lights my way.

> *"The whole earth is filled with awe at your wonders; where morning dawns, where evening fades, you call forth songs of joy."*
> Psalm 65:8 (NIV)

The sun rises, dances, reflects and washes through the window, to pour out like liquid gold upon the walls. Here, in this moment—dawn seems to be the simplest, most lovely, purest manifestation of God's love. With it comes hope, clarity, and peace. As I meditate upon Scripture and pray in this quiet, glowing atmosphere, it's like I've entered "holy ground."

Dear Lord, I invite You to wash Your light into every space of my home, my heart, my life, my thoughts, actions and deeds. Remove any shadow and let Your Spirit glow, dance, and be reflected from my very soul. May every space that I enter, display something of Your radiance. For it is Your light that transforms, renews, cleanses, illuminates—one soul at a time—until the world knows You, as its Source, the Son. Amen.

The power of the sun is made possible by the Light of the World. Is He visible in You?

Luke 11:34-35, Philippians 1:9-11, John 1:4-5, Psalm 18:28, Psalm 139:7-12, John 12:44-46, Ephesians 5:8-9, Ephesians 5:13-14

How does light or the lack of it—bring out certain emotions?

Prayer of the Sky

One day I was pondering how many changes that the sky goes through, in any 24 hour period. From the first break of dawn, to the falling of dusk, to the first appearance of stars—from the shifting clouds to developing rain and streaks of lightening—this canopy above us communicates God's love, majesty, and creativity—and to me, forms a prayer …

I am the sky above you,
In my fingers are the clouds.
I hold the sun,
In all its splendor,
And the stars in a veil-like shroud.
I am a gift if you will see me,
High above the atmosphere.
I bridge the earth and the gates of heaven;
God is there—He is here.
As I change and unfold like a canopy,
I am a witness of God's love.
And everyday I am writing a message,
Of His glory—
Just look, above,
To me … the sky.
But pray, not, to my heights,
I only serve to point you,
To the Father, Creator,
Lord, of power,
And of might.

For as you gaze into the heavenly realm, the sky above your head, may you also look into the eyes of Jesus, and be wholly led! Amen.

"The heavens declare the glory of God, and the sky displays what his hands have made. One day tells a story to the next. One night shares knowledge with the next without talking, without words, without their voices being heard. Yet, their sound has gone out into the entire world, their message to the ends of the earth. He has set up a tent in the heavens for the sun, which comes out of its chamber like a bridegroom. Like a champion, it is eager to run its course. It rises from one end of the heavens. It circles around to the other. Nothing is hidden from its heat." Psalm 19:1-6 GW

Through the Veil

The mist nestled,
O're the fields, the plains.
The clouds hung heavily,
In the sky.
Here and there, they met,
To obscure one's view.
But even through the veil—
I saw You, Adonai.

Lord, help me to see light as a means of Your creation, speaking directly into my soul. I vow to notice its effects in all forms, and to look for Your majesty in each one. Amen.

It was a beautiful crisp morning, when I captured this image, as the sun swiftly, rose. Fog and clouds—lowered, hovered—to linger and touch. Though a veil formed, the sun was visible; its rays broke through. So it is with the Lord's presence—even in the shadows, even in times of difficulty, illness, uncertainty.

If you feel a mist rest upon your mind, or clouds lower o're your soul —seek Adonai. If a veil happens to fill your eyes and runs down your cheeks, reach out toward God's grace. He is near, aware, and His love will always shine through—every shadow—to cut through the gloom and drench your heart in purest light.

Whether vale or valley, cumulous clouds or accumulating concerns —God's love will always come shining through. Trust that His light will win out over the darkness. For He is as present on earth, as He is in heaven. He is in every dawn, for He is the Source of all illumination, now, and in the Kingdom to come.

Isaiah 44:22, Deuteronomy 4:39, Jeremiah 23:23-24,
Psalm 34:18, 2 Corinthians 4:6, Psalm 23:3b-4

Though fog consists of vapor, it can entirely envelop a landscape, obscuring our view. It can do the same, emotionally and spiritually. That's why we need the Source of Light to shine through the veil— right into the center of our being, our hearts.

Clouds

There are ten major types of clouds. We usually only hear of the four most familiar terms: cirrus, stratus, cumulus, and nimbus, but there are six other types identified as well. Clouds are collections of very tiny droplets of water or miniature ice crystals. They form, when air is heated by the sun; as it rises, it slowly cools and reaches a saturation point, where water condenses forming these crystals. The ten types also form bands in the atmosphere—low, middle, and high —corresponding to where they usually appear in the sky.

"In the beginning, God created the heavens and earth" ... clouds were made on the first day of creation.

The two photos shown, represent a couple of these different types. As I walked and snapped, God brought the Israelites to mind. I was taken back to Exodus, to a time when God's people were in the wilderness. Actually, they were just coming out of Egypt. Pharaoh had recently let them go, freed them from being his slaves.

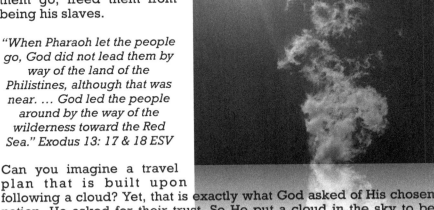

"When Pharaoh let the people go, God did not lead them by way of the land of the Philistines, although that was near. ... God led the people around by the way of the wilderness toward the Red Sea." Exodus 13: 17 & 18 ESV

Can you imagine a travel plan that is built upon following a cloud? Yet, that is exactly what God asked of His chosen nation. He asked for their trust. So He put a cloud in the sky to be their beacon, by day; at night, he gave them a pillar of fire.

"The Lord went in front of them by day in a pillar of cloud to lead them along the way, and by night in a pillar of fire to give them light, so they could travel both day and night." Exodus 13:21 ISV

Clouds fascinate me because of how quickly they change. They have always captured my imagination. I can only imagine the feeling the Israelites had, when they heard that commission. "Yes folks, we are going to follow a cloud." ... Sometimes our journey with God, feels likewise. In some ways, God's Spirit is like a vapor (both visible and invisible). He is part of us, above us, around us, below us, always.

In Hebrews 12:1 (GW) we are told, "Since we are surrounded by so many examples of faith, (or a great cloud of witnesses), we must get rid of everything that slows us down, or distracts us. We must run the race that lies ahead of us and never give up." The cloud led the Israelites, verse 22, "The pillar of cloud by day and the pillar of fire by night did not depart from before the people." But notice the wording, "the Lord went in front of them." (Verse 21) They may have been following a "cloud," but God was present; He, was in the cloud.

God's Spirit is ever-present; He will not depart from us, either. If we walk in obedience, trust, and faithfulness, He will guide our journey, and lead us to the promised land. Like the Israelites, there are times when we seem to arrive via the wilderness, but God is our compass, our Divine Guide. So as you look at the clouds, you are indeed looking-up, and that is just as Jesus would have it.

Spectrum of the Heart:
Above the Weatherman

Thank You, Lord, for the sunshine that appeared on a day that was predicted to be cloudy. It displays that You are sovereign, majestic, all-knowing, and more powerful than anyone or anything on earth. Your holiness as Creator, is so awe-inspiring to see played out—in the weather, in the seasons, in the arranging of our lives.

And man's predictions, show him (or her) to be foolish in comparison, to You. However, those who trust You, are not relying in their own strength, but are the true seekers of wisdom. And You say, these hearts You will answer; to this request, You will respond.

In fact, Matthew 7:7-8 (NIV) tells us: "Ask and it will be given to you; seek and you will find; knock and the door will be opened to you. For everyone who asks receives; the one who seeks finds; and to the one who knocks, the door will be opened."

So in a sense, the sunshine that's pouring forth from heaven, instead of clouds today, seemed to remind my heart that You are always reaching out to us, wanting us to understand You. Though we are imperfect, fallible, fragile and weak—You long to connect, empower, encourage, defend, and strengthen us. So may we look to You, above the weatherman. Because when we focus on the Son, it matters not if the day holds clouds. It only matters, that You are all that we will need. Amen.

God lives, rules and reigns, above the weatherman. This brings comfort to my soul. For He is Lord of all that comes at us. He is our peace in any storm.

Our Eyes Are ...

Our eyes are like,
A clear glass window pane.
They give us a view,
Pure and shining,
Sometimes, clouded, with rain.

Our eyes are like,
A stained-glass piece of art.
They give us a faceted view,
Of prism-like rainbows,
Creating dimension,
And love, from God's own heart.

Our eyes are like,
A camera's lens.
With each new blink,
We have a fresh landscape,
And a world without end.

Our eyes are like,
A microscope,
A kaleidoscope—
They bring the world,
Up-close,
To show us beauty, joy, hope.

Our eyes are the window,
To our souls.
They are the instruments,
By which,
God's light, should flow,
Also through which, He makes us whole.

Our eyes are a gift. Our sight is a wonder. And if we have insight, we have been given a miracle. For with everything that we see, may we see beyond it, to the Creator.

For He is the window, the One, Who clearly allows us—to experience His goodness, His kindness, His faithful care. He, is the stained glass piece of art—allowing us to view our lives, as a work-in-progress—being held up to His light. He, holds the camera, and sees the landscape of His entire Will for us. He, holds the microscope—to our doubt, fear, faltering faith. And if our eyes are fixed upon Him, He is the filter through which our lives—are refined, cropped, enlarged, touched-up and made beautiful.

Our eyes open the world to us, and the world into our inner being. They are the instruments through which we view God's lovely creation. They are also the mirrors of our emotions. They are the place, that can purely shine with God's glory.

What do your eyes reflect? Are they lit with the love of Christ?

Our eyes are ... wonders, miracles ... and receptacles of light—to be His light, to the world.

Crystal Rain

Out of this corner of darkest rooftop, shone blue sky.
From the skylight, hung crystal droplets.
To my eye, the glass dewdrops, appeared as rain.

Dear Jesus, let your love rain down upon me, in the darkest moments of confusion, fear or doubt. Let your light and hope and peace surround me, until I see only Your crystal-clear nearness. May Your Spirit descend like dewdrops, so that my mind and body, feel as though a soothing shower has infused me with strength. For here, I learn to trust You. Here, I see You more clearly. Here, the embrace of Your loving-kindness comes into focus, as the cares of this world fade into obscurity. Amen.

Out of every corner of darkness, can be found, some essence of light—shining, falling, illuminating. For even the gloomiest spots, are not so, within the soul of a child of the King. Why?

Because light cannot dwell in the same space as despair. So look for the precious gems that God wants to speak into your heart, so that the rain you feel brushing your face, also brings a rainbow of promise, to sweep over your soul, to confirm: you are not alone.

"The Lord reigns, let the earth be glad; let the distant shores rejoice. Clouds and thick darkness surround him; righteousness and justice are the foundation of his throne. Fire goes before him and consumes his foes on every side. His lightning lights up the world; the earth sees and trembles. ... Light shines on the righteous and joy on the upright in heart. Rejoice in the Lord, you who are righteous, and praise his holy name." Psalm 97:1-4, & 11-12 NIV

Crystal rain, fell from darkness, only to be illuminated by the Light. God can use any corner of darkness in our lives, to bring His Spirit nearer, in brilliant detail. He transforms the shadows into a shower of grace, joy and praise, if we will simply raise our eyes to His and expectantly seek His presence. All else, then, seems to fade away, leaving us drenched in His reign of restoration and peace.

Jesus is referred to as the Light of the World. What does that mean to your heart when you feel tired, weary or troubled?

Lord, I am thankful for the following versions of light.
1) ....
2) ....
3) ....
These in particular, remind me that You are near,
no matter the hour of the day or night.

Spectrum of the Heart:

A Fresh Canvas

Dear Jesus, this new day is like a blank slate, a fresh canvas, a fresh opportunity, to begin again. For this, I praise You, Lord.

With each dawn, comes the ability to let the mistakes of yesterday, go; let the lessons, rise. It opens with hope, because it signifies that if we are here, alive—then You are not finished with us. We are meant to do something, contribute something to our world. It means that we can lend a hand, spread some joy or encouragement, or shine a light of Your truth to every corner of our workplace, play-space, and community.

The very blessing of opening our eyes and taking a breath into our lungs, should be miracle enough, to propel us to see this day, as a starting place. It's a way of motivating us. We may not be where we want to be, but we have the chance to grow, learn, seek You, and let Your love infiltrate our hearts a little more each day.

A fresh canvas is an artist's dream. It's where an inspiration comes to life. Lord, help us to see our lives as You do, each day through Your eyes. Grant us, souls that strive to soar as we follow in Your footsteps, we pray. Amen.

"Therefore, if anyone is in Christ, he is a new creation; old things have passed away; behold, all things have become new." (2 Corinthians 5:17 NKJV) This verse, means that we are made new (born again) when we surrender our hearts (and lives) to Jesus. He becomes our Lord and Savior, and we seek His Will, in how we live.

But what if … we viewed each day in the Christian life, as a fresh start? What if we yielded each one to the Lord? What might He create in us? What might He do for us? What might He remove from us (past hurts, darkness, burdens and the like), if we but sought to look at each dawn, as the fresh canvas that God is offering us? What shades of His character might He bring out in us?

How might this concept, transform how we view Him and ourselves?

We received this combination room atomizer/night light, as a gift from a family member a few years ago. While we don't use it to release the essential oils as intended due to health issues, it has become one of our favorite things because of its changing light pigments. You can select colors, or allow it to circulate with a spectrum of shades.

One morning I had left it on, after we had completed our morning routine. I noticed the effect that daylight had upon it, versus the evening's darkness. My photos are of the same setting; yet notice how the same shade appears violet in the daytime, and royal blue at night?

Dear Lord, may Your Spirit be alive to radiate Your attributes in every light, at every hour of the day and night. May the shades of Your love and grace, glow from our inner selves to shine, not from any holiness of our own—but from the righteous covering You provide— through Your mercy and forgiveness. It's Your Light of Salvation that creates the changing of our hearts and lives. And we are grateful for signs of transition, maturity, and growth. Amen.

The effect of God's Light within the mind, heart, and soul—is to magnify the fruits of the Spirit from within, to our world, without—be that, our home, neighborhood, community, or wherever we work or travel to.

The effect of Light on light, means that God is continually renewing us—to reflect Him, no matter where we are, no matter the time of day or night.

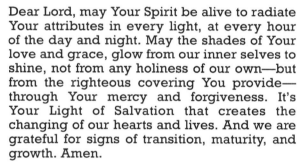

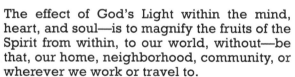

Barren Branches, Palest Sun

High up in the tree limbs,
Barren branches stood, ebony and tall,
Against an early morning,
Where the palest sun seemed to stall.
It got caught in a halo,
In the midst of a wispy veil,
As if it was held by invisible threads to show me,
It was enfolded in its milky trail.
Light reflected around it,
In a shadowy luminous glow,
Forming an iridescent rainbow,
Clouds danced, in a rhythm, ever so slow.

High up in the heavens,
Our Father stands powerful and tall,
In all His might and glory,
He is available at our first call.
Our prayers may form a halo,
Like a glittering crown around His throne.
He gathers them in His hands like branches,
To enfold our requests and praises near His heart, His home.
His love and light are reflected upon them,
And He listens and answers every one.
He touches each soul with a promise,
Like a rainbow before He's done.

There was something about the barren branches and the palest sun shining through, that reminded me of halos and veils, and the wispiness of our prayers wafting to heaven. And I could picture them encircling the throne, and envisioned God's arms as the branches, pulling them unto Himself. As He personally answered every request and praise, the light dances and a rainbow forms, to give us a promise and show us that He has heard each plea.

No matter if the sun is visible or not, the Son is available! That is a promise worth believing, and one to hang your halo on. God's love never stalls; it is always moving, always encircling us. You are held in the circle of His Light always. There is no dimming. He will forever be the Lord of power, might and strength.

"Your arm is endowed with power; your hand is strong, your right hand exalted. Righteousness and justice are the foundation of your throne; love and faithfulness go before you. Blessed are those who have learned to acclaim you, who walk in the light of your presence, Lord." Psalm 89:13-15 NIV

Look Up, Out, Down, … and Around

Look out, to the horizon,
To where the sun begins to shine.
It's where today, meets the future,
When the light, starts to climb.

Look up, into the heavens,
To the glorious sky, above.
And see the majestic-star-lit-canopy,
That displays the wonder of His love.

Look down, at the shells on the seashore,
To the tiny-miracles in your hand.
For their twisted, sculpted beauty,
Shows us how everything, has a plan.

Look around to see creation,
All the beauty He has made.
His glory is like a symphony;
Can you hear its praises, being played?

Look out, to the horizon,
To where the Son begins to shine,
He holds today and the future,
In His palm, where the light starts to climb.

I'm often telling you, to "look up." But it is actually in looking up, down, out, and all around us, that we see the evidence of our Creator and Lord. In every little thing, big thing, in the sun, or the moon and stars at night … in the mountain peak, or crashing wave of the ocean —His love is displayed.

The more we notice the beautiful things God has made for us, the more I think we see His true beauty.

So look up, look out, look down and all around; for everything that we can see and touch, and even imagine—is designed so that we recognize His hand print, and so that we give Him our highest praise!

Sunset's Shock and Awe

I love when one image,
Takes us to another place and time,
Carrying us back to a special memory,
To a window in our mind, sublime.

As I stood taking in the beauty of this sunset, I was in shock to remember. I was in awe of the present moment. I was blessed to see the combination of both, in one scene before my eyes.

There was something about this sunset,
And the way the colors danced upon the clouds,
That made me think of our time in the southwest,
As the sun hid behind a veil-like shroud.
The trees almost look like rock formations,
The foreground like the desert floor.
The rays lifted my eyes to heaven,
It brought so many thought-pictures, to the fore.
The moment captured something beautiful,
You can almost see mountains have taken shape,
As the wisps look like smoke, rising,
Like all of Creation, when dawn awakes.
I stood in shock as I realized,
It felt like I stood out in the West.
It was a joy, just to remember,
It's a blessing, when you know you're blessed.

This image had an etherealness about it,
And I stood humbly in awe.
In the wash of colors from the dust to sky above,
I hear the echo of the angels call ...
Perhaps the shadows forming,
Are the celestial beings gathered in the clouds,
Dancing, moving, praising;
Earth and heaven are joined and are wholly bowed.
The trees lift their arms in exultation,
The Light, His presence is surely here.
As I look upon God's beauty,
Everything else seems to disappear.
So while I stand on the East Coast,
And remember the West,
I am in shock and awe of my Savior,
I am indeed, feeling blessed!

"The Lord reigneth; let the people tremble: he sitteth between the cherubims; let the earth be moved. The Lord is great in Zion; and he is high above all the people. Let them praise thy great and terrible name; for it is holy." Psalm 99:1-3 KJV

Dear Lord, great is Your name, and greatly to be praised. In the East, in the West, in the desert and in the rainforest, You are ever-present. Your beauty makes me stand up and take notice. I am amazed at how much You love us. All of earth and heaven join in moments such as this, to deliver Your message, everyday. Amen.

"... How awesome is this place! This is none other than the house of God; this is the gate of heaven." Genesis 28:17b NIV

It was sunset one evening, rain had just moved through our local area. As I was about go upstairs, the sunset caught my eye through the front window. I got my camera, and went out on the front steps. The image before me, made me feel like I was being given a glimpse into heaven. The way the sun was coming from behind the clouds, the different shades of blue and gray in the sky, all formed this collage to make me pause. As sunlight lit each cloud and seemed to dance with the close of day, my mind was filled with God's grandeur.

> *"O Lord, our Lord, how majestic is your name in all the earth! ...*
> *When I look at your heavens, the work of your fingers, the*
> *moon and the stars, which you have set in place, what is man that*
> *you are mindful of him, and the son of man that you care for him? ...*
> *O Lord, our Lord, how majestic is your name in all the earth!"*
> *Psalm 8:1, 3-4, 9 ESV*

In this moment, it was like something beautiful was captured between God and myself. And now, I share it with you, because I hope you will behold Him; for that moment was over in the blink of an eye. The clouds shifted quickly, and the opening closed, creating a new image. Our lives are like this, too. We have this moment, one day at a time, one hour at a time. It is my prayer that you won't miss any moments, any glimpses into heaven, or any opportunities in the day in front of you.

> *Is God bringing to mind a moment that you missed?*
> *How did He, or how can He yet, redeem it?*

In that opening, that time and space, it was like God's love poured through, it was almost like a hug. I hope it appears that way to you, also. Because His love is grander, bigger, wider, fuller, and deeper than my camera can capture, or your mind can comprehend. May the glow of His love rest upon you, and may you sense His ray of hope, coming through any cloud in your life. The Light of the World came to give us a glimpse into heaven, by giving His Son, and maybe the sun is just one reminder of His love.

Fire meets Ice

In seeing this sunset, I had one singular thought ... "fire meets ice." The light was just fading, as it hit the edge of the lake that had begun to freeze.

Like a blaze of sunset,
Red, rose and gold,
Lit the horizon line;
These shades,
Met in splendor,
Upon the frozen lake,
—To shine.
Fire meets ice,
Here, is God's majesty.
Can you not see,
His display of authority?

Like a flame to the world,
Is His Salvation within us.
As His light fills our soul,
To warm,
The hearts near and dear,
—Fire meets ice.
Do we have passion,
For His mission?
Can others see Him,
Displayed,
In our lives?

From the moment that we become His child, we are to be like an ember on a hill, shining with a pure and holy light. And though we are sometimes met with the world's icy hostility toward God, we are to be like the sunset, unfurling His message of hope, everywhere we go.

> *"The unfolding of Your [glorious] words give light; Their unfolding gives understanding to the simple (childlike)."*
> Psalm 119:130 (AMP)

Like a blaze of sunset,
May our hearts,
Be ignited.
May all who meet us,
See His splendor,
As fire meets ice. ...
Melting, yielding,
Lovingly showing,
Until the colors of His rainbow,
Unfold,
All across the earth.

May our love for You, Jesus, never fade. May we be like fire upon ice, reflecting Your beauty and love. And may we bring warmth to the world, that is sometimes cold. Amen.

Prisms on Ice

Upon the crackled ice,
As twilight fell,
Sunset left a trail,
—Of prisms.
They danced,
And lit these floating islands,
To glisten,
In the eventide,
That swiftly descended.
Around them,
Flowed open water.
Above them,
A milky sun,
With vestiges of tranquil hues,
—All combined,
To swish beauty over the sky and sea.

When have you needed to rely on God to be the island of your soul? When has His light reflected to declare you as His own?

And the image of stillness,
Hovered over it all,
Until a prism of God's Spirit,
Lit my heart, within.

Prisms of ice warmed my soul, until stillness settled, to bring the tranquility of God's Spirit, within. It was like He became my island, in the current of life. It is the Lord Whose light shines, as a beacon from our inner being, reflecting that we belong to Him.

- When you feel at sea … is Jesus your anchor?
- Does His light shine from within, so that His love is reflected into all that you do and say?
- When the winds of hurt assail you, do you seek the Son for warmth, healing and grace?

Evening and Morning

There are some scholars, who feel we have our day and night, reversed. We look at a day, as beginning—with the sun rising upon the horizon. Yet in Genesis, a few translations actually state evening and morning, created a day. Why am I pointing out this distinction? Because we may see each 24 hour period, in an entirely new light.

What if we viewed the beginning of a day, as starting in a period of rest? How would this change our perspective? What if, what we view as the end, is really the beginning? And meant to be our soul's refreshment? Would we have a greater sense of peace? Joy? Would we view God's Spirit and presence any differently?

There is a hush that seems to descend upon all of nature as the sun sets. And I began to wonder, if that is what God means for us to have, as the beginning of our next day. Instead of looking at this time of tranquility as the end of the day, perhaps He means for us to experience the calm, as the commencement of the next.

I wonder if we might sleep a little better at night, or trust God a little more, if we were surrendered to this idea. For "as it was in the beginning," is a wise concept to embrace. And if we are willing to look at all things in a fresh way, we might see that every evening and morning, can bring us closer to His presence.

References: The Jewish Sabbath begins a few minutes before sunset on Friday evening, until the first stars appear in the sky on Saturday night. It is ushered in by the lighting of candles and the reciting of a blessing.

"God called the light 'day,' and the darkness he called 'night.' And there was evening, and there was morning—the first day." Genesis 1:5 NIV

Softly and Loudly

It was just moments after the sun had set. Rose, gold, aqua, lavender, and blue-gray, all seemed to kiss on the golden evening's air. The curtain began to close on the day, and a tranquility began to settle over the water, over the shoreline.

Even the traffic on the bridge was quieted for the night. I have come to love this magical time. Now, don't misunderstand me—I love to catch sunsets; those glorious glimpses have a beauty all their own. But during this year, I have found a loveliness, to these few minutes immediately following the sun's setting.

> There is a hush that enters,
> When the sun has fallen.
> The colors draw out, and up,
> O're the atmosphere.
> In the solitude, I find the silence,
> Speaks loudest,
> That my God, is near.

Twilight, feels like earth is saying its prayers for the night. It brings its final offerings of beauty and grace before the King. Quietly, humbly, it is shaded in peace. With gentleness, it seems to sing a hymn of praise to the Creator. The very atmosphere changes and becomes calm. Yet it speaks to my soul, clearly, loudly: "The Lord reigns. He is ever present. He is in the midst of the earth. He cares about you, me, about all that He has made."

Let this stillness wash over you. Let Jesus draw you into His arms. Let Him be your bridge, your guide. For with every breath, His Spirit is alive within you. May your communion with the Lord, feel like His kiss upon the atmosphere of your heart. For His love is that close. Let it fall, fresh, to speak softly and loudly, to your soul.

Let His nearness embrace you, like the promise of His faithful care which shall reign through the watches of the night, until the first light of morning.

> *What hour of each day, speaks most softly to your soul?*
> *Which one, speaks most loudly, that God is near?*

> *"And each morning and evening they stood before the Lord to sing songs of thanks and praise to him." 1 Chronicles 23:30 (NLT)*

Thank You's—Embracing Light

Whether you are greeted by the colorful illumination of an alarm clock, a bathroom light, the sun streaming through the window, or see it reflected upon a wintery landscape ... light, is all around us.
It shines 'round about us, from all directions.

What are some of the light sources for which you are grateful? What might a "Thank You" note look like, sound like, to the Light of the World, if you counted every source of light that you encounter on a given day? Which one(s) would be most pro-foundly, missed, if they were to disappear?

Soul's Introspection—Embracing Light

*"Arise, shine; for your light has come, and the glory of the
Lord has risen upon you." Isaiah 60:1 (NASB)*

What is the first lighted object that you see each morning? Is it an
LED clock, a nightlight's glow, or dawn coming through your
window? How does light affect your mood, and the start of your day?

*"In the morning, O Eternal One, listen for my voice; in the day's
first light, I will offer my prayer to You and watch expectantly for
Your answer." Psalm 5:3 (VOICE)*

*"My soul waits for the Lord more than the watchmen for the morning;
indeed, more than the watchmen for the morning." Psalm 130:6 (NASB)*

Dear Adonai, may the light of Your presence be like an embrace
today. Teach me, to feel Your warmth as a personal touch, just as I
can experience the rays of the sun upon my skin. Help me to see You
as the source of my strength. Today, I am trusting that You will shine
brightly upon the path that helps me closely follow You. Amen.

*"Let the morning bring me word of your unfailing love, for I have
put my trust in you. Show me the way I should go, for to you I
entrust my life." Psalm 143:8 (NIV)*

*"But as for me, I will sing of your strength, and I will hail your
loyal love in the morning, because you have been my high
stronghold and a refuge in my time of trouble." Psalm 59:16 (LEB)*

*"Then, oh then, your light will break out like the warm, golden rays
of a rising sun; in an instant, you will be healed. Your rightness will
precede and protect you; the glory of the Eternal will follow and
defend you." Isaiah 58:8 (VOICE)*

Do you remember a time when a parent or adult rescued you from
darkness, and how it made you feel safe? Explore those feelings.

*"When Jesus spoke again to the people, he said, 'I am the light of the
world. Whoever follows me will never walk in darkness, but will have
the light of life.'" John 8:12 (NIV)*

*"Let your light shine before men in such a way that they may see your
good deeds and moral excellence, and [recognize and honor and]
glorify your Father who is in heaven." Matthew 5:16 (AMP)*

The Gem of Meditation

The Pause:

I love the way that any light source seems to envelop a space. No matter if is a candle, a lamp, or the sunshine coming through a window—it seems to create a holy illumination. I enjoy tracing how it travels around a room or throughout the entire house, during a given day and into the evening hours. And I have even noticed how our cat follows its path, to lie in its warmth. And I am fascinated to watch God's light invade a soul—to purely shine—from their countenance, from acts of kindness, into a growing, developing faith.

How have you witnessed light move, in a transformative way?

....

How have you seen God's Spirit—illuminate, change or shape—a life (your own or someone else's), to bring hope and encouragement?

....

How has the Light of the World, Jesus, met you in a place of darkness, to teach you that He is love, personified?

....

The Praise:

Dear Jesus, I am thankful that You are the Light of the World. I am grateful that I face no situation, no temptation, no fear, no shadow, nothing—alone. I praise You, God, for being the One Who holds me close and walks with me at all times. As I take time to pray and commune with You, I find that I am embraced, met, by Your loving-kindness and feel surrounded by Your grace. Amen.

....

....

....

....

....

Under a Canopy of Stars

Focusing-In

Triangles,
facets,
geometric
shapes—
form within a
circular tube—
to create star-like
images. In our
minds, we can
dream, as if we are
under the heavenly
hosts, gazing upward.

Suddenly a toy—fills the
daytime with God's glory
—bursting, shining,
glittering and sparkly right
before our eyes. In it, we can
see our Creator's creativity—
in every hour of the day/night.

The images are as vivid as the
canopy of stars that the Lord brings
out nightly, so faithfully. In each, we
find evidence of His watchful care to
remind us, that we are as these—called
by name, known, loved.

Will you let the stars remind you that God's
a bit starry-eyed over you?

Section III

Under a Canopy of Stars

The Heavenly hosts were made to shine.

God calls each star by name. The moon changes its shape
nightly, marking time, marking the tides. Under a canopy of
velvet sky, His glory glistens, silently, yet speaks volumes
to the heart that beholds Him, as Lord.

Psalm 19:1-6 (ICB)

"The heavens tell the glory of God.
And the skies announce what his hands have made.
Day after day they tell the story.
Night after night they tell it again.

They have no speech or words.
They don't make any sound to be heard.
But their message goes out through all the world.
It goes everywhere on earth.

The sky is like a home for the sun.

The sun comes out like a bridegroom from his bedroom.
It rejoices like an athlete eager to run a race.

The sun rises at one end of the sky,
and it follows its path to the other end.
Nothing hides from its heat."

When you behold the canopy of stars, or stand awe-struck
by the beauty of the glow of the moon, may you feel God's
enveloping grace, as light and warmth to your soul.

North Star

The telescope, much like the kaleidoscope, magnifies not just the stars of space, but brings us into a sanctuary of solitude. Here, we find ourselves alone with the audience of One, in a private moment of communion, to ponder with wonder, His glory.

The North Star is, as you would guess, the marker for heading North. It is not the brightest star in the sky. It actually comes in, currently, at 50th place. Many use the Big Dipper as a guide, because the North Star, is actually the last star in the handle of the Little Dipper—which is helpful in finding it. It has been a guide for sailors for centuries, and is a favorite among stargazers of every age.

Since God made the heavens, the moon and the stars, I am always reminded of His grandeur when I gaze into the night sky. I love the clear evenings when the velvet darkness is hushed, and the starry host look like crystals hanging by invisible threads. For in these moments, I remember that My Father holds them in place, exactly where they are. They come up like clockwork, every night with the rotation of the earth, to shine down His glory and love.

In the solitude of night, I can often feel God's presence so nearly, so dearly. I can get my bearing and hear His voice, with a clarity that the noises of the daytime hours, do not allow. So if you need to hear His voice, try looking up at the sky.

Don't wish upon these heavenly bodies, but instead, say a prayer, offer a word of thanks or a song of praise, to the One Who created them. In doing so, you may find that you have indeed been guided by the North Star, Jesus, Himself. For in this private space of a lovely starlit canopy, and before an audience of One, you may find rest for your body, mind, and spirit.

Sweet Dreams!

> *"You are as majestic as the morning sky—glorious as the moon—blinding as the sun! Your charms are more powerful than all the stars above." Song of Songs 6:10 (CEV)*

Lord, are the stars,
Your version of diamonds,
With perfect cut, color and clarity?
Is the moon,
One large pearl,
With its luster,
And iridescent luminosity?
Are the planets and galaxies,
Shaped and faceted,
Like precious jewels—
Hanging—
Yet, mounted by Your Holy hand?

For in them,
I see Your majesty,
Your glittering beauty,
Your authority,
—Over all creation.
They are,
—God breathed,
So that we,
Breathe,
You, in.

Jesus, please "set" my life by Your Will, so that it shines for Your glory. 'Cause I long for every activity under heaven, to be an offering of praise, unto Your throne. Amen.

Star Praise

When I gaze into the heavens,
And see the wonders that You have made,
View the glittering canopy above me,
I remember Your care for all of my days.
I cannot help but praise You,
My Father, Lord, and God;
For without You, I can do nothing,
I rely on Your strength and mighty rod.
As the stars come out to light the heavens,
I am reminded of Your vigilant, watchful love.
Your faithfulness that is new every morning,
Is like dew-drops,
And is as pure as a snow white dove.
I honor and bow before You,
Jesus, Jehovah, my King.
And every night with the twinkling stars above me,
I too, raise my voice to sing,
Praise and prayers of exultation,
That my heart and soul, long to bring.
You are a God of awesome power,
Ruling over every person, animal, and thing.
I am amazed at the glory You have created,
Too beautiful for my mind to grasp;
It is Your hand until eternity,
That I will ever, clasp!

"God, the Holy One, says, 'Can you compare me to anyone?
Is anyone equal to me? Look up to the skies. Who created all
these stars? He leads out all the army of heaven one by one.
He calls all the stars by name. He is very strong and full
of power. So not one of them is missing.'" Isaiah 40:25-26 ICB

Dear Lord, thank You for the beauty and crystalline marvel of the stars. They are like twinkling promises of Your love, grace and goodness, as a canopy draped over the earth. Your tender mercies are new every morning, and every night they are reminders that Your care never ceases. We praise You, Father, for creation, for the glimpses that it gives us into heaven, into Your character, into Your love! Amen.

*"Praise him, sun and moon; praise him,
all you shining stars." Psalm 148:3 NIV*

Prayer to an Audience of One

This tree is growing right in our own neighborhood. And one evening as I looked up, I loved how it appeared that the nightly stars, seemed to adorn its limbs. It looked like it had been strung with lights, as if it was Christmas-time ... yet it was a natural effect, created by light, shadows, and angles.

It drew my eye toward the heavens, the Maker of the starry canopy. In this moment of stillness, I sought an Audience of One—in a prayer of praise— for this special sight. His illumination of this tree, also lit my heart, with His love.

Dear Jehovah,

When I am still and in communion with You, I find peace. I find Your Spirit attending me with every breath. And with it, comes Your comfort and rest; thank You, for being as close as a whisper to my heart.

You know my every thought—yet You long for my voice to praise You, to worship, to bring my needs and requests before Your throne, in a gift of submission. It is this holy conversation that joins earth and heaven—time and space—for all eternity. It is a promise to my soul to know that You are always listening, attentive to my first cry, or utterance of joy, or greatest need.

You are like my North Star, ever guiding me. For without You, I am nothing; I have nothing. But with You, I can do anything, because You go with me, as my Savior and Friend. And as I pray, to an Audience of One, I am assured that Your Spirit joins my heart to Yours, thus, my words and thoughts must be amplified throughout the halls of heaven, to give You my highest praise. Amen.

- Bring our Praises and Petitions: Philippians 4:6
- Pray for others, & offer prayer with joy: Philippians 1:3-6
- The Moon and Stars display His loving-kindness: Psalm 136:7-9
- Lift up your eyes to the Creator of the Stars: Isaiah 40:26
- The Lord hears our voice and supplications: Psalm 116:1

The Lord says that the number of stars are greater than the grains of sand on the seashore. How does the fact that He knows these numbers and calls the stars by name, bring you comfort—that He knows your every need and your whereabouts at all times?

"He counts the number of the stars; he gives names to all of them. Great is our Lord, and abundant in power; his understanding is unlimited." Psalm 147:4-5 (LEB)

Moon Dance

It was midnight ...
That hour of darkness when all is quiet,
When one day is ending,
And a new one begins.
At the stroke of twelve,
I captured the dance of the moon.
The sky seemed to mirror my emotions,
They felt in as much turmoil,
As the clouds appeared,
As they ebbed and flowed,
'Round the moon.
They seemed to move like dancers,
Caught up in their own steps,
Creating a cocoon of light and shadow.

Our lives are made up of steps,
Sometimes they flow in a perfect rhythm,
And are perfectly timed.
At other times,
We can feel off-center,
Or be left feeling unbalanced ...
In that cocoon of light and shadow,
Not knowing which way to turn.

"The sun shall not strike you by day, nor the moon by night."
Psalm 121:6 (NKJV)

As I watched the moon and clouds,
Change in shape and position,
An optical illusion was created.
Because to my eye,
It appeared that both were moving,
Not just the clouds.
They seemed to sway as if to music,
To a hymn or song of praise that my ear,
Could not hear.

Maybe at midnight in heaven,
There is, indeed, a moon dance.
And tonight,
Or this morning,
I got a front-row seat to God's throne room.
It was a lovely view.
I think I might hear music, after all.
The sweet sound of praise,
And the whisper of God's love echoed,
As the moon, dances by!

On that Night of Miracles

On that night of miracles,
The wise men followed a star.
It lit the heavens,
To pave the way for worship,
And bearing gifts to the Christ Child.

It rested above the little town of Bethlehem,
Where Jesus lay swaddled in the manger.
And on any given night,
We can remember,
By simply going outside,
Into the twilight,
To behold His majesty in creation.

Have you ever chosen a star as your very own, to wish upon? Pray upon? To think upon—as possibly the one that appeared, and has remained—to lift our eyes to the Lord's divinity? Have you ever thanked God for all of the gifts that He has bestowed upon your life: breath, each new day, His faithful provision and care? And have you ever offered Him gifts: tithes, offerings, your time, talents, love and adoration?

"After hearing the king, they went their way; and behold, the star, which they had seen in the east, went on before them [continually leading the way] until it came and stood over the place where the young Child was. When they saw the star, they rejoiced exceedingly with great joy. And after entering the house, they saw the Child with Mary His mother; and they fell down and worshiped Him. Then, after opening their treasure chests, they presented to Him gifts [fit for a king, gifts] of gold, frankincense, and myrrh." Matthew 2:9-11 (AMP)

How might looking at the night sky from time to time, bring the miracle of Jesus' birth, a little closer to your world? To your heart? And help you feel His nearness with just a simple gaze?

Father God,

All of creation bears Your imprint,
    Just as you made heaven 'n earth,
    The moon 'n stars.
    Your love reaches to the highest places,
    Even to Jupiter and Mars.
        It transcends beyond the horizon,
        And goes beyond the lowest hell.
        There is nothing outside of Your knowledge,
        No praise that cannot tell …
            Of Your glory and splendor;
            You rule over all of time and space.
            As I seek Your holy presence,
            I bow before You,
            My God of power, might, and grace.
                I stand in total wonder,
                And am in awe of Who You are.
                Creation bears Your imprint,
                —Every person, heart, planet,
                      And shining star.

I bow in wonder, before Your throne; for all of heaven and earth are Your kingdom, yet my heart is Your home. The sky holds the stars, yet You are the One Who holds gravity's hand. Nothing is beyond Your power or notice. And everything that You have created bears the image of Your likeness. For these reasons, I praise. For these things, I give thanks. For these blessings, I know You are God.

By the Light of the Moon, She Remembers ...

There is a crescent moon above her head. It reminds her of her childhood, when she believed in fairy tales. It sends down a beam to the earth below and lights a path that her eyes seem to follow. She is captivated by the dance of light and the veil of shadows, that is created. And on this night, she remembers God's love for her, because her husband  has passed away. She tries to feel the presence of Jesus, because she misses the one who used to hold her close. Her name is "widow;" her story is loneliness. But her song, is love.

For within her heart she ponders their journey. Maybe she drops a tear for every shared year. As she walks down this path of memories, she holds a box full of the letters and tokens of the things that they held dear. She sits in her room in the corner, her rocker's motion and the ticking of the clock, are the only sounds. But in her mind, she can hear the music playing; she sees them dancing in days-gone-by.

She can almost feel her love's embrace, feel his kiss upon her cheek. She can still recall the scent of his aftershave, feel the smoothness of his face. She remembers the twinkle in his eye when he found something funny. She hears the echo of his voice calling her name. The home they shared and where they raised their children, will never, be quite the same.

She takes one day at a time now. Yet, she maintains a heart that is giving and kind. She reaches out to others because she hasn't left love behind. She has kept it in her heart for safe keeping. It is the gift they shared that she continues to impart. She is a blessing to others, because she shares what she has learned of God, of life, and knows this is where all things, begin.

She has not stayed locked away; and by now her smile has returned. She shines with the light of Jesus, and dances with Him 'neath the moon. For as she flows with the music that she can hear only in her mind, she is rocked in His arms forever, known with a love that will last for all time. She bears the fragrance of the Savior, for her life bears the image of His grace. And when you look into her eyes, it is like looking into Jesus' face.

Maybe that is who widows (and widowers) are … perhaps they are angels in disguise. For who can know the love of God more deeply, than the ones who have loved and lost, and have so much of Him to share? For these dear ones, God's children, often wear the silvery crown of age. Yet, they exemplify love so freely, they are treasures like a cherished book's pages. They have much to teach us, if we will look inside their hearts. The light shining from within them, is a love story written from God's own heart.

> *"Gray hair is a crown of splendor; it is attained in the way of righteousness." Proverbs 16:31 NIV*

The Star Above Me

I had to stop and retrace a few steps, to verify that I had seen—what I thought I saw. The moon was held perfectly in the center of this set of strung lights. And the effect seemed to form, the perfect Moravian star.

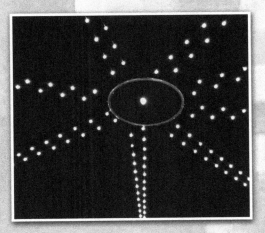

I gazed up toward the heavens,
And there dancing in the sky,
Was the image of a star above me,
—A beautiful light, drew nigh.

85

The moon was held in the center,
As the rays formed perfect lines.
Against the velvety darkness,
It seemed to glimmer and shine.
It looked so much like a Moravian,
In its shape and form,
And as it illumined all below it,
Its glow somehow felt safe and warm.
It wasn't hard to imagine,
The one that shone long ago,
O're the little town of Bethlehem,
Or the love the Christ-child,
To earth, would bestow.
He came to light the recesses of our hearts,
To shine His rays into the darkest places ...
And if we will gaze upon His beauty,
He will radiate the same, upon our faces.

The lights formed an interesting image, but it wasn't until the moon was perfectly centered, that it took on the appearance of the Moravian star, and pointed me to the Savior. When He is the center of our world, the center of our lives, our focus, we allow Him to create a design with our lives. Being held, just like gravity by His Spirit, is where we find the freedom to fly, to shine, to sparkle.

Lord, keep my eyes ever focused to look for the stars above me; for in seeing them, I see something of You. Let them remind me of You as a babe, but also of the love that constantly shines down upon me. Illumine my heart—until my face, my life, my actions, my words, my everything—radiates You. Amen.

"Praise Him, sun and moon; Praise Him, all
stars of light!" Psalm 148:3 NASB

The stars seem to form a canopy in the night sky.
They remind me that You hover over me, watching
and lovingly tending me—even on the darkest night.
I am thankful for their existence Lord, since I also
know this also indicates _____ to my soul.

There's a full moon tonight that's winking,
From heaven's blue-black sky.
It's silvery light hangs like a lantern,
Brushing earth in a glow, as night draws nigh.
And I got to thinking it's perfect,
It's complete in its beautiful ball.
There are no pieces missing;
It's held in place by the Lord of All.
And I wondered if we could see ourselves,
From this perspective, through the Father's eyes,
If we would dream a little bigger,
If it would be simpler to realize ...
That God's light always surrounds us,
In an everlasting circle of love.
May we know that when we diligently seek Him,
He views us, as perfect, from heaven above.

"O Lord, our Lord, your majestic name fills the earth! Your glory is higher than the heavens." Psalm 8:1 (NLT)

"His dynasty will go on forever; His kingdom will endure as the sun. It will be as eternal as the moon, my faithful witness in the sky!" Psalm 89: 36-37 NLT

The full moon this evening made me wonder: What would we be able to do for God's kingdom—if we saw ourselves as He sees us? In seeing its perfection, I thought ... this is how our Father views our heart, if we have received Jesus as Lord and Savior. In Him, nothing is missing, we are made whole. So as you gaze at the night sky, ask Him for a dream. And know that whatever He places in your heart, is perfect. One perfect moon, One perfect Lord; it's one perfect night to dream!

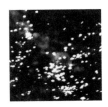

The moon changes shapes all throughout the month. Have you ever wondered why?

Oh Galaxies of Heaven

The moonbeam shines down,
O're all the land.
Light and shadow are formed,
By His mighty hand.
The stars how they twinkle,
This lovely night.
He casts them majestically,
Before our sight.
Right into the galaxy's path they ride,
The glories of heaven are opened, wide.
Velvet black sky,
Twinkles and glows,
With majesty and divine secrets,
Only it, seems to know.
O Galaxies of Heaven,
You leave me in awe,
For you are but the footstool,
Of Your Creator,
My Lord, and All and All.

Do we miss the simple beauty and divine secrets that our Creator displays for us, nightly? Do we miss, what is obvious? Do we neglect to thank Him, for the things of wonder that He has made? For I wonder, how can you look at the twinkling, majestic, velvety heavens—O Galaxies of Heaven—and not be mesmerized, by this Lord?

Dear Lord, I stand amazed, or rather I bow, for I cannot stand; my knees grow weak at the beauty You have created. I love how these things show me Your majesty. O Galaxies of Heaven, are but stardust in comparison to Who You are! Amen.

"Look at the myriad of stars and constellations above you. Who set them to burning, each in its place? Who knows those countless lights each by name? They obediently shine, each in its place, because God has the great strength and strong power to make it so." Isaiah 40:26 VOICE

Starlit Days

This sculpture sits on a grassy knoll in a garden. If you catch the hour just right, as we did, it reflects its own design within the interior of the metal dome. I found it beautiful, to have a—starlit, day.

Dear Jesus, because You are called the Bright and Morning Star and Your Spirit dwells within every soul that calls You, Lord—we can know something of starlit-days (and nights). Thank You, for this physical reminder from the garden, that You are always with us—at all hours, for every need. You are the Son that radiates truth, peace, joy, hope ... correction, instruction, justice ... goodness, mercy and forgiveness. And we are grateful that You leave us signs along our path, that point to You. Amen.

Do you reflect the Spirit of God to those around you, as this sculpture does, so naturally? If the Lord held your life up to the light, would He see His attributes coming into clearer focus, each day, each month, each year? Do those people in your life—your family, your friends, etc.—know that you are a child of God, if you are? Are you seeking to know Him, if you are not?

The Son shines upon every heart to draw them into communion—to see Him, know Him, love Him, serve Him, and reflect Him.

Dear Jesus,
How could I not,
Look at You,
And be amazed?
How could I see the stars,
And not, simply gaze,
At Your beauty?
How could I not,
Feel the wind as Your refreshing,
Spirit's breeze?
How could I not,
See its movement,
Dancing in, and through the leaves?
How could I not,
See Your power,
In the lightning,
Of this wee morning's hour?
How could I not,
See Your faithfulness,
Rising, falling, in the tide?
How could I not,
See Your holy glow,
In the first rays of dawn?
How could I not,
See Your glory,
As my source of joy,
To carry on?

"How could I not?" became a prayer in the middle of the night. For with this simple question, came a profound recognition: everything that God has created, leaves me with a sense of holy-admiration. Yet not at these things, but the One Who makes each and every one of them. It is unto Him, that all glory and honor and worship is due. It is unto Him, that I proclaim my faith, my joy, and Salvation.

"Blessed be the name of the Lord from this time forth and for evermore! From the rising of the sun to its setting the name of the Lord is to be praised! The Lord is high above all nations, and his glory above the heavens!" Psalm 113:2-4 RSVCE

How could we not, indeed? For just as this lightning strike connected earth to heaven, so too, does praise to the Father's ear, rise like incense. And somehow our surrender, brings power, to leave us amazed!

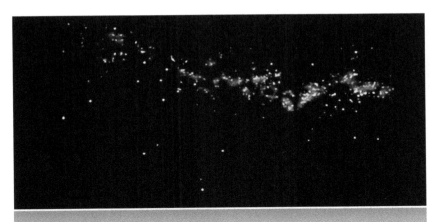

Twinkle,Twinkle.
Little star ...
I gaze into heaven,
Above me so far.
I see the glory of Jesus,
And His wonderful face.
I feel the embrace of love,
Beyond all time and space.
As the moon and stars gather,
For their nightly, artistic show,
They light up the earth,
Here below,
With a majesty and beauty,
That does not compare,
With anything, anywhere.
For as I look into the sky,
I see God's Holy hand.
Sparkling and shifting like this,
Could come, from no other plan.
Twinkle, Twinkle,
Little Star,
You help me remember,
That God is not very far,
From my presence,
Only a prayer away,
One word in request or worship,
And His ear is instantly, bent my way.
As I gaze into heaven,
It is You, I see,
My heavenly Father,
Ever, watching over me.

"I look up at your macro-skies, dark and enormous, your handmade sky-jewelry, moon and stars mounted in their settings. Then I look at my micro-self and wonder, why do you bother with us? Why take a second look our way? Yet we've so narrowly missed being gods, bright with Eden's dawn light. You put us in charge of your handcrafted world, repeated to us your Genesis-charge, made us lords of sheep and cattle, even animals out in the wild, birds flying and fish swimming, whales singing in the ocean deeps."
Psalm 8:3-8 (MSG)

The moon and stars rise at His command; they obey at His voice, and twinkle at the touch of His fingers. If He can hold all of time and space in gravity, He can hold our concerns, our every need. Look up to the heavens, look into the eyes of the Father. Behold the One Who holds the answers, and Who holds you with eternal love—because He does. His love is like a canopy of blessing and peace. Every star that twinkles may be God winking at us, reminding us that His eye is always upon us, as He keeps watch over His children to bring us perfect rest.

> *Where we see a veil, the Father, Son and Spirit are the Light, shining on earth and in the heavens.*

The Milky Moon

There was a milky moon,
Visible this morning,
Way before the break of dawn.
It was covered by a veil,
Softly glowing,
Shedding palest light across the lawn.
Yet I wondered,
If the reverse side,
That shone upon heaven's shore,
Would be brighter, fuller, clearer ...
Lit by my glorious Lord.
Through the veil,
His Spirit travels.
It shines within the soul,
Of the child of Christ,
To illuminate their heart,
With purest delight.
Though a veil can overcome us,
We must remember the Light within.
For in God's grace,
And faithful indwelling,
He shines hope, never, to dim.

The milky moon, shone with a warm, gentle glow. It looked like a lantern that was lit from behind a curtain of lace. And I wondered if the view from heaven was just the opposite—bright, brilliant, dazzling. How much like His Spirit in us. Our circumstances may change and cause us to feel various degrees of His light. But it is always present in the soul, in whom the Light of World, dwells.

A veil of clouds cannot dim the radiance of His peace in His followers. For like the milky moon that appears one way to our eyes on earth, the view from His throne is glorious. His Spirit traverses between the two, to lead and guide us with purest grace, to shine light upon our way.

Only You, God

Can you hold the wind back?
Can you stop the waves,
From their never ending adulation?
Only You, God!
Can you cause the stars,
To give their nightly,
Glittering, ovation?
Only You, God!
Can you make the flowers, grow,
Can you place the mountains,
And valleys on earth, just so?
Only You, God!
Can you make the eagle soar?
Can you cause the colors,
Of the leaves to change?
Only You, God!

Only our God,
Lord,
Author of Life,
Could do these things.
That is why,
We can place our trust,
In Him and know ...
That we are safe in His care!
Only You, God,
Could create,
All of creation—
All the wonders,
That we see.
I cannot fathom,
Those who refuse,
To honor, Thee.

Only You, God, have done/do, these things. I give You honor and praise. For with every miracle that I see, hear, and experience—I find myself more and more in love with Who You are. I am astounded by how You care for every thing and everyone, that You have ever made.

The wind, the waves, the stars,
All dance, move and shine,
At His command.
    The flowers grow,
    The birds soar,
    How this thrills,
    This heart of mine.
        When I see the mountains,
        And the valleys rise and fall,
        How I crown Thee,
        Oh Jesus,
        King, my Lord,
        My All and All.
            Only You, God.
            Only You!

"Can you connect the chains of the constellation Pleiades or untie the ropes of Orion? Can you bring out the constellations at the right time or guide Ursa Major with its cubs? Do you know the laws of the sky or make them rule the earth? Can you call to the clouds and have a flood of water cover you? Can you send lightning flashes so that they may go and say to you, 'Here we are?' Who put wisdom in the heart or gave understanding to the mind? Who is wise enough to count the clouds or pour out the water jars of heaven? ..." Job 38:31-37 (GW)

Spectrum of the Heart:

Lord, You are the "Space Between"

Father God,
You are the only One Who hears my "utterances"—the
things that I can't even begin to put into words. When I
revere Your majesty, or come to praise You, or cry out in pain,
or fall on my face before You—You are there.

You are ... the space-between,
... the sun and the moon,
... heaven and earth,
... pain and healing,
... cuts and scars,
... joy and happiness,
... peace and contentment.

Lord, I lay all that I am, have, and will ever be, at Your feet.
Use me, make me, mold me. Satisfy every longing with
Your love, Your Spirit, and Your promises.
Amen.

Romans 8:24-27, Psalm 23, Psalm 18:6, Isaiah 49:10

As every moon strikes its pose,
May your heart be reminded,
That God—with it goes ...
To fill every space,
From here to eternity,
With His light and love.
Under a canopy of stars,
He sees you, and knows you by name.
He's whispering His nearness,
Unto the depths of your soul ...
Every day ... every night ... always!

Moon through the Evergreens

The moon shone brightly,
Through the evergreens.
Sweetest illumination,
Lit the needles, to gleam.
Against a velvet sky,
Holiness, seemed to purely glow.
It became one of Winter's,
Treasured, wonderland-shows.

Moonlight, lit the evergreen branches with such beauty, that it appeared as though God's own holiness rested like a blessing, upon the night. And with the coming of twilight, on most evenings, we are treated to the moon's changing glow.

Oh, how these branches,
Displayed Your glory.
For Your radiance, God,
Is earth and heaven's story.

God's holiness is all around us, always shining down from heaven, to touch our lives. When we see His radiance and then lift up adoring praise, it is like directing this light back to His throne. As the moon shone through the evergreens, holiness brushed all of earth. With its anointing, my soul was touched to give God honor, on this treasured wintery night.

"But each day the Lord pours his unfailing love upon me, and through each night I sing his songs, praying to God who gives me life." Psalm 42:8 NLT

On August 21, 2017, most of the country and much of the world, witnessed—the total Solar Eclipse. While the time of its appearing was different in each state or geographical location, the shadows that formed before and after it, were much the same. And one of the treasures of the day—in our neighborhood, occurred—on our own street. There was a sharing of the protective glasses, home-made viewing-boxes, and images. This natural wonder, brought us together, to observe the majesty of our Creator.

How good and great and marvelous is the Lord of All, to show us His majesty via a moving display of His artistry! How wonderful to see that a single event, could bring us outside to fellowship with one another, under one sun, to worship *the Son*. It was a spectacular sight to behold His glory, and also a thing of beauty to see our friendships displayed on the block. As I heard the laughter, and oohs-and-aahs, I gave God praise, for He is an amazing Lord. This God of the universe Who flung the sun, moon and stars into the canopy above us—loves us, to the heavenly realms and back!

There is nothing that can eclipse the favor or grace or mercy, that He has bestowed upon His children. So as you remember the wonder of this special event—know that this same Father— shines His goodness upon you today, and always. All over the country—and the world—He is Creator, Father, Healer, Comforter, Protector, and Friend. And it is a blessing to know that nothing in nature, no spirit, no opinion, nothing

formed against us—can eclipse the plans—that He has for those who love Him, obey Him, and follow His call.

I pray that we will each be inspired by Who He is, so that we follow the Son, from here into eternity!

For a refresher, read, Romans 8:31-39

Canvas of the Universe

Dear Lord, when I see,
How You paint the sky,
How You stretch the canvas of the universe,
Before my eyes ...
I cannot help but worship,
I cannot help but give You praise,
As Author, Artist, Creator,
The Maker of our Days.
When I see shadows and clouds dance,
Or the twinkling stars at night,
Watch a meteor shower,
Or the approach of dawn's, first light ...
When I see the moon reflect You,
With its purest luminescent glow,
I see Your blaze of glory,
In the heavenly, atmospheric show.
When I see a sun rise,
Or feel the warmth of its power,
I see glimpses of Your majesty,
Holiness and grace, in every hour.
For as I look at the sky above me,
I fall on my knees to worship You;
All that dances in the heavens,
Seems to bow before You, too!
Amen.

"Commit everything you do to the Lord. Trust him, and he will help you. He will make your innocence radiate like the dawn, and the justice of your cause will shine like the noonday sun." Psalm 37:5-6 (NLT)

I love how each new day, seems to hold a fresh painting of God's majesty in the heavens. Each day, we have the opportunity to behold Him as Artist, Creator, Inventor, and the Maker of all that is on the earth or contained in the universe. But I wonder if we notice how beautiful, how lovely, each of these images truly are? Do we see the colors that He perfectly blends like a skilled painter? Do we notice the technique in the dance of light and shadow? Do we feel the warmth of the sun, and receive the touch of His embrace through its rays? Do we see the moon as a reflection of, not just the sun, but the glory of the Son? Do we ever try to count the stars, to verify, that we cannot begin to count them? Do we take in, that this canopy alone, gives us a panoramic view of God's goodness and grace?

The sky may not actually be able to pray, but it helps me, visualize my Father. Everyday, I see something in the atmosphere that makes me realize what a big God we serve. I behold something of His power in the clouds that build before a thunderstorm. I feel His presence when I pause on a beach, waiting for the sun to rise. And in that moment of twilight, when the moon is just a shadow, I am reminded that His care is ever-present. These things, give me reasons to keep my prayers flowing to the Creator, of these creations. For in these things, I see the wonders that He has made. We are in part, being shown our Lord in all of nature. And I think when we behold Him in the sky, our prayers, will reflect the nature of His image.

Knowing God, by the Lights of Heaven

Father, we woke to a quarter-storybook-moon. It was visible, as the beginnings of dawn formed on the horizon, and I felt Your nearness. Your presence hovers over the morning, in the evening, in the in-between of day and night. You can be found in every circumstance that we go through. Thank You for always being present, at the ready—to shine hope, strength, or peace, into our every need.

Thank You, that as the moon and sun, rise and set, Your love rotates around us in a constant, never-ending circle of peace. I breathe in, and know that You are with me. I breathe out, and feel Your Spirit fill me with thanksgiving. Amen.

With every glittering star, every night we see the moon, and every day we follow light's orbit 'round the earth, we have a front-row-seat to see our God at work. He is never still, but always at work on the earth, in the heavens, and in the hearts of those who seek to know Him. We can experience His power by being aware of His might that is on display, daily, nightly, to prove His steadfast love.

Dear Jesus, I thank You for the nightly lights—the moon and stars. These glittering orbs bring me joy because ...

Unfurl the Curtain

God unfurls a curtain,
Night falls into place.
As He shakes it into motion,
The moon and stars,
Fill the sky and space.
The twilight is filled,
With a glittering field,
Myriad kinds of light,
To the shadows, yield.
God's power is displayed,
His might is arrayed,
For each of these,
Reflects the light of His soul.

We are like the night, until we become His child. Then, as we learn to know Him, walk with Him, grow in our faith and trust—little by little, we are lit from the inside. One tiny seed at a time, like stars, begin to shine from us until we look like the sky on a crystalline night. As we mature, we are like the moon, drawing others to the light, the love, the joy, the very character of God. His Spirit resides in our soul to draw back the curtain, and let His love shine through us.

Dear Lord, unfurl the curtain of my heart. Plant Your seeds like the stars, until there is the glow of Your Spirit shining brightly, to show my love for You. Amen.

Thank You's—Under a Canopy of Stars

Do you have a favorite star or constellation? Do you enjoy star-gazing, wishing or praying to the Maker of a certain starry host? What "Thank You's" fill your mind, when you consider that God has named each of these luminous, glitters orbs, individually? And that He cares for you, likewise?

....

....

....

....

....

....

....

....

....

Soul's Introspection — Under a Canopy of Stars

"Then God said, 'Let there be light-bearers (sun, moon, stars) in the expanse of the heavens to separate the day from the night, and let them be useful for signs (tokens) [of God's provident care], and for marking seasons, days, and years; and let them be useful as lights in the expanse of the heavens to provide light on the earth'; and it was so, [just as He commanded]." Genesis 1:14-15 (AMP)

"When you look to the heavens and see the sun, moon, and stars—all the array of heaven—do not be led astray to bow down and worship them. The Lord your God has provided them for all people everywhere under heaven." Deuteronomy 4:19 (HCSB)

Psalm 33:6 says this: "By the word of the LORD the heavens were made, and all the stars by the breath of His mouth." Does this fill you with wonder, at our Creator?

"He replied, 'You are good at reading the weather signs of the skies—red sky tonight means fair weather tomorrow; red sky in the morning means foul weather all day—but you can't read the obvious signs of the times!'" Matthew 16:2-3 (TLB)

"God fashioned the two great lights—the brighter to mark the course of day, the dimmer to mark the course of night—and the Divine needled night with the stars. God set them in heavens' sky to cast warm light on the earth, to rule over the day and night, and to divide the light from the darkness. And God saw that His new creation was beautiful and good." Genesis 1:16-18 (VOICE)

"Praise the Lord, O heavens! Praise him from the skies! Praise him, all his angels, all the armies of heaven. Praise him, sun and moon and all you twinkling stars." Psalm 148:1-3 (TLB)

Lord, Your creativity is displayed in the constellations. With each shape You demonstrate Your sense of creativity and that You are always reaching out to connect to all of mankind. Tonight, I will try to locate as many of them as I can. And I will behold You, with wonder.

"The Lord provides the sun for light by day, the moon and the stars to shine at night. He stirs up the sea and makes it roar; his name is the Lord Almighty." Jeremiah 31:35 (GNT)

The Gem of Meditation

The moon sheds its glow in an ever-changing stream from heaven, with rays that touch earth. The stars glitter in the velvety canopy above our heads, to remind us that Your thoughts toward us, are more innumerable than the grains of sand on the seashore. These heavenly bodies are miraculous creations, indeed, for they seem to be suspended in mid-air—held by Your omnipotence, declaring Your glory on a nightly basis.

How do the lights of the night sky, speak of God's wonders, to your soul?

....

....

....

How does the fact that God spoke them into existence in such numbers, into such a great expanse, teach you that He cares for you intimately and with infinite detail?

....

....

....

The Praise:

Dear Lord, in this loveliest of nightly displays, I am in awe of You, as Creator, Artist and Architect. For in the design of pure white light upon purple twilight and velvet onyx, I see Your grace, radiated, upon earth—but also into my heart. May these wonders, leave me pondering the depth and breadth of Your mercy and forgiveness. And may You use their beauty, to instill within my heart, a sense of pausing to behold You, as my Lord, my King. Amen.

....

....

....

From the Inside, Out

Focusing-In

We can be inside a house
—looking out—but gain only a limited view.
We must go outside—to see the intricacy that was
hidden from sight. Then, the whole image becomes
clear.

A Kaleidoscope's exterior—may be fairly plain, or
brightly colored and patterned. But from the inside, they
explode with a profusion of images and changing scenes.

God lives on the inside of us (our hearts) to indwell the soul
and transform body, mind and spirit—into surrendered
followers that He treats as children—part of His family.

It's this process that is the miracle. We are His
workmanship. Are you yielding to His design,
so that you reflect Him on the inside, to
your outside, world?

Section IV

From the Inside, Out

We are God's workmanship. And He is always moving, shaping and changing all of creation, and likewise, those of us who are His children, from the inside, out.

A Sand Dollar is a wonderful illustration of God's invisible wonders, made visible. To me, this is proof that God creates all things with intricacy and the finest of detail. He cares for us, with this same degree of intimacy, also.

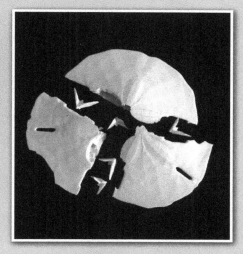

Ephesians 2:4-10 (VOICE)

"But God, with the unfathomable richness of His love and mercy focused on us, united us with the Anointed One and infused our lifeless souls with life —even though we were buried under mountains of sin—and saved us by His grace. He raised us up with Him and seated us in the heavenly realms with our beloved Jesus the Anointed, the Liberating King.

He did this for a reason: so that for all eternity we will stand as a living testimony to the incredible riches of His grace and kindness that He freely gives to us by uniting us with Jesus the Anointed. For it's by God's grace that you have been saved. You receive it through faith. It was not our plan or our effort.

It is God's gift, pure and simple. You didn't earn it, not one of us did, so don't go around bragging that you must have done something amazing. For we are the product of His hand, heaven's poetry etched on lives, created in the Anointed, Jesus, to accomplish the good works God arranged long ago."

God began at conception, by forming us in His image. Then, when we invite Him into our hearts, He begins the workmanship of grace —of imprinting us with His Spirit. This is so that our lives bear testimony that we have been transformed, from the inside, out.

Like a Kaleidoscope

If you take a kaleidoscope,
In your hands,
And hold it up to an object,
It can change flowers, rocks or sand,
To create new patterns,
Making them come to life.
And I wondered …
Is this how the Lord,
Sees the plan,
Of our days?

When He holds us up,
To the light,
Do the things that He allows,
To the left and the right …
Move and shift,
Changing our hearts?
Do they transform us from within?
Do the things that break us,
Draw us, to Him?
Do they create patterns,
That display His ways?

If God took a kaleidoscope,
To your soul,
And held it next to His image,
Would it be a duplicate,
Or be made of holes?
Would the pattern created,
Be colored by His love?
Have you been washed,
By His cleansing flood?
Would you be sparkling with His light?
Are you being transformed,
By day, by night?

"Oh, magnify the Lord with me, and let us exalt his name together!"
Psalm 34:3 (ESV)

Lord, as You look at our lives, may the patterns that You see from the things that touch us, reveal Your love and attributes, within. May we be the living, hopeful, delightful image of You, to the world. Change us, move us, shift our thinking. Take our faith, deeper. Make our trust, stronger, until our hearts are perfect reflections of You, as refractions of Your Light. Amen.

Erosion's Treasure

As we have gone on day-trips to the beaches along Lake Michigan—we've noticed erosion—serious erosion. It's like the shoreline is being cut-away, sculpted, each time we travel there. Trees have been felled, uprooted. Sand, has been shifted. Areas that were once able to be walked upon, no longer have space to do so. The tide runs right up to the bank. In fact, the shoreline in some places now resemble cliffs.

But in one of our visits, I captured this interesting photo in which the sand has been worn away, revealing rocks that are visible, as treasures. They were wedged beneath the surface, creating designs that would have otherwise, been hidden. From what is being broken, I found a form of beauty.

Dear Jesus, when I feel worn down, battered, scared, tired ... please allow me to see a glimpse of the design You're creating, within. For when you show me even a piece of the internal workings, I am encouraged to trust. I am given faith to believe that the barren places will be filled; the hurts will be healed; I am given a firm foundation for the next wave. And I know that You will complete what You've begun, because You alone control all that touches me. Amen.

"Behold, you delight in truth in the inward parts, and
in the hidden parts you make me to know wisdom." Psalm 51:6 LEB

Look for the design below the surface of pain, grief, illness, loneliness. Search for God's love and the embrace of His presence. For just as the tide—ebbs in, ebbs out—He is faithful. The Lord is simply creating a sculpture that can endure the winds of time and eternity.

> *"All this is for your benefit, so that the grace that is reaching more and more people may cause thanksgiving to overflow to the glory of God. Therefore we do not lose heart. Though outwardly we are wasting away, yet inwardly we are being renewed day by day. For our light and momentary troubles are achieving for us an eternal glory that far outweighs them all. So we fix our eyes not on what is seen, but on what is unseen, since what is seen is temporary, but what is unseen is eternal." 2 Corinthians 4:15-18 NIV*

Erosion, revealed the treasure of rocks as art, to my heart. God uses our pain, trials, and difficulties—to transform our inner being. We must trust Him with everything, knowing He is in control of the design.

> *Kaleidoscopes, take an image and transform it into segments of light and new creative patterns. What does the Lord want you to see from a different angle or perspective? Has He removed anything from your life (eroded, but thus revealed something beautiful)?*

Has He bowed you in any way, in order to lift your eyes to focus upon Him?

....

....

Lit by You

Twilight, nestled on the horizon.
Blue-gray clouds,
Embraced the night.
Shades of foam-green,
Touched the water;
This lighthouse lantern,
Was the only light.
As we approached,
We observed its turning.
Then, as we drew closer,
We discovered the internal glow.
Here, the waves on the causeway,
Were flowing, moving ...
The lake was alive,
Lit, by a magical show.

When twilight nestles,
On your horizon,
And storm clouds gather,
In your circumstances or mind ...

> *"The earth and everything it contains are the Lord's. The world and all who live in it are his. He laid its foundation on the seas and set it firmly on the rivers."*
> *Psalm 24:1-2 (GW)*

... Let God's embrace,
Wrap 'round you, like comfort.
He is the lantern,
The only true Light.
For as you draw close,
He will strike a flame,
Inside you;
He'll place His Spirit's glow,
Like Living Water,
To display that you,
Are His marvelous show.

It was a magical time to capture this lighthouse. As we approached, we could see only the turning of the top lantern. But as we parked and walked to it, suddenly, the inside illumination appeared. And I thought—it is like a soul—lit by the presence of God, reflecting Him, on the causeway of our lives.

It must appear magical to the Lord, when His peace, love, joy, kindness, and mercy, flow from within us. It must be amazing to see us channel some part of Who He is, to the world. It must be marvelous from His view, when He sees a 360-degree-life, that shines for His glory.

Oh, to be lit by God—until I radiate Your light and love, and goodness—all around me. That is my prayer. I know I'm not there yet, Father, but by Your grace, keep the flame, aglow. For to give You honor, is my soul's desire. Amen.

What is your prayer, to be lit by the Lord?

....

....

The lighthouse may be lit by man's genius, but the soul that holds the flame of God's Spirit, is a wonder indeed—let it shine forth—with His holiness.

> *"And we all, with unveiled face, beholding the glory of the Lord, are being transformed into the same image from one degree of glory to another. For this comes from the Lord who is the Spirit."*
> *2 Corinthians 3:18 (ESV)*

Internal Housing

Inside these shells, live snails. Have you ever found it amazing that God would provide such covering? Such refuge? Such shelter to these smallest creatures that He has made? Well, one day I saw this concept, as an analogy for His indwelling presence in our hearts.

Think of it ... God, the supreme Being, our Creator, Maker, comes to live inside our "center," when we invite Him into our hearts. He comes to reside in our soul—the essence and eternal part of us. Jesus' Spirit is woven into every fiber of our thoughts, motives, actions and deeds, if we are surrendered to His Will, purpose and plans. He becomes our Intercessor (Romans 8:26-27) and Guide, Shepherd (Psalm 23:1) and Friend.

Here, He works to create new life, new dreams, new goals—because they begin to be shaped by Him, at the moment of our Salvation. Here, He places within us spiritual gifts (1 Corinthians 12:4-11) that we can use to serve Him and others. Here, within our internal housing, He becomes our refuge and strength for the waves, the shifting sand, and the tides that ebb and flow.

God formed us in our mother's womb. It was a space much like these little shells. It is within the space of our internal housing—the heart and soul—that He transforms us into His likeness.

"Now may the God of peace [the source of serenity and spiritual well-being] who brought up from the dead our Lord Jesus, the great Shepherd of the sheep, through the blood that sealed and ratified the eternal covenant, equip you with every good thing to carry out His will and strengthen you [making you complete and perfect as you ought to be], accomplishing in us that which is pleasing in His sight, through Jesus Christ, to whom be the glory forever and ever. Amen."
Hebrews 13:20-21 AMP

Dear Jesus, You are my safe place, from the inside, out. It is from my innermost being, that I bring all that I am, to love and serve You. You are my Shelter. You are my Comforter. And though I live in but a "shell," I know that my soul belongs to You, so it's easy to surrender the tide of following, to Your keeping. Amen.

The Sand Dollar

The Sand Dollar, to me, is one of the most unique and beautiful treasures of the ocean. It is a member of the sea urchin family, and when alive, has a purple hue. I love that it is imprinted with a starfish and holds seagulls (or doves) within its shell. Nothing else is quite like it, in all of the sea.

The Sand Dollar is the color,
Of purist white sand;
It's imprinted, embossed with a star,
Only, by God's hand.
It is shaped in a circle,
With slits that are formed by the tide.
The cycle of life is represented,
With a secret held inside.
For when it is broken,
It reveals a gift, lovely tokens to receive.
Five perfect seagulls,
Are reasons to believe …
In the God Who formed the seashells,
With such intricacy and detail;
He formed us, knit us together,
And His love never fails.
The Sand Dollar tells a story,
Of the beach, the sand, the deep blue sea.
Its combination of shell, starfish, and seagulls,
Are reminders to me …

... God creates beauty from the inside,
That is a gift, meant to be shared.
But sometimes we are broken,
Before we discover what's truly there.
It is often through difficulty,
That we find hope, faith and love,
As we grasp onto the strength that lies within us,
We see it's been given generously, from above.
So when you go through times of trial,
Look to this treasure, found in the sand,
And remember that as He cares for the sea creatures,
You too, are held in His hand!

He cares for you with the same detail as He put into the Sand Dollar. You are as complexly woven from conception: your heart, your intelligence, your emotions, your body, your soul, have been formed, just so. Nothing is by chance, but by His divine plan.

Each muscle, every pump of blood through our veins and heart, are regulated by the One Who regulates the tides. Every person and circumstance that He allows to touch our lives, serves a purpose to imprint something, upon our hearts.

The same One Who holds the stars in place, is the same God Who causes the sun to rise and set. And if He has all of these things in the palm of His hand, and He does, He has you. Your life, your hopes, your faith, your goals and dreams—your everything, is within His grasp. He is with you, above you, beneath you, around you, and in you, if you are His child.

Within each of us are hidden gifts to be shared, just like the Sand Dollar. But we must seek and trust God to find them, and use them. We must be yielded to the tides of life that shape us, refine us. Just as the sand and ocean shape each seashell, God is creating us in His image, day by day, tide by tide. So don't be afraid to ride the waves, He has you. Trust in the design that He is creating.

Let God shape you; beauty (or handsomeness) begins in the heart! For the inner secrets that He is working on, are shining through. You are getting better-looking everyday.

> *I love Sand Dollars. Upon their exterior is imprinted a 5-pointed star, and the imprints of the nails that marked Jesus' hand and feet at Calvary. Some, see a poinsettia on the reverse side. But it is upon breaking it, that we find the 5 doves of peace. What circumstance in your life, has caused you to look inward, to find a treasure of God's design?*

The Circle of Love

She has no needle and thread. She has no yarn and knitting needles. She has no loom or hands to guide her work. She is a bird, creating a cylindrical miracle, a place for her eggs, her young—a nest. With precision, she chooses just the right twigs and leavings, and weaves this finest circle to form a version of cocoon, which will serve as their home.

Dear Lord, may we see Your intimate love for us, in the intricacy of the bird's weaving, her nest. May we find her stitchery compelling, and as an analogy of Your care and provision. Help us to see how You give her instinct, insight, wisdom and creativity, that could only flow from her Creator. For in the forming of this loving circle, I see how You display, Yourself. As You supply one thread, one twig, one piece of lichen at a time, it is a reminder to us that the heart that trusts, will be given refuge and a home, within the circle of Your love and grace. Amen.

If you wonder if God is working in and for you—look at a nest. With great detail, He is using every piece of your past, present and future, to show you His faithfulness. But you must do your part—make room in your heart—for Him, to be at home!

Jeremiah 29:11-13, Ephesians 2:9-10, Philippians 4:19

The DNA of God

Have you ever considered that God has DNA? Well, let's break down the concept of what DNA means—it is in our cells, our finger print, it's what makes us unique from one another, from a molecular perspective and through heredity. The imprint, the very hand of God, is etched upon your face. His signature, is written in the color of your eyes. His heartbeat pulses, in perfect rhythm to yours.

Genesis 1 says, "Let us create" meaning the Father, Son and Holy Spirit were all present at the conception of the heavens and the earth. Genesis 1:27 goes on to tell us that all of mankind, is made in the likeness (or image) of our Creator. That sparkle in your eye, the special quality of your smile, the sound of your voice—all reflect, in some way—your Maker, the Lord, God Almighty.

His invisible traits, are made visible, in the snow-capped mountain peak. They are manifested in the intricacies of the flower from bud to bloom, or are seen in the majestic glide of a bird in flight. His attributes have been known in the changing of the seasons, in the motion of the ocean's waves. God's fingerprint is upon every creature, every creation, every human life that has ever, or will ever, be born.

His imprint is upon every seed that will sprout, to grow, mature, bloom and flourish. It's in the rain that waters and nourishes the earth. His existence is in the sun's rays and moonbeam's softest glow. All of nature is like a mirror, reflecting, magnifying, glorifying Him. And we are made, with the express purpose of doing, likewise.

Within our makeup is the desire to know the One Who made all things. Because to know our Creator, is to see, feel, and experience, some part of His DNA within our own heart. And to do so, allows us to also experience His divine love, intimately. That is the nature of His goodness and grace. That is why He's made all creation with such detail and variety—so that no one could miss Who He is, and how He diligently cares for all that He has made.

The DNA of God is upon everything and everyone that has ever been created. This is so, so that we can know and love Him, as He loves us. May our journey of discovery, lead us to magnify Him, so that we leave hereditary imprints that show our faith and devotion to our Lord.

Did you ever pause to think about the precision with which we are made? But He also gives us a choice: Everyone is made in God's image, but not everyone invites Him into their heart, and surrenders to His ways, purposes, and plans.

It is only when we are yielded and become moldable—that the Potter, can change us, form us, and use us as His vessel. I don't know about you, but I want His imprint to be deep, visible, to run through every fiber of my being. I want my life to bear the mark of Christ. For the closer I walk to Him, the more His DNA will match my own. His signature will write the story of my legacy, and His heartbeat will carry mine into eternity.

Have you invited God to imprint His Spirit upon your heart?

The Kaleidoscope

I have been fascinated by kaleidoscopes, since I was a child. You can hold these "magical wands" up to the light, and with the tiniest twist, have an entirely different image appear before your eyes. Here, I have used a kaleidoscope effect with a flower arrangement, that I had hand-made to create this work-of-art. It almost looks like a painting. Each detail is magnified, turned into a prism, given different dimensions and angles. Each flower, each part of the arrangement has taken on a new look, or has been transformed by an optical illusion. The ribbon, tulle, greenery, wire, each part is highlighted, as if click-by-click, it was brought into focus.

We are like a kaleidoscope. We have many facets. We are born into families that give our lives angles and dimensions. We have life-experiences that shape us—some are magical, some are sharp edged, but all of them magnify our character, and form the work-of-art, that we become. God shines His light upon us, then turns us, and brings our souls into focus. He magnifies certain things in our lives to transform us into His image; to create a beautiful reflection of Who He is.

In His hands we are like a kaleidoscope to be viewed and experienced by others. What affect are you having on those around you? Do you have a vibrancy? A depth, and dimension that magnifies the love of Jesus? As you are turned, God's love is unfurled like a flower, and a striking faceted image is created. What "magical" impact will you have on your own environment?

> *"So here's what I want you to do, God helping you: Take your everyday, ordinary life—your sleeping, eating, going-to-work, and walking-around life—and place it before God as an offering. Embracing what God does for you is the best thing you can do for him. Don't become so well-adjusted to your culture that you fit into it without even thinking. Instead, fix your attention on God. You'll be changed from the inside out. Readily recognize what he wants from you, and quickly respond to it. Unlike the culture around you, always dragging you down to its level of immaturity, God brings the best out of you, develops well-formed maturity in you." Romans 12:1-2 (MSG)*

Layering

I went downstairs to find our digital picture frame, frozen, in this double-exposure. In the background, we (Doug and I) are posing with my brother and his family (Bob, Bonnie, and Alicia). This snapshot was taken one Summer day roughly 8 years ago. In the foreground, I was having a little fun with Doug at a local lake, which is from about a year and 1/2 ago. The super-imposing of the two together, appeared as a version of "layering" to my eyes. And I immediately thought: the same is true, in our lives.

Our families are our "firsts:" in experiencing what love is, what rules are, what respect means. They are where we are taught "right from wrong," given our first values and belief system. Here, we learn something of our identity—as being part of something—and being a representative of a name.

In this indoor and outdoor space called home, we learn our work-ethic, and how to care for others. This is the environment where we learn to forgive and be forgiven, and to offer and are offered, grace. And if we are fortunate, as I was, we are introduced to Jesus here, within the family-circle by witnessing one or both parent's love for Christ. These are just some of the layers that are developed from earliest childhood, that remain in place all of our lives.

Then, we go off to college, move, marry into another family, change jobs, have children/grandchildren—go through all kinds of transitions—in every age and stage. These, further layer our experiences and broaden our horizons. We grow spiritually, in maturity and understanding of God's Word, and learn to listen and obey Him, in new ways also.

The foundation that we are born into, is the first layer of our lives. If we open our hearts to Jesus, His Spirit creates a "born again" status that can add to this base, reinforcing, or even replacing an unwholesome atmosphere. He remakes us day by day, in His image, super-imposing His Will and purpose into our hopes and dreams. That's what it means to love and follow Him.

God, layers His love upon your life from the moment that you were formed; He's been loving you ever since. But when you willingly surrender your heart and life to His care and become His child, the true building, begins.

What are some of your firsts, with your original family?

What of this foundation, did you carry into your marriage/family? Which patterns or behavior did you commit to leave behind?

What are some of your "firsts" or unique traditions, that you've created in your own home?

Did you have the influence of Jesus' love in your early childhood?

Let the Lord structure your steps and create the life that He sees. For the layers that He fashions will look a little like my picture: they may not be perfect, but they will look like art, in the eye of the beholder. For the tapestry created, will be touched with His love—above, beneath, behind, in front, and on both sides of you. Trust God to make the whole of your journey—into His image—a blessed, and abundant life.

"So we have stopped evaluating others from a human point of view. At one time we thought of Christ merely from a human point of view. How differently we know him now! This means that anyone who belongs to Christ has become a new person. The old life is gone; a new life has begun! And all of this is a gift from God, who brought us back to himself through Christ. And God has given us this task of reconciling people to him. For God was in Christ, reconciling the world to himself, no longer counting people's sins against them. And he gave us this wonderful message of reconciliation. So we are Christ's ambassadors; God is making his appeal through us. We speak for Christ when we plead, 'Come back to God!'"
2 Corinthians 5:16-20 NLT

Layers, make us who we are. God begins layering us from the inside, out—it's how our lives are formed—adding family, adding friends, adding places and experiences. And this photo was a reminder that our past, present and future, are held in God's hands, like a frame— of His faithfulness—which shapes us, day-by-day. If we are His child, we too, represent His name and attributes, wherever we go. May He be the foundation, upon which our story, unfolds.

Fearfully and Wonderfully Made

As I knelt to capture the beauty of this royal purple iris, I noticed not only its finite striping and greenery, but in particular, its background. It was this, that reminded me of the interior of a kaleidoscope. Like fragments, the chartreuse foliage created a backdrop, for the iris' vibrancy, to come, alive.

Nature, God's creations, are amazing with their soft lines and angles, and in their unique and varied tones. Each, was made individually and hand-crafted by the Creator. His eye and touch are as a fine Artisan, to perfection. You are no less a marvel in your design.

Psalm 139:13-16 tells us, that we have been created with this kind of skill, woven together, with our days recorded by the very One who knit us together in the womb.

"For you created my inmost being; you knit me together in my mother's womb. I praise you because I am fearfully and wonderfully made; your works are wonderful, I know that full well. My frame was not hidden from you when I was made in the secret place, when I was woven together in the depths of the earth. Your eyes saw my unformed body; all the days ordained for me were written in your book before one of them came to be." Psalm 139:13-16 NIV

"Fearfully, wonderfully" … do you think of yourself that way? Have you ever considered that the Lord made no one, exactly like you? Do you know that He has every part of your life planned, detailed? He knows every hope, dream, desire, goal, and has your past, present, and future all mapped out. Did you ever stop to ponder the many facets of your personality, your natural abilities and spiritual gifts? Because the attention that God showed this iris and its setting, can demonstrate to our hearts, that He took the same kind of care at our inception, and beyond.

Everything that He allows to touch us, encompass us, whether it is past, in the present, or in the future—is like the inside of the kaleidoscope—showing us that He is always aware of the changing interior as well as the exterior. And no matter how our world changes, He is always at work in us, to create art, beauty, and His own character as part of the design.

Dear Lord, help me to appreciate the time You took to create me. Help me watch closely for Your Will and purposes to be made manifest. And help me to kneel often, to see Your grandeur in all of its facets, as evidence of Your careful attention upon everyday of my life. Amen.

God works in the background, to produce His image upon each of us, in the close-up. And as He turns the wand of our days, He refines us, by drawing us into the circle of His love and grace.

We were formed from the inside, out, within the space of the womb. While in this comforting-confine, He was perfecting our features, fingers, toes and body. How does the knowledge that God made you intricately, encourage you that He is not done with His purpose and plan for your life?

Dandelion Seeds

The details of nature and God's creation, never cease to amaze me. In one tiny dandelion puff, that will blow in the wind, are a multitude of seeds. I began counting from the top view, (only going down 10 tiny seedlings, in a circle) and easily viewed about 300 within seconds; imagine the total number in the whole design. And when you look at the close-up—each seed has a base, a stem, and a "flower," which resembles a feather. Note, that the second image, is leaving the silhouette of a star-shape, behind?

We are God's workmanship, created in His image. How our bodies function, our organs, our heartbeat, how our blood flows—are all pieces of an amazing puzzle, and a miracle of nature and God's creation. In every heart, I believe God sows a seed, a passion—something we love or care about, that is to be our gift to others. We are meant to "blow in the wind," to give of the gift(s) that He has given us, as an offering of praise.

The very hairs on our head are numbered (Matthew 10:30), so too, are our days (Psalm 139:16). We need to be firmly attached to a base, Jesus, in order for our lives to be growing and fruitful. In the dandelion puff, each stem is connected to one another; we are, also. We have the ability through one word of encouragement, one smile, one hug, one prayer, or one act of kindness, to be the love of Christ, to live out the circle of faith. And when God views us "close-up," we want to reflect His design.

The dandelion, in its simplicity has a striking beauty, a delicate softness, and a unique lesson to offer. We are part of a "whole," but individual seeds (or gifts) to be air-lifted, into the winds of time and the lives of others. The seeds blow and land where they will, often self-planting, but are God-driven. Wherever He carries you, is your place to be planted.

Could someone around you use a feather touch, a little softness, love, and grace? Let the wind carry you, and let God guide where you land. That is the rich soil, where your soul is to live-out its mission. May your seeds be fruitful! You are part of an amazing, complex puzzle that's all connected to the One Who made all things. Only God can see the whole picture, but in His hands, each of our parts is made whole. One tiny seed, available to His call, in its simplicity, is beautiful!

Dandelion seeds are held in the center of this "flower" until they reach a mature stage. Then, they lift-off, to be dispersed into the air. God works on us from the inside, out—physically, emotionally and spiritually—preparing us, so that we can love and serve Him and others. We are the seeds that He uses, to produce a harvest of souls for His kingdom.

Dear Jesus, may Your image be imprinted from the inside, out—so that the seeds of Your love and influence—leave a lasting silhouette, that we belonged to You. Amen.

> *"You should not use outward aids to make yourselves beautiful, such as the way you fix your hair, or the jewelry you put on, or the dresses you wear. Instead, your beauty should consist of your true inner self, the ageless beauty of a gentle and quiet spirit, which is of the greatest value in God's sight." 1 Peter 3:3-4 (GNT)*

Rotten on the Inside

We were peeling and coring an apple to enjoy with our breakfast, when this is what we discovered: it was rotten, on the inside. To the very core, it was brown, mushy, and unappealing. We did not go any further with this one, as you might imagine. Who would want to partake of such a fruit?

We pulled a fresh one and began the process again, to find a tasty, sweet, tart accompaniment to our eggs. But this simple apple, formed a great illustration of our lives. We are born with a sinful nature—rotten—which in fact, dates back to the days of earliest creation, and the story of another apple and the first couple, Eve and Adam.

If you recall, the serpent enticed Eve with it, and Eve enticed Adam. That's the abridged version. But the eating of it, was in direct disobedience of what God commanded. He had placed them in the perfect surroundings, the Garden of Eden, and had given them free rein, with the exception of this one tree. (Genesis 3)

From one couple's misdeed, came the fall of mankind. But from one perfect Son of God, Jesus, came our opportunity for redemption. So while we were born, separated from God, Jesus was our sacrificial Lamb and guilt-bearer to restore us. But we must choose whether we will eat of forbidden fruit or partake of the Bread of Life.

God invites us into fellowship with Him, from the inside, out. He whispers to the heart His invitation of Salvation. And through a work of grace and forgiveness, He transforms our lives, through the indwelling of His Spirit. He removes our desire to have our own way and instead, chose His. He removes our mushy thinking, to replace our thoughts with His Word and ways. And over time, He places seeds of faith that grows into trees, into orchards, that yield abundant produce.

Our heart and soul are where God works—on the inside—to invite us to be His child. It's where He works to transform us, and to build faith and His attributes to be shared. From within, is where He guides us, teaches us, disciples us—so that we learn to submit to His Will in our lives. And it is within the confines of our inner being, that He changes and challenges us to be living, growing fruit, for His kingdom.

Each of us begin as sinful beings—rotten on the inside—from our birth. But thank goodness we do not need to stay that way. With the gift of God's grace, we are redeemed, changed, and transformed into seed-bearing followers of Christ. As we feed upon His love, He renews us, making us productive, like trees, to grow and thrive.

Romans 3:23, Romans 6:23, Romans 12:2, Titus 2:14,
Ephesians 2:8-9, Isaiah 61:10, Isaiah 41:18-20

In what area of your life have you wanted your own way, but
God has pointed out to you that this would be sin? How has He
helped you correct your choice of thought, action, or deed?

The Inside Story of the Cord

By now, you may have noticed,
That God has me, noticing, many things.
And my latest fascination occurred,
When I was cutting a braided cord—a type of string.

    As my scissors sliced the rope to cut it,
    The inside was filled with the softest threads …
    While it was white and textured on the outside,
    Inside, it held a rainbow of color—and to Jesus, I was led.

I was thinking … we are like this,
No matter how we look on the outside,
We have the same kind of heart, mind,
And blood running through us;
Yet, He is the tie-that-binds.

    And if we are yielded,
    Even on the days that we feel frayed,
    His love can run right through us,
    —'Til His majesty is arrayed.

        So, to have the inside story,
        Of a braided piece of cord …
        We need look no farther,
        Than the glory of the Lord.

As we were cutting rope to roll and secure a rug for the season, I was fascinated to find these soft, multi-colored threads, within. God is always surprising me with these simple, yet special details. And as I held this coil to form my image, I thought how His love, presence, and character, are also multi-faceted.

To understand His story, we can sometimes see it displayed most clearly, in the lives of one another. For though our hearts are bound to Him, we must at the same time, be reaching out, too. His blood was poured out, for ours. His heart and mind and eyes, are always attentive to us. And as He endured the cuts, Jesus was being woven into the fabric of every believer's soul.

One piece of cord, with all its multi-colored hues, reminded me, of all that Jesus died to give me. That is the story and the testimony of His life. May it soak into your very soul, all the way inside your heart, till it is the story that you tell—not just with words, but with thoughts and actions.

When you feel a little frayed or frazzled, or when life cuts you to the quick, will you look for what God may be exposing of His character and love to be shared?

God holds this Terrestrial Ball in His Love

God walks in heaven, He walks on earth, and this terrestrial ball is held in His hand.

It looks like the world,
Our terrestrial ball,
Held in the arms of darkness,
Where only the meteors fall.
Every nation and tribe,
Every language and tongue,
Will bow before God,
With praises willingly sung.
We will join as one voice,
There will be no discord;
Peace will reign,
Unto You, my holy Lord!

You will be exalted,
There will be no more tears.
Only joy will follow us,
Into this life so dear.
So when the shadows creep,
Or come at you in waves,
Look up at the blue sky,
There's no reason not to praise!
We are held in His arms,
Just like the moon and stars,
We are ever in His presence,
He is never far.
If you ever feel alone,
On this terrestrial ball,
Just take the hand,
Of Jesus, Lord of All!

> *God's love covers*
> *the earth from end to end.*
> *His care stretches*
> *from the heights of heaven*
> *to the depths, below.*
> *It encircles the globe,*
> *to reach every heart*
> *— to touch us*
> *— within.*

There is nowhere we can go, on earth, in heaven, or anywhere under the earth, that can keep the Father's love and presence from us. He is Lord of the universe, Lord of every nation, tribe and tongue. And when I think of every culture, every race, being united in one accord in heaven, it brings tears to my eyes. What we cannot achieve on earth, will be accomplished in glory.

So until that time, behold the moon and the stars, the earth, sky, nature. See Him in all of His grandeur. Notice how He allows us to witness His majestic character, power and might. May peace reign in your heart, because God reigns over everything. Let Him reign and rule your life. Because to be held in the arms of Jesus, is to be embraced by all of time and space.

The Crown around the Throne

Every nationality is represented upon the earth. Every tribe and tongue is present and accounted for. Each group, each individual, is precious in the sight of God because He created them. As the children's song says: "Jesus loves the little children, all the children of the world, red and yellow, black and white, they are precious in His sight, Jesus loves the little children of the world."

In Revelation 7:9-10, there's a description of heaven, of multitudes gathered 'round the throne of Christ. And one day as I let my mind tarry on this image, I pictured all the worlds' believers as the most beautiful kaleidoscope, as if through the Creator's eyes. How wondrous each face looked, focused upon Him in worship and adoration. And oh, to be part, just one facet of this throng, this circle, fills my heart with expectant praise!

On earth, we sometimes notice our differences. But in heaven, every knee will bow, and every rainbow skin-tone will exalt Him, as Messiah. In complete unity, we shall serve our Lord, and live in a state of perfect peace.

See: Psalm 90:2, Psalm 139:14, John 1:12

God will revel in the kaleidoscope of souls that form a "crown" around Him. He will call each one of us by name. In a place described with rainbow colors, we'll forever praise and proclaim ... that He is Lord, Master, Messiah, and Creator. Together, in harmony, "hallelujahs" will resound.

Every person is like a faceted jewel of the crown that will bow before the Lord. What a lovely kaleidoscope it shall be, when no more hate or discord rises, and only love, God's love, unites and binds us unto Himself, eternally! Oh Lord, what joy and song fills my heart at that image. It brings peace for some future day, when we shall join hand in hand, to give You all the glory that You deserve.

Lyrics to Jesus Loves the Little Children are by:
Clarence Herbert Woolsten (1856-1927) and are
based on Matthew 19:14.

The Children's Praise, is His Joy

Several times a year, the children of our church, open our worship service. They file out onto the stage and sing God's praise. Today, the young ones came to mind, so I decided to feature them, because of their joy.

Dear Lord, thank You for the children of earth. Thank You, that with each new life, You bring a blessing, as You create each one in Your image. When these young ones lift their voices and hands to give You glory, this helps me raise my eyes and heart, to You.

May You bless each child on the stage (and all over the world)—at every stage of their lives. And may You draw them close to Yourself. Because as they are taught to clap, to sing, and to worship You, they absorb Your Word through lyrics, and learn of Your love and goodness.

I have fond memories of singing in church; I still sing with my whole heart. Because to worship my Lord and King, is to know joy, and to give Him praise. And I think that, can bring Him no greater glory. So may all of the children of the world—of every age—be filled with reverence of the Creator, and bring this blessing before His throne. To praise You Jesus, is our greatest joy! Amen.

> *"My dear friends, we are already God's children, though what we will be hasn't yet been seen. But we do know that when Christ returns, we will be like him, because we will see him as he truly is. This hope makes us keep ourselves holy, just as Christ is holy." 1 John 3:2-3 (CEV)*

Has your heart expressed some exultation, today?

Psalm 149:3, Psalm 95: 1-2, Matthew 21:16, Psalm 33:8

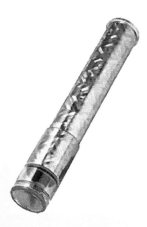

From the Outside Case

Have you ever felt a little like a kaleidoscope? Ordinary, plain, waiting for someone to pick you up and peer inside? To love you and show you that you're wanted and valued? Well, good news—God, your Creator, is the One Who made you originally, and loves you completely.

You may feel ordinary …
You may have been picked on as a child.
You may think you have little to offer,
But God's eye is upon you.
His love is encircling you.
His heart is reaching out to you,
To show you His love,
And your individual worth.
Reach out your hand,
Open your heart.
Trust Him with your life,
Your decisions, your choices, your next step,
And you'll be the one,
Coming alive,
Sharing the gifts that He's instilled within your soul,
To give Him glory,
And to create beauty in the world.

A kaleidoscope cannot be appreciated until it's taken from a shelf, held, touched, turned from an inanimate object and spun, viewed, that it seems to come to life. Likewise, no life is whole, complete or multi-faceted, until we surrender to God's Will and guidance and plan. Then and only then, can He create art from our brokenness, and form patterns within us, that glow to reflect His grace.

Man looks at the outward "case," but God is creating beauty and His image—upon the internal—the heart. It's here, that the facets of His character and love, come alive, to shine.

Meditate upon: 1 Samuel 16:7, Ephesians 2:10, Philippians 1:6

- What gifts do you possess, naturally and spiritually, that Jesus wants to use for His glory?

- What feels ordinary within you, that God is telling you, He sees as potential and your specific area of testimony or service?

- How can viewing a simple kaleidoscope bring encouragement to your heart, to show you that God is not done with your life?

- Can you see new dimensions of God's care for you, in the way He is shaping your circumstances, your path in life?

Spectrum of the Heart:
Faces

Dear Lord, as I begin the day, I am blessed to seek Your face. You're my first thought upon opening my eyes. Next, I'm grateful for Doug's face, beside me—the first and last that I kiss, morning and evening. Then, I am thankful for Tilly's little whiskered face, as she chirps and meows, or jumps on the bed to get my attention. These, are the faces in my daily world, upon waking. Each, brings a different sense of Who You are.

> *Each face is unique—in shape, eye color, in feature, in skin color, in width, in our expressions. We are each made in the image of God. Someone's face comes to mind that you love. What emotion do you feel? Someone's face comes to mind that you struggle to love ... what emotion do you feel? How can knowing that every face (and person) are made in the image of God—transform how you love others or appreciate their gifts?*

Help me to see each face that I meet today, as Your reflection. May I notice eye color and expression. May I listen to the stories that are shared, and those that need discernment to understand what lies beneath. Grant me sensitivity to encourage, offer a compliment, to let no one on my path, pass, without acknowledgement. For every face, every life, is Your special, precious creation. Each one, holds an opportunity, to extend Your love and grace.

Faces, display or conceal, emotion. It's up to us, to show God's love and seek His Spirit's help, in being a light of hope. It is only through seeking the face of God, that we can do this. It is only by drawing near our Creator, that we can love every created being, as He would, and does.

"Just as water mirrors your face, so your face mirrors your heart." Proverbs 27:19 MSG

Smiles come from the Inside, Out

From the time that Tilly started to mature into an adult cat, we noticed that at certain angles, it appears as if she has a "painted-on" smile. It gives her the look of being perpetually happy, and feeling blessed. It is a reminder that when a smile lights our faces, we have a glow, a certain light, that comes from within.

At a certain angle,
At a certain height ...
She's got a painted-on, smile.
It goes from whisker,
To whisker,
Like a pure-white, mile.
And it makes me grin,
Just looking at her.
It is a reminder,
Of all that's good.
For when God was creating,
This little girl for us,
He knew that any moment,
From every angle,
We would see His love,
Shining through.

Isn't it funny, how a smile can transform a face? Have you ever noticed how this singular expression—that expresses our mood—changes the light in our eyes, the very complexion of our faces? Ever notice how just the presence of a smile, radiates the message of warmth and friendliness, from the inside, out?

None of us, will be happy or joyful, at every moment of every day. We will each go through things that try us, define us, make us, mold us, and change us. But if, on a regular basis you are without a smile —you may want to ask yourself why. Because if the Spirit of the living, loving Lord, lives on the inside—you have much to smile about, much to be grateful for. And when we go through the desert or the valley, Jesus, is with us.

We, as God's kids, should bear the mark of His light within our souls. And to me, that means a smile on our face to radiate His glory. As often as possible, it should adorn our countenances. Because a constant frown, cannot draw anyone toward God's mercy, grace, kindness, forgiveness, comfort, hope, peace.

If a smile does not come easy to you, practice in the mirror. Even if you have to begin with a "painted-on" smile looking back at you for a few days, try it out. See if your mood doesn't improve. See if your perspective doesn't become a little more positive. See, if the Lord doesn't draw others to you.

Now I am not advocating being "fake." As I said, we each go through times when grief, or loss, or concerns weigh us down. We should be genuine in who we are, and not be afraid to be a witness in those times as well. But we can smile—through—minor irritations, little bumps in the road. And if we choose to do so, we just may find, some new friends along the way.

Smile,
> It makes your heart lighter.

> Smile,
>> It's like a gift you can give.

Smile,
> It's an offering of encouragement.

> Smile,
>> It shows you love Jesus,
Everyday, that you live.

Psalm 16:11, 28:7 and 92:4-5, Proverbs 15:30, and 17:22, Galatians 5:22, James 5:13

Tiger Lily, posed in a box that contained a Christmas gift. Our lives, are a gift from God, everyday. A smile, is not just a blessing to others, but a way that we honor Him. It is a way we show that we have a merry heart, and a life that is open to new possibilities. Have you got your smile on?

> I love that Jesus, painted one on Tilly; she reminds me,
>> how good it looks, on every face.

The Inside-Out Butterfly

Doug and I had gone to a local garden that has a seasonal display of butterflies. One of my favorites, is this one. When her wings are open, you see a brilliant blue specimen that is speckled with white dots and is finely etched with gray-black shading. But the funny thing is, when she is closed, she looks like a bigger-version of a common moth. Then, its coloring is simply, brown, white and black. You would never presume that such beauty, lies within her.

In the time that we spent in the butterfly area, it was easy to capture this butterfly, closed. Each, was enjoying its catered feast of fruit and other delectables. But in flight, they were swift, dancing this way and that. On this particular day, I only caught one, resting on a pot.

What God really brought to my mind, is that while our outer shell or appearance changes with each year, (sometimes it feels like each day), God is concerned with our heart, our mind, and soul. It is the internal qualities and character, that He is focused on. When things land on and around us, He is looking at how we respond, how we act, how we move on. Do we soar above petty issues? Do we fly into His arms when we are attacked? Do we trust everything to Jesus? Do we allow the Creator, to create beauty, within us?

The longer I have photographed butterflies, the more I notice a couple of common components. 1) They must fight to come to life (from the cocoon), to fly, and they seem to have to fight for life. 2) In picture after picture, I usually notice scars, tears, marks of their journey. Sound familiar? Whether it is grays in our hair, or lines upon our face, or internal or external pain, we each bear the marks of our experiences, hurts and difficulties.

However, I have found that when I give these things to Jesus, and trust Him, I believe He is developing the inside, the everlasting part of me, as His display. So no matter where you flit or roam, what bruises you, or clips your wings—stay in the fight: Your inner beauty (handsomeness) is being developed. You're growing stronger for the flight before you. And if we stay close to the Lord, I think He keeps us flying into His kingdom—light, and free from the net of the enemy.

Psalm 51:6, 1 Samuel 16:7, Matthew 23:27,
Psalm 139:1-2, 2 Corinthians 4:16

Dear Lord, let our lives be lived, inside-out. May Your character be reflected in and through us, to display Your majesty, and give You glory. For though we often feel like a moth, give us wings of faith to fly and soar, in the freedom that You died to give us. Because You bear the marks and scars of Calvary, we are covered by grace. I will praise You with my heart, voice, and "wings!" Amen.

> *I found this butterfly stunning, with its outer appearance of drab brown yet whose winged display, was a glorious, vibrant, shimmering blue. The contrast was amazing. It reminds me of a soul's conversion. It is a wonderful analogy of Salvation. Have you had this encounter? If so, did God dramatically change your life, behavior, or habits? If you do not yet know Christ, is He whispering to your spirit? Salvation is a gift of grace. But grace is not a one time action. It is a continual process, much like the butterfly from cocoon to lovely wing. Have you "taken flight?"*

Within the Rainbow of Lights

As we walked beneath this man-made rainbow, the Lord seemed to whisper a covenant into the wintery breeze:

Within an arboretum,
Within the sphere of a rainbow of lights,
We came upon this spectrum,
—This canopy.
We came up to it,
Before it was lit,
In the early evening.
Each frame of the arch,
Was wrapped in a different hue:
Red, orange, yellow,
Green, blue, and lavender,
Stood silhouetted, against a wintery sky.
But the effect held a similar promise,
As the ones that God paints in the sky.
"Come into the shelter,
Of My arms, child.
Come, behold Me, on this snowy day.
Come and walk in this space of evergreens …
I am here.
I am above You.
I surround you, always.
Within the rainbow of lights,
—Know, that you are loved."

"The glorious radiance resembled a rainbow that lights up the clouds on a rainy day. This was nothing less than the glory of the Eternal that appeared to me. When I saw the vision of the Eternal and His glory, I fell upon my face and heard a voice speaking to me." Ezekiel 1:28 VOICE

No matter where we find a rainbow, may it remind us that Jesus is near—illuminating, speaking, listening, and walking with us.

Do you have an emotional response when you see a rainbow? ....
Have you ever felt that God was making a specific covenant or promise to your heart? ....
....
What is your deepest longing or need right now?
....
Will you see His love stretch above and around you, as a rainbow of hope, peace and joy?
....

White as Snow

Snow, fell from the inside of earth's highest atmosphere, to touch the trees and boardwalk with a form of grace and purity. Undefiled, it landed upon every surface, to glisten, to transform. Quietly, it displayed the message of forgiveness, within the soul that is surrendered to Jesus.

Father God, I thank You, for the freshly-fallen-wonderland that was created, overnight. In the first rays of dawn, it was lovely. All that was brown and barren, was now covered as an illustration of Your grace. What looked desolate, now appeared, picturesque.

It reminds me of the verse in Isaiah 1:18 (ESV): "'Come now, let us reason together,' says the LORD. 'Though your sins are like scarlet, they will be as white as snow; though they are as red as crimson, they will become like wool.'"

Thank You, Jesus, for this down-like softness that has brought forgiveness to mind. Each limb seems to hold mercy, each distant view is a reminder that Your loving-kindness is everlasting.

The inches,
piled along the walkway,
teach my heart,
that Your healing,
is like a covering,
that fills every crack and crevice.

As You have done this for me,
help me, do so willingly,
sacrificially, for others, also.

For today,
the snow,
was more than just a beautiful setting ...
it was a necessary touch,
upon my soul.
With purity,
may I follow after You.
Amen

From within,
we are given a covering of grace,
that is a gift to the world,
outside our doors.

Before a butterfly can become a being of winged-beauty, it is formed and developed from the inside, out, within the confines of a cocoon. We are made similarly within the womb. Many things in life, follow this pattern such as the apple which comes from its seed, many shells hold delicate contents, and baby creatures sometimes come from eggs. What other examples come to your mind?

....

Lord, I am thankful that I am so wonderfully made.

As I ponder ....

about the workings of the human body,

I am in awe of You.

Dear Jesus, I am filled with wonder at ....

.... and

....

....

upon the earth and

....

....

in the heavens.

Soul's Introspection—From the Inside, Out

Are you a collector of sea shells? What types or colors draw your eye? Have you ever held one to your ear, to hear the echo of the waves? How do the things of the sea bring your focus to our Creator?

"I will give thanks and praise to You, for I am fearfully and wonderfully made; wonderful are Your works, and my soul knows it very well. My frame was not hidden from You, when I was being formed in secret, and intricately and skillfully formed [as if embroidered with many colors] in the depths of the earth. Your eyes have seen my unformed substance; and in Your book were all written the days that were appointed for me, when as yet there was not one of them [even taking shape]." Psalm 139:14-16 (AMP)

Most people have things they like and dislike about their own body. How does the above verse make you rethink your appreciation of the time and effort God took to create you? How does it make you want to invest in, becoming more like Him?

"For this very reason, make every effort to supplement your faith with goodness, goodness with knowledge, knowledge with self-control, self-control with endurance, endurance with godliness, godliness with brotherly affection, and brotherly affection with love." 2 Peter 1:5-7 (HCSB)

How have you crossed a divide or reached out to a stranger, in order to love them from the inside, out?

"Blessed are those who find wisdom, those who gain understanding, for she is more profitable than silver and yields better returns than gold." Proverbs 3:13-14 (NIV)

A potter take a piece of clay between their hands and molds it into a shape, a vessel to be used, or to be displayed. Jesus, does the same with our hearts, minds, and lives. In Isaiah 64:8 it says: "We are the clay, and You our potter; And all of us are the work of Your hand." How have you witnessed the Father molding your life, or events in your life, to keep you in the center of His Will?

"The Lord's light penetrates the human spirit, exposing every hidden motive." Proverbs 20:27 (NLT)

"Create in me a clean heart, O God, and renew a steadfast spirit within me." Psalm 51:10 (NKJV)

The Gem of Meditation

The Pause:

I cherish the image of the Sand Dollar to convey the "inside, out" concept. Why? Because it is a lovely seashell—from the outside. Yet, when it is broken, it reveals hidden treasures—5 doves or seagulls—that are tucked inside its sturdy covering.

Jesus comes to dwell in the heart, the hidden depths of who we are. He does His hidden work of Salvation within the soul, the eternal part of us. And it is in the secret place of the womb that He formed each of us, so individually, so wonderfully and uniquely.

From the inside, out, He made all of creation. From the inside, out, He transforms a life. From the inside, out, we are made in His image to reflect Him and give Him honor and glory. We are the hidden treasures of earth, to become gems that shine for all of eternity.

What most intrigues you about something in creation that displays this process?

....

....

What most fascinates you, about the workings of the human body, where You see God's complex design?

....

....

The Praise:

Dear Heavenly Father, everything that You have made from light, to all things with breath, to all things growing and blooming—display Your creativity and majesty. I bow before You and glorify Your name, at the visible ways in which You display Your invisible attributes. Teach me to see and acknowledge how skillfully and amazingly You have made all things, including me (even the breath in my lungs). For with all that I am, I long to serve You, and sing of Your goodness for all my days. Amen.

What is your greatest praise, today?

....

Facets of God's Love

If *love* were represented by a color—what would you choose? To some, it would be red, because it evokes the idea of romance and expressions of the heart. To some, it might be blue, because it seems to bring a soothing, peaceful response. Perhaps you'd pick green, to remind you of Psalm 23's pasture-like scenes. Or maybe you'd choose pink or purple or orange, for their vibrancy and artistry. Or maybe Autumn's jewel-like hues, because they remind you of cool, crisp, refreshment?

No matter what shade you associate with love—whether a single primary color, a crayon-box type title, or one from the rainbow—God is reaching out, down, around —to surround your heart with His unconditional acceptance, mercy, and grace.

A kaleidoscope creates facets; so too, is God's love displayed in myriad ways— purely, joyfully, playfully, artistically —in all that He's made, in every step of His mission and ministry. Drawing close to God, is to know what it means to know and to be known.

This is what it means to have a Father, Abba Daddy, Comforter, Healer, Provider, Protector, Savior, and Dearest Friend.

Section V

Facets of God's Love

God loves us perfectly, without flaw, unconditionally. All of nature reflects His nature purely, from beginning to end.

Can you find the heart in the middle of the tree limbs? The sun shone at just the perfect angle on this late afternoon, and it was a message to my soul that God's love reaches outward, downward, to each of us as an invitation. Nothing can hold it back. Nothing can keep it from wrapping around us, to bring us peace, hope, and the very presence of His Spirit.

Romans 8:38-39 (NLT)

"And I am convinced that nothing can ever separate us from God's love.

Neither death nor life, neither angels nor demons, neither our fears for today nor our worries about tomorrow—not even the powers of hell can separate us from God's love.

No power in the sky above or in the earth below—indeed, nothing in all creation will ever be able to separate us from the love of God that is revealed in Christ Jesus our Lord."

The facets of God's love, surround us in all of nature. From the sea, to the sky, to the trees, to the birdsong—everything that He has made—is a lyric, a line-by-line detailing of His care for all humanity. May it touch your heart today, for the first time, or with a fresh passion, that inspires your appreciation and praise.

I loved finding the heart in the center of the tree. While you may say it was only an optical illusion—it was there—visible to those of us who paused in this moment. God is reaching out with love to you, always. How might you be seeing it? How might you be missing it? Will you take greater notice in the future of His presence—in nature, but in your circumstances, in your day-to-day routine, as well?

Up in the Tree Tops

Up in the tree tops,
High above ....
Lives my Savior,
The God of love.
Yet what is amazing,
Everyday to me,
Is that He is evident,
In everything we see.
I can see Him in the blue sky,
In the changing branches, and leaves;
I can feel His presence,
Hear His voice in the breeze.
I can see His beauty,
In a glorious sunset,
Or in the dance of the ocean waves,
His faithfulness, I've met.
No matter where I wander,
As I gaze to or 'fro,
My Father—invisible,
Is visible, everywhere I go.
Up in the tree tops,
High above ...
Even in my heart,
Lives, the God of love.

> "If I ascend to heaven, you are there! If I make my bed in Sheol, you are there! If I take the wings of the morning and dwell in the uttermost parts of the sea, even there your hand shall lead me, and your right hand shall hold me. If I say, 'Surely the darkness shall cover me, and the light about me be night,' even the darkness is not dark to you; the night is bright as the day, for darkness is as light with you."
> Psalm 139:8-12 (ESV)

I was looking out my little kitchen window one morning when we lived in Hawaii, to have the thought that ..."up above the tree tops, lives our Father." Yet, as high as the heavens are above us, if we have accepted Jesus as the Lord of our lives, then He lives within our hearts, too. I loved this idea. And as I look at God's wondrous creations, I find myself worshiping the Creator. Though He is invisible, He is visible, through all that His hands have made.

From the blue sky, to the trees, to a mountain, to the waves of the ocean; from a sunrise to its sunset, to the labyrinth-like patterns of the clouds or details of a flower, our God displays His creativity, His majesty, power, and faithfulness to us, daily. And as He shows us these things, they also demonstrate the evidence of His love. What a wondrous Daddy, indeed!

So whether you have a window-view of tree tops, the ocean waves, a snow-capped mountain, a corn-field, or a sky scraper—if you look closely, there is something there, that will point you to the Father. But if you want a close-up, just look in a mirror. You are made in His likeness. You are made in His image, to reflect Him. We are the visible evidence, of the invisible God. And knowing He lives within our hearts, means we have access to His Spirit at every moment of the day or night.

Up in the tree tops, high above ... lives the God of love. But if you call Him Lord, He lives within you, too. And if you ask Him, He will help you become more aware of His beauty. He will make all that is invisible, visible to your soul. Because when we truly grasp that He is in us, we might just see a whole lot of things—through the light of His love.

> *"For the Lord is a great God, a great King above all gods. The depths of the earth are in His hand, and the mountain peaks are His. The sea is His; He made it. His hands formed the dry land. Come, let us worship and bow down; let us kneel before the Lord our Maker."*
> *Psalm 95: 3-6 HCSB*

Have you ever danced before the Lord, simply grateful for His love, for the gift of this day, in simple adoration? If not, why not?

143

The earth is God's writing,
His scroll rolled out of praise—
From the sunrise to the sunset,
He shows Himself, as the Ancient of Days.
The heavens declare His glory,
Glittering stars and shining moon,
From the eagle to the seagull,
The robin, to the lake loon ...
From the mountains and valleys,
Wildflowers and bees.
The endless sand on the seashore,
To the Autumn's jewel-like leaves ...
From the firefly to the snowflake,
From the first bulb of Spring,
All of creation,
Cries out—with joy, to sing.
These, all point to His wonder,
They are just tokens of His grace.

"Oh give thanks to Yahweh, for he is good; his loyal love is everlasting."
1 Chronicles 16:34 (LEB)

For splendor is His adornment,
Majesty, illumines His face.
And my soul cannot help,
But also praise …
You, Jesus, my Savior,
For Your glorious ways!

In the beginning, everything that was created, was proclaimed to be
perfect, good, as it was made. From void, nothingness, came light,
soaring and singing birds, all kinds of animals, plant-life, flowers,
and insects. Days and seasons were created. Human life was created
in the very image of God. And after each, He said, "It is good." These
are God's writings, His recordings, so how we can not notice them?
How we can not issue forth praise? How can we not see how good
and kind, loving and merciful, and wonderful and perfect, is our
Lord?

The earth and heavens are His scroll, unfurled for the human heart.
But will you believe? Will you receive all that He longs to
communicate to your heart? For it is love, true love, that is displayed,
everyday!

Love is the Scroll,
To be unrolled …
Will you read it,
With your heart?
It is the very heart of God,
Written for you.

> *Genesis 1, Psalm 24:1,*
> *Deuteronomy 10:14,*
> *Isaiah 42:5, Proverbs 30:4*

Encircling Love

Light arose,
Like each new morning,
Except clouds enfolded,
The horizon line.
So the colors of dawn,
Lifted higher,
To display themselves,
—Outwardly and upwardly—
Into the sky.
In every direction,
There was rose, pearl,
Lavender, gold and blue;
These surrounded,
A silver storybook moon,
It's true.

And I saw Your love, God,
Everlasting,
Never-ending,
Unfathomable—
Reaching out.
It encircles every nation,
Embraces all of mankind.
And giving You,
My adoration and praise,
Was all that I could do,
In that moment,
—At all times,
My Lord.

*John 3:16, Psalm 36:5, Psalm 103:11,
Ephesians 3:17-19, Psalm 136:26*

The encircling love of Jesus was displayed so beautifully, on this morning. It is available to every heart, always. Has His light, touched your soul?

*What is your earliest
memory of being loved?*

Love, Light, Power and Presence

It's an Irish prayer of blessing; I had this lovely saying quoted to me, the first time I had ever flown. I was in an airplane heading to Dallas, on business; it was also the first time I had traveled without Doug. The plane was going through turbulence. Of course, my maiden flight, would be filled with adventure!

The lady next to me, probably in her sixties, asked me if I had flown before, I answered, "no." Somehow, she sensed that I was a believer; that topic came up quickly. She took my hand and recited these words:

"The Love of God enfolds me,
The Light of God surrounds me,
The Power of God protects me,
The Presence of God watches over me.
Wherever I am, God is."   (by James Dillet Freeman, 1941)

Not only did that prayer give us both a reminder of God's care and His presence, but before we knew it, the turbulence had stopped, the plane eased its rocking and jarring of our teeth. This beautiful lady had given me a gift of her gentle and sweet spirit, and words that flowed with love.

For some reason God brought this prayer to my mind today, right now. It is for someone specific. You need to know that God is reaching out to you. His hand is holding yours, and He is with you through whatever you are going through. His love, light, power and presence, are available to comfort and sustain you. He is holding you close through the turbulence, through the teeth-jarring, that is rocking your world.

"The Lord is the One who will go before you. He will be with you;
He will not leave you or forsake you. Do not be afraid or discouraged."
Deuteronomy 31:8 HCSB

Father, I pray that this simple, but profound, Irish blessing would bring peace and comfort to one heart today, as it did to me during my first flight. This may be a first flight of a different type, for whomever you have placed on my heart just now, but I ask for these four things: Your love, Your light, Your power and Your presence would be so close, that no difficulty would prevail.

May peace descend like a dove, and remove all doubt and fear. Thank You, Lord, that You are as near as a whisper, as close as one breath that we inhale. In Your love, Amen.

The Finger-Painted Heart

God was finger-painting ...
He created a work of abstract art;
In the sky above me,
He was speaking a message into my heart.
Though it was in shades of blue,
With clouds of wispy white ...
This shape bears the message of His love;
He was drawing His affection in plain sight.
He has been here ahead of me,
And His majesty is displayed.
His glory, goodness, and faithfulness,
Was beautifully, arrayed.
All I have to do to see Him—is,
Look around me, to know that He's near.
I am always observing creation,
Because His sketches say,
"I'm right here."

We had gone on a day-trip one weekend. And as I looked off to my right, on our way home, I saw this set of hearts forming in the clouds. It looked like an abstract work-of-art. I loved that it evoked the thought that God has been here, just ahead of us. It seemed to impart the idea that He had traveled before us, and had written a message to us, to lead us safely homeward.

Every day that we live, is a gift; and God is writing our story. Our lives are giving a message to the world around us. Are we displaying the shades of His goodness, and faithfulness? Do we allow God to work in and through us, to tell the Good News? Are we sketching His character in a visible, tangible way, to those around us?

We are each created with a unique purpose and design—much like a piece of art. We each have the imprint of the Creator. And I pray that we each bear the affection of His heart. I hope we are looking around us, to see Him; but I hope He is also seen in us. God is "right here." He is evident in creation, He is as near as a prayer. And I hope we make Him, near to others. For that is the message of love.

Spectrum of the Heart:

Showers as a Blessing

Dear Lord, even if the day is stormy, I will see the rain as a shower of blessing. I will see Your watering of the earth, as a sign of Your care and provision for my every need. I will feel Your Spirit, like a waterfall of goodness—cleansing, restoring and filling me with Your strength, joy and love.

For as I hear the pitter patter of rain striking the windowpane, my soul seems to be anointed with Your overflowing kindness. In every circumstance and happening in my life, I feel drenched with Your grace. The rain reminds me that You reign over all of earth and heaven. I trust You, Father, because many times, rain, is followed by a rainbow. And I know that no matter what happens, You hold every day of my life, in Your hands.

*"God stretched out the northern sky and hung
the earth in empty space. It is God who fills the clouds with
water and keeps them from bursting with the weight. He hides the
full moon behind a cloud. He divided light from darkness
by a circle drawn on the face of the sea." Job 26:7-10 GNT*

As I captured this rainbow, I felt blessed indeed, to stand in the remaining drops of rain and simply absorb the shower of Your love. For surely there was a whisper in the light shower, that only my soul could hear. And I answered, with praise. Amen.

Drenched

Jesus
says,
"I am
a rose
of Sharon,
a lily
of the
valleys."
in Song
of Songs
2:1
(ESV)

In my photo,
The Rose of Sharon,
Is drenched.
The rain has come and saturated its petals.
The leaves and stems,
Every part of the flower,
Has been covered in heaven's dew.
And as I focused my lens,
I wondered if we are drenched,
In His love,
In His mercy,
In His grace,
In His power?
Are we living under the reign,
Of His submission?
Do we allow Jesus to saturate our minds,
Our moods, our emotions,
With His thoughts and ways?
Are we seeking His strength,
And listening for His voice?
Do we allow Him to enfold us,
In our everyday decisions?
Do we allow Christ to cover us,
When trials or testing, like rain, come?
Lord, may we be drenched,
In Your goodness,
And Your favor,
Until the dew of Your Spirit,
Saturates, our very soul. Amen.

"Drip down, O heavens, from above, and let the clouds pour down righteousness; let the earth open up and salvation bear fruit, and righteousness spring up with it. I, the Lord, have created it." Isaiah 45:8 NASB

Are we drenched by Your Spirit?
Drenched, with Your love?
Quenched, by Your mercy?
Until we are baptized in Your goodness, from above?

A Rosy View of Love

Roses are amazing from bud to full bloom. They are lovely in their scents that perfume the air. And they are a mystery of creation with their thorns, set against such beauty. Love, is like a rose—wondrous, intoxicating, inviting, but it can also hurt. God's love is unconditional. By His wounds, we are healed.

If you take a walk through a flower garden ... there are few, where you would not find, the splendor and beauty of a rose; it's the symbol of love, to mankind.

The rose is a delicate flower, with velvety petals and perfumed fragrance, which captures our hearts. When it is carefully tended, gently pruned, touched by sunlight and rain, it flourishes. The Master's touch opens the petals, until it reaches full-bloom. With love, care and nurturing, its roots deepen and send up "new shoots." It adds loveliness to our world.

Love is like a rose—a delicate, precious gift, giving off a
sweet fragrance of agape, familia, or passionate emotions. When
love is carefully tended, gently pruned, touched by
enough happiness and sorrow, it flourishes. The Master's touch
"opens" our hearts until we share His gifts of the Spirit with
others. With care, nurturing, and protection—it grows,
and its roots deepen. It adds loveliness to our world.

May every relationship that we have,
bear the aroma, of the love of Christ.

*"For we are the sweet fragrance of Christ [which ascends] to God,
[discernible both] among those who are being saved and among those who
are perishing; to the latter one an aroma from death to death [a fatal,
offensive odor], but to the other an aroma from life to life [a vital fragrance,
living and fresh]. ... For we are not like many, [acting like merchants]
peddling God's word [shortchanging and adulterating God's message];
but from pure [uncompromised] motives, as [commissioned and sent] from
God, we speak [His message] in Christ in the sight of God."*
2 Corinthians 2:15-17 AMP

*There are many forms of love—from agape,
to familial, to passionate. If we a child of God—
He loves us with each form, and we are to love
Him, likewise. What are some ways that you
feel all three from the Lord? What are some
ways, that you express all three to Him?*

Prisms Shining

When we lived in Virginia, I would decorate the bureau that sat in
our entry way, with seasonal designs. Often, I enhanced my creative
floral creations with light, such as the prism-inducing one, that is
present. We have a few that we rotated for the applicable themes.

We came to the time of our moving, and learned that we were not
the only ones to enjoy their illumination. Our side windows had
openings near the top that were difficult to "dress" with draperies, so
they were left open—in part, because they were unique in shape,
and we did not want to cover their artistry. We enjoyed both the
sunlight and moonlight that were visible. But unbeknownst to us, our
prisms were visible to the neighbors.

Upon our exit, I shared a few goodies with the folks across from us. And the wife of the family, shared that they would miss us—walking and holding hands, the loving glow that emanated from us (our love), but also from the windows of our home. I was so touched by her words of kindness.

How precious to be remembered for our love and light—internally, externally, and for one another. Others in our neighborhood sent us emails and cards and remarked in-person with similar sentiments. Love, cannot be contained within a home. It cannot remain within our hearts. It must be shared, just as Jesus shared His love for us, for all mankind, more than 2000 years ago.

Prisms shone from our home to bring peace to the hearts of others. That's what a relationship with Jesus does, in the heart, mind and soul, of His child. Is your light shining, in your world?

> " ... and you shall love the Lord your God with all your heart, and with all your soul (life), and with all your mind (thought, understanding), and with all your strength. This is the second: 'You shall [unselfishly] love your neighbor as yourself.' There is no other commandment greater than these." Mark 12:30-31 (AMP)

Crown of Life

Since the kids in our neighborhood were being home-schooled due to the Corona Virus, we were treated to many displays of their artistry. Our sidewalks, rocks, and even windows, contained any number of drawings and appliqués to display their imaginations—come to life.

This, happens to be one of my favorite designs. There was something about a rainbow wreath (or crown) made of hearts, that I loved. We passed by it a few times before I was able to capture a photo, but it is a good reminder of Jesus' all-encompassing love for mankind.

Love embraces us. It shines forth. It colors every circumstance, every home, every heart with hope, with vibrancy. And it is the one quality that every person—wants, needs, and longs to receive. Love, crosses boundaries. It connects us. It helps heal us, when we feel isolated, afraid, or alone. It helps us maintain courage and strength, to go on.

One day, the children of God, shall be as this "a royal diadem," a crown of living, breathing souls surrounding the throne of King. In all shapes and sizes, colors and nationalities, we shall proclaim Him and praise Him, as Messiah. The circle of love shall be complete, unending, fathomless. For as we bow before our Maker, we shall know and be known—fully, perfectly, wholly loved.

The love of God is like a circle, because it creates in us a sense of completion, while at the same time, makes everyone (who calls upon the name of the Lord), welcome. There is always room to be included in the crown of His family. There is no heart that is or will be excluded, from the coming design that shall be formed of those who worship around His throne. For those who love Jesus, He loves forever. And this love knows no end. May He be praised. And may each of us be found around the throne, to crown Him, Lord of All.

Isaiah 62:3, Philippians 4:1, Philippians 2:9-11,
James 1:12, 2 Timothy 4:8, 1 Peter 5:4, Psalm 86:10,
1 Chronicles 16:25, 1 John 4:7

Love is the crown of life, shining forth today, to bring us hope for tomorrow and for all of eternity.

The Color Wheel

White, in the center of the color wheel, grounds all the colors that surround it. What comes to mind when you picture this hue? To me, I think of innocence, purity, cleanliness, holiness, wholeness. From it, rainbows, spiral outward, in every hue to affect our emotions and atmospheres.

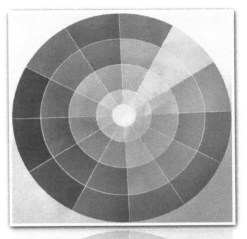

We associate colors with certain seasons, certain senses, tastes and smells. Colors can encourage us, calm us, even change and elevate our moods and attitudes. For instance, sunny yellow, makes a space feel warm and inviting. Greens and blues, seem to evoke a soothing response like the sea and the sky. Violet, brings out our energy, harmony, artistry and creativity. Pink, pulls from us happiness and joy. Red and orange, draw out stronger responses—passion, anger—and remind us of flames being kindled.

Within each of these circles are segments, which further delineate these tones into lighter and darker depths, which range from pastels to bold. In their subtly or strength, they bring memories of places and outdoor spaces, to our minds. Color, has a remarkable ability to influence us. And God's brilliant assortment, is evident in His every creation.

- What colors do you surround yourself with—in your home? In your office?
- What is your favorite outdoor space? Is it filled with vivid colors or a subtle palette? Is your choice of coloring—via paint, or growing things? Is it open or fenced-in?
- If you close your eyes and pick your favorite—what color do you envision?
- What is your first memory of color?

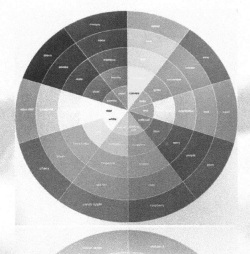

Here, is a full spectrum color wheel. Note that it contains grey, brown and black, (as opposed to the one previous), and is labeled with names, similar to those in a crayon box. What was your favorite "crayon-color," as a child? What shade would you choose, now?

What landscape in creation, best portrays a color wheel in your mind? Have you ever given God praise for its intricacy and beauty?

Perhaps God paints the earth in living-color, to draw our hearts more easily like a child, to discover His immeasurable love, in its fullest array.

Dear Jesus, may You awaken my child-like wonder, in the colors in Your world. Help me see their nuances, as the degrees of Your love in every circumstance. Teach me to trust You, in the subtle, in the bold—until my life is like a rainbow—a beam of hope from my first breath, until my last. For as the color wheel so beautifully illustrates, all the shades are made apparent and vibrant, when they meet purity in the center. May the center of my life, always be found, in You. Amen.

The Connection of Love

We were attending an outdoor church service, when I observed this scene: a little tike began to draw on the pavement. In his childish art, I could make out a plane, a car, a truck. Although a bit abstract, there may be a budding artist forming right before our eyes. But what caught my attention? Each of his little vignettes—were joined with a connecting line. He drew each vehicle separately, but then created of them, one picture. I found this, intriguing.

> "I have loved you with an everlasting love; Therefore I have drawn you with loving-kindness."
> Jeremiah 31:3
> (NASB)

After the service I chatted with his mom. She told us his name, that he was 3 1/2, and that I was correct in my spying out of his art—as many forms of transportation.

She said that he has all of these as toys, and that they are currently his favorite things.

Everything that God has made, is likewise, individual. Whether it is a sunrise, a flower, a new baby, a stalk of grain ... in His hands, creation as a whole, represents Who He is to us, every day. We decide how much we notice, how much we observe ... but never doubt that each object or landscape or grouping, is meant to draw us, near Him.

The other interesting thing? I found it a blessing to worship outside on this particular morning. In the midst of our singing, the birds sang along. In the midst of our worship, one child drew items, then connected them as if to display God's love doing the same with every creature and creation, unto His own heart. As we listened to His Word being taught, they floated into his young mind and into the neighborhood—sharing the Good News of hope.

God's love connects all of creation. It connects us one to another. It connects our hearts to the One Who made us. It is an invitation to live-out our days sharing the work-of-art, that He is making of us. And His love, is miraculously drawn, into the fiber of our very souls.

Jeremiah 31:3 tells us, that the Lord "has drawn us with loving-kindness." To me, this means two things. 1) He created us—drew us, sketched us, made us—with love. 2) He draws us—invites us, comforts us, pulls us into sweet friendship and fellowship. How does this verse make you feel? Does this double meaning bring a fresh perspective of these words? Does it broaden your understanding of His heart for yours?

He Loves Me ...

Do you remember as a kid, playing the little game ... "He/she loves me, they love me not?" If you don't—here's how it goes. You would choose a flower such as this one, that has multiple petals, and begin to remove them one by one, while speaking these alternating lines.

Whichever line you ended with, was supposed to give you the answer of his/her heart. It may or may not have been the truth, however. As with anything else, any inquiry, requires that we go to the source, if we want an accurate result.

Aren't you glad that God's love does not work this way? I know I am! The love of the Father is everlasting, never-ending, wrapping around every heart that He's ever created. His love travels around the globe, into every space, and touches His every creation.

His love is available as an invitation, via Jesus' death at Calvary. And it provides forgiveness, mercy and grace—to every soul who answers the whisper of His Spirit within their heart. We do not have to ask or waver with the question, does He love me/love me not. We are assured of it, because Jesus died and rose again—going to a great sacrifice, to prove it.

"But God, with the unfathomable richness of His love and mercy focused on us, united us with the Anointed One and infused our lifeless souls with life—even though we were buried under mountains of sin—and saved us by His grace." Ephesians 2:4-5 VOICE

I encourage you to say the line: Jesus loves me—(your name here) a few times. Let this truth sink in—all the way to your soul. How might this help you to love Jesus a little more? How about others in your circle? How might it mend a few tears, or bring cohesion to your community?

Conveyance of the Heart

Love is conveyed through words, and expressed through kindness and action. It moves beyond, and outside, the space of the heart—to include, invite—others into its sphere. It is giving in nature, filled with hope and light. It can express and reflect the emotions of the soul—from joy, to sorrow, to uncertainty.

Love is gracious and forgiving. It speaks words of healing, encouragement, and offers peace and restoration. It seeks justice and to build others up. Love is faithful and true. It keeps its word, its promises, and is on time. Love is intangible, yet tangibly felt, discovered, experienced, and embraced.

Question: Did you read these definitions and think of your spouse, significant other, a family member, or a friend—and think, "yes, someone, loves me like that?"

Question: Do the above lines describe how you (and I) love? Or strive to?

Question: Do you see this, as a perfect outline of love?

Because in truth, it's the way Jesus loves us. It's the way we are commanded to love Him and our neighbor (our spouse, family members, our co-workers, those in our community and in our world).

Love casts out fear, believes, stands strong, and binds us together. It is what held Jesus to the Cross, more than the nails! And it is one of the most precious gifts that we'll ever give or receive.

Any day, is a good time to give some expression of love—in the form of thoughtfulness and kindness, with our words, with our actions. It's a good time to offer forgiveness, grace, or encouragement.

"No, he has told you what he wants, and this is all it is: to be fair, just, merciful, and to walk humbly with your God." Micah 6:8 TLB

The conveyance of Jesus' heart was love—to us—to flow through us —into those around us.

Deuteronomy 6:5, Luke 10:27, 1 Corinthians 13:4-7, Ephesians 4:32, 1 John 4:18, Psalm 103:12, Micah 7:19

Gifts from the Heart

Each of us have gifts to offer—from the heart—that can show one another the love of God. Here are a few of the every day things, that can make an extraordinary difference in someone else's day.

One image is from a card that was sent to me. The other, is from a food pantry in which I was a volunteer. What I loved? Flowers were included in this day's choices. While these were perhaps unnecessary, they brightened many a face as folks walked in the door, and brought delight to those who chose them along with their other grocery items. Never underestimate the power of giving kindness, and of yourself.

Here are a few offerings:
- A smile (especially, if someone is not wearing one)
- A word of encouragement
- A card, an e-mail, or text with a heartfelt line of care
- Reach out—to a hurting friend, to someone who is grieving ...
- Saying "I love you," "Thank you" and "I forgive you" are also welcome gifts
- A hand written-note—(even a few lines) brightens a trip to the mailbox, and may lift someone's spirits
- Pay for someone's coffee, or an elderly person/couple's meal

- A small token—for no reason —"just because"
- Give something or share something—with someone who cannot repay you
- Give of your time, of yourself, not just a monetary expression—be creative
- Plan an activity with your loved one, but also with a shut-in
- Say a prayer
- Shovel a sidewalk
- Share some "lovin'-from-your-oven"—cookies, cupcakes, or homemade soup from your kitchen—conveys caring hands and a kind heart
- Do the least favorite chore of your kid, or your spouse, for them as a surprise
- Ask a stranger "How are you doing?"—then really listen/care when they respond. Take this one step further, and be prepared to offer help, if it is applicable and/or appropriate.
- Offer/run an errand for a sick neighbor/friend
- Include flowers, or candy or something "unnecessary" when you give to someone in need

- Remembering birthdays, anniversaries or the other special occasions of your family and friends, conveys loving-kindness
- Help someone in need—not just financially, but give emotional support. Also check your local area—do you know which churches, food banks, shelters, etc.—offer aid/assistance for the things—that we as individuals, cannot always do on our own?
- Offer a hand of welcome to new neighbors
- Open a door
- Ask God to open your heart to those that you tend to "prejudge"

The list is endless. If we are aware, we can give love every day—God's love.

It is the greatest gift that we have to give back to Him. It is the sweetest offering that we can give others—because it displays that His love, lives in us.

In Mark 12:30-31, the Lord gives us the instruction to love Him, then to love others as ourselves. This same command can be found in Luke 10:27, and Matthew 22:37-39. Deuteronomy 6:5-6 goes on to tell us, to "put them upon your hearts." Love, is important to God, and He was the premier example of this emotion. (John 3:16-17). So anytime we act like Him, think like Him, speak like Him, or display this quality—we are surely giving Him honor.

The Heart of Prayer

If you draw a heart in the air,
As a child would do,
You will see in the end,
That it returns to you.
But not until,
It rises upward;
Not until,
It goes outward.
And to me,
This is a way,
To shape our prayers.
It is a reminder,
To lift our praises,
Every care,
And to cover,
One another's,
Needs.
For every time,
We say a prayer,
We show our love,
For those around us—
Which in turn,
Points our hearts,
To the Lord.

> "I love him, because Yahweh
> has heard the voice of my
> supplications. Because he has
> inclined his ear to me, I will
> call all my days."
> Psalm 116:1-2 (LEB)

The heart that prays, extends love by lifting others up. We are reaching outward, connecting one another with God's grace. And as we touch those we care about, our focus is turned on the One who loves us, unconditionally.

Prayer, is like sending our innermost thoughts through the tube of a kaleidoscope, directly to the heart of God. Then His Spirit takes them, and gives them facets, interceding on our behalf to turn them into prisms, that shine as we cover our family, friends, strangers, our nation. What rainbows must be created, as He turns our whispers into treasures of love.

Love like a Rock

On the rocky shoreline,
Soaked by the tide,
Was a stone,
In the shape of a heart.
It was embedded in the sand,
Left here by the Great I AM;
It bears a message for you and me.
It is the sign of love,
Given from His hand, above ...
Red, like the blood,
He shed at Calvary.
Amidst the white, gray and tan,
And the seaweed upon the land,
It was His letter,
For all who will see ...
God left His heart on the ocean floor,
Displaying mercy, forgiveness and more.
Father, for this sign,
I bow in praise!

As I walked along this rocky coastline, imagine my surprise, (or not), to find a perfectly shaped red heart, amongst the mixture of stones. It was as if God had left a message for us to find—a reminder of the mercy, love, forgiveness and grace, that He left behind—when He gave His life at Calvary.

So if your path is a little rocky, or your heart feels like it's on the floor, let His kindness wash over you. Let His peace and compassion, embrace you. For at the Cross, the tide of our sin was released. Let the Lord heal you and restore you, baptize, and renew you.

Calvary was the sign unto us, that His love has freed us. It was His open love letter to our hearts. Have you answered, replied? Is His Spirit embedded in your life? Do others feel joy, and sense your praise and love for Christ, rising from you?

His heart, His love, is like a Rock—steadfast, immovable, unshakeable. It does not change with the wind, or shift with the tides. It is trustworthy, and worthy of praise. He offers, not a heart of stone, but one of love alone, for all time!

> *"In this the love of God was made manifest among us, that God sent his only Son into the world, so that we might live through him. In this is love, not that we have loved God but that he loved us and sent his Son to be the propitiation for our sins. Beloved, if God so loved us, we also ought to love one another." 1 John 4: 9-11 ESV*

Every Hue

Red and yellow, black and white,
Rust and gray, were before my sight;
Green and beige in every hue,
Decorated, the sandy dune.

Each was brought out,
By the tide.
Their colors made vibrant,
By the cleansing, God supplied.
Every soul upon the earth,
Is loved and cherished, given worth.
Renewed, Restored,
By His cleansing flood,
When we receive,
The gift of His grace-filled blood.

Every tribe and creed,
Will one day bow,
And into heaven,
God will allow ...
Red and yellow, black and white,
Each soul He's saved,
By His invitation, power and might.
What a crown of love we'll form,
Worshiping our King, so bright.

I think God made every hue in creation to reflect to our hearts, that every one will be represented around His throne. What glory shall shine from every countenance, as we lay down our crowns to worship and adore Jesus, our Lord! Are you held in the arms of the Rock, so that He is bringing out every hue of His grace in your life?

> *"And I heard a loud voice from the throne saying, 'Look! God's dwelling place is now among the people, and he will dwell with them. They will be his people, and God himself will be with them and be their God. He will wipe every tear from their eyes. There will be no more death or mourning or crying or pain, for the old order of things has passed away.'"*
> *Revelation 21:3-4 (NIV)*

Creation, Whispered and Shouted

The various cries coming from the amazing variety of birds, is a shout; the sweet chirps coming from a single nest, that's a whisper.

The waterfall that rages o're the cliff, that's the shout; the mountain stream that flows gently through an alpine wildflower meadow, that's a whisper.

The whole of earth's flowers and vegetation from an arial view, that's the shout; beholding a single seed or plant coming to life, that's the whisper.

The mighty ocean's wave, turbulent, guided by the storm, that's the shout; but its gentle, sweeping, peaceful tide, that's the whisper.

Watching the sun rise in all its fiery glory in shades of red and gold and lavender, set against a crisp blue sky, that's the shout; watching the silvery glow of a moonbeam dance among, between the clouds to touch the earth, that's the whisper.

The lion who roams and prowls and roars with such power, is the shout; while the kitten, cuddled in your arms, in your lap, purring softly, is the whisper.

Cicadas, singing collectively on a summer afternoon, that's a shout; while a butterfly, soundlessly, yet with mesmerizing colors and patterns weaving in a flitting dance o're the meadow, that's the whisper.

God has made wondrous, bold, beautiful, stunning and creative things, for us to see and enjoy. They are like a shout of His might, glory and power. Then, He's made the unique, the fragrant, the intoxicating, to draw us in, closer, to whisper of His sovereignty, grace, joy, peace, and hope. And if we were to observe and understand all of creation—God's intention would be to show us His nature—the very essence of His love and faithfulness.

With a shout,
    With a whisper,
        Creator God,
            Has made all things.
                Above, beneath, beside,
            They belong to Him,
        Whether beast, flower,
            Or creature of vibrant wings.
    How majestic,
            How marvelous,
                Is, all that's on display.

Within the beat of my heart,
Runs a melody,
Of unceasing praise.
With a shout,
With a whisper,
All creation reflects,
Who You, are Lord.
And we are the blessed recipients,
Of all the good gifts,
That You give.
So give a shout,
Give a whisper,
Call upon His name.
Let your love of our Savior,
Be quietly and loudly,
Proclaimed.

> *"For since the creation of the world God's invisible qualities—his eternal power and divine nature—have been clearly seen, being understood from what has been made, so that people are without excuse."*
> *Romans 1:20 (NIV)*

Creation, has been whispered and shouted, so that everyone can see something of God's grandeur and holiness. Through it, His nature is clearly on display. And by it, His character and attributes have been made known. Are you listening? Are you observant? Do you feel the height and depth and breadth of God's love for you, in the beauty that surrounds you each day?

From the rising of the sun to its setting is an illustration that we are given of God's love for us. How does this analogy, that is so very visible each day, bring you comfort and assurance?

From this One Spot

From this one spot,
All I see is water;
It's a gentle reminder,
Of God's unfathomable grace,
Mercy and measureless love.
It represents an infinite supply,
Of Your faithful care.
It encourages us to be cleansed,
Of all sin.

We bring it before You, Jesus,
Letting it here to be carried with the tide,
As far as the East is from the West.
It symbolizes how You move,
Around us, encircling us,
With favor and blessing.
It's like a well-spring,
Refreshing, our minds,
Our souls,
Our dreams.
It lifts my spirits to see,
The colors shift and change,
To reflect Your beauty and splendor.
From this one spot,
It's like I get just the tiniest glimpse,
Of heaven's glassy sea.
For these sparkling waters,
Surely glisten and shine,
With the radiance of Who You are.
From this one spot,
I find my heart, overflows,
With praise,
To know You, as Creator,
Lord, and Savior.
Forever, You remain,
Boundless, uncontained.

> *"From one man he made all the nations, that they should inhabit the whole earth; and he marked out their appointed times in history and the boundaries of their lands. God did this so that they would seek him and perhaps reach out for him and find him, though he is not far from any one of us. 'For in him we live and move and have our being.' As some of your own poets have said, 'We are his offspring.'"*
> Acts 17:26-28 (NIV)

From this one spot, wherever you are—in your circumstances, in your heart, in your dreams—God is reaching out to you, with His fathomless love.

Spectrum of the Heart:
Fed by the Stream

In the center of our neighborhood, runs a man-made stream. It is a source of life to the wildlife in the area. Ducks, birds, and even a local cat, can be found here enjoying its flowing nutrients. But what I also discovered, was how the grass grew, from beneath. I thought this was a wonderful lesson of God's love, within us.

Dear Jesus, may You be so alive in my heart, that new growth is present at all times. May I be like grass that grows taller, even when the waters seem to flow over me ... even when I feel like I am struggling to get air. You are my Living Water, the One that I depend upon to refresh me, to strengthen me, and to cause me to bow, yet stand tall. For it is unto You that I bring the offering of praise. You are my oxygen. And like the deer, I long to be in Your presence, to be fed from Your gracious hand, always. Amen.

"As the deer longs for streams of water, so
I long for you, O God." Psalm 42:1 NLT

We, like the wildlife, are fed by the stream of God's love. May He be our source of life, until His Spirit bubbles up, to gush forth and draw others to His heart.

Through the trees,
Swept the light.
It faded past the shadows,
To the meadow, below.
And there it cast a glow,
—Like liquid gold.
It spun through the Aspens,
Illuminating the forest floor,
And touched the mountain peak,
In the background, beyond.
My eyes raised upward,
To the Light, above.
It was like beholding,
God's golden rays of love.

"Behold, the eye of the Lord is upon those who fear Him [and worship Him with awe-inspired reverence and obedience], on those who hope [confidently] in His compassion and lovingkindness, ..."
Psalm 33:18 (AMP)

Your Light, Oh Lord, is all around us. Just like the sun, Your love touches every surface, every thing in heaven and earth. You make all of creation glow with Your radiance. And when Your hope sweeps o're a soul, it is lit from within, to draw others to You.

Through the trees, swept the light—but from this quiet moment of pause—what I saw, was Jesus all around. He was the golden glow that touched mountain, valley, every tree limb and leaf. He is the Light that dwells within every heart that He calls His own.

God's love, is the light that flows from heaven—into our hearts and onto all of creation.

A Spectrum of the Heart:
The Song of Love to Heaven

> "The birds
> of the sky
> nest by the waters;
> they sing
> among the
> branches."
> Psalm 104:12
> (NIV)

Birds, sing, outside the window.
Lord, they seem to create a symphony,
as each unique cheep and chirp and twill,
combines into a lyrical sound.
Like praise, they rise to Your throne.
Uniquely, You have made each of us, Your children, likewise.
May we use our gifts, time, talents, resources and loving acts,
in harmony, to bring You glory.
Let not competition or ambition,
keep us from joining hands and hearts, within Your kingdom,
in order to bring You honor and glory.
And may the anthem of our motives, thoughts, deeds and service,
be as a song of love, lifted,
—offered freely, daily, as a gift, to Your highest heaven. Amen.

Nourishing

Rain, falls, to nourish the earth. It makes all things grow. It is God's love poured out upon the land in order to make flowers, plants and crops, flourish. It feeds the streams and rivers and waterfalls. These, give life to the animals, birds, and sea creatures. Snow, falls in its season to continue the cycle, to form sculptures—snowflakes, drifts, icicles—shapes, that are held until the temperatures rise.

Love is liquid, fluid. Love is moving, enriching; it's a life-giving nutrient. And it flowed from the veins of Jesus, into the hearts of all mankind. It was shaped like drops of sweat at Gethsemane. It is His love's-blood that provides our freedom, grace and the means of our forgiveness. And it develops in the growing space within our hearts —by planting seeds of Salvation's faith.

God's love shapes us, moves us, changes us—internally first—then with external fruit, that becomes evident as we walk with Him. His love reigns down upon us. It reigns over us, because He is sovereign, supreme, over all that He has made. His love is like a fountain, rising, since when we surrender our lives—His Spirit comes to dwell within us.

Love is a living thing; it's a flowing thing. It's a nourishing, cleansing, restoring, renewing thing. It is needed for us to survive. And Jesus' love was perfect. It is available in every season. And it is His desire that we love Him as He loves us. It's His desire that we love others, likewise.

*"God's voice is glorious in the thunder. We can't even imagine
the greatness of his power. He directs the snow to fall on the earth and
tells the rain to pour down. Then everyone stops working so they can
watch his power." Job 37:5-7 NLT*

May God's love that ran so richly through His veins, flow into ours,
so that we are like rain and snow, nourishing everyone that we
encounter with seeds of faith.

Part of the Group or Part of God's Family

God created each one of us
uniquely. We each have different
DNA, fingerprints, eye color,
facial features, physical builds,
personalities, likes and dislikes.
We have been given natural
abilities, strengths and
weaknesses. But we are made
up of the same things—body,
soul, mind, spirit. How amazing
is it to contemplate, that we are
alike, yet individual; yet all, bear
the image of our Maker? How
intricately we have been formed
—in every bone, muscle, and
tissue—in our thinking,
reasoning, discernment, and
ability to soak up and retain
knowledge.

From my stash, I came across
this photo. It is an arial view of
humankind. And I thought it was
a great illustration of how God
sees us—like a kaleidoscope of
our tastes (how we dress/present ourselves) linked together
(having the same Creator), and as a multi-generational people in
every nationality—a beautiful rainbow that He made to bring
Himself glory.

As my mind continued to turn, I began to see each person, as
transformed—when we invite Jesus into our hearts. It is in this
rebirth that we truly begin to come to life. It's called "born again." It
means—to be saved by grace, to come to a place when we
surrender our heart to the Lord, and want to submit to His way, His
Will, and follow where He leads.

He has created us like this picture—to dwell in harmony, to work together, pray together, praise together, live with the purpose of peace with one another. We were made to complement one another. In fact, when we become His child, He gives us what are known as "spiritual gifts." Each person receives at least one of these. But the thing that I have witnessed, over and over, is that our good God, often uses what He has already created, then blesses it, supernaturally.

What do I mean? If you are a child of God—you have invited Him into your heart, but you are not sure where your spiritual gift(s) lie—look to your natural gifts as a beginning place of examination. Ask God if His original design, has been enhanced. For instance, if God has given you a natural talent or ability—does He intend for you to use this as a way to teach, minister, encourage, be a caregiver?

You see, maybe we do not realize it, but our spiritual gifts are not given to us in a one-dimensional light. God preordained our days (Psalm 139:16). He knows the number of hairs on our head (Luke 12:7). He knows our rising and sleeping (Psalm 139:2), our comings and goings (Psalm 139:3). He knows those who will give their hearts to Him, and those who will reject Him (Ephesians 1:4-5).

God made you as a masterpiece, at conception. But it's in the supernatural that His design, comes to life. It's here, that He works to create patterns, brings out His character, softens our edges, etc. Being born again, doesn't mean that we are perfect. But it does mean that God's Spirit changes us, day by day, into His reflection. It means that the facets of His love, joy, peace, and grace radiate toward Him and others.

We choose, in this life, whether we want to be "part of the group," or included in God's family. The life that answers His invitation will surely find, not only eternal life, but will be woven into the heart of the kingdom-work on earth, and serve the King, forever. Today, is the time to decide. Will you let the Lord, transform your heart, mind, soul and spirit, from natural to supernatural? From self-centered, to God-centered? Will you let Him have His way in your life, to give you not only spiritual gifts, but the gift of eternity in His presence?

Souls

I'd like you read this list, slowly. I'd like you pay attention, to your internal responses as you do.

American
Lutheran
Painter
Muslim
Native Indian
    Christian
    Artisan
    Hindu
    Asian
    Chef
        Hawaiian
        Samoan
        Financial Broker
        Lawyer
        German
            Teacher
            Norwegian
            Architect
            Jew
            Baptist
            Frenchman
                African American
                Caucasian
                Banker
                Englishman
                    Farmer
                    Presbyterian
                    Electrician
                    Plumber
                    Florist

The purpose of the exercise is this ... each of these "labels" applies to a soul. Each, represents a person or group of people—by their ethnicity, or occupation, or religion. There is great diversity in this list, just as there is, in all of God's amazing—humankind.

We vary from one another in everything from our facial features, eye color, hair color, as we do in our thinking, values, and upbringing. We all vary in our DNA, talents, skills, and abilities. Yet, we are alike. We love in the same ways, experience pain and sorrow in the same ways. We bleed in the same ways. We each face adversity and difficulty at some time(s) in our lives.

And each of us have three things in common, spiritually.
1. We have an eternal soul. (Psalm 139:14, Ezekiel 18:4)
2. With it, Jesus gives us a choice. Will we invite Him into our hearts, so we will dwell with Him forever? Or will we remain in our sin, darkness, and be separated from Him, forever? (John 11:25, John 14:6, Revelation 20:11-15, John 3:16-17)
3. One day, every knee will bow before Him (Philippians 2:9-11).

Our souls are the "perfect" part of our design that has been created in the image of our Maker, Creator. This is the part of us that endures, forever. God loves each one of us, unconditionally. (Jeremiah 31:3) He is just, and will judge each person, individually. In heaven, there will be no more labels. There will only be His children gathered 'round His throne to give Him praise and adoration.

In this life, we wear labels. We are often told from earliest childhood, that we are "good, bad, rich, poor, pretty, ugly, worthy, unworthy, etc." But God made us with an express reason for being here—to love Him, serve Him and to love others. It is the mission and ministry of every person that He ever made. But we must choose, if, we will step into the role that He intended.

Every soul will bow before Him. Each, must make a choice. It matters not—who our parents are, what they believed, what we have done, or what they have—only, that God wants you to be part of His kingdom. And now, is the time to decide!

If your soul is saved, what are you doing—to help bring a new sister or brother, into the family of Christ? If we look into the eyes of those we meet with the love of Jesus, we'll not see a list of labels, but of souls that need to know Him, and we'll want to extend the offer of His grace.

Provided are two prayers. You're invited to pray each. Which does your soul respond to?

Dear Jesus, I can't do this life on my own. Today, I am asking You to come into my sinner's heart and save me. I believe that You gave Your life as a substitute for my guilt, at Calvary. And I believe that You rose again, to bring me the resurrection power of Your Spirit, within my soul. I offer You my mind, my heart, my body—as Your temple. Please guide me, teach me, and lead me, from this day forward. Help me follow the decrees of Your Word and Your voice, so that I grow in my knowledge and faith, day-by-day. Amen.

Dear Jesus, I am a soul that is saved, but I ask You for a greater passion for the lost. Take away any divide in my mind—of ethnicity, occupation, or religion. Grant me—less fear and greater courage—to step out of my comfort-zone and to share Your love, from the depths of my heart. Help me to memorize Your Word and to be able to "give an answer" if You provide an opportunity, for me to openly talk about my faith. But most of all, may the way that I live, speak, make decisions, do my work, go about daily life—be a witness—that I am Your child, and that You are my God. Amen.

Souls, all look the same in the sight of Jesus: precious, loved, favored. So they should, to our eyes, as well.

One Heart of Love

We are given ...

2 Eyes ...
2 Ears ...
2 Hands ...
2 Feet ...

But only 1 Heart ...

So it must be,
Big enough ...

To Love ...
To Give ...
To Share ...
To Reflect, Jesus.

But all of the other things,
That we are given,
—2 of—these,
Are the tools that we have ...

To see Love ...
To hear Love ...
To express Love ...
And to walk out,
Its characteristics.

How can a simple act of kindness or a compliment brighten your day? Can you be an encourager, with such a simple act?

One blessed heart,
Jesus,
Gave us His Love,
So that we would,
Live out—Love—
To the World!

Love Communicates by Joining Hands

One day, while out walking, I came across a lovely Indian lady. She spoke very little English. Our forms of communication were touch, attempted speech, and hand gestures. It was clear she was trying to find something in the area. I gave her a hug, continued to try to discern her destination, made her feel safe, and we walked together.

We got to a specific intersection and needed to cross the street ... she placed her hand in mine. No real communication had transpired between us, yet volumes were spoken in that moment!

Love and trust cross the boundaries of culture, race, religion, and class. In the clasp of hands we joined hearts, and I know, God smiled!

We walked about another mile, I prayed for God to bring someone who spoke her language, and sure enough a young man came along —with kindness and directions, to bridge the gap!

That is what God does: He takes our willingness to keep walking, even if we don't have the words, or know where the path is leading. He will use touch—hand gestures, hugs, love, and trust—to guide us. Follow His path, His hand is outstretched! If you are available, you may just find, that you can be the hands of God. How can you communicate His love?

"This is My commandment, that you love one another, just as I have loved you." John 15:12 NASB

What are some unique ways that you love? Have you ever bridged a gap, or crossed any divide to show compassion or kindness to a stranger?

Gazing with Wonder

Your eyes connect across a room, across the street, or with the one who holds your affection. You sit with a friend, and they share the depth of their excitement or pain. You can see it, feel it, displayed in their gaze.

Our eyes, hold our emotions; they give us not only vision to see the world, but also allow the world to see something of our feelings—joy, light, love, sorrow, pain—is reflected, highlighted, mirrored. These tiny windows, help us glimpse not only the wonder of God's creation, the beauty in each other, but also allow each of us to see some of His grandeur in every thing that He has ever made.

I've looked into blue eyes,
That matched the loveliest of skies.
I've looked into gray eyes,
That matched a stormy sea.
I've looked into brown eyes,
That were as warm as cocoa.
I've looked into green eyes,
That looked cool and serene.
I've looked into eyes,
That were bright, shining, like stars.
I've looked into eyes,
That wordlessly spoke of such pain.
I've looked into teary eyes,
Joyful eyes,
Soul-searching eyes,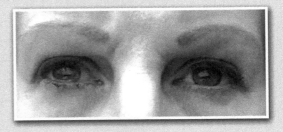
Love-filled eyes …
Each of them,
Were windows,
To the heart, within.
And I wonder,
If you've ever looked,
Into the eyes,
Of purest grace?
Have you ever looked into,
The eyes of the One,
Who unconditionally,
Made a way …
For each of us,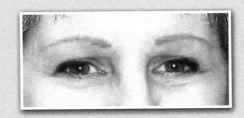
To be, His beloved?
'Cause it's this set of eyes,
That sees you,
Knows you,
Believes in you.
Jesus loves you,
And wants to call you,
His own.

Will you,
Lift your eyes,
Up to Him?
Will you,
Open your heart,
To be His home?

Our eyes, open us, to the world. They open the world, into, our inner being. Our eyes, often display the hidden things of our heart, that we do not even have words to communicate. But Jesus, sees us; He knows us. His eyes shine with delight, when He looks at every one of us, His creations.

Look up,
Look into,
The eyes of grace.
Let them hold you,
In the gaze,
Of purest love.

Every time you look into someone's eyes, or something beautiful in creation ... may you be reminded that the God of the universe—has His eyes upon you. They shine with love, light, and grace. They are filled with acceptance, delight, and invite you into relationship, to become His beloved child.

Jesus sees you. He never sleeps nor slumbers. His gaze holds you closely, affectionately. Draw near. Look into the gaze that loves you, completely, unconditionally, for always.

Dear Jesus, let each of us—feel to the depths of our soul—that we are the apple of Your eye. May Your love, Your grace, Your hope and truth, permeate our emotions, our thoughts, and circumstances, until we can feel Your embrace of kindness, goodness, and tenderness, like a physical touch. Thank You, for watching over us. Thank You, for your observant notice and care. Help us, fix our eyes upon You. Amen.

To leave you with a little more wonder:
Psalm 17:8, Psalm 121:8, Psalm 32:8,
Psalm 34:15, Job 34:21, 1 Samuel 16:7

*"But as Scripture says: 'No eye has seen, no
ear has heard, and no mind has imagined the things that God has
prepared for those who love him.'" 1 Corinthians 2:9 (GW)*

Eyes only for You

Our eyes are like a camera lens. With each blink, we capture a fresh frame. Did you ever think about this? Each time our lashes touch our cheeks, we have a new perspective. And in less than a second, we can go from seeing a landscape, to focusing in on the minutest detail.

Our eyes are sharper and faster at this transition, than a mechanical device. Our Creator—created us with these built-in-miracles, to absorb, to observe—not only His creations, but to see the very hand and presence of God, in bursts, that are faster than the speed of light.

- But do we notice the beauty right before us?
- Do we see Your glory God?
- Do we see the landscape, the fullness of Your grace that is constantly unfolding?
- Do we observe the detail, the colors, the nuances—of sky, earth, birds, flowers—of every human face?
- Do we focus on what a miracle it is, to be given physical and spiritual vision?

With every blink Lord, let me see, not just the beauty of Your creations, but You. Make me observant to the landscape-view, the close-up, the in-between, and that You are guardian of every perspective. For as You lead everyday of my life, I entrust all that I see, all that I experience, to Your power, Your omnipotence. I will walk by faith, because I know that You hold my future, frame by frame, in Your hands.

181

Awake, asleep,
With each blink,
Each time my lashes,
Touch my cheek,
May I see You, God.
For this life,
Is Yours.
Every detail,
Great or small,
All my days,
Are but a miracle,
Guided by,
Your gracious ways.
And as I look through,
I know that I am,
Living each day,
With—eyes, only for You.

When was someone observant and attentive to one of your needs? How did that feel? When were you able to meet someone else's need(s)? Was it better to give or receive?

If we live each day, with eyes only for the Lord, we will see Him in everything that is before us. We will see creation with a fresh perspective. Every landscape will be like a painting. Every close-up will come alive, with detail. This kind of insight awakens His Spirit within us. It helps us recognize God's glory, in what others may consider ordinary. It makes our minds sharper and causes our spiritual senses to be more alert, to discern His Will and follow His leadings more closely.

If our eyes are focused on the Creator, we are captivated by His nature, everyday, every moment, until we see Him face to face. In this way, we give Him honor and glory!

"The eye is the lamp of the body. If your eyes are healthy, your whole body will be full of light." Matthew 6:22 NIV

Though Dimly

If you look in a mirror, you see your own face or whatever image you have presented in it, reflected perfectly back to you. Two mirrors together, create a circle. But the combination of three, is the beginning premise of how a kaleidoscope came into existence.

Endless images are created, as mirrors are added, to enhance a single frame. A profusion of colors explode, as we move and change what we place within the viewfinder. Angles and repetitive designs now dance, at the spin of the dial. Whatever you hold it up to—becomes magnified, multiplied, forming a version of art, within an encapsulated tube.

And while the kaleidoscope was invented by a Scottish scientist, mathematician and physicist, Sir David Brewster in 1816, he had nothing on our Creator, Who gave us galaxies, mountains, oceans, waterfalls, wildlife, animals, and reptiles, in every type and variety and hue under the sun. There are sunrises and sunsets, storms with thunder and lightning, starry hosts winking from on high, wildflower meadows dotted with bees and butterflies. And birds that sing, to give Him constant praise. In fact, I wonder if these were part of Sir David's original inspiration?

Each blink of our eyes and turn of our heads, displays more of God's glory, more of His story. And the three parts of the Trinity—Father, Son, and Holy Spirit that were all present at creation—are still at work, alive, to continue revealing earth and heaven's grandeur and majesty, today. In fact, they are manifested, right within the confines of our hearts.

Each of us, with our fragments and broken places (things reflected, things learned, and faith gathered) come to the Father to be made into artful, useful designs of His perfect Will. In His hands He polishes, hones our rough edges, puts the pieces into perfect order to be transformed.

Then we learn to know Jesus via a humble babe, and as the Lamb of God via the Cross. At Calvary, two beams of wood gave us three gifts to change everything:

1. We witness Jesus' love as He became our sacrifice, took our place and paid our sin-debt.
2. Here, He offers grace to forgive us, if we come like a child to ask and receive Him as Savior and Lord.
3. His death and resurrection are meant to free us, offering us the gift of eternity in His presence.

When we invite Jesus into our hearts, the Holy Spirit teaches us to understand God's Word, to follow in His footsteps, to commune with the Lord and seek His company. He is our Intercessor, indwelling our soul with a seal of God's love and the promise of His presence with us through mountain highs or valley lows.

A kaleidoscope, takes a static object and creates of it, a vivid three-dimensional image that seems to come alive. That's what the Trinity does in us, as well. That's also the perspective from which we can view Revelation. The multi-dimensional, multi-faceted world beyond —will be fascinating and beautiful, indeed.

> *"For now [in this time of imperfection] we see in a mirror dimly [a blurred reflection, a riddle, an enigma], but then [when the time of perfection comes we will see reality] face to face. Now I know in part [just in fragments], but then I will know fully, just as I have been fully known [by God]." 1 Corinthians 13:12 AMP*

Though we see and experience God's masterpieces in the here and now, these will be but a dim reflection of what heaven will contain, as we behold the risen Lord, face to face.

Immeasurable

God's love is as measureless,
As the ocean's width, breadth and depth.

It reaches as far,
As the East is from the West.

It knows no boundary,
Like the wide open spaces,
Of the Western states.

It travels across every continent,
The universe, the globe,
And into every galaxy, and beyond.

It's as enduring as He is,
From beginning to end,
And from everlasting to everlasting.

It's as all-encompassing,
As the velvet onyx sky,
Filled with starry hosts.

God's love reaches out to us, (mankind),
No matter where we live,
Work or play.

It is invisible,
Yet visibly,
Felt, seen, and experienced.

Immeasurable,
is the love of God,
so that it cannot
be missed
or contained
or tamed.
And it is available
to one and all.
He loved us perfectly
at our birth.
He loves
and redeems us,
at our re-birth.
He loves us
always, eternally.
Oh what a gift
to the soul!

His love transcends all time and space. It was demonstrated at Calvary where He physically took our place. But His love indwells the heart and soul—internally, eternally—that is surrendered. His Spirit teaches us to live, sacrificially, according to His Will, and by faith. This love, has been a witness and a testimony that has been passed down through every generation from the time that He was born as a babe. And He died and rose from the grave, to rule and reign, always.

God's love is present in every heartbeat, every blooming, growing thing, bird, animal, creature and creation that He has made. He's imprinted His love upon the dewdrop, within the nutrient of rain and snow, within the river's flow, the thunder's echo, the mountain's peak and the shadowy valley.

It will never die. It will never be extinguished. It will never be drowned out. It will never fade or rust or decay. It will never perish. It will forever be, as He is—pure, perfect, holy, righteous, grace-filled.

And from it, flows abundant fruits from the Spirit: love, joy, peace, long-suffering, gentleness, goodness, faith, meekness, temperance. These are the attributes of Jesus' life. They are the marks of His love, in us.

The Shades of God's Love

Darkness still covered the shoreline in shadows. White contrails were softly illuminated, by the first rays of the morning's dawn. Blue sky and shades of gold, rose, and lavender danced between the two. It was a new day, a fresh beginning. And my heart responded, not only to the breathtaking beauty of the scene before me, but also to the Maker, the One Who created such artistry and put it on display— for anyone who pauses to notice.

In the shades of Your love,
I walk, I dance.
By the light of Your Spirit,
I'm touched by Salvation's romance.
 As I gaze upon the waves,
 That lie tranquil and still,
 I know I'm held in Your arms of grace,
 Until, until …
  In the shadow of Your love,
  I take hold of Your hand,
  Moving within the living rainbow reflected here,
  At the edge of the sand.
   Suddenly I am calmed;
   My mind is at peace,
   For the shades of Your grace,
   Cover me,
    Until, until …
    Eternity meets me today,
    Until the moment,
    That I behold Your holy face.

The early morning dawn and the colors that washed over the horizon brought my soul, quietude. The shades of God's loving-kindness seemed to communicate His gift of unmerited favor—like a rainbow of promise—to all who look for Him, and to anyone who calls upon His name.

> "He saved us because of his mercy and not because of any good things that we have done. God washed us by the power of the Holy Spirit. He gave us new birth and a fresh beginning. God sent Jesus Christ our Savior to give us his Spirit. Jesus treated us much better than we deserve. He made us acceptable to God and gave us the hope of eternal life." Titus 3:5-7 CEV

The Lord shades us in His love, to keep us stepping and dancing, in the close company of God.

> "Love is patient and kind. Love is not jealous or boastful or proud or rude. It does not demand its own way. It is not irritable, and it keeps no record of being wronged. It does not rejoice about injustice but rejoices whenever the truth wins out. Love never gives up, never loses faith, is always hopeful, and endures through every circumstance."
> 1 Corinthians 13:4-7 (NLT)

Most of us have heard these verses as part of a wedding or sermon. Right? Well, one day in my personal devotional time, the Lord reversed them. What do I mean?

He spoke them into my heart as double negatives. For instance—love is not impatient. Love is not unkind. Love does not ... I found it interesting and impactful to hear them this way (verses 4 and 7). And while this may not be proper grammar, it provided another lesson in what love is, and is not.

How might this little exercise assist you, in seeing God's intention of the love chapter? How might it clarify how we are to live and emulate His life?

Thank You's—Facets of God's Love

Heart designs are often synonymous with the communication of love. And I appreciate finding them in nature. To me, ones like my Ginkgo leaves below, are constant reminders of God's unending, fathomless love for us, in every season.

In the spaces below, list some of the things you love,

....

some of the people you love and those who love you,

....

a few reasons that you appreciate God's unconditional love.

....

What is the sweetest act of love that you have received?

....

What is the sweetest act of love that you have given?

....

With which sense do you most keenly feel or experience love?

....

"For God so loved the world, that He gave His only begotten Son, that whoever believes in Him shall not perish, but have eternal life. For God did not send the Son into the world to judge the world, but that the world might be saved through Him." John 3:16-17 NASB

Have you ever written a love letter to Jesus?
Now is your opportunity:

....

....

....

....

....

....

....

....

....

....

"Kindness, peace, love—may they never stop blooming in you and from you." Jude 1:2 (VOICE)

Soul's Introspection—Facets of God's Love

"Your steadfast love, O Lord, is as great as all the heavens. Your faithfulness reaches beyond the clouds. Your justice is as solid as God's mountains. Your decisions are as full of wisdom as the oceans are with water. You are concerned for men and animals alike." Psalm 36:5-6 (TLB)

"How precious, O God, is your constant love! We find protection under the shadow of your wings." Psalm 36:7 (GNT)

All of creation is rolled out as a scroll of God's love for us. What speaks to your heart, line by line?

"The loyal love of Yahweh does not cease; his compassions do not come to an end. They are new in the morning, great is your faithfulness." Lamentations 3:22-23 (LEB)

"Cause me to hear Your lovingkindness in the morning, for in You do I trust; cause me to know the way in which I should walk, for I lift up my soul to You." Psalm 143:8 (NKJV)

If you were to describe love in practical terms, what would they be? What if you chose fanciful terminology? Now read your list back, and think of it, as God's love, condensed, and expanded beyond your imagination!

"But you, dear friends, carefully build yourselves up in this most holy faith by praying in the Holy Spirit, staying right at the center of God's love, keeping your arms open and outstretched, ready for the mercy of our Master, Jesus Christ. This is the unending life, the real life!"
Jude 1:20-21 (MSG)

God's love is measureless, fathomless. In fact, no picture, or words, or painting, or ideas can really convey this to our minds. So how do we wrap our thoughts around this concept? What helps you understand His unconditional grace, acceptance, forgiveness, mercy, etc.? How do you make it personal?

"Show your kindness to me, your servant. Save me because of your love." Psalm 31:16 (ICB)

"Look at how great a love the Father has given us that we should be called God's children. And we are! The reason the world does not know us is that it didn't know Him." 1 John 3:1 (HCSB)

The Gem of Meditation

The Pause:

God's love is likened to being as high as the heavens. His forgiveness and mercy are analogous to stretching as far as the east is from the west. Jesus' arms were extended upon the Cross in outward extension, as an embrace to all mankind. The Cross itself, travels from earth to heaven's heights to invite connection with our Sovereign God. And its beams go horizontally, to remind us to love others as Christ loved us.

God's love is immeasurable, fathomless, depthless. It cannot be contained. Nothing can separate us—from His presence, His notice, His care or deliverance. How amazing is this knowledge? How wonderful in times of difficulty and stress, to come and worship this God, Who knows us completely, yet loves us unconditionally!

What amazes you about God's love? How do you love God, in return? How do you share His love with others?

....

....

....

The Praise:

Dear Lord, thank You, for images such as the heart in the tree (which began this chapter), or flowers as a crown, or heart shapes in the clouds, or daily graces that demonstrate Your tender affection for us. We are grateful. Thank You, for Your sacrifice at Calvary, and the invitation to know You and walk in sweet fellowship with You, daily. Your love surrounds us; it is our oxygen, the breath that fills us, and it is our praise and gift, to give You glory. Amen.

How can you love God in a new way? Do you have any fresh insights, into the depth of His care and affection for you?

....

....

....

....

From the Shadows

We were out walking, immediately following a thunderstorm. Remnants of dark clouds remained, even as the sun streamed through the sky to create rays and illuminate the atmosphere. My mind conjured the well known and beloved passage from Psalm 23. Especially the line: "yea, though I walk through the valley of the shadow" .... "thou art with me."

From earth, it appeared as if the cloud blocked part of the sun. But if you were looking at it from heaven, you would see the design, in reverse. The cloud would be behind the light. That's a great perspective from which to view times of illness, loss, grief. It helps us to remember that our good and loving God, has not left our side. It reminds us that He is present in the shadows, that He is the visible image of the invisible God. (Colossians 1:15-17)

And just as rays were formed to stretch in every direction of the sky —God's grace, hope, peace, mercy, healing and presence— likewise, are as near as our first whisper of prayer, to connect us to His throne-room.

No shadow is formed,
Without a light source.
Let the Light of our Savior,
Enfold You, in times of pain,
To remind your heart,
That there shall be joy, again.
For where there have been tears,
There is also a Lord,
Who bottles them, collects them,
To turn them into jewels.
And one day,
If we are His child,
There shall be no more ...
Darkness,
Or sorrow,
Or death.
May that truth,
Bring a ray of comfort,
For today,
And everyday,
Until we see the Son,
Face to face.

From the shadows, Light, dawns to envelop our hearts, with God's love.

Epilogue

I hope you've enjoyed Volume I, of *Creation's Kaleidoscope: Embracing Light Devotional.* Here, we've explored everything that God has made—from the very beginning. We've watched, how *Out of Darkness,* void, all things came to life. We've experienced His *Embracing Light,* which spans every 24 hour period, and all of time and space. We've traversed *Under a Canopy of Stars* to trace God's grandeur and majesty. *From the Inside, Out,* He's fashioned miracles to draw us close, to feel and know the *Facets of God's Love.*

As we have done so, we've paused to meditate upon His Word, we've asked and answered some questions. We've spent some time thanking God, and praising His holy name. And we've lifted our eyes, to focus on His divinity and sovereignty. It's my prayer, that this devotional has shone the Light of the World into your soul, so that His love for you, is reflected to those around you.

Volume II, will continue to expand upon creation and the kaleidoscope theme, but you'll have to watch for it ... to discover where God's Spirit and inspirations ... take us next!

Thanks for taking the journey with me. May God's light surround you to bring you blessing, joy, peace, hope, comfort, and His eternal love.

With warmest regards,
deborah goshorn-stenger

Here's a little of my story as a Writer/Photographer, which began to form at a very early age. Over the last year or so, the Lord has been showing me, how He's been leading me to this current path, for a very long time. For instance, I remember in second grade being rewarded with small gifts and treats from "Mrs. Miller," as we students, vied for the title of "spelling-bee champion" each week. In sixth grade, I recall "liking" to memorize prepositions and diagraming sentences, while others in my English class, groaned. And as soon as I could print, it seems I had an affinity for stationery, cards, pencils and the like. In fact, my brother (John) used to give me his extra notebooks and supplies at school-year's end, and to me, it was like Christmas, had come early.

Interestingly enough, since I had given my heart to Jesus as a child, He brought to my mind a picture of myself as a very young girl, writing out Scriptures and explaining to my dolls and toys, what these verses meant to me. Perhaps it was the Lord, placing a dream in a small mind, of what would one day be a gifting of His Spirit?! At age 10, I received my first Polaroid camera, and I discovered that faces and places could be captured, and treasured; I was hooked. Then, it was in my early teens that I began to write poetry. What began as a hobby, I later shared with family and friends; and this, has now become my "calling."

Creation's Kaleidoscope is very personal to me, because as the story of Genesis 1 unfolds, it's also a testimony of how God takes the simple, to change it, transform it—if we allow His light and love—to shine through it. He's been my inspiration, my hope, my joy and peace through many moves (14 to date), through on-going illnesses, through loss and personal struggles of many kinds. God uses our whole lives—fragments and all—if we, surrender it all.

If you're searching for God's purpose in your heart, in your decisions, in your vocation—ask Him to show you what He's been writing (perhaps as far back as childhood) as the foundation for your life's work, acts of kindness, and service—unto Him. Because sometimes, the key to loving Him and encouraging other sojourner's for His kingdom, lies in the patterns, that He's been creating, all along.

God's nature is to teach us, inspire us and love us, through every day of our lives. He wants us to find and fulfill His Will and purpose. Lord, I pray that Your story is imprinted upon every heart—until each—brings You, glory. Amen.

Also by *Deborah Goshorn-Stenger*

The *Creation's Kaleidoscope* Series:

<u>Available Now</u>
Embracing Light (Volume I)

Devotional	Paperback and Ebook
Journal	Paperback
To-Go	Paperback, Exclusively on our website

<u>Please check our website for release dates for Volumes II/III.</u>

Let Everything that has Life ... Praise (Volume II)

Devotional	Paperback and Ebook
Journal	Paperback
To-Go	Paperback, Exclusively on our website

Prisms of God's Glory (Volume III)

Devotional	Paperback and Ebook
Journal	Paperback
To-Go	Paperback, Exclusively on our website

To Contact us: 2PauseandPraiseCreations.com
or by mail at:

2 Pause and Praise Creations
5315 Long St, Suite 518
McFarland, WI 53558

"The Lord bless you and keep you; the Lord make His face shine upon you, and be gracious to you; the Lord lift up His countenance upon you, and give you peace." Numbers 6:24-26 NKJV

Dear Readers,

Will you leave a kind or thoughtful review?

Now that you've finished reading this devotional, will you tell us what you think? How has it spoken to your heart? How has it helped you to grow in your relationship with Jesus, or given you a greater awareness of Jesus' love, through creation? How did tracing light from dawn to darkness, show you that God is present in your life?

We'd be honored if you take time to leave us a comment (wherever you've purchased our product, i.e. Amazon, Apple, etc.). We'll use your feedback to guide any updates to this manuscript, as well as consider your inputs for future projects.

Would you like to be added to our mailing list?

Do you want to be notified of upcoming releases and exclusive materials? If so, we invite you to join our mailing list.

You can do so, at our website:

<u>2pauseandpraisecreations.com</u>

Thank you so much!
Doug and Deb

196

THE CREATION
OF VALUE

BOOKS BY IRVING SINGER

Meaning in Life
1. The Creation of Value
2. The Pursuit of Love
3. The Harmony of Nature and Spirit

The Nature of Love
1. Plato to Luther
2. Courtly and Romantic
3. The Modern World

Mozart and Beethoven: The Concept of Love in Their Operas

The Goals of Human Sexuality

Santayana's Aesthetics

Essays in Literary Criticism by George Santayana (Editor)

*The Nature and Pursuit of Love: The Philosophy of
Irving Singer (Ed. David Goicoechea)*

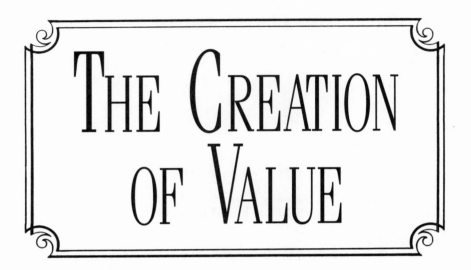

THE CREATION OF VALUE

Volume I of
Meaning in Life

IRVING SINGER

The Johns Hopkins University Press
Baltimore and London

Originally published as *Meaning in Life:*
The Creation of Value by The Free Press, A Division of
Macmillan, Inc., New York, N.Y.
Johns Hopkins edition, 1996
05 04 03 02 01 00 99 98 97 96   5 4 3 2 1

The Johns Hopkins University Press
2715 North Charles Street
Baltimore, Maryland 21218-4319
The Johns Hopkins Press Ltd., London

Library of Congress Cataloging-in-Publication Data will be
found at the end of this book.

A catalog record for this book is available from the British
Library.

ISBN 0-8018-5453-9
ISBN 0-8018-5451-2 (pbk.)

To Ben

CONTENTS

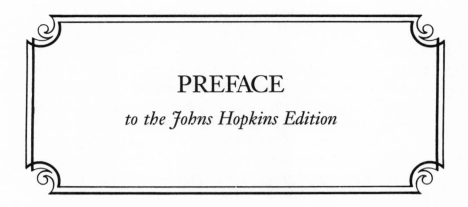

PREFACE

to the Johns Hopkins Edition

When I first wrote this book, I did not know that it would be the beginning of a trilogy. Perhaps because good work had been done by other philosophers who grappled with similar topics, I hardly recognized how much more would be needed in order to round out the perspective I was proposing. On some points I restrained myself because I feared that swelling in the prose might wreak havoc with the overall balance of my presentation. At several places in the argument I left much unsaid. I wished to articulate a succinct, though occasionally schematic, statement of my naturalist, humanist, pluralist approach. In the company of the two books that serve as sequels to it, the present one may still be taken as an attempt of that sort.

The encompassing framework of all three books is established at the outset of *The Creation of Value*. It appears in the distinction I make between "meaning in life" and "the meaning of life." Though in ordinary parlance the phrases are often used interchangeably, they evoke questions about the world and about our experience that are not the same. We all yearn to discover objective truths, or, better yet, a single overarching truth, that can provide a comprehensive explanation of what there is in the universe while also assuring us that ultimately everything is for the best. At the very least, we want to feel that the cosmos is not governed by random forces or wholly material laws of nature: we want to believe that we have sufficient reason to think that what conforms to our ideas of goodness and value, and therefore matters to us, ordains somehow what nature must be like.

In trying to make sense of traditional doctrines about this unitary meaning of life, I examine in the introduction and first chapter of this volume arguments for and against denying that the concept itself has meaning. I reach no final conclusions in this controversy, but rather use it as a vehicle for directing attention toward problems about meaningfulness as it structures a life that is purposive and adequately fulfilling for human beings (or other creatures) to care about anything. I maintain that meaning in life—and the meaning in our own lives—results from creative efforts on our part. It is not a prior reality awaiting our discovery. Though we talk about a "search" for meaning, what we are seeking is primarily a form of creativity that will *make* our lives meaningful.

I therefore analyze meaning in life as a pattern of existence that engenders whatever values are required to go on living creatively. I suggest that this is what many, perhaps most, people who ask about a meaning *of* life are really concerned about. Even if there is no prior being, or category of being, that can yield an objective and independent meaning of life, living things have meaningful lives by creating values from within themselves. In that sense meaning in life *is* the creation of value.

With this as my guiding principle, I devote the rest of the book to matters such as the following: the meaning that death can have in relation to life; how it is that human beings create meaning despite their perplexity, indeed anxiety, in the face of

questions about their reality that are often puzzling and sometimes incomprehensible; the importance of wonderment and
vital instinct as natural reactions that can eventuate in a growth
of meaning; the difference between a meaningful life and one
that is merely happy; the desire of many people to live a life that
amounts to something and is thus "significant"; the possibility
that this significance, which is more than just meaningfulness,
consists in having a creative life that increases the level of
meaning and happiness in others as well as in oneself. The book
ends with a discussion of what would constitute a love of life. I
also speculate about a further love definable as love for the love
in everything that is capable of love.

What I did not realize until I finished the first edition was
the extent to which my work on it would create, in me at least, a
need to carry my deliberations into diverse areas of collateral
inquiry. In a number of passages I mention the relation between
meaning and love, the latter being a subject I had addressed in
previous books. But having given my panoramic account of
meaning in life, I began to perceive its relevance to a more
systematic view of love that had been germinating in me for
some time. In the first volume of my trilogy *The Nature of Love*,
I had approached love as an affirmative but equally imaginative
response to persons, things, or ideals we appraise and simultaneously bestow value upon. By living through the experience of
formulating my ideas about the creation of value—not only in
the chapters of this book but also in the classes and public
lectures that preceded them at MIT, Johns Hopkins, and elsewhere—I found that I had at hand a focus for my continued
exploration of love, meaning, value, and their interactions with
one another.

The Pursuit of Love, the book that issued from this development, seeks to reveal how the appraisals and bestowals in terms
of which I had originally characterized the nature of love are
themselves the products of imagination creating a life that is
worth living in association with the persons, things, and ideals
that have meaning for us. Having before me the orientation I

had sketched in *The Creation of Value*, I could then distinguish between the different values that contribute to the meaningfulness of varied kinds of human love: self-love, the parent's love for a child, the child's love for a parent, peer love, friendship love, the love of one's clan or nation, the love of humanity. I devote separate chapters to sexual love and religious love, since these involve a complexity of values that warrant special treatment. I analyze sexual love into elements that I call the libidinal, the erotic, and the romantic. I demonstrate how greatly they manifest a longing for meaning and the creation of value, as opposed to purely physiological or mechanistic determinants. In studying religious love, I emphasize the play of imagination that constantly gropes for a meaning of life even if its doing so only evinces an eagerness to create systems of value that can possibly overcome our residual fear that nature has no interest in our personal welfare. Exploring this aspect of religious love, I discuss the love of nature itself and the means by which that may be related to a love of life.

Crucial as *The Creation of Value* was in generating *The Pursuit of Love*, its importance for *The Harmony of Nature and Spirit*, the third volume of the trilogy, is even greater. By the time I had completed the first two books, I saw how the many problems demanding clarification could be investigated more thoroughly and in a format that would not intrude upon the outline I had chosen for the first volume. Though each of the three volumes can be read independently of the other two, *The Harmony of Nature and Spirit* not only branches off from the speculative trunk which is the book you are reading now but also attempts to extend its major thrust.

Returning to *The Creation of Value*'s distinction between meaning and happiness, the last volume considers how one might have both within the dimensions of a good life. I describe the joining of these two values in the context of a broader harmony between nature and spirit. To show how that harmonization depends upon imagination and idealization, I offer a theory that is more elaborate than anything I had written about

them in either the earlier books of this trilogy or in *The Nature
of Love*. Out of these reverberations I derive the idea that art in
all its varieties, including the art of living a good life, is the part
of human nature that devotes itself to achieving unity between
consummation, and therefore happiness, and the different meanings relevant to particular art forms. I suggest that art is itself the
harmony of nature and spirit. Since spirit must originate in
nature through means that art creates and beneficially employs,
I argue that the aesthetic element in life is foundational to
religion as well as ethics. That enables me to amplify what I had
tentatively proposed, at the end of *The Creation of Value*, in my
allusions to the love of life and the love of love in everything that
experiences love. This amplification occurs in comments about
empathy, sympathy, and compassion as different modalities of
social and religious love that embody their own type of meaningful existence.

In preparing *The Creation of Value* for its Johns Hopkins
edition, I have made some changes that express redirections in
my thinking that accumulated after the book was first published.
In the last chapter, for instance, I had briefly interpreted
Nietzsche's notion of *amor fati* (cosmic love), revising it to suit
ideas of mine about a significant life, the love of life, and the love
of love in everything. In the process, I now feel, I may have
amalgamated these disparate concepts in a way that confounds
their differences among themselves, and with regard to what
Nietzsche meant.

Nietzsche presents as his "formula for greatness in a human
being" the capacity to love indiscriminately everything that
happens in the cosmos even though one believes, as he did, that
the universe as a whole is inherently meaningless and horrid. My
interpretation tried to make this view intelligible. But I failed to
emphasize that a life that is significant, a life that amounts to
something of importance, can very well exist without cosmic
love. Moreover, I sounded as if I thought that a significant life
presupposed the having of a love for the love in everything—
which is to say, a love for the ability to love that any animate

creature might have, if only in loving itself and wanting to perpetuate its being. I now see more clearly why this would be too stringent a requirement. While loving the love in everything may enrich one's love of life in others and in oneself, it cannot be a necessary condition for attaining a significant life. That belongs to any mode of living that creates and augments the values of meaning or happiness. The love of the love in everything can sometimes bolster the love of life. But it is a different ideal, and not one that is essential for a life to be significant.

In *The Harmony of Nature and Spirit*, I study these ideas afresh. In the present edition of *The Creation of Value*, I deal with them by using language that is more circumspect than before. The reader can decide for him- or herself whether either of these tactics is fully satisfying.

I. S.

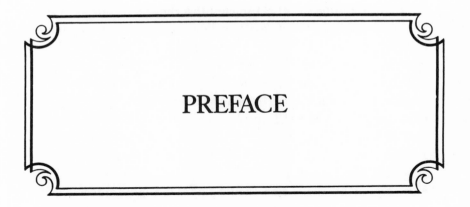

PREFACE

This book is a personal testament in the form of a philosophical exploration. Much of it can be read as an intellectual odyssey. Like many others, I turned at an early age to writings about life and meaning in the hope of finding a coherent world view consistent with my own sense of reality. I soon discovered that the sheer articulation of problems and answers in this area created major difficulties for anyone who aspires to intellectual honesty. Faced by the enormity of the issues, I felt that one needed not only pervasive humility but also a way of putting all possible theorizing into the closest rapport with one's immediate experience of the world— with vague intimations or intuitions or ideational probings that often elude precise analysis while clamoring for sympathetic understanding.

In writing about these questions, I have therefore sought to clarify, if only for myself, the cognitive twists and turns through which my thinking has evolved. Beginning with panoramic queries about "the meaning of life," I suggest that they be reconceived and redirected in order for us to learn how human beings can attain lives that are meaningful and perhaps, in a special sense that I later introduce, significant. The entire book is based on a distinction between searching for a prior meaning of life and the creating of meaning in one's life apart from any such concern. I cumulatively try to show how the latter enables us to have a life worth living.

In making this attempt, I have no arcane message to profess, no doctrine that I recognize as ultimate or authoritative for those who do not see the world as I do. Contentious as I may be and eager to refute arguments that I find challenging, I am more interested in making suggestions than in reaching definite conclusions. Studying the meaning that may be available in life, I have sought to illuminate the complexity of doubt and confusion that reflective human beings generally encounter. At the same time I also want to provide the outlines of a point of view that others can accept or reject, improve or criticize, in accordance with their own experience and predilection.

The book is not addressed to specialists in any field. It is based on a series of public lectures that I delivered in a program on medicine and the humanities at the Johns Hopkins Medical Institutions. The audience consisted of members of the general community, and most of them were not trained in philosophy or in literature—the two disciplines that overlap in my approach. My lectures were designed to convey a perspective that I have developed over a number of years, drawing on the efforts others have recently made in related fields but not pretending to represent them. In expanding and greatly revising the contents of those lectures, I have retained the initial intention and written with the same kind of audience in mind. Those who wish to do further research will find in the endnotes many references to other books and articles.

The ideas I discuss or formulate are presented mainly as tentacles that reach out and explore various problems of life and death. Having made our inquiry, we may eventually decide that some of these problems are insoluble. But that will not matter if our exploration into them is a fulfillment on its own. The outcome of philosophy is always precarious, and often unforeseeable. At least, it ought to be.

There are several people I wish to thank for the help they have provided in relation to this work. I am grateful to the Committee on Cultural and Social Affairs of the Johns Hopkins Medical Institutions, and in particular George B. Udvarhelyi and Richard A. Macksey, for having invited me to give the originating lectures. Among people who read earlier drafts of the manuscript, I am especially indebted to Herbert Engelhardt, Adam Frost, Dan Leary, and W. V. Quine. Adam Bellow, my editor at the Free Press, offered good ideas and inspired advice that I was happy to use in the final version. As always, my writing at every stage owes a great deal to the innumerable comments of my wife Josephine Singer. Finally, there are the students in courses at MIT who enriched my thinking by responding critically to it. I dedicate the finished product to my son, as a representative of their questing spirit.

I. S.

THE CREATION OF VALUE

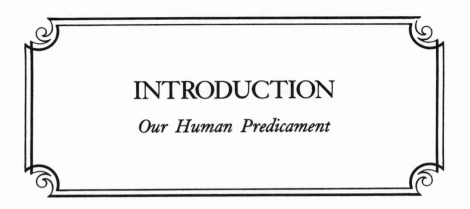

INTRODUCTION

Our Human Predicament

Throughout history educated people generally assumed that philosophy, like religion, is capable of elucidating the meaning of life. In the past, philosophers often made this attempt. But the twentieth century has been different. Questions about the meaning of life have been dismissed or neglected by many of the greatest thinkers in the last hundred years. Even if they were right to do so, we must nevertheless wonder why it is that human beings are both attracted to such matters and constantly baffled by them. I begin with a quotation from an interview that George Bernard Shaw gave in 1901. At the end of many queries about various subjects, the interviewer asks for "one word as to the meaning of the world-comedy." Shaw replies as follows:

> It is this thoughtless demand for a meaning that produces the comedy. You ask for it in one word though we are not within a million years, as yet, of seeing the world as it really is. We are

1

intellectually still babies: this is perhaps why a baby's facial expression so strongly suggests the professional philosopher. . . . Well, we are all still as much babies in the world of thought as we were in our second year in the world of sense. Men are not real men to us: they are heroes and villains, respectable persons and criminals. Their qualities are virtues and vices; the natural laws that govern them are gods and devils; their destinies are rewards and expiations; their reasoning a formula of cause and effect with the horse mostly behind the cart. They come to me with their heads full of these figments, which they call, if you please, "the world," and ask me what is the meaning of them, as if I or anyone else were God Omniscient and could tell them. Pretty funny this: eh? But when they ostracize, punish, murder, and make war to impose by force their grotesque religions and hideous criminal codes, then the comedy becomes a tragedy. The Army, the Navy, the Church, the Bar, the theatres, the picture-galleries, the libraries, and the trade unions are forced to bolster up their pet hallucinations. Enough. You expect me to prate about the Absolute, about Reality, about The First Cause, and to answer the universal Why. When I see these words in print the book goes into the basket. Good morning.[1]

We must all feel something similar, at least those of us who are concerned about clarity of thought. We also respond sympathetically to something Freud said, near the end of his life, in a letter to Marie Bonaparte: "The moment one inquires about the sense or value of life one is sick, since objectively neither of them has any existence. In doing so one is only admitting a surplus of unsatisfied libido."[2]

We may well agree with much of what Freud implies. A healthy person does not brood about the meaning of life. He gets up in the morning and throws himself into activities that involve his energies and provide personal gratifications. When his emotional interests are thwarted, there can be a certain amount of "unsatisfied libido" but then he will remedy the situation by taking action in some other direction. Preoccupation with the meaning of life might thus signify inefficiency in discharging libidinal excess. As Freud points out, this eventuates in "grief and depression."

In this view questions about the meaning of life have no inherent value. Presumably Freud had investigated these questions himself, or else he could not have asserted that neither the sense nor value of life has any existence "objectively." Having made his investigation, however, he was convinced that such inquiries are merely symptomatic of a pervasive sickness experienced by those who pursue them.

Later in his letter Freud admits that he may be "too pessimistic." But even if we take his comments literally, what follows from them? Since most people ask about the meaning of life at one time or other, perhaps we should conclude that the majority of human beings are sick to some extent and at crucial moments in their existence. The fact that we systematically raise unanswerable questions may indicate a form of philosophical sickness that belongs to us generically, as part of what it is to be human. In this respect Nietzsche was possibly right when he said that man is "the sick animal." To ask for the meaning of life would then be an expression of one's humanity rather than just a symptom of psychological or moral disability.

When I once mentioned Freud's idea to the philosopher W. V. Quine, he nodded in agreement with Freud. When I then quoted Nietzsche's aphorism, Quine replied: "Yes, but some of us are sicker than others." This is doubtless true. But there is no reason to think that all questioning of this sort is merely pathological. The attitude typified by the assertions of Freud and Quine ignores a dimension of cognitive exploration that many people have cherished. Human consciousness would be greatly impoverished if it eliminated its habitual concern in this area. Not only would we lessen our ability to speculate about the world, but also we would deprive ourselves of a framework within which more immediate and manageable problems can be approached. At the limits of every scientific discipline there remain troublesome issues that one cannot dismiss simply by calling them metaphysical or extra-scientific. Even if these questions are ultimately unanswerable, they elicit imaginative responses that enrich and embellish life.

To this extent an inquiry into the "sense or value" of existence does not at all indicate sickness. On the contrary, it may be the only healthy and creative way that we can express a type of curiosity distinctive to our species. Illness is generally an undesirable state of mind or body, but reflecting on the meaning of life may sometimes transmute our ontological malaise into feelings about ourselves and about the universe that integrate experience. This would be an achievement worth cultivating. To eliminate such interests is to revert to a lower order of consciousness. That path is regressive, not liberating or truly responsive to the possibilities of intellectual development.

The issues that we shall be addressing are particularly urgent in our society. Though they pertain to the human condition as a whole, they also have special relevance to current attitudes. By the time the 1980s were drawing to a close, that decade was often described as a period of "instant gratification." The Western world, above all the United States, was motivated as never before by hopes of rapidly eliminating all inherent barriers between wanting something and getting it. By the beginning of the 1990s, some cultural critics argued that utopian aspirations of this sort are not only unrealistic but also conducive to facile pleasures and addictions that eventually end in demoralization. Our entire culture is often depicted as suffering from a crisis that may well undermine the values on which it is based. A large part of Western ideology, at least in the democratic traditions, has always been oriented toward giving people whatever will satisfy their desires. But how can that be justified if it means providing transient goods that foster a pervasive inability to accept and truly profit from reality?

This crisis, which now exists throughout the more advanced countries, presupposes a widespread belief that the pursuit of happiness is universal, that it can succeed in principle, and that for all men and women it is what the American Declaration of Independence calls "an inalienable right." These assumptions have guided humanistic efforts for the last two hundred years, and they reflect enlightened attitudes that are worthy of respect. It would be barbaric to suggest that people ought not to seek happiness. Nevertheless, we should consider the possibility that our current difficulties often result from a sense of meaninglessness to which favored human beings are commonly prone, and more so than those who must struggle for mere survival. If this is true, pursuing and attaining happiness might appear to be paradoxically self-defeating. The happier we are, the harder it becomes to find the meaning in our lives that is essential for remaining truly happy.

Seen from this perspective, our contemporary concern about meaning is peculiar to the modern world. It arises from our relative wealth and freedom in a context of malaise, even despair, about man's ability to achieve lasting and genuine happiness. The experience of Leo Tolstoy, who died in his eighties in 1910, can illuminate our predicament. He anticipated many of our current problems and developed solutions that are often taken for granted nowadays. His belief in passive resistance had a direct effect on Gandhi as well as Martin Luther King. But more relevant here is the emotional turmoil that uprooted his life at the age of fifty. It convinced him that his existence had no meaning and that he should terminate it as quickly as possible.

In his memoir *Confession,* Tolstoy describes the circumstances that preceded his breakdown. In some respects, they resemble the condition of many affluent baby boomers in present-day America who feel a sense of emptiness even though they may have satisfied their own personal ambitions and lived up to the demands of their society. Having succeeded in a profession, and possibly in the raising of a family, they begin to wonder obsessively about the choices they have made. They are perturbed by the possibility that their lives may really be "meaningless." This preoccupation often becomes a painful midlife crisis.

For some fifteen years Tolstoy had enjoyed the warmth and security of family happiness. He had numerous children and a wife who was devoted to him and to his work. He was recognized as the greatest living Russian author. He was wealthy, a member of the nobility, a man whose every word was listened to with great attention throughout the world. But then, as he tells us, he started experiencing "moments of bewilderment, when my life would come to a halt, as if I did not know how to live or what to do."[3] These moments turned into a continuous fixation. For weeks, months, even years he could not free himself of doubts and anxieties that weakened his composure. When he thought of what he had achieved, what he was doing, what his plans for the future involved, he could not help asking himself: What is it for? Where does it lead? What does it matter to me? He could find no answer to such questions and he began to feel that he could not live any longer. "I could breathe, eat, drink, and sleep; indeed, I could not help but breathe, eat, drink, and sleep. But there was no life in me because I had no desires whose satisfaction I would have found reasonable."[4]

Tolstoy also tells us that his prodigious powers of physical and mental exertion remained unabated. He labored in the fields with his peasants as he had before, and he continued to pursue his intellectual labors for eight and ten hours a day without ill effects. But he was wracked by what he calls a "fear of life." He felt that life had no meaning whatsoever. It led to a complete annihilation which he dreaded yet felt he should hasten through suicide. He says he hid a rope for fear that he would hang himself in his room, and he stopped going out to shoot lest he suddenly turn the gun on himself. "I myself did not know what I wanted. I was afraid of life, I struggled to get rid of it, and yet I hoped for something from it."[5]

As a way of alleviating this mental agony, Tolstoy turned to philosophy and science for answers to the questions that tormented him. He soon concluded that science systematically avoids matters related to the meaning of life and that all persuasive arguments in philosophy served to prove that life can have no meaning. Studying the greatest thinkers of the past—he mentions Socrates, Schopenhauer, Solomon (Ecclesiastes), and Buddha—he felt that they merely confirmed his own negative conclusions. They too seemed convinced that life is pointless, that it has no goal beyond itself, that despite the many casual delights that induce us to prolong our existence, we should welcome death as a release from the sheer futility of everything.

Having found nothing in science or philosophy to cure his distress, Tolstoy next asked himself how other people managed, particularly those who were educated like himself and capable of living in the manner to which he was accustomed. He observed that such people generally took one of four ways out of their difficulty. The first defense was simple ignorance about life's lack of meaning. Persons who had not yet reached his own level of sophistication might still have access to this. They appeared to enjoy rudimentary pleasures, but he was sure that he could not learn much from them. The second way out he calls "epicureanism." Assuming that life has no meaning, most cultivated people clung to their privileges and luxuries in order to preserve the gratuitous advantages that had befallen them. Though they knew it was only through good luck that they could savor whatever enjoyments were available, they merely sought further distractions in an attempt to ignore the horrifying truth. Tolstoy tells us that such deceptiveness issued from "moral dullness" and a lack of imagination which was foreign to his nature: "I could not imitate these people, since I did not lack imagination and could not pretend that I did."[6]

The third way of dealing with life's problems that Tolstoy lists is suicide. He calls this the path of "strength and energy," and he says that once a person realizes life is not worth living—as he himself believed at this point—killing oneself is "the most worthy means of escape."[7] The fourth posture was the one that he himself exemplified. He characterizes it as "weakness." Though he was sure that death was preferable to any further life, he somehow endured, hoping without reason that a meaning would become manifest in one fashion or another. Tolstoy remarks that this attitude "was disgusting and painful to me, but I remained in it all the same."[8]

It is remarkable that, in sketching these four modes of response, Tolstoy says nothing about people in his immediate society who were both imaginative and capable of truly enjoying their condition as human beings. He seems to assume that every sensitive person must have been miserable and quivering on the brink of suicide just as he was. Speaking sociologically, we may well insist that this is quite improbable.

In his memoir, Tolstoy says that he now understands why he did not commit suicide. He tells us that he clung to life not just out of weakness, but because he somehow intuited the "invalidity" of his thinking. Instead of depending entirely on his rational faculty, as he had been doing, he began to see that reason is only a partial aspect of one's being. At a deeper level there was a force he calls his "consciousness of life."[9] Intellectuals who relied on a filigree of reason to sustain themselves were not representative of mankind.

Most people, he now believed, avoid despair and find some kind of meaning in existence by retaining frequent contact with their consciousness of life. It was as if ordinary folk, the peasants above all, had an "irrational knowledge" that he and his equals had throttled in themselves. The peasants had a harder life; they suffered from physical deprivation and were denied many of the pleasures that came so easily to more fortunate individuals; yet they had access to a vital sustenance that made it impossible for them to think that life has no meaning. Without much schooling and without systematic thought, they had learned how to live in a manner that eluded him. They acted out of faith rather than reason, and he concluded that only faith comparable to theirs could make life meaningful.

From this, Tolstoy inferred that for him—and in general for anyone who had developed as he had—the only solution consisted in harmonizing his rational nature with some kind of faith that would enable him to go on living. He could not eradicate the habits of reasoning that had accumulated throughout the years and indeed defined his own particular talent. He could not pretend that he was just another peasant who blindly accepts whatever a secular or ecclesiastic authority promulgates. But unless he found a faith that resembled the irrational knowledge so many peasants had, he was sure that he would not attain the strength of life he desperately sought.

Tolstoy says that he came to love poor and simple folk, and that he gradually succeeded in learning how to emulate their attitude toward life. He states that this helped him toward religious feelings he thought he had long outgrown. The peasants' faith in God was fundamentally the same Christian faith that he had imbibed from early childhood. He had turned away from it because his reason rejected its dogmatic superstitions. He had also noticed that priests and others in the church often used religion as an excuse for self-indulgence. Living as the peasants did, he now found that orthodox views no longer seemed repellent. For a while his religious conversion led him to rejoin the Russian Orthodox church, and even to accept dogmas that had previously been most offensive to his reason.

At a later stage Tolstoy once again rebelled against orthodox theology, while still trying to remain a Christian. He reverted to the teachings of the gospels as the unquenchable source for the faith he admired in the peasants. Though he was excommunicated by the church, he thought he had finally discovered the meaning of life. By renouncing the illogical assertions of the dominant religion, he could satisfy his reason; by having faith in a supreme deity who both enacts and ordains a love of mankind, he felt united with the consciousness of life that propelled him forward from moment to moment.

Tolstoy's struggles have been interpreted in different ways. Most biographers see him, in this period of his life, as a Christian reformer who sought to cleanse Christianity of extraneous elements. Some place him in the long line of mystics who trusted their religious experience more than they trusted the institutional proclamations of the church. Nowadays adherents to various sects can find in his pacifist and humanitarian beliefs much that they consider definitive of their religion. On the other hand, Tolstoy was so troubled a human being throughout his life that clinical analyses of his conversion may also be justified.

At least one psychiatrist has argued that Tolstoy was undergoing the kind of severe depression or melancholia that frequently occurs in midlife. Men who have had great successes, who have been as virile and sexually active as Tolstoy was, often feel that life loses all its meaning once their libidinal potency declines.

Like him, they sometimes have a devastating fear of death while also thinking that suicide may be the only solace for their distress. Even if they are able to work out a viable adjustment, as Tolstoy seems to have done, preoccupation with ultimate philosophical questions is in their case largely displacement behavior masking the emotional disturbance that besets them at this stage in life.[10]

As I shall later argue, this interpretation seems too extreme, and overly reductive. It can hardly discredit Tolstoy's belief that his conversion was authentic as well as being crucial for his continued existence. Who is to say that even the most commendable of religious attitudes may not occur in persons who are psychologically diseased? For our purposes, Tolstoy's example is interesting as an early version of what many people in our society experience despite their previous accomplishments, perhaps even because of them. Whether or not Tolstoy's solution is acceptable to us (it is not acceptable to me), his search for meaning can serve as an introduction to the modern world. As he did, we may have lingering doubts about many optimistic tenets that our parents or grandparents found convincing. We too may feel that possibly pessimists are right, or nearer to the truth, when they maintain that life is really just a tragedy.

The seventeenth-century philosopher Thomas Hobbes said that in its "natural condition" the life of man is "solitary, poor, nasty, brutish, and short."[11] Hobbes thought that civilization could remedy many of the limitations in our being, and he himself lived cheerfully into his nineties. Nevertheless, he believed that we best understand human existence when we place it within a context of general adversity. In a similar vein, Francis Bacon's essay "On Adversity" points out the advantages of seeing life in its somber rather than its brighter aspects. As with "needleworks and embroideries," Bacon says, "it is more pleasing to have a lively work upon a sad and solemn ground, than to have a dark and melancholy work upon a lightsome ground."

To approach life as a tragedy in which we all participate may be a wholesome beginning even though it is only a partial perspective. It is often useful to assume a worst-case scenario. The result may not be as "pleasing" as Bacon suggests, but it can possibly have a fortifying effect that helps us to endure in a satisfactory manner. The lives of most men and women have always been difficult—liable to moral, mental, and physical suffering, and either too long (for those who find no point in it) or too short (for those who do). Large numbers of people in the twentieth century have rejected the simplicity and assurance of almost every optimistic dogma. In earlier ages they might have hoped that all human losses would somehow be regained—if not in the physical world, then in another realm that various doctrines described as the ontological basis of our own reality; if not as a good to be experienced in the present, then as a utopian prospect for the future on earth or in heaven or in some mythological combination of the two.

This kind of faith is scarcely intelligible to millions in the world today. For many of us it is not a viable option. We believe, as a matter of scientific fact, that life on this planet is an unusual and possibly unique phenomenon occurring within a cosmic setting that may otherwise be an enormous wasteland. We also believe that the character as well as the continuance of life is ultimately governed by material forces beyond the control of any conscious being. The universe would appear to be nothing but a field of energy. Eventually everything that now exists may totally dissolve, as Prospero says in Shakespeare's *Tempest,* and "leave not a rack behind."

More than any of its predecessors, our generation may therefore feel that life is not only a tragedy but also one that we perform before an empty house. Within the overall experience there can be incidental types of gratification, as there are for actors in a play. Some people find contentment in life by limiting their attention to consummations that satisfy their sensory and emotional needs without greatly taxing their intellect. If they are lucky and have been spared financial pressures while remaining in good health, they may even taste what the Italians call *il dolce far niente* (the sweetness of doing nothing). For many people this version of earthly paradise is all they want, though it is usually reserved for life after retirement.

Others seek, and sometimes find, a period of happiness that differs from mere contentment. In its ability to satisfy a wider range of interests, social as well as personal and active as well as passive, happiness bespeaks a harmony between the separate individual and his or her environment. It includes intervals of pleasure, but is more characteristically a general sense of well-being and efficiency in getting what we want. At moments of great achievement or success, we may also experience that burst of positive feeling for which we use words like "joy" or "ecstasy."

These gratifications are not trivial aspects of the human condition, as pessimists in philosophy have often claimed. Though we shall mainly be concerned with questions about meaning, we need not doubt the importance of contentment, happiness, and joy. But even in their own dimension, these brighter possibilities that everyone desires may amount to something less than one might have expected. Pleasures quickly fade and are hard to recapture; contentment often degenerates into boredom and a bovine weariness with life; permanent happiness is evasive not only because we are easily deluded in our hunger for anything that might make us happy, but also because our quest depends on external circumstances that can cease to cooperate at any moment. Aristotle rightly said: call no man happy while he is still alive.

As for joy, that summit of our affective being idealized by nineteenth-century romanticism as a virtual infusion of divinity, even those who must know the experience best find it to be infrequent and unpredictable. We may think that creative men and women have the greatest access to beauty and to joy. And yet, regardless of what has been achieved, an artist must always face the agonies of each particular art form. These present themselves anew in every work, and they inevitably curtail any momentary joyfulness. Joy may register the completion of what we have done in the past, but it does not guarantee that we shall be able to continue. The geniuses who have so clearly earned the reward of joy or ecstasy are precisely the ones who suffer most acutely from the constant struggles that creativity involves. Life is not a path of determinate length and direction such that creative individuals who have traveled furthest can feel that they are closer to some absolute and all-resolving goal. The past cannot be relived, and the future is never fully knowable until it becomes the present. The more that human beings accomplish, the more they generally realize how little they have done.

Still we may feel that the great achievers are people who have the most meaningful and significant existence. Surely they are best equipped to show us what life can yield. Even if life is tragic, do they not reveal how it can be turned into a work of art—not a comedy, perhaps, or even a melodrama that has a happy ending, but a tragedy that plumbs the depths? Tragedies impose mythic and aesthetic coordinates upon some particular reality chosen for imaginative re-creation. Is it too much to hope that human beings can deal with all of life that way?

Few of our major philosophers in the twentieth century have had much to say about these questions. Particularly in the traditions that have dominated philosophy in the English-speaking countries, problems concerning the meaning of life were largely ignored until recent years. In one place, however, Ludwig Wittgenstein makes some brief remarks that are worth considering. After asserting that "the meaning of life, i.e. the meaning of the world, we can call God," he offers the following reflections:

> Dostoievsky is right when he says that the man who is happy is fulfilling the purpose of existence.
>
> Or again we could say that the man is fulfilling the purpose of existence who no longer needs to have any purpose except to live. That is to say, who is content.
>
> The solution of the problem of life is to be seen in the disappearance of this problem. . . .

> But is it possible for one so to live that life stops being problematic? That one is *living* in eternity and not in time?
>
> Isn't this the reason why men to whom the meaning of life had become clear after long doubting could not say what this meaning consisted in?[12]

Wittgenstein intimates that those who know the meaning of life may reveal it in how they live, although they find themselves unable to analyze its components. This is surely true, since experience—particularly affirmative and satisfying experience—does not always lend itself to detailed examination. To say, however, that "the solution" to the problem of life involves its disappearance leaves open the possibility of a definite resolution that might someday enable philosophers to discard this problem entirely. Wittgenstein does wonder whether one could ever live in such a way that life would stop being problematic, but he seems to think that this can occur for those who are happy or content or no longer depend on "any purpose except to live."

But all of this requires much more discussion than Wittgenstein provides. Not only do we need greater clarification about the meaning of concepts such as "purpose" or "living in eternity," but we must also decide what kind of "problem" the problem of life can possibly be. Philosophical problems are not always solvable. How do we determine whether or not problems about the meaning of life can be resolved? Even if they cease to trouble us, can we know that we have found a solution? Is it not possible that we have merely slipped into a manner of living that sedates our probing sensibilities?

Above all, we must ask ourselves whether we understand what the original problem was. Do we really know what we are requesting when we ask for a meaning of life and wonder whether or not it is inherently tragic? Possibly the greatest difficulty consists not in finding a solution but in elucidating the meaning of our questions. When Gertrude Stein was dying, her friend Alice B. Toklas is reported to have said, "Gertrude, Gertrude, what is the answer?" Miss Stein replied: "Alice, Alice, what is the question?"

As another illustration, consider a passage in *The Hitchhiker's Guide to the Galaxy* by Douglas Adams. The computer named Deep Thought announces that he has finally determined the meaning of life and that, by his calculation, the answer to the great question is forty-two. The humanoids who have been eagerly awaiting his findings, generation after generation for seven and a half million years, are thunderstruck. They had expected a different kind of answer to the "Ultimate Question of Life, the Universe and Everything." But Deep Thought explains that their problem arises from their confusion about the question. "So once you do know what the question is," he says, "you'll know what the answer means."[13]

It should be noted that Deep Thought has nothing else to say about the answer. He only claims that knowing the question will enable us to know what the answer means. This seems to me like the beginning of wisdom about the nature of philosophy. If we expect our inquiry to provide definitive and satisfying solutions, we are likely to be disappointed. Each of its answers, assuming they are fertile and not stillborn in themselves, will always generate new problems that must also be resolved. Though philosophy can stimulate the imagination and lead to intellectual advances, its greatest benefit consists in encouraging us to clarify our intuitions. We all know what reality is, Socrates said, because we are all equally immersed in it. But most of us have confused ideas about ourselves and about the world. Through philosophy, however, we may fabricate what I. A. Richards called "speculative instruments." These can help us to straighten out our thinking.

Plato and other philosophers were less cautious than Socrates, and perhaps philosophy can do more than merely give clues about how to make our ideas clear. Nevertheless, that is where we must start this kind of exploration. Before we can try to look for solutions, we must first determine which are the intelligible problems. Even if we say, as one troubled youth did, "To be or not to be: that is the question," we need to understand the nature of all such questioning.

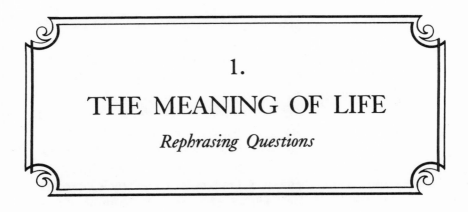

1.

THE MEANING OF LIFE

Rephrasing Questions

To a large extent, questions about the meaning of life emanate from the body of continuous investigation that constitutes the history of philosophy. And within that history, one finds an ambivalence that also pervades the mentality of ordinary people who have thought about this cluster of basic problems. We long to know the secrets of the universe and what it means, in itself, apart from human interests. At the same time, however, we seek a meaningful way to live our lives, whether or not we can find a separate meaning in the cosmos.

These two types of questions, which have usually been lumped together by philosophers as well as laymen, are really very different. Even the twentieth-century idea that life is "absurd" becomes more manageable once we recognize this difference. Having encountered difficulties in our search for a meaning of life as a whole, we may nevertheless hope to answer questions about the nature of a meaningful life. Is it something we find or something we create? How is it dependent on purposes, values, ideals? How is it related to happiness, and does it give us assurance that men and women can face up to their predicament as finite creatures? In working at these issues, we may be able to construct an outlook that reveals a life worth living even if we remain partly pessimistic about human existence.

As a prelude, it may be useful to review the speculations of three nineteenth-century philosophers who foresaw many of the problems that will follow us into the twenty-first century. Despite their dialectical differences, Hegel, Schopenhauer, and Nietzsche make a unity within themselves. On points of detail their views are often remarkably similar. Each was convinced that nothing of life, and certainly no human being, can long survive in itself. They hold out little hope for personal immortality or the escape from death that Western religions promised.

In other ways, of course, their philosophies differ greatly. Unlike the two later thinkers, Hegel is an optimist and an idealist insofar as he believes that reality is meaningful as a totality. Though individuals are annihilated once they have played their tiny role, they all contribute to the ongoing development of the cosmos. They do so by searching for value and self-awareness. Hegel identifies this quest, which he considers fundamental in the universe, as a yearning for moral or spiritual goals. This striving explains the material order of things as well as the struggles of conscious beings. Hegel believes that all reality moves toward total union with absolute spirit. Such union is also *re*union since it entails a return to primordial oneness, though each new particularity undergoes a kind of separation merely in existing as itself.

If Hegel is right, life may well be called a tragedy for everything that participates in it. It is tragic for each entity perceived as a being whose organic drives and cherished values will be defeated sooner or later. But in contributing to the search for greater spirituality, which motivates their behavior whether or not they realize it, all things have a permanent place within the cosmic performance. Their tragic existence contains an inherent creativity that reveals the progressive attainment of ever-increasing meaning, goodness, and beauty.

Since Hegel assures us that these ideal determinants are objectively present in the world, we might well conclude that life is not really tragic. Taken as a whole it would all seem to be an ontological comedy, an enterprise that justifies our deepest hopes. It is nevertheless a tragedy for the participants, since they survive their brief appearance only in having a meager effect upon the ineluctable flow that quickly engulfs them. One might therefore say that Hegel sees life as a tragi-comedy: tragic for those who perform in it but infinitely rewarding for the evolving and impersonal spirituality that marches toward fulfillment throughout this process.

In its own sophisticated manner, the Hegelian comedy of life resembles the divine comedy that Dante portrays. In the *Paradiso* the blessed spirits are not entities of the sort they were on earth. In effect they have been annihilated, as Hegel would also say, for now they have no being apart from God. They radiate his luminous goodness, from which they are no longer separated. But in their unity with God, are they really persons? Are they not merely resplendent expressions of the divine presence? Hegel seems to think so. He duplicates Dante's vision except that he sees the final beatitude as residual or latent in each moment, as operative in existence at all times. For him this pervasive spirituality shows forth the meaning of life and explains the being of anything that occurs.

Schopenhauer, who was Hegel's contemporary, opposes his philosophy and condemns it as hideous wish-fulfillment. He denies that there is any benign principle in the cosmos that can mitigate or justify the suffering one observes. Schopenhauer thinks that all life must be tragic, since every event is governed by laws of nature that have nothing in them that could be considered ideal. The fundamental principle existing in the universe is dynamic, material, brutal, non-purposive, and more or less without direction. Schopenhauer calls this principle "the will" since we feel it most directly in our volitional impulses.

Rejecting Hegel's faith in underlying spiritual goals, Schopenhauer argues that existence is simply a reservoir of energy spewing out in no meaningful pattern—like explosions in an atom or a distant galaxy. Nature germinates individual manifestations of itself but then reamalgamates them without a trace, everything that exists belonging to an enormous recycling process. The totality keeps changing but without any discernible rationale. In living things, only an instinct for self-preservation is constant. At times, Schopenhauer refers to the will as "the will to live." Nothing else could count as an explanation of life.

Schopenhauer believes that animate existence is more often a form of suffering than of happiness or pleasure. Life on earth is a calamity whose only cure is death. But though he is pessimistic in this respect, he also thinks that knowledge of his philosophy will help us live agreeable and rewarding lives. Once people understand that the metaphysical will to which they are subject is unconcerned about their welfare, they can adapt to this fatality in constructive and satisfying ways. They cannot defeat the will and they must reconcile themselves to being parts of a recycling process. But also they can show their revulsion at the mindless cruelty of existence and attain essential dignity in their reaction to it.

Schopenhauer articulates a system of meaningful responses to the tragedy of life, and he outlines a moral philosophy based on feeling compassion for the suffering of everything that lives. The sense of dignity, which he posits as the source of any possible salvation, results from various attitudes or attainments that he recommends: philosophical awareness provided by his metaphysics; scientific and technological knowledge that enables us to re-direct the will despite our subjugation to it; contemplation of the quasi-Platonic forms through which, he thinks, being always shows itself; creativity and aesthetic delight that employs such contemplation in the making and enjoying of works of art; and in general, renunciation of bodily interests that merely perpetuate the will's imperious appetite.

In offering liberation of this sort, Schopenhauer's philosophy is neither gloomy nor wholly defeatist. He himself seems to have had a comfortable existence, writing as he wished, playing his flute for pleasure, and taking walks with his little dog. One can live a good or at least bearable life, he thought, but only after one has stared the horrors of reality in the face and withdrawn allegiance from the metaphysical force that produces them. Though we cannot defeat the will, we can and should say no to it. This was what Ivan Karamazov in Dostoyevsky's novel would later call giving back the ticket to the universe. Generations of thinkers who were influenced by Schopenhauer—for instance, Freud—inherited a comparable attitude of nay-saying. But it was this part of Schopenhauer's doctrine that Friedrich Nietzsche found most unacceptable as his own ideas matured.

Nietzsche agrees that the will is devoid of meaning, that it is vicious and the cause of more suffering than happiness, that there are no gods to whom we can appeal, and that the only paths of salvation are those that lead to philosophy, science, art, and the kind of morality that emerges from such pursuits. What Nietzsche could not stomach was the element of negativity in Schopenhauer's philosophy. He himself had, both mentally and physically, a more delicate constitution than Schopenhauer, and he felt that saying no to the universe would prevent one from being able to live productively.

As an alternative to nay-saying, Nietzsche recommends *amor fati* (love of destiny, or things as they really are). This attitude entails a heroic and healthy-minded acceptance of reality *even though* it is horrible and wholly destructive to everything that participates in it. For Nietzsche this love of the hateful cosmos is the highest attainment humanity can reach: "My formula for greatness in a human being is *amor fati:* that one wants nothing to be different, not forward, not backward, not in all eternity. Not merely bear what is necessary, still less conceal it—all idealism is mendaciousness in the face of what is necessary—but *love* it."[1]

Nietzsche synthesizes the philosophies of Hegel and Schopenhauer. For Hegel, existence—harsh and horrid as it often is—could only be the means by which spirit joyfully progressed. Though life was a tragedy for everything that lives, it would eventually provide a happy resolution for the totality of being. Nietzsche is convinced that this totality must be meaningless, devoid of spirit, as Schopenhauer had said. And yet he thinks participants in life might create—through amor fati—a heroic comedy by courageously accepting it all despite the fact that everything is ultimately tragic and even vile. In this way, Nietzsche feels, one might see life realistically without undermining the pursuit of noble ideals that Hegel considered paramount.

There is much in Nietzsche's philosophy that speaks to people of the twentieth century. But his ideas about amor fati and the meaning of life are unconvincing to me. If Schopenhauer was accurate in depicting the horror of all existence, as Nietzsche believed, why should one *accept* reality rather than reject it as much as possible? Why should we identify with the aggressor, so to speak, instead of hating our subjection to the will? Would it not be more honest to cry out in terror—as in the famous painting of *The Shriek* by Edvard Munch—or at least to recognize coolly that there must always remain a basic discontinuity between our values and the world in which they make their freakish and unrepresentative appearance?

Nietzsche may have thought that love is so essential that no one, not even a liberated pessimist like Schopenhauer, could enjoy a single moment of existence unless he contrived to love reality despite its utter worthlessness. He may also have felt that only one who loves the world while knowing how bad it is can find the fortitude needed to improve it through moral conduct. But if the Nietzschean philosopher-saint loves everything that exists, how can he reject the bad elements? The worst parts of existence also belong to reality, and he has determined to love and therefore to accept it all completely. Nietzsche's synthesis of Schopenhauer and Hegel is, at best, very problematic.[2]

Hegel's optimism may seem ridiculous to us in view of its unswerving certitude about the goodness of the universe, but it alerts us to the importance of ideals and to the human capacity for self-fulfillment in the act of pursuing them. Hegel's greatest strength consists in his recognition that human beings can and do enjoy life by striving for spiritual goals. Consummation of this sort presupposes an attunement to nature and the world in which we live. Hegel understood that we could not have the ends, the interests, and the values that define our being unless we believed that reality sustains us in some way. Schopenhauer's philosophy is weak precisely at this point, though it is clear-sighted about the material context in which human idealization occurs. Combining the insights of Hegel and Schopenhauer, we need not recommend a love of all the terrible things that happen in reality—as Nietzsche's notion of amor fati requires—but we may be able to develop a view of the world that is realistic and yet sensitive to the possibility of meaning. Nietzsche is to be revered for having shown us, with greater power than anyone else, how ghastly human experience will be in the coming years unless our philosophers succeed in working out the details of a viable synthesis.

❊

But what exactly is involved in the problems we are exploring? What is one saying when one asks for the meaning of life? People who raise this question usually want to know about more than life alone. They want to know where existence "comes from." They want to know the why of it: why we are "here," and why anything—or rather everything—should be as it is.[3] To the scrupulous philosopher as well as the plain-speaking skeptic on the street, such use of language must occasion puzzlement. What can "meaning" signify in this context? Out of all the many types of linguistic usage that cluster about this term, two senses of the word "meaning" seem to me especially relevant. One of them is cognitive; the other is valuational.

When we use "meaning" in its cognitive sense, we are looking for some kind of explanation, some clarification about an occurrence or event. We hope to find out why something has the properties it has. We want to gain insight into an existing or possible state of affairs. We wish to learn about its consequences, its implications for further observation. This usage applies to the denoting of an actuality as well as to the connotative function of a word. When we say "What does it mean if water fails to boil at 212 degrees Fahrenheit?" we seek a cognitive type of meaning. The same is true when we ask for the meaning of the term "Fahren-heit."

On the other hand, we often use the word "meaning" in relation to personal feelings and emotional significance. It then reveals and sometimes declares our highest values. It manifests ideals that we cherish and pursue, that guide our behavior and provide the norms by which we live. "Friendship means a great deal to that man; when his friends have need of him, money means nothing at all." This way of using words like "means" or "meaning" is easily combined with the first kind of usage. In saying that a mother's attitude toward her child reveals the meaning of love, we are suggesting that her response exemplifies a value system that may well be studied for its cognitive import.

People who search for "the meaning of life" are trying to articulate analogous questions about the world. They want to know what would enable us to understand the diverse and frequently bizarre phenomena that constitute reality. But also they wonder whether things can be as they are because of some benign intention of a quasi-human sort that pervades the universe. Theories about a deity who has created everything are often secondary to this concern. Ideas about God's essence—whether he is infinitely wise or good or powerful—pertain to mainly technical problems in theology. To argue about the Supreme Being's attributes is to engage in an exercise that probably has minor importance for most people. William James was quite right when he claimed that the "cash value" of such deliberations resides in our primordial need to reassure ourselves about an ultimate good will in the cosmos, a basic friendliness toward us and what we value, a final haven or support for our ideals and aspirations.

James thought that the "need of an eternal moral order is one of the deepest needs of our breast."[4] Whether this is true of everyone, and whether or not the need is satisfiable, it helps explain our search for meaning in both senses of the term and regardless of specific religious belief. We know what it is to pursue ideals that express human values and elicit relevant emotional responses. The crucial question for most people is whether anything of the sort is justified by objective conditions in the universe. We may be willing to remain ignorant about the chances of our own immortality, and even about the ultimate fate of whatever we consider to be good. We mainly want to be assured that a controlling power exists in terms of which all things could be explained—if only we had intellects capable of understanding its nature—and that it is purposeful in some manner we might recognize as having consummate value.

❄

By introducing the idea of purpose, we have taken an important step. Life often includes purposes that organize our actions in fixed and sometimes predictable patterns. "Why did the chicken cross the road?" We are expected to find the answer witty because the question has led us to anticipate a motive more interesting than wanting merely to reach the other side. That kind of purpose we take for granted. Life is filled with many like it. But is there one or even several purposes *of* life, over and above the purposes *in* life?

In earlier generations some philosophers believed that the purpose of life is the progressive advancement of the most highly organized species. Others claimed it is just the continuance of life itself. Nowadays one might be tempted to argue that the purpose of life is the replication of DNA. But to each of these replies, we can ask: What is the purpose of *that?* If we say that the final end has no purpose, since it simply *is,* we have concluded that ultimately there is no purpose of life. There would be purposefulness in life, most notably in human life, but no all-embracing purpose for life or being as a whole.

Different as they are, these accounts would seem to share a similar conception of what a purpose is. But that term also needs clarification. There are two primary senses of the word that have been used in Western philosophy. One, which may be considered "idealist," derives from Plato; the other we may call "pragmatic." The idealist sense is best exemplified by Plato's description of creation in the *Timaeus*. He there portrays the world as having been created by a demiurge or Grand Artificer who contemplates the realm of forms and then imposes them, as best he can, upon brute matter. Plato thinks of the forms as eternal possibilities; and he claims that since the Creator is good, he "desired that all things should be good and nothing bad, so far as this was attainable."[5]

Plato formulates this model in order to show how the world may be seen as purposeful. He assumes that the creative agency has in mind not only what is good but also what is best. The Platonic forms are hierarchical, with the Good presiding over all other possibilities as the highest and most desirable object. This doctrine is rationalistic inasmuch as Plato maintains that contemplation employs abstract reason that takes the inquisitive soul beyond the sensory world. In the *Republic,* and elsewhere, he argues that only deductive reason—as in mathematics, logic, and metaphysical intuition—puts us in contact with reality. Only through deductive reason can we envision the ultimate form, which he sometimes calls the Beautiful as well as the Good.

In effect, Plato is saying not only that the world itself is purposeful, but also that activities within the world become more fully purposeful by employing reason and contemplation to realize the best that is attainable. The implications of this approach can be illustrated by touching on a problem in aesthetics. Philosophers have often wondered what is involved in making art. In Plato's view, artistic creativity imitates the action of the demiurge. According to Plato, painters, poets, composers, etc., contemplate a realm of possible forms to which they have access through their powers of abstract reason within the confines of their individual talent. They then impose these forms upon the materials of their art in the hope of achieving a predeterminate good. This good serves as a goal that guides the aesthetic process from its beginnings. Only by recognizing that his initial intuition shows forth reality and the meaning of life, can the artist—or anyone else—pursue the purposes ingredient in human creativity.

Much of Plato's philosophy is magnificent. But there are many difficulties in the conception he offers. They become especially apparent when we remember that in ordinary life, and even (some would say preeminently) in moments of great inspiration, purpose-fulness does not lend itself to any such analysis. The second approach, which I call "pragmatic," emphasizes the discrepancy between purposive behavior and reliance upon abstract reason of the sort that Plato advocates. Instead of depicting human beings as godlike entities who contemplate eternal possibilities, the prag-matic approach encourages us to study what happens when intelligent animals engage in behavior that we would deem pur-posive.

Think of a dog, let us say a relatively inexperienced puppy, that has not eaten for some time and presumably feels hunger. Imagine that it can see a bowl of food on the other side of a long chain fence with barbed wire on top. What are the likely events that could reveal the nature of purposive behavior? The dog might leap forward, only to be stopped by the fence. He might try to climb over or dig under it. There may be other unsuccessful experiments. Finally he gets the "idea" or "insight" (both of which I put in quotes because these are phenomena about which we know little or nothing) that leads him to run around the end of the fence. He then eats the food, lies down, and remains quiescent until some later desire stirs him into further activity.

The pragmatic conception interprets purposefulness as part of a process that satisfies organic needs. Purpose consists in appetitive striving that is finally eliminated by the attaining of consummatory goals. During the appetitive phase, the purposive animal undergoes a pattern of trial and error until it manages to get what it wants. Having got it, the animal rests. Its purposefulness is not a function of abstract reason or the contemplation of Platonic forms. It is only the doing of what is necessary to satisfy desires in a systematic, orderly, and therefore "sensible" fashion that happens to work in a given environment.

In books such as *How We Think* and *Logic: The Theory of Inquiry,* John Dewey develops the pragmatic view in great detail and shows its relation to what we normally mean by intelligence. In *Art as Experience* Dewey counters the Platonic approach to creativity by insisting that the ends an artist pursues throughout the making of his object cannot be separated from the means that he employs. Far from being the intuition of a formal and inherently perfect possibility that might have served as a prior goal, artistic effort is a coordinated succession of maneuvers motivated by needs and desires. The process terminates once an acceptable level of relevant satisfaction has been achieved by the artist. His behavior includes appetitive and consummatory phases comparable to what the hungry dog experienced, though far more complex and certainly more conceptual.

Each of these two approaches has its admirers and its critics. We need not adjudicate between them, or even determine whether they may be harmonized in a synthesis that reconciles their differences. The first one needs to overcome skepticism about the faculty of abstract reason that it invokes as an aprioristic attunement to ultimate reality. The second one must justify its claim that even the most elevated of human activities—in art, in ethical conduct, in religion—is based upon motivation similar to what occurs in animal behavior directed toward the satisfaction of organic needs. Of more immediate importance is the possibility that neither view of human purpose and its sources elucidates a meaning of life. Each may only make sense as an account of purposefulness *in* life. Examples of appetitive behavior and abstract reasoning abound. They are readily observed, though philosophers differ greatly in their theorizing about them. But what are we to say about extrapolations to the entire universe?

❋

If we follow Dewey, we are likely to end up with a materialism that sees the cosmos as a field of contending forces in which purpose exists only to the extent that conscious creatures strive to gratify their own interests. If we follow Plato, we ascribe to some divinity or universal being a concern for higher values that humanity may pursue in an attempt to rise above its mundane condition.

In various ways, philosophers have tried to undermine suggestions that there might be this kind of superior purpose. For instance, if we said that a demiurge or a God of the Judaeo-Christian variety created the world in order to bring about as much goodness as possible, would we not be involving ourselves in an infinite regress? For we should have to ask whether God's purposiveness was itself occasioned by a prior purpose. It is not self-evident that a Supreme Creator must want to maximize goodness. If that desire is ascribed to his "essence," we might still wonder whether such an essence manifests some further, more ultimate purposefulness. We may have made an advance in seeking for the meaning of life, but the quest will have shown itself to be endless.[6] Nor will we have made much progress if, in the pragmatic mode, we suggest that everything seeks its own completion as if it were all part of a cosmic organism trying to satisfy its natural appetites. For then, too, we awaken questions about the purposefulness of that animate totality.

Some philosophers argue that if there were indeed a comprehensive purpose of life, that alone would deprive us of traits human beings have always valued and sought to preserve. We pride ourselves on being free and autonomous, capable of heroic achievements when we live in accordance with our ideals. If, however, we are constituents of a cosmos that has been designed to fulfill a purpose, our status does not differ greatly from that of a tool or instrument fashioned with a predetermined end in mind. The form and use of a kitchen utensil is defined by the function it was designed to carry out. If humanity, or life in general, was created to serve a purpose beyond itself, our being would be analogous to that of a manufactured artifact. There seems to be little in this state of affairs to justify the exultation that religious people sometimes feel in thinking that God's plan reveals the purpose and the meaning of all reality.[7]

Within the linguistic orientation that has characterized much of contemporary philosophy, queries about life's purpose are often rejected in a more radical manner. We are encouraged to believe that such language may really be nonsensical. In order to have meaning, our remarks must have a logical form that is syntactically and semantically adequate for expressing a meaningful question.

We assume that a sentence such as "What is the purpose of life?" makes sense because it has the same grammatical form as sentences like "What is the purpose of pre-heating the oven?" This question is intelligible and has relevance to an observable purpose in life. But though the first utterance has a similar *grammatical* structure, there is no assurance that it has any meaning whatsoever.

To see how we might be fooled in this respect, compare the following sentences: "When it is 5 p.m. in New York, what time is it in Los Angeles?"; "When it is 5 p.m. in New York, what time is it on the sun?" Since clock-time is defined in terms of the angle at which the sun's rays strike some location on the earth, the second of these sentences is nonsense. Whatever its pretensions, a question about time on the sun is internally inconsistent. It has no coherent logical form, and is therefore not really a question. To take it seriously is to waste one's energy. Should we not say the same about putative questions about the purpose of life? Despite the beguiling arrangement of their grammar, are they not equally nonsensical?

This linguistic argument seems very powerful to me. We have often observed purposes in the world, and we know what someone asks when he raises questions about a particular pattern of behavior. But though we are immersed in the cosmos, it is not clear that we can have experience of the cosmos as a whole. We cannot stand back and regard the universe in its totality, as we might do with one or another of its parts. We have no awareness of a second universe with which to compare our own. For the most part, our language is a function of what we can experience or imagine on the basis of experience. We participate in life; we experience it directly; and that can give us knowledge of the purposes within it. But if these purposes must be grounded in a larger purpose that underlies the entire universe, nothing that we try to say or ask about the meaning of it all may really make sense.

And yet, questions about the purpose or meaning of life are not necessarily self-contradictory, or inconsistent, like questions about time on the sun. They are certainly vague, and must always involve perilous extensions beyond ordinary experience. They must be treated as metaphoric and symbolic rather than literal or factual. But this alone does not deprive them of intelligibility. It merely puts them in a category that is closer to poetry than to science. This need not be a serious impediment. Our linguistic capabilities are infinitely diverse. Though there may be good reasons for renouncing the quest for a meaning of life, we should not dismiss such interests merely because they require a language that is hard to understand.[8]

❊

If our concern about the meaning of everything cannot be rejected in advance, on purely linguistic grounds, theories about what that meaning might be are worth studying. Traditional Western religions trace it to an entity they call *super*natural because it exists apart from space, time, and all other coordinates of nature. This Being has a plan in accordance with which he (in the usual ascription of gender) has created the universe. Moreover, he has given everything the ability to live in accordance with his design. The cosmic plan, together with this innate capacity, provides an underlying purpose such that once we understand it we perceive the meaning of life. Millions of people have accepted that account as persuasive and reassuring, a fount of spiritual sustenance throughout their lives. How can this system of beliefs be rejected as nonsensical or logically inadequate?

To begin with, one would want to know what is meant by a universal "plan." Is it similar to the blueprint that an architect draws up before building a house? God, or whatever we call the supernatural being that establishes the purpose of life, presumably creates the universe in an attempt to carry out his prior design. All of nature strives to accomplish his intention, and we may liken this to construction workers following the architect's blueprint. But to talk in this way is to assume that one can refer to an intentionality *outside* of time and space comparable to what occurs within. That is the basic flaw in the analogy.

What can it mean to assert that something is "outside" of time and space? We might argue that numbers exist apart from time and space; and if someone were to claim that for all eternity $2 + 2 = 4$, we would know what is being said. But we would never suggest that numbers have the same properties as things *in* time and space. We do not say that numbers come into or go out of existence. We may even deny that they exist at all. We certainly do not believe that their relationships reveal a "purpose." In talking about a purposive being whose creativity gives value and a goal to all existence, it is as if Western religions confused abstract entities, such as numbers, with things in time and space. It is not a question of determining whether we can fathom the cosmic plan, or prove that a cosmic-planner exists, or manage to fulfill his purposive program. It is a question of knowing whether our mind is able to formulate these notions with any degree of clarity.

One's motive for seeking a meaning of life is quite evident. The problems of living would be greatly simplified if everything could be shown to make sense in terms of a goal toward which it was or ought to be tending. Even if this goal was inescapable or predetermined, we could still acquiesce and happily perform whatever actions are required. Of course we might also conclude that since all decisions must somehow follow the ineluctable order of things, it does not matter what we choose. Some might find this liberating, others might deem it injurious to their sense of freedom; but everyone could feel that an objective explanation has been discovered. Whatever the emotional response, the power of the human mind would at least have been established. Our species would have proved its ability to solve the greatest of all puzzles.

In the history of ideas, many great philosophers (beginning with Plato and Aristotle) have defended the belief in an Ultimate Being or Highest Good that provides objective ends each thing or person must pursue in order to fulfill itself. In theology equally great thinkers, such as Aquinas, have tried to codify our intuitions about the supernatural. This is not the place to engage them in debate. Instead I suggest, as others have in the last two hundred years, that such concepts issue from our human attempt to magnify and idealize what is merely natural. Far from transcending nature, we glorify the aspects that matter to us. In the process we both aggrandize our imagination and inflate our own experience.

Human beings seek a prior meaning in everything as a defense against doubts about the importance of anything, including man's existence. Though we see people expend a great deal of energy on matters of personal concern, we are also aware of human limitations. We know that we are mortal, living for fairly short periods, and that nothing we may do or feel can have a major influence upon the universe. There appears to be a disproportion between the seriousness with which men and women approach their multiple interests and the relative insignificance of these interests within the cosmos as a whole. If, however, the world itself pursues a goal toward which we all contribute, this basic disproportion would be resolved. What matters to us surely does matter if the course of reality includes it within some truly objective design. To affirm that there is a supreme meaning of life is to give the intellect an opportunity to escape the disquieting conclusion that *nothing* people do can possibly have more than slight importance.

The belief that human purposiveness has no real significance belongs to the philosophical view called "nihilism." This, in turn, is related to the idea that our existence is inherently "absurd." The beginnings of absurdist thought may be traced to David Hume. He argues that there is no knowable true statement from which one can deduce the existence of anything (except in a tautologous fashion). In other words, as far as we can tell, everything that is exists for no necessary reason. Hume reached this conclusion because he thought that causality is always ascribed to events that occur in a regular but ultimately arbitrary fashion. Every existing entity is just a *surd*—its occurrence is not necessitated by anything else even though it appears in a constant sequence with events that precede or follow it.

From this, one may conclude that there is no meaning of life, only a pervasive complex of basically inexplicable structures.

Objects and events just happen to be as they are. There is no inherent reason for them to be or not to be, even though our minds become habituated to their usual appearance. They are not planned in any objective sense, and their existence cannot be explained by reference to a prior being.

In books such as *Nausea* and *Being and Nothingness,* Jean-Paul Sartre uses Hume's idea to express the nature of all factuality. Nothing that exists, he says, has any ontological necessity requiring it to be; and therefore its existence can never be "justified" or shown to be required for the existence of anything else. That is what Sartre means when he postulates the "contingency" of everything human, and of being in general. Since I am contingent, nothing fundamental in the world would be different if I did not exist. There may be interesting existential consequences of my never having been—for instance, my children would never have existed—but such considerations are irrelevant, since my children cannot be justified either. They exist, if they happen to do so, only as haphazard occurrences and not as the exemplars of an ultimate meaning in the universe.

In the writings of Albert Camus similar ideas about the absurdity of life are extended in a way that is especially pertinent to our discussion. Camus focuses upon the discrepancy between man's "longing for happiness and for reason" and his inevitable awareness that there is nothing in the universe to satisfy this longing except in a meager or ephemeral manner. The cosmos does not care about human welfare. Camus remarks that "the absurd is born of this confrontation between the human need and the unreasonable silence of the world."[9] It is as if the life of every human being, from beginning to end, was simply a ridiculous rearranging of the chairs in the dining room of the *Titanic* after it has hit the iceberg. For us the iceberg is our finitude, our mortality, and the absurdity of our life lies in our inability either to forgo our customary strivings or to ignore the fact that reality shows no interest in dignifying and preserving them.

Developing a related theory of the absurd, Thomas Nagel says it results from an opposition between what he calls man's "self-consciousness" and his "self-transcendence." He means that the seriousness with which human beings live their lives conflicts with their capacity to transcend this attitude by seeing themselves as "arbitrary, idiosyncratic, highly specific occupants of the world, one of countless possible forms of life."[10] The absurd arises from a discrepancy between our inclination to take our values seriously, as if they were really important, and our awareness that nothing in the universe justifies their existence. Like Camus, Nagel concludes that ultimately and objectively there is no basis for believing that anything matters.

In proposing their conceptions of absurdity, these philosophers assume a contradiction, or at least a split, between man and the world, and also between two aspects of human nature. Man is portrayed as inherently divided between his purposive desire to pursue whatever goals he values and his being as a self-transcending spectator who recognizes that the world is wholly unresponsive either to him or to his values. The world does not seem to mind destroying, sooner or later, everything man cares about. His sense of absurdity is therefore a painful counterpart to the intellect's demonstration of human pretentiousness.

Is this line of reasoning really cogent? For one thing, it is hard to imagine where the "serious" side of man could have come from if there is nothing to maintain it. Thinkers like Sartre and Martin Heidegger defend the absurdist approach by arguing that human life is predicated upon nothingness inasmuch as nothing has value or meaning until man brings these categories into existence. Strictly speaking, that is not correct, as these writers also perceive on occasion. For everything a sentient being wants will be valuable and meaningful to it, to some extent at least. This holds for all creatures that are able to have desires, even if it is true that only human beings can formulate the *concept* of value or meaning. In any event, it does not follow that values issue out of nothing or that the world does not sustain them.

What is meaningful to a human being originates in the vital necessities of the human condition, and that results from nature as it exists in us. It would indeed be absurd to expect inanimate objects or beings in some remote galaxy to share our own system of values. Human beings belong to nature in ways that are defined by the evolution of life on this particular planet. The seriousness of man does not *contradict* the world but rather springs from it as a new but wholly compatible expression of phenomena that may or may not occur elsewhere.

To assert that human interests are always pretentious or disproportionate, and therefore absurd, is to use a metaphor that does not apply. Rearranging the chairs on the *Titanic* is absurd because one then acts as if there is reason to prepare the dining room for passengers who will notice the placement of furniture, whereas everyone has already begun to scurry for the lifeboats. It is likewise absurd—to use one of Camus' examples—for an individual armed with nothing but a sword to attack machine guns, since the man who makes the attempt must know (as we do) that it cannot succeed. But one who tries to live a meaningful life does not manifest a similar confusion. He is not necessarily assuming that his values matter to the universe at large. He may act as he does with full recognition of the context in which he acts. Though the meaningfulness of his existence may be shortlived or highly circumscribed, that need not doom his efforts to futility. To say that one's interests are absurd would be to claim that here, as in the case of the *Titanic* or the solitary swordsman, one's knowledge about reality inevitably contradicts the gamut of beliefs implied by one's behavior. That claim seems to me wholly unwarranted. What could be the content of these damaging beliefs? An assumption that one's values are preordained or that one's life will go on forever? Or that it may consist of unalloyed pleasure, infinite achievement, increasing fervor, and continuous onward momentum? Sometimes people do act as if this is what they believe. But even so, the question remains: Does the pursuit of meaning *presuppose* such ideas? There is no reason to think that it does.

Since the absurdist philosophers assert that values issue from nothing and that the world therefore provides no ground for meaning, it seems strange from the very outset that they should consider man's condition to be inherently absurd. For that implies there is some other way for human beings to exist, though they absurdly fail to do so. But if there is no such alternative, as these philosophers insist, the concept of absurdity cannot be relevant to actual existence. I am willing to agree that men and women often yearn for unattainable goals, and that this sort of attitude may well be called absurd. But why should *all* human striving be characterized that way?

The absurdist philosophers observe, or assume, that the universe has no overarching purpose and, apparently, no concern for human welfare. Since people nevertheless continue to pursue cherished goals, the philosophers see a contradiction between the purposefulness in man's struggle for life and the general purposelessness of the cosmos. This is what they consider the source of human absurdity. I have been arguing that no contradiction, and therefore no absurdity, can be derived from the stated facts. If someone does think that his values matter to some ultimate being, while deep down he knows this cannot be true, his attitude reveals an obvious inconsistency that may justify calling it absurd. But the absurdists are unable to show that our pursuit of goals must always involve this type of contradiction. On the contrary, they themselves usually exhort us to live in a purposive manner that will be free of delusive hopes about corroboration from the universe. They call this an acceptance of our basic absurdity, but it would be more correct to say that acting for realistic goals without harboring false expectations means *avoiding* the alleged contradiction. If we do that, our life is not absurd. Since the absurdists believe that man can follow their recommendations, they cannot cogently argue that his condition is absurd by its very nature.

✳

At this point we may reconsider motives that drive us to ask for the meaning of life. As a purely practical matter, would we not reduce the agony of our existence if we were certain that we are instruments in a grand and purposive design? Alone and afraid in a world we never made, we often yearn for marching orders from a superior power whose greater authority will direct our energies while making us feel sure that they are being properly used. And if we believed in such a power, would that not absolve us of absurdity?

Many people have said that it would, and have claimed that it does in their case. They must nevertheless confront the problem of validation. If a voice from the clouds suddenly booms forth instructions about how we should live, we must still determine that we are not having an auditory hallucination. And if we are told to act contrary to our own deepest feelings and intuitions, are we really obligated to accept the dictates of the superior being? Even if we acquiesce, what have we learned about the meaning of life? Submission to the higher power might simplify our lives and even help us go on living, but in itself it would not indicate what the meaning of life is. For we would still need to know why the words of this individual must be taken as the ultimate authority. Perhaps it gets its own sense of importance by arbitrarily giving orders to inferior beings. Perhaps it is carrying out the commands of a power higher than itself, even though reality as a whole has no meaning whatsoever.

One might reply that having access to vividly articulated prescriptions for behavior is so great a joy that we should not care about their final validation. That makes sense. But if we do not really care about final validation, then neither are we seeking a meaning of life in any objective sense. Instead we will have subtly redirected our original investigation. Rather than searching for a prior meaning of life, we would be asking what is needed for someone to have *a meaningful life*. This is a different kind of question: it orients us toward possibilities that emanate from man's estate regardless of any external meaning that may or may not surround it. Even if there is no meaning of life, or if this meaning is unknowable, or if the entire question is nonsensical in some respect, we may nevertheless hope for illumination about the circumstances under which human beings are able to achieve a meaningful existence.

Though Camus and the others say the human condition is absurd, they establish only that men and women act as if they can have meaningful lives while also believing that the universe does not give a damn. And if people act this way, are they not creating values and a meaning for themselves? The absurdists might agree. But in thinking that all human interests are merely arbitrary, all equally absurd, they cannot explain why people do (or should) prefer any particular attitude toward man's inescapable absurdity. Suggesting irony as an appropriate response, Nagel says: "If *sub specie aeternitatis* there is no reason to believe that anything matters, then that does not matter either, and we can approach our absurd lives with irony instead of heroism or despair."[11] But Nagel is obviously advocating, or at least favoring, irony as a suitable and meaningful reaction, just as Camus had proposed heroic defiance as the means by which human beings can overcome the absurdity in life. To say anything of this sort, however, is to admit that human existence is not wholly absurd. It then behooves us to determine the nature of meaningfulness and how it may be attained.

In a recent book, Nagel suggests that the conflict between self-consciousness and self-transcendence can possibly be minimized. He is not sanguine about this prospect, however. He concludes that "the possibilities for most of us are limited," and indeed that it is "better to be simultaneously engaged and detached, and therefore absurd, for this is the opposite of self-denial and the result of full awareness."[12] But once we realize that life is not absurd, since we are able to create meaning in it, we see that Nagel's dichotomies are untenable. Values do not exist *sub specie aeternitatis;* but neither are they merely arbitrary, as Nagel seems to think.

The basic error in the absurdist approach consists in a kind of fallacy of abstraction through which these theorists observe the human condition. Though they realize that people constantly pursue values and construct ideals, the absurdists examine man's experience out of context. They ignore the ways in which our species is always acting as a part of nature. Men and women have the goals and purposes that are meaningful to them because a biological structure in their needs and satisfactions underlies, either directly or indirectly, their creation of meaning. It is not at all absurd that human beings have the values that they do. These belong to us as just the natural entities that we happen to be.

Nor is it absurd that we have values that are distinct from those of a fish or a bird or any other species significantly different from our own. Each set of values arises out of material and social circumstances that make an organism to be as it is, which is to say, as it has evolved in nature. When natural preconditions are satisfied, the organism is rewarded by consummations that reinforce a viable mode of living. That is how our values come into being. That is the soil in which a meaningful life originates.

There is a sense in which the evolution of species may be considered arbitrary, for we can imagine a world in which everything could have developed differently. In that sense, nothing in life is objectively necessary. But in the reality that we know—nature as it exists, species having evolved as they did—it is not at all absurd that human beings should seek the values and create the meanings that they do. This aspect of our being is no less natural than everything else that constitutes our fundamental humanity.

✳

Thus far I have been discussing two approaches to the meaning of life: the traditionalist, which includes most of religious belief in the West, and the absurdist or nihilist. Despite the differences between them, they are alike in one crucial respect. Each addresses questions about the meaning of life as if it were a single something, and moreover, something *findable*. Though their answers to these questions are diametrically opposed, both approaches look for a unitary, all-embracing set of answers that somehow might be *there*, waiting to be revealed. The traditionalists would seem to see the world as a quasi-mathematical problem for which there must be a definite solution. If we can only refine our reasoning powers or cleanse our hearts, they say, we are sure to discover what we seek. Against this optimistic view, the absurdists despair of ever succeeding in such a quest. They conceive of the philosophical problem in similar terms, but they believe it is resolved only by the honest recognition that there is no meaning of life. The tragedy of man's condition thus consists in his having the propensity to act as if he had found a prior meaning that ratifies his decisions while all the time he senses at the deepest level of his being that no such meaning exists.

But are we sure that we even know what such a meaning could actually be? If we say that the world is or resembles a soluble problem, we use an analogy that may be wholly inappropriate. We have no acquaintance with different universes, as we do with different problems in mathematics, some of which can be solved while others cannot. To *ask* about a meaning of life that we might discover is not nonsensical. We can understand how the human imagination is operating when it poses such questions. To answer them in the manner of the traditionalists or the absurdists is fruitless, however, for they offer no way of verifying that a universe such as ours does or does not have an independent meaning capable of being found. How could we justify or defeat either assumption? What would count as evidence for or against it?

Whether or not the universe has a meaning to be found, the world as we know it is clearly one in which meaning *comes into being*. We frequently observe meaning being created, whether or not these new creations conform to a further meaning that precedes them. Rather than asking for the meaning of life as if it were a single or comprehensive pattern that permeates all existence a priori, we do better to investigate how it is that life acquires or may be *given* a meaning. This meaning is generally ambiguous, as Simone de Beauvoir argues in her book *The Ethics of Ambiguity*. Criticizing the absurdists, she states: "To declare that existence is absurd is to deny that it can ever be given a meaning." Beauvoir prefers the idea of ambiguity because "to say that it [existence] is ambiguous is to assert that its meaning is never fixed, that it must be constantly won."[13] In other words, ours is not an absurd existence in which we seek for absolute meaning although we are convinced that the universe does not afford any such thing. Rather we are creatures who create meaning for ourselves without having objective and unambiguous criteria by which to determine how we should do so.

We therefore need to examine the conditions under which human beings, and other organisms, make life meaningful. To the extent that life becomes meaningful in this accumulative way, its total meaning is increased. This is something we can verify by reference to empirical data. And indeed, when people ask about "the meaning of life," it is often meaning as a developmental phenomenon in nature that really interests them more than anything else.

With this in mind, we can make an additional response to the pessimistic comment of Freud's referred to earlier. We may now say that there is nothing inherently sick about asking for a meaning of life, provided one recognizes that apart from such considerations life is and can be meaningful in itself. If, however, the metaphysical musings arise out of despair that anything man does will ever give sense or value to life, the pathological implications are obvious. The same applies to doubts that we might have about our individual ability to attain a meaningful life. If we function as healthy beings, we act with assurance that people like ourselves are capable of creating sense and value in their lives. To the extent that they do so they augment the meaning of life in ways that would not have existed otherwise. Without meaning of this sort, human existence degenerates into misery and general chaos.

As a variation on this idea, one might say that life itself includes the creation of meaning and value as part of its innate structure. In accordance with the parameters of their individual natures, different organisms—above all, different animals— manifest indigenous modes of meaning without which they could not survive. If a human being asks for the sense or value of his life, he is either revealing uncertainty about which mode is suitable to himself, or else speculating about further ways of achieving a meaningful life. That can be painful, but our species creates meaning by undergoing this dialectic of doubt and innovation. It is by immersing ourselves in "the destructive element"—as Joseph Conrad said—that we are able to have meaning in life.

We must therefore rephrase the usual questions. Instead of seeking the meaning of life as if it were something preexisting, we must study the natural history of mental acts and bodily responses that enable organisms such as ours to fabricate meaning for themselves. We speak of "finding" a life that is meaningful, but the meaning is something we create. Whether or not we believe there is a prior system of intentions built into reality, we need to ask questions of a different sort: How do we actually create meaning? What is the phenomenology of a meaningful life? What will give a meaning to *my* life? Is life worthwhile? Is it worth living? What makes a life significant? Does anything really matter? Can one learn how to live? If so, how does one do it?

I shall return to these questions, but here I would like to linger on the last one. It appeared most graphically in Tolstoy's account of his midlife crisis and subsequent discovery of faith. Tolstoy achieved his own salvation by observing how the peasants lived. Being close to nature and relatively exempt from the depravities of modern society, they seemed to have acquired what he had missed—the intuitive knowledge of how to live. In their case this meant minimal expectation, simplicity of heart, a curtailing of personal arrogance, and spontaneous submission to their lot as human beings. These were the attitudes Tolstoy considered essential for the faith that gives meaning to life.

Other thinkers have offered their own guides to a meaningful existence: the cultivation of creativity itself, aesthetic contemplation, the pursuit of spiritual or humanitarian ideals, the full employment of one's energies, the realization of individual talents, the search for truth, the experience of love in one or another of its modalities.

However we finally analyze these alternatives, they all belong to a spectrum of life attaining meaning it does not have until we bestow that meaning upon it. I refer to the human race, of course, but not exclusively. In most, and possibly all, forms of life meaning arises from the more or less creative response of a particular organism to its environment. Since the environment may include another bit of life, the creation of meaning can be a reaction to what is meaningful in someone else. My attitude means a great deal to my dog. He creates this meaning, and thereby augments the meaningfulness of his life, by the value he gives to occurrences that others may not even notice—small gestures of mine or my momentary moods. By cherishing his responsive meaning, I make my own life more meaningful. In general, meaning will always depend on the value-laden behavior that living creatures manifest. Meaning in life is the creating of values in accordance with the needs and inclinations that belong to one's natural condition. Valuation is the making of choices by individuals striving for a meaningful life in nature. The values and meanings that emerge are, in this sense, facts of nature—not at all transcendental, as various metaphysicians have thought.

Nor is there a single pattern of meaning that runs throughout the universe. The values of a bird are not only different from, but also incommensurate with, those of a fish. Though each may overlap with the other, and human meaningfulness can often resemble both, we need not posit a discernible identity that remains constant throughout. Even if each form of life is driven by a desire to survive—or to perpetuate itself in its own being, as Spinoza would say—this alone does not reveal a generic purpose that everything has in common. For that implies the existence of a particular program or underlying meaning that creatures must all have in the act of surviving as they do. We have little reason to think that any such uniformity resides within the endless variety of meaningful events that life comprises. Even if the many types of meaningfulness derive from a quest for gene replication, these types remain infinitely diverse among themselves.

❋

Having recognized the dangers in speculating about a prior meaning of life, we can now focus our discussion on meaningfulness in living things. We may see them as separate units within a diversified class of meaningful lives, and we may possibly assert that the cosmos acquires greater meaning only to the extent that it includes a totality of lives that become increasingly meaningful. We may even conclude that this growth in universal meaning *is* the meaning of life. I shall return to that idea at the end of this book. Here I merely note that our interest in meaningfulness need not culminate in a stultifying positivism.

However we interpret the nature of meaningfulness, we must realize that it is always changing. It alters as living things create their own modes of meaning. We human beings differ from members of other species in our astounding capacity to innovate, to generate new meanings for ourselves. We are not more purposive than other animals, and we frequently seem to be less gifted than they are as far as personal happiness is concerned. Anyone who has ever watched a bird building its nest will agree that it usually goes about its business with a kind of confidence, security, and single-mindedness that is rare in men and women. Doing what comes naturally, animals often appear contented, sometimes even serene. Walt Whitman admired them for that:

> I think I could turn and live with animals, they
>   are so placid and self-contain'd,
> I stand and look at them long and long.[14]

But though this conception of animal life may be attractive, these creatures attain their level of fulfillment largely by pursuing routine purposes in much the same way throughout a lifetime and from generation to generation. What is meaningful to them is usually constraining rather than expansive. Their placidity is correlated with a lack of intellect or imagination. They are limited in their ability to entertain novel or alternate meanings. Our species is unique in its great creativity with respect to meaningfulness. Our systems of meaning vary tremendously from moment to moment, from one individual to another, and from society to society. On the one hand, we are quickly bored by older meanings and are constantly trying to replace them with newer ones; on the other hand, we have the power to enrich what is meaningful by fashioning cultural and artistic traditions that may grow and develop for centuries.

What we define as culture or civilization is itself a complex of institutions and customs that enable people to acquire patterns of meaning throughout a historical continuity. Civilization is always conservative inasmuch as the future determines itself by means of responses—many of them habitual—that preserve what was meaningful in the past. But it is also progressive, since it gives the imagination material for extending earlier attitudes through sophisticated reactions that make possible vastly unforeseen and often unforeseeable variations. In general, nothing will survive unless it is revitalized in accordance with what has current meaning. Even the dead hand of the past, as in outmoded customs or bureaucracies, retains its power over the present only by a constantly renewed acquiescence among those who submit to it. This subservience is, paradoxically, part of their search for meaning. That creative venture is the human opportunity. It reveals *our* program: not only to ask for the meaning of life but also to bring it into being in the endless ways that constitute our creativity.

The capacity to create new and greater meaning does not exist without its perils. I shall address this problem further on. But here I can say a little about the factors that threaten meaningfulness. Physical decay and many types of disease, including mental illness, are often unable to diminish it. Indeed, some of the most meaningful lives are lived by persons who undergo severe pathologies of either mind or body. A meaningful life can and often does result from efforts to overcome such impediments. Some philosophers think that death itself is just another impediment, and that we negate it by having lived a life that achieves its proper meaning. Socrates talks this way in Plato's *Phaedo*. I think instead that we must treat death as the great destroyer of meaning since it is the termination of each life in nature. But human beings know that they will die, and this awareness may itself provide a source of meaning for them. Moreover, the death of one person is an occurrence in the lives of those who survive. For them, too, it can take on creative meaning.

What then is the relationship between death and meaningfulness? Is death the meaning of life, as philosophers and theologians have often said? Or is life the meaning of death, in the sense that we can understand mortality only in relation to the facts about our finite being? Once we have analyzed our ideas in this area, we may find that we are better able to approach the many difficult questions about meaning as it exists in human experience.

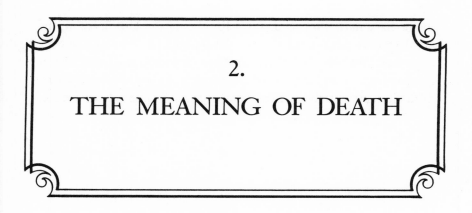

2.

THE MEANING OF DEATH

People who write about "the meaning of death" often do so in order to impart news of another world beyond our mortal span, a spirit-world or at least a realm that transcends the limitations of nature. Lest anyone be deceived in this respect, I must warn the reader that I have no such tidings to convey. I have nothing to report about a white light at the end of the tunnel that reveals a continuance of life after death. My long-deceased grandmother has never welcomed me with a cup of chicken soup to the land of those who survive their death in some Elysian field. To paraphrase William James, I am only a philosopher, which is to say someone who has been trained to attack all the other philosophers. It is the *concept* of death that primarily interests me. How do we use that word? Just what does it refer to? Is death simply a termination of life, or does it have other meaning as well?

What is philosophically interesting in the idea of death will appear immediately if we contrast it with the concept of *dying*. The two are very different. Dying is a physical and psychological process whose beginning may be subject to interpretation but whose ending clearly occurs when vital activity ceases. Whether dying can be defined more precisely as culminating in the loss of brainwaves or heartbeat, or whatever, is not a matter to concern us here. For regardless of how such important issues are resolved, the fact remains that we can readily understand what is meant by "dying," whereas it is not at all obvious what "death" means. One might assume that each refers to a state of being, death taking place after dying has completed itself. But if death is nothing but a termination, it is not a state of *being*. Strictly speaking, it is not a state at all. What then are we talking about?

We naively speak of "dying" and "death" as if these were ordinary process-product terms. Consider how we talk about sleep. We treat falling asleep as a condition that results in our being asleep. The former is a process and the latter is a product that results from that process. Dying is also a process. But is death a product comparable to being asleep? It would be odd to believe this since the person who is asleep is the same as the one who was falling asleep. But death is not like that. We cannot say that being dead is analogous to being asleep, unless we think that the person who was dying is still the same although he has died, somehow continuing to exist in this new condition which has resulted from the process that brought it about. If, however, one who is dead no longer exists, as most of us believe, death cannot be related to dying in any way that is parallel to the relationship between being asleep and falling asleep. What then do we mean by death? We use the term with great facility but its logic is obscure.

If we keep in mind the differences between death and dying, it may not matter that the language appropriate for one of these concepts sometimes serves metaphorically for the other. More essential is our understanding of what each concept entails. As a way of beginning, let me quote from an essay that George Santayana wrote after reading Freud's book *Beyond the Pleasure Principle*. Freud had suggested that death is the goal of life in the sense that all organisms are programmed with an innate drive toward their own annihilation. Freud thought this drive supplemented, and interacted with, the equally instinctive drive to perpetuate one's life as long as possible. Santayana interprets this to mean that life is, as he entitles the essay, "A Long Way Round to Nirvana." He then says the following:

> That the end of life should be death may sound sad: yet what other end can anything have? The end of an evening party is to go to bed; but its use is to gather congenial people together, that they may pass the time pleasantly. An invitation to the dance is not rendered ironical because the dance cannot last for ever; the youngest of us and the most vigorously wound up, after a few hours, has had enough of sinuous stepping and prancing. The transitoriness of things is essential to their physical being, and not at all sad in itself; it becomes sad by virtue of a sentimental illusion, which makes us imagine that they wish to endure, and that their end is always untimely; but in a healthy nature it is not so. What is truly sad is to have some impulse frustrated in the midst of its career, and robbed of its chosen object; and what is painful is to have an organ lacerated or destroyed when it is still vigorous, and not ready for its natural sleep and dissolution. . . . The point is to have expressed and discharged all that was latent in us; and to this perfect relief various temperaments and various traditions assign different names, calling it having one's day, or doing one's duty, or realising one's ideal, or saving one's soul. The task in any case is definite and imposed on us by nature, whether we recognize it or not; therefore we can make true moral progress or fall into real errors. Wisdom and genius lie in discerning this prescribed task and in doing it readily, cleanly, and without distraction. Folly on the contrary imagines that any scent is worth following, that we have an infinite nature, or no nature in particular, that life begins without obligations and can do business without capital, and that the will is vacuously free, instead of being a specific burden and a tight hereditary knot to be unravelled.[1]

I find much in this statement that is wise and true to reality as I have known it. Though I will discuss further questions that Santayana does not broach, his perspective seems to me wholesome and correct. He sees that death is a function of life, a termination and possibly a completion of events that we recognize to be native to our existence. This view is preferable to ideas, such as those that various religions regularly refurbish, of death as the meaning of life. Religious dogmas assume something of the sort whenever they depict life as a preparation for a future dispensation to which we shall have access only after we have sloughed off our earthly coils. Some sects even accord the moment of death greater importance than any that precedes it, as if the meaning of a person's life could be revealed by how he dies rather than by how he has lived.

While repudiating such conceptions, we may also want to reject Freud's notion that death is an instinctive goal of life. That idea gives death a function in natural processes, but possibly misinterprets what the function is. I shall develop this argument below. But first I want to study what might be called a "non-natural" meaning of death that has had considerable influence in twentieth-century philosophy.

Without having recourse to religious categories of the usual type, Heidegger argues that man's being is inherently, ontologically, a being-toward-death (*Sein zum Tode*).[2] According to Heidegger, human existence is permeated by a realization that it is finite and heading toward nothingness. Our being must therefore involve the anxiety one constantly feels in knowing that one is always subject to death. Heidegger claims that this anxiety is not merely psychological, since if that were the case a person might or might not have it. Rather, he thinks, it is inseparable from human existence: in one way or another man is always aware of "the possibility of [his own] absolute impossibility." Life not only tends toward death as a goal or terminus, but also death occurs in human beings as a potentiality that is ever-present to us through our constant foreboding of what awaits us at some undetermined moment in the future.

Characterizing the being of man in this fashion, Heidegger distinguishes two types of response to it. Most people deal with death in a manner that he calls "inauthentic." They attempt to forget or ignore their destiny as finite creatures that will eventually be destroyed by death. They think of death as something that happens to other people, or else as a calamity that they need not consider until it occurs at some distant time their imagination cannot fathom. In order to live a life of "authenticity," Heidegger insists, we must confront reality by a continual awareness of our fate. One then accepts it in the sense that one treats death as a necessity and ceases to fabricate fanciful means of trying to deny it. In this act of acceptance Heidegger discerns heroic grandeur or ultimate dignity. By no longer falsifying the character of his own finitude, the authentic person makes a kind of noble acquiescence and even willing choice. He has attained the "freedom-to-die," which is to say, freedom in the face of death.

Heidegger's concept of the inauthentic is illustrated by something that the cartoonist Al Capp once said. He remarked that when he gets up in the morning he immediately turns to the obituaries in the newspapers and studies the ages of those who have died. If their average age is greater than his own, he feels relieved by the fact that he has additional years to live. If the average age is less than his, he is delighted to see that he has passed the danger. (But what if the average is exactly his own age? Does he stay in bed that day, to minimize all risks?) The inauthenticity of the attitude portrayed by Capp's whimsical account consists in its implicit belief that one can so easily escape the anxiety that motivates a person to make such calculations. However comforting they may be, nothing can liberate him from the ever-looming fatality that is inherent in human existence. Since recognition of it belongs to our very being, a refusal to live in accordance with this knowledge must always lead to inauthenticity. The evasive maneuvers need not be as humorous as Capp's, but they are all equally self-deluding.

We can readily see what is valid in Heidegger's conception of authenticity. There is little virtue, and nothing admirable, in deceiving oneself either about one's own mortality or the mortality of others. But Heidegger wants to say something more than this alone. He claims that we are inauthentic unless we treat death as an element in *all* of our experience. Since we know we will die, he asserts, we cannot have an authentic life without constantly attending to that fundamental fact about ourselves. He then concludes that, painful as it sometimes is, ontological anxiety—anxiety about this "ground" of our being—is a necessary part of all authentic existence.[3]

I find Heidegger's analysis unconvincing. It neglects, or understates, much of a contrary nature that also belongs to the human condition. Even an adequate awareness of possible and eventual death will rarely amount to the preoccupation incorporated in his concept of anxiety. Heidegger does not believe that we must brood on our coming demise to the exclusion of everything else, but he does maintain that anxiety about death is ontologically ultimate since it colors and pervades our entire being. To say this, however, is to minimize the role of other coordinates that often dominate our experience and have greater importance. In wishing to live, we take action against our impending doom. We seek to delay annihilation as long as possible, we try to protect others from it, we pursue ideals that cultivate and perfect the possibilities of life, we focus upon the experience of immediate consummations that defy death by their sheer vitality.

In all these ways we manifest a being that is directed not *toward* death but away from it. To this extent, one might define human existence as a "being-to-overcome-death." Though we know that death will triumph in the end, and though we recognize the constant "possibility of impossibility," our being is more fundamentally oriented toward the preserving and maintaining of life than to anxiety about its termination.

In his critique of Heidegger's ideas on death, Sartre raises somewhat different objections. Since Heidegger defines human existence as a being-toward-death, Sartre says, he treats death as if it were a completion of life, as if it were something that life tends toward as a consummatory goal or meaningful outcome. In that event, death would be tantamount to what Sartre calls "a resolved chord at the end of a melody."[4] He considers this notion totally mistaken.

We can easily see what Sartre means. A melody begins at a moment in time just as a life does, and it ends with similar decisiveness. In the case of the melody, a resolving chord has retroactive significance. It suggests the meaning of what has preceded it. In that sense it has a value and musical function at every point in the melody. The question is whether death has any analogous role in the life that it terminates. Heidegger would seem to say it does. Sartre argues that life and death are not related in this way.

In Sartre's view, death is always foreign to life, a curtailment imposed from without. It is like a pair of scissors that snaps a thread. Unless the thread were liable to such snapping, this could not occur. But the action of the scissors results from causes and events that have nothing to do with the inner constitution of the thread. Sartre sees human existence as a succession of projects and projections that consciousness initiates. Death is their termination. It is not the fulfillment of their intention, but rather a final barrier that descends upon them arbitrarily. We may know that we will die *some* day, but our actual death is unpredictable. It can happen at any time, regardless of our expectations.

Sartre gives the example of a man who courageously prepares to die on the scaffold and determines to make a brave appearance at the end in order to round out his life with dignity. This would be comparable to viewing death as the resolving chord. But before the man can be hanged, he dies of influenza. *That* is what life is like, Sartre states, and it shows why death is not a culmination but only an absurd termination. Death is not a part of life: it only supervenes upon it. Death occurs as a foreign agency, and for no reason that reveals the fundamental nature of the life it dispatches.

Sartre concludes that death never defines human existence. An individual's being consists in what is possible to him. But my death is not my possibility, he claims, since it is merely that which eliminates everything that was possible to me. My death is "an always possible nihilation of my possibles which is outside my possibilities."[5] Far from being basic to what I am, my death is never a reality for me. Once I die it becomes a reality for others: the survivors experience it as something that has happened to me. I myself can never have that experience. Even if I imagine what my

death will be like, my conception must be inadequate and somewhat inaccurate, if only because there is no way of knowing exactly
how my life will end.

Since death is outside of life and serves as nothing but its
elimination, Sartre insists that death cannot give meaning to life.
"Thus death is never that which gives life its meanings; it is, on the
contrary, that which on principle removes all meaning from life. If
we must die, then our life has no meaning because its problems
receive no solution and because the very meaning of the problems
remains undetermined."[6] According to Sartre, life acquires meaning only as long as it freely chooses its possibilities, the values it
projects upon the world. They constitute its being and create its
meaningfulness out of nothing. Death, like birth, just happens. It is
a brute fact imposed upon whatever exists. It cannot confer on life
any sort of meaning.

This conclusion may help to free us from Heidegger's
approach, but I believe it is equally suspect. In a sense the two
views, antithetical as they may seem to be, are unacceptable for
similar reasons. Heidegger failed to emphasize that meaningful acts
are devices for surmounting death even though we recognize its
inevitability. They enable us to overcome death by creating and
expressing values that not only manifest life but also further its
ongoing existence in ourselves. Every moment of fulfillment or
consummation symbolically defeats the idea of death. It is as if our
experience proclaimed to the world: "Though I will die, at least I
have achieved this much." Through deeds that are humane, artistic,
or merely nurturing, the imagination propels us into a time when
we will no longer be but whatever we care about will survive and
possibly prevail. We know we will die, but we deploy our energies
toward possible occurrences that project themselves through life as
it continues in the future.

Sartre understands that meaning arises from the projection of
these possibilities. He also perceives that they exist within a
context of human finitude. His concept of "facticity" codifies the
way in which man's freedom is always conditioned by givens such
as the materiality of his body and his dependence on events in

nature. Death is for Sartre just another facticity, something that merely happens to human beings, and that is why he thinks it removes the possibility of meaning instead of contributing to it. To say this, however, is to ignore the fact that human projects are normally undertaken and pursued with a sense of temporal realities. Whether they are designed to benefit ourselves or others, they are enacted with the awareness that we will not live forever. They derive their meaning not only from the freedom with which they are chosen but also from our knowledge that sooner or later death will cut them short for us. In functioning as the boundary to our being, death signifies that everything we do must be completed within a more or less brief period of time during which we are continually at risk of annihilation.

It is this recognition, operating as a structural element in our creation of meaning, that Sartre neglects. In his ideas about death, as in much of his philosophy, he sets up a highly problematic dualism between life and death, freedom and facticity, consciousness and body, man and nature. In doing so, he misrepresents the ways in which these contraries interpenetrate throughout ordinary experience.

This shortcoming appears most clearly in Sartre's remarks to Simone de Beauvoir about his own imminent death: "It seems to me natural. Natural as opposed to my life as a whole, which has been cultural. It is after all the return to nature and the assertion that I was a part of nature."[7] Moving as these words may be, they nevertheless reveal a great confusion. Sartre wants to say that insofar as his life was cultural, it exceeded the natural forces that would soon bring it to an end. What he disregards, however, is the way in which the cultural derives from the natural, manifesting forces in nature that are needed for its existence, even though the goals of culture can always deviate from its origins. In a sense, Sartre admits as much when he says that the return to nature, through death, is the "assertion" that he was all along a part of nature. But if his life was always part of nature, how can there be a *return* to it when death occurs? In destroying life, death is no more natural than the processes (some of them cultural) that it eradicates.

Neither is it any less natural. In the life of nature, death is an ingredient that we confront throughout our efforts to pursue meaningful projects within the finite circumstances available to us.

When we live with an awareness of the limits death entails and also symbolizes, we begin to feel the wonder in our ability to do anything at all. In view of the littleness of our lives, even our minor achievements may seem grandiose. Accompanied by a realistic sense of mortality, our decisions about how to live take on a meaning they would not otherwise have. When I was a child I used to be thrilled by the words "they died with their boots on"; and though this phrase seems puerile to me now, I still find it meaningful. It conveys the idea of people dying in the midst of a purposive but perilous activity, people becoming heroic by militant involvement in a mission they have chosen even though it may lead to death—a culmination they do not seek but which belongs to the nature of the enterprise.

There is no sense of absurdity or despair in the slogan I have quoted. On the contrary, it expresses a feeling of suitability, even rightness. Living with your boots on, as a soldier does in battle, it is fitting and a kind of achievement that one should die that way. When death comes, it validates the risk we assumed in creating the project that gave our lives meaning. Death does not always strike in an unforeseen and irrelevant manner, as happens to Sartre's condemned prisoner. Heroes are not always killed by a chance occurrence—the flu epidemic—that mocks all noble aspirations. They sometimes die in a way that affirms the meaningfulness of their courageous behavior.

Thus Heidegger does not sufficiently appreciate the importance of our having a being-to-overcome-death, while Sartre ignores the extent to which the creation of meaning involves an awareness of death as the ending that signifies the finitude in all our projects. Our lives become meaningful in the struggle to defeat death even though we realize that everything we attempt belongs to a natural condition delimited by death. One might say that all human experience is doomed or futile insofar as death will happen regardless of what we do about it. But there is no absurdity or ontological failure in this. It is just a part of our mortality, which is natural to our condition. Though the meanings we create will disappear sooner or later, they further life in the present and prolong it for a while in the future. To that extent they succeed in overcoming death, and they do so in the only way available to creatures such as we.

If this is how we think of death, we will see it as neither the prelude to some glorious hereafter nor as the final chord that imparts a resolution to all that preceded it. But we can still envisage death as an event that may possibly serve as the appropriate and timely completion of the life it terminates. Life and death are both fortuitous in some respects. It is arbitrary, in the sense that it just happens to be the case, that we live in a period of history when warfare or famine or cancer has not yet been conquered and therefore people are prevented from living as long as they someday may. It is always fortuitous that anyone should die when and how he does, since the world could have been such that those particular causes of death might not have existed. But it is not arbitrary or fortuitous that beings like ourselves, who participate in nature as we do, should die at some time and in one way or another.

Partly following Sartre, Thomas Nagel claims that death is an absurdity because, from an individual's "internal" point of view, one's own "existence seems . . . to be a universe of possibilities that stands by itself, and therefore stands in need of nothing else in order to continue."[8] But this is not true to our experience. We generally, and perhaps always, know that our possibilities are inseparable from the limitations indigenous to our being. We can *feel* that we may live forever, as we can imagine anything that is not logically self-contradictory, but that feeling must always be suspect. It is not based on observation, and except in moments of illusion it usually has little effect upon the quality of our consciousness or the decisions that we make.

Most people realize that death is one of the major facts of their life. And when we live our lives with a genuine recognition of this particular fact, acting resolutely in response to it, giving life meaning *because* we know that we will die in the not-too-distant

future, death ceases to be a meaningless termination. It will not
have solved or resolved anything, but it exists as a constraint that
reveals what it is to be alive as human beings are. Acknowledging
its presence within the trajectory of our existence can also have a
useful consequence. In dilatory creatures such as we, it is possible
that nothing much would be accomplished without the awareness
that time is bounded for us. Confinement can become creative
concentration. As the poet Richard Wilbur puts it, "limitation
makes for power: the strength of the genie comes of his being
confined in a bottle."[9]

I can illustrate these suggestions, so different from the
perspective in either Heidegger or Sartre or Nagel, by the song of
Guiderius in Shakespeare's *Cymbeline:*

> Fear no more the heat o' th' sun
>> Nor the furious winter's rages;
> Thou thy worldly task hast done,
>> Home art gone and ta'en thy wages;
> Golden lads and girls all must,
>> As chimney-sweepers, come to dust. (IV, ii)

Shakespeare's lines imply that death can be a meaningful
occurrence, not merely ending a life but also effecting a kind of
relevant completion. All is not lost if we succeed in doing our
"worldly task." It is reassuring to think that life in this world can
even be regarded as a task, which is to say, a purposeful activity.
The practice that Shakespeare uses for his metaphor—the sweeping of chimneys—satisfies a social need. It is an honorable
occupation, and those who perform it may point to the ashen dust
in their hair as proof that they have carried out their service. So too
may lads and girls, whose hair changes from gold to gray and whose
bones turn to dust, undergo death as a natural and correlative result
of having lived.

The Shakespearean lines can be taken as meaning that death is
a benign outcome, like payment to one who has done his job. Later
in the scene death is actually called a "quiet consummation." This

may seem to us unjustifiably roseate. The ground in which we are buried may strike us as something less than the home to which the honest laborer goes after his day's work. But even so, the word "home" reverberates with a sense of belonging to a familiar and possibly familial setting. Though we need not consider death a boon or consummation, we eliminate some of its horror if we accept it as the befitting conclusion to a natural process.

Sartre's analysis rules out the idea of any rightness or suitability in death. In proposing a different view, I am not suggesting that death always, or often, occurs as a happy ending. I am not saying that in itself it gives life meaning. I only want to leave open the possibility that we can live in such a way that death has an appropriate, and therefore meaningful, place in our being. The projects that determine human experience can be realistic or unrealistic. When they are realistic, they define themselves in terms of boundaries imposed by the physical and organic determinants of life. They are known to be structured not only by their vital momentum but also by their inherent limitation. For each of us this occurs in death. If we deny it, whether for religious or sentimental reasons, we are out of touch with our own existence. If we accept it as part of what it is to be a human being, we surmount it in advance. Death is incapable of depriving life of "all meaning," as Sartre maintains, if the projects that give a life its meaning are undertaken with a staunch recognition that even at their best they cannot last forever.

Though life begins with birth and ends with death, human consciousness exists in the apparent timelessness of the present moment. It is therefore understandable that conscious beings like ourselves may sometimes feel alienated from their temporal restraints and even consider them an absurdity. But death is not absurd, just as birth is not. Without the latter, we have no existence; and unless technology can radically alter our current state, the same is true of the former. These are elements of our life in nature, regardless of what we might prefer. It would be fanciful, and even irrational, for us to think that we are able to live without dying and yet belong to the same natural order that has created us.

If we choose, we can rebel against our finitude, as Dylan Thomas does in the lines about his father's proximate death: "Do not go gentle into that good night,/Old age should burn and rave at close of day;/Rage, rage against the dying of the light."[10] An old man is less likely to have this attitude than his young son, but the feeling is not inappropriate though possibly unfortunate. Raging against death is hardly the best method for delaying it, and the vehemence of our rejection can prevent us from attaining a meaningful response to the final outcome. I am suggesting that we do so when we accept death, not in the sense of glorifying it or confusing it with a consummatory good but rather in seeing it as one of the coordinates without which we would not exist. Acceptance of this sort is essential if we are to achieve the greatest meaningfulness in our actual condition.[11]

❄

The concept of anxiety that Heidegger and Sartre employ in their attempts to show how man should cope with death is worthy of close attention. I defer that discussion to the following chapter since it is related to questions about the creation of meaning. The fear of death differs from anxiety in being focused on the specific event which is the destruction of life in us. Psychologists, of whom Elisabeth Kübler-Ross is the most renowned, have done excellent work analyzing the stages that people go through in the process of dying. Philosophers have traditionally asked a different kind of question. They have wanted to determine whether it is *rational* to fear death. Some have thought that we might be cured of our fear if only we recognized that this feeling—unlike many others— cannot be justified by reason. It would be rational, for instance, to fear something that we know to be harmful. But if being dead is unknowable or a state of nothingness, we need not assume that it does us any harm. One could then conclude that there is no rational basis for dreading it. Once people realize this, will they not be able to control or even exorcise their painful fear?

Idealist philosophers have often argued against the fear of death by claiming that our little life is not rounded by a sleep but rather encased in a meaningful universe that transmutes death into a beneficial event we should gladly welcome. Arguments of this sort appear in Plato's *Apology* and Hegel's *Lectures on the Philosophy of Religion,* among many other philosophical works. It is more pertinent, however, to consider the beliefs of philosophers who treat death as a total, irreversible destruction of each individual and yet who claim it is not rational to fear it.

The most famous argument along these lines is the one that Epicurus offered in ancient Greece. Epicurus said: When we are, death is not; when death is, we are not; therefore, it is irrational to fear death. Epicurus was addressing people who worried about punishments they might receive in an afterlife that traditional religions have often portrayed. Having rejected faith in any such immortality, Epicurus could take comfort in the belief that there is no possibility of retribution beyond death. And to those who may have feared death because they thought they would suffer after dying, his reasoning may well have been persuasive. But it scarcely deals with the problem of most people nowadays, who are not apprehensive about hellfire but who are afraid that they will be annihilated by death. What they fear is precisely the circumstance Epicurus specifies: that they will not be when death is.

In other words, Epicurus' slogan fails to show that the fear of death is irrational in those who fear they may be terminated completely. To tell them they will be nothing after death and thus there is nothing to be feared cannot be helpful. The feeling of dread, which Epicurus was trying to alleviate, is often very strong, and if it is to be deemed irrational, this must be demonstrated by a more elaborate argument.

In that attempt Lucretius suggested the following: Life is a finite span from birth to death; before birth there was an infinity of nothingness out of which we arose, and after death there will be an infinity of the same kind; it would never occur to us to fear or bewail our not having existed during all those eons that preceded our birth; therefore there is no reason why we should fear the comparable non-existence that will ensue after death. Lucretius assumes, of course, that if it is irrational to fear some particular state of affairs, it is equally irrational to fear one that is equivalent or very similar.

Lucretius is right in thinking that we would consider it irrational to have fears about non-existence prior to our birth (though we might regret and even lament that we were not alive during the heyday of Greek culture, or the Renaissance, or some other era). But he is mistaken in thinking that our fear of death is at all comparable. Before we were born, we did not exist and therefore had nothing to lose. We fear death because we fear the loss of life, much as a mother fears the loss of her child, or a lover the loss of his sweetheart, or a miser the loss of his money. In each case people fear that they will be deprived of a good they possess. And can anything be more clearly good than life itself—at least, for one who enjoys his existence and appreciates the many satisfactions that belong to a life worth living? For such a person, the fear of death would seem to be supremely rational.

The patriot who dies for his country and the revolutionary who dies for the cause he believes in may say they fear death less than they fear betraying their ideals. This attitude does not prove it is irrational to fear losing one's life, but only that devotion such as theirs can lead a person to make enormous sacrifices for something he cares about. Dedicating ourselves entirely, we may even find that our fear of death has disappeared. This, however, does not mean that the earlier fear was irrational. Nor can Lucretius' argument be salvaged by anything else that motivates our willingness to return to the non-existence that preceded birth. It is always rational to want to retain whatever life we have and value. The situation is not the same, or in any way equivalent, before we have it.[12]

In Schopenhauer's conception of death we find a very different type of argument. People fear death, Schopenhauer says, because they think of themselves as separate substances, each unique and ontologically independent. This is erroneous, he insists, since we—and everything else that lives—are but manifestations of an ultimate metaphysical force that courses through all of nature. This force, which follows deterministic laws and in itself has no purpose, is "the will." As we saw, he uses that term to characterize the underlying reality because he thinks we come closest to intuiting its presence through our volitional and instinctual being, which includes our sexuality. The will is a will to live; it shows itself primarily as a striving for its own preservation. Since intellect is useful for the perpetuation of life, it has successfully evolved in man. To the extent that it furthers survival, the intellect serves the will and remains congruent with reality. But no sooner does intellect come into existence, Schopenhauer states, than the will has difficulty controlling it. The idea that human beings are separate from the rest of nature and have independent lives whose individual destruction is a calamity—all this bespeaks the waywardness of intellect.

We *are* the will, Schopenhauer claims: our life is only an expression of it. When we die, our personal energies are merely reprocessed by the cosmic force that has briefly appeared in us and will now appear in something else. From this point of view, death does not destroy our individuality, since we never really had it in the first place. Death is a transitional moment of no great consequence to the will. The intellect gives death undue importance and that is what generates our fear. The fear of death must be irrational because it is based upon a fallacy. Far from being negative or undesirable, death serves to eradicate delusion. It removes a major misconception—the notion of our separateness—that the intellect has foolishly instilled. Since the will survives and since we are nothing but local manifestations of it, there is no reason to dread its transfer into other entities. That is all that happens when we die.

Without examining the problems that belong to metaphysical theories like Schopenhauer's, I shall only point out one obvious flaw in his doctrine. Schopenhauer says it is irrational to fear death since this emotion issues from the intellect's delusions about our separate being. But even if this is true, the fact remains that humans are what they are partly *because* of their intellect. Even if we are exchangeable and expendable parts of an impersonal force in nature, our actual experience of ourselves is nothing like that. We exist in the world as individuals, as beings whose consciousness and self-awareness are unique to each person in his or her particularity. We are living nodules that may intermesh with one another but never lose all vestige of delimiting differentiation. If we had no intellect and our experience were other than it is, we might have no sense of independent being. But since we have this, and only this, way of living—even though Schopenhauer's own intellect questions the reliability of intellect in general—it is not surprising that we should feel great apprehension about whatever eliminates the condition we recognize as our own. Radically deluded though we may be, thanks to the metaphysical errors of the intellect, that is what we *are* by our very nature. Consequently, it seems perfectly rational for us to fear the momentous event that can and will annihilate us.

I conclude that there is no basis for considering it necessarily irrational to fear death. Unless we are convinced that greater benefits will compensate us for the loss of cherished goods enjoyed in the process of living, the fear of death is always rational. I do not mean that this feeling is inevitable or unavoidable; and certainly it is counterproductive when it becomes a painful obsession that interferes with our ability to savor life and go on living. On many occasions the fear of death is needed for self-preservation. Without a salutary fear we might run risks that would markedly decrease our chances for survival. In the long run our gene pool would suffer and the species might even be imperiled. From this we can infer that it is sometimes *desirable* to fear death. That must depend on the consequences in each case, but it does indicate that one can imagine circumstances in which the fear of death would indeed be wholly justified.

In the final analysis we fear death because we love life, at least enough of it and in sufficient degree to believe that our existence is worth continuing. In a vigorous organism both the fear and the love arise from instinctual roots and are often inseparable. To impose criteria of rationality may therefore be considered pointless. But our reason is also part of nature, and it is natural for us to seek some rationality in what we feel. However strong and deep within our psyche, no emotions are self-validating. That is why we cannot say that the fear of death, or even the love of life, *must* be rational—only that it is not inherently irrational.

❋

If it can be rational to fear death, one may nevertheless wonder why that fear is absent in many people whose rationality would never be questioned. I have long thought about the paradoxical fact that, on the whole, young persons fear death more acutely than older ones, even though the latter are statistically closer to their demise. The elderly are no less rational, and they have had greater experience of death as an unwanted intrusion upon the lives of others. Yet they generally suffer much less from the fear of death than they themselves may have done when they were young. In addition, the fear of death is often inversely correlated with the quality of experience and the feeling that one's life has been fairly successful. While they stand to lose more by dying, men and women who are happy or have meaningful lives tend to fear death less than others do. Though the sense of having lived well may enable human beings to face their fate with equanimity, the situation remains anomalous. Where one has access to a greater goodness in life, should one not have greater fear that it will be obliterated by death?

Freud's explanation for this paradox is related to his theory about the "death drive," which he considered innate in everything that lives. His conception is somewhat unclear, but it would seem to take the following form: We all have in us an instinctual need to return to the inorganic state out of which life evolved; this regressive impulse limits the search for new experience and further exploration on the part of our equally instinctual life-force; when people get older, they survive by adjusting to the diminution of energy in themselves as they approach the goal their death drive has been seeking; it is therefore easier for them to become reconciled to the eventuality that appeared so repellent when their vital impulse was both powerful and predominant.

Freud need not be understood as suggesting that all human beings have a *wish* for death. Though he is often misquoted in this fashion, his metaphysical hypotheses—which he himself found puzzling and unverifiable—may be given a more moderate interpretation. Instead of claiming that everyone wants to die, he may only have meant that we possess a basic capacity for accepting death as the programmed goal of life.

If we read Freud this way, we can explain the lessened fear of death in older persons as a constitutional response that appears under suitable circumstances. Though perhaps we should not call it an instinct, the progressive acceptance of death might be considered a potentiality that is biologically determined in all people. As with other biological phenomena, this attitude can also reflect the influence of cultural and individual differences. It may nevertheless occur as a development that is more or less constant in human beings once they reach old age.

Further research may also indicate that the ability to overcome the fear of death increases after one's sexual drive starts dwindling. This could be an evolutionary device related to the utility of discouraging survival among the aging members of a population, whose value for the next generation will have lessened. It might well be the case that our acceptance of death, in the sense that we no longer fear it greatly, is correlated with the decrease in our ability to react quickly and vigorously to anything that threatens the existence of our genetic group. The capacity for immediate responsiveness declines with age, even when the individual's own welfare is at stake. Though many people learn to enjoy life only as they get older—George Bernard Shaw was right when he said that youth is too wonderful to waste on children—the elderly often lose their emotional potency as well as their muscular strength, their sensory acuity, and their intellectual rapidity. In other words, we conquer the fear of death only after our vital forces have been weakened by disabilities and impairments that nature imposes with the passage of time. Death becomes less fearful to us because the energy that enables us to fear anything has been diminished.

Carrying these suggestions a little further, we may posit four or five different stages in our response to death. In the earlier years there is often a narcissistic sense of immortality. The young child acts as if, and in some respects believes that, he will live forever.

Even if he has heard about the death of others, he may have no conception of it as something that could happen to him. He may be afraid that those he loves, and those whose love he depends on, will die or disappear. But that is quite different from the fear of his own death. There is a great variability in the length of time during which this first attitude continues. In children who suffer from illnesses that they know or suspect are terminal, it may be quickly superseded by responses that would otherwise occur much later.

With the onset of puberty, we normally attain the unpleasant realization that death threatens us as it does everyone else. Where the younger child may have played with the idea of being dead, as he also pretends to kill everyone who opposes him, there now arises with vivid consternation the awareness that death will someday strike him down exactly as if he were no different from all other living things that die. Older people often idealize the innocence and boundless vitality of youth. I think they have forgotten how terrifying the first acquaintance with the fear of death can be for many juveniles. Its occurrence partly explains the fascination among the young for horror movies that objectify and express the terror they feel. To some extent, it may also account for much of the violent and troubled behavior that characterizes this period of life. Through a dialectical confusion to which all strong emotions are subject, it may even throw some light on the relative frequency of suicide among adolescents. When it is painful and persistent, the fear of death augments the difficulty of living and thereby makes the prospect of immediate, total escape seem more attractive than before.

Among those who live on, which is to say the vast majority, there generally evolves a slow but gradual acceptance of death as a final termination. This may often take the form of mere adjustment: we become habituated to our fear of death and that makes the idea more tolerable, or at least less terrifying. In either event our mortality tends to become less of a preoccupation than before. We stop feeling the torment that we may have experienced in our earlier years; we become accustomed to the fact that everyone dies, ourselves included. We may still fear death, and to some extent that emotion may be present in all human beings, but it no longer affects us as once it did.

Also, we become used to surviving. We have endured all these years without dying; we have eluded the infinite number of catastrophes that are always possible in life; and so we tend to assume that things will go on the same way. The automobiles that missed hitting us, however barely, will continue to miss us. Illnesses that might have killed us, but didn't, will not kill us when they recur. It becomes easy to believe that we will be able to cope with future calamities as we always have. In a similar vein Mark Twain, when he was almost seventy-five, said that he did not fear death since there were so many catastrophes he had dreaded throughout his life which never materialized. He felt that death, too, would not equal its advance billing.

One should not idealize this stage of life, as optimistic philosophers do when they treat the increased acceptance of death like a blissful twilight that nature offers as a remedy to earlier suffering. In some people this attitude doubtless issues into a period of great peace and serenity; and we may consider that to be an innate capacity in everyone. But in most of us the acceptance of our coming death probably means that we have finally given up trying to unravel ultimate problems and are saving our remaining emotionality for efforts needed to stay alive. Accepting death as an approaching reality may thus signify greater insensitivity on our part rather than profound clarification. It may actually mask a subtle form of inauthenticity. That can be resisted, of course, but it is always possible in human beings.

For many people a further experience follows, or accompanies, the ones I have mentioned. We often transmute the fear of our own death into a greater fear that death may come to those we love. Through love people bestow exceptional value upon other persons and sometimes upon ideals or physical objects. The recipient of our love becomes so intimate a part of our being that the beloved's continued existence may matter to us more than our own. Self-sacrificial love in the saint, the hero, the devoted spouse, the parent defending his or her child is motivated by emotions that frequently include an overwhelming fear of death: not a fear of one's own death, though this may still exist to some degree, but a fear of mortal dangers that can befall the object of one's love.

In the history of ideas, love and death have often been associated with one another. Though a character in Shakespeare claims that "men have died from time to time, and worms have eaten them, but not for love," various traditions in the Western world have maintained that people do die for love and even that love proves itself in the willingness to die for what one loves.[13] In the philosophy of the twentieth-century writer Gabriel Marcel, one finds the suggestion that love is a way of saying to another person that "you shall not die."[14]

If we take this idea literally, it may well seem to be ridiculous. The beloved is just another human being, and nothing we can do will confer immortality. But possibly Marcel means that love is an affirmation of the beloved which bestows endless importance upon that person. In loving someone, an individual encases the beloved in values that may live on after the lovers die. Love includes the hope that their bond will have created a permanent goodness. The lover is telling the beloved: "Even if you died tomorrow, you will survive because our love has been a real and ineradicable achievement in life." That is what T. S. Eliot means when he says, in "A Dedication to My Wife," that neither wind nor sun can kill the roses in the rose-garden which is their love.[15] In this sense love does conquer death.

❊

In sketching these aspects of human development, I am not claiming that they reveal anything like a death-related instinct. On the other hand, they seem to accompany the aging process in ways that are not entirely learned from the environment. We are not taught to fear death acutely in adolescence, or to accept it with forbearance when we get older. Nevertheless, most people do learn how to adapt to physiological and psychological changes that occur throughout the years. One could therefore say that, to some extent, the progressive alteration in our attitude toward death must involve the accretion of learned responses. This does not prevent us from believing that the different stages follow one another in accordance with a complicated pattern that is basically innate. Further evidence may reveal that Freud's speculations, primitive and metaphysical as they were, can have fruitful consequences for research provided they are suitably revised.

For this new research to succeed, it must always recognize that what we mean by death has to be explained in terms of a natural dynamic that constitutes life. There is no meaning of death apart from its meaning in life. Death is so great a problem for human beings only because it intrudes upon our search for a meaningful life. All thinking about death reflects what we consider meaningful to us in life itself.

Our investigation thus takes us back to questions about the nature of meaningfulness. The Japanese novelist Mishima thought that life has meaning only when it is beautiful and therefore, he concluded, one should die before the ugliness of decay sets in. Whether or not he was right, many people have treated the aesthetic as a paradigm of meaning in life. Even if life is sound and fury signifying nothing, as Macbeth thought, it is also a production in which a player "struts and frets his hour upon the stage." But there are different ways of strutting and fretting. And a stage exists within a creative transaction. The player is the embodiment of an art form, and each of his gestures can be meaningful to him as well as to his audience. The question we must now ask is how this (or any other) meaning comes into being.

3.

THE CREATION OF MEANING

In this book I have been trying to suggest a naturalistic and empirical approach to questions about life and death. I argued that the meaning of death consists in its relevance to processes within life itself, and I suggested that instead of hoping to find the meaning *of* life we should seek insight into the nature of meaningfulness. Even if we make sense of the idea that there is a single meaning to life, and that this meaning has a prior status that may be discoverable, we still have to determine how life can be meaningful for us.

Those who accept Western religion believe that God's plan provides a foundation for meaning, and we may all agree that their faith simplifies their life by assuring them that everything they do and everything that happens to them is meaningful. But this pattern of belief is based on non-verifiable assumptions that exceed the limits of natural events and ordinary experience. Take away the transcendental props, which nowadays have become wobbly after centuries of criticism, and the grand edifice cannot stand. The challenge in our age is to understand how meaning can be acquired without dubious fantasying beyond the limits of our knowledge.

In "A Brief History of My Opinions" Santayana depicts his struggle with this problem. He describes his boyhood experience as a Catholic who loved what he calls "the Christian epic" but eventually concluded that neither it nor any other cosmic system could be taken as literal truth. "For my own part," he reports, "I was quite sure that life was not worth living; for if religion was false everything was worthless, and almost everything, if religion was true." Looking back at this moment in his life, Santayana interprets his pessimism as the by-product of a conflict within himself between Catholicism and "complete disillusion." He indicates the outcome when he tells us: "I was never afraid of disillusion, and I have chosen it."[1]

Santayana lived a meaningful life. The crisis he portrays frequently occurs among adolescents who come to realize how fragile are the doctrines they have inherited but now find untenable. There is also the sense of disillusionment that often accompanies a child's growing awareness that—like everything else in nature—he too will die. But having found the strength to put aside dogmas he no longer believed, Santayana could then create and carry out projects that were meaningful for others as well as for himself. Though he disintoxicated himself (a term that often appears in his writing) of optimistic assurance that all was for the best, he managed to live a productive and rewarding life.

Santayana's case, like many others, reveals that avoiding the traditional search for meaning need not put us at a disadvantage in our creation of a meaningful life. Though we no longer have authorities whose certitudes can direct us, we acquire the freedom to mold our own destiny. Santayana's approach requires greater courage perhaps, and so it may be harder to attain. But this alone would make it more outstanding as a personal achievement. Nevertheless, Santayana does not explain how his attitude can be distinguished from bravado or mere defiance. For if life is possibly worthless and our values have no objectivity beyond our own decisions, the creating of meaning may be just a superficial display and not especially important. What looks like courage may only be a refusal to accept the bitter consequences of believing that ultimately everything is futile.

This intuition underlies the thinking of Heidegger and Sartre about ontological anxiety. Their concept pertains to the creation of meaning as well as to the nature of death. Heidegger and Sartre assert that death not only issues into nothingness, inasmuch as it terminates life, but also that it symbolizes the inherent nothingness of being. Since the world arises out of nothing and will someday return to it, nothing really matters. They infer that anxiety (as an ontological condition) is the inevitable result of our awareness that nothingness is fundamental in reality. Anxiety is our unavoidable response to the contingency of existence and the lack of final sanction for any ideals or strivings that may guide our behavior. We define ourselves through freely chosen acts, but what we are and what we value must always be predicated on the underlying nullity of everything. Like Heidegger, Sartre maintains that we create meaningful and authentic lives by facing up to this grim fact. But that can happen, they insist, only in the context of ontological anxiety about nothingness.

Neither Heidegger nor Sartre is referring to psychological anxiety. That occurs when we are apprehensive about something in our experience without exactly being aware of what it is. But ontological anxiety is not addressed to anything. It directs itself not to an actual or conceivable something but to the nothing—which is the ground for everything—that Sartre calls "non-being curled at the heart of being."

Unless we can make sense of the notion of absolute nothingness, neither Heidegger's nor Sartre's conception of a meaningful life will be defensible. In a classic article Rudolf Carnap demonstrated the non-sense, the literal nonsense, of treating nothingness in this bizarre and confusing manner.[2] When Heidegger tries to clarify his approach, he admits that there may be no noun that can possibly convey the meaning of nothingness. For every substantival term must deal with a something, while nothingness is the total opposite of that. In his heavy-handed way, Heidegger jokes with the reader. If I am talking about nothing, he says, why should anyone bother with what I have written? Unless I can say something about something, why should anyone read me? He concludes that since there is nothing that *is* nothingness, his meaning can only be conveyed by a verb; and so he remarks that "Das Nichts nichtet." This translates as: "Nothingness nothings."[3]

The move from the noun to the verb cannot extricate Heidegger from his ontological difficulties. One can see why many philosophers who prize honesty of thought refuse to take his effort seriously. It lends itself to parody such as Tom Stoppard's in *Rosencrantz and Guildenstern Are Dead.* In Act III the ship is becalmed that carries the two false friends of Hamlet to England (and to death, though they do not know this). Rosencrantz is bored by their prolonged inactivity. He and Guildenstern have the following conversation:

> *Guil.:* Don't give up, we can't be long now.
>
> *Ros.:* We might as well be dead. Do you think death could possibly be a boat?
>
> *Guil.:* No, no, no . . . Death is . . . not. Death isn't. You take my meaning. Death is the ultimate negative. Not-being. You can't not-be on a boat.
>
> *Ros.:* I've frequently not been on boats.
>
> *Guil.:* No, no, no—What you've been is not on boats.
>
> *Ros.:* I wish I was dead.[4]

In part we laugh at this by-play because we feel that critics like Carnap may well be right in arguing that Heideggerian talk about ontological nothingness is nonsensical. We can understand what it is like for something to turn into nothing. First it existed and then it did not. Looking at a computer's monitor, we see a something which is the visual image. Then someone unplugs the machine and we see nothing of the sort. Similar alternations between something and nothing recur throughout our experience. They do not, however, implicate the total and absolute nothingness that Heidegger calls an ultimate ontological category. One might say that his language is poetically metaphoric. That would be acceptable if we could understand his metaphors. I am not convinced that we can. And if we cannot clarify the meaning of nothingness in this special usage, neither will the Heideggerian concept of anxiety function as he would like.

On the other hand, I feel within myself a definite and sympathetic responsiveness to Heidegger's intention, and this feeling cannot be discounted. For if he were merely talking gibberish, how could there be anything in me that resonates to his language? Heidegger is renowned for his claim that the prime question in philosophy is: "Why, in the universe as a whole, is there something rather than nothing?" Heidegger was not the first to have formulated this as a philosophical question. It appears in the writings of Leibniz, in Hume's *Dialogues Concerning Natural Religion,* and much further back in the history of philosophy. If it were a meaningless or nonsensical query, it could not strike us as having real profundity. Yet the question has a strong, albeit ambivalent, effect. Even though I doubt that anything intelligible is being said, I also feel that this is the most important issue that we could possibly consider.

Here again I can illustrate what seems nonsensical by citing a familiar joke. I am thinking of the Jewish story about two old friends who meet after an interval of many years. One asks the other what kind of life he has had. "A very happy one," is the reply: "On the whole, life has been good to me. And you?" "Not bad. I've nothing to complain about. But to tell the truth, if I had it all to do over again, I'd just as soon not have been born at all." "Ah yes," the other sighs, "but who can be so lucky?"

Why do we laugh at this answer? Because it is ontologically paradoxical. In order to exist, one must be born. (The man is not referring to his life as a fetus.) In non-existence there is no capacity for anything. How then could one have been lucky before existing; how could one have "been," whether lucky or otherwise?

If we extend this quandary to the universe as a whole, do we not see the impossibility of trying to conceive of absolute nothingness? And does this not reveal the oddness in asking the philosopher's question about why there is something rather than nothing? Physicists get into a similar difficulty when they incautiously say that everything began with the Big Bang and then ask what *preceded* it. This kind of question does not belong to physics at all, particularly if one assumes that the physical world originated with the Big Bang. If there was something before that, it cannot be understood in the language of physics. If *nothing* preceded the Big Bang, this too is inexpressible in physics. What then can it mean to ask what there was before there was anything?

But if the question is truly meaningless, why does it affect us so powerfully? Why does it constantly hover at the periphery of consciousness? Why do we feel that in *some* sense we do understand it? Its meaning is perpetually out of reach but almost within our grasp, like a forgotten name for which we keep groping. I have no satisfying solution to this dilemma, but I suggest that beyond the anxiety about nothingness as Heidegger and Sartre use that term there is an anxiety that must always be more ultimate. This is anxiety about ourselves as creatures who are able to use language in so strange and uncertain a fashion. There would be no cause of that anxiety if we could either understand what is being asked or else discard such utterances as merely nonsensical. But we seem to be unable to do either. Nor can we ignore the issue or reject it as a trivial confusion. We may dismiss the joke about the preferability of being unborn, but we cannot escape our nagging and disquieting puzzlement about there being something in the universe rather than nothing. The anxiety I am describing arises from our propensity to formulate problematic questions of this sort. It may not cause distress in everyone, but it lurks within us as a predicament that is typically human.

This kind of anxiety has a positive as well as a negative aspect. The positive contributes to the creation of meaning, as I shall presently show. But the negative warrants further attention. I am suggesting that it is a radical malaise we feel as thinking beings who use words that grip us with a sense of great, possibly greatest importance even though their meaning eludes our comprehension.

This is different from anxiety we might feel in trying to think about a situation that is unknown and even inconceivable. A person might fear death not only because he wants to live but also because he is pained by the fact that he cannot conceive of himself *as dead*. No one can imagine the state of being nothing rather than the something one now is. That is unknowable as well as inconceivable.

Nevertheless, the death of anything, even oneself, is not incomprehensible. We have often seen the termination of life processes. We are very familiar with the fact that events in nature come to an end. I strike a match and thereby ignite a flame. The fire exists by consuming energy. When its material resources are exhausted, it goes out. It would never occur to me to ask where the flame is once it has been extinguished. I understand what is meant by its having existed and now being nothing. In a similar fashion, I may think of my own life as beginning in time, continuing for a while as the flame does, and then disappearing whenever it has used up the matter that was essential for its existence. Though these processes, and the world from which they emerge, are largely unknown and even unknowable to me, I can recognize them as the workings of nature.

My annihilation as the outcome of my having existed may therefore be comprehensible even though the nothingness which results is unimaginable. I cannot know or imagine what it is like to be nothing, but I can understand this eventuality as the terminus of my finite being. What I cannot comprehend is the possibility of *everything* being nothing. One has the feeling that just as some particular flame goes out, so too could *all* flames expire. And if all flames, then why not all things as a whole? And if everything—all matter, all events in the universe, all space and time itself—were to end, each in its own way, would we not have absolute nothingness? One *seems* to understand what is being said. But actually the language defies comprehension. For if there were absolutely nothing, there would be no universe at all. There would just be a void. But what kind of being is *that?* It is not a consistent possibility for us to entertain. It boggles the mind.

This tells us something about our ability to think. It is wholly comprehensible to us that the flame I just ignited should not exist. It is wholly comprehensible that I, or you, or anyone else should not exist. We can surely envisage such possibilities. In doing so, we imagine the universe as it was before, but now deprived of one or another of its former entities. What we cannot comprehend is the universe being deprived of itself. We may *say* that all things can disappear just as any of them might, but the notion stuns and even troubles us. It is as if we were speculating about the end of reality. But it was reality that we were trying to comprehend. How can we do so if we eliminate that concept entirely? We cannot. And yet neither can we avoid having feelings of bafflement and metaphysical discomfort.

Out of this reverberation, obscure as it may be, arises the ontological anxiety that is basic to our condition and that only human beings undergo. It is part of what makes man the sick animal; no other animal suffers from this sickness. To the extent that all people are solipsistic and tend to identify reality with their own experience, the idea of their individual death can occasion a related anxiety. It is not only that we cannot imagine ourselves as nothing but also—if there is no reality apart from our own experience—our death may seem to be wholly incomprehensible. How can there be a world without *me*, since the only world I have ever known is the one that appears (directly or indirectly) to myself? If it could think, every flame and every atom in nature would have a similar thought. In overcoming our primal solipsism, we eradicate this form of anxiety. But in its more general reference, the underlying malaise may be inescapable, even in positivistic philosophers who ridicule any mention of it.

❄

In its negative aspect, ontological anxiety can make us doubt all efforts to think intelligibly about ultimate questions. Indeed, are we even sure that we know what rightly counts as "ultimate"? Being creatures who are aware of our own shortcomings, we have good reason to distrust our mental faculties. We often find ourselves guilty of self-delusion and liable to cognitive distortions of many sorts. But the uncertainties that belong to our ontological anxiety can be more pervasive. For they affect our knowledge of ourselves as conscious organisms that must define and determine their roles in the universe. We are by nature thinking beings, and if we cannot escape anxiety about the inherent structure of our thought processes, how can we hope to create purposive ideals that are congruent with reality instead of deflecting us from it?

This negative aspect may help to explain the conflict and depression that occur in many young people. I remember going through a very painful period, when I was fifteen or sixteen, during which I was troubled by reflections such as these: Not only will I die and be expunged but so too will the earth, the solar system, and possibly everything else that exists in the universe; whatever anyone achieves can have only local importance and short-lived value; in itself nothing is permanently or objectively good or bad; and therefore everything adds up to nothing and nothing really matters. And throughout these reflections, as a kind of ground bass to my misery, I sensed a residual inability to think clearly about such problems, as if they required a language I had not learned and never would. I gradually outgrew the depression that accompanied these ideas, and I am not suggesting that my depression was caused by them rather than vice versa. But they are ideas that often exist in human beings, particularly at moments of crisis, and above all in those who are beginning to suspect that there may not be a beneficent authority in the cosmos. If our ontological anxiety had only this negative pole, one might find it difficult to understand how anything but extreme pathology could ensue.

Fortunately, this type of anxiety can have a positive side. Once our hopeless questioning has reverberated in us, we may also intuit the mystery and the wonder in everything being what it is. The source of our anxiety will not have changed but our attention will now be focused on the mere fact of existence rather than the obscure possibility of non-existence. We may also experience, at least occasionally, what Wittgenstein called "astonishment that anything exists."* Instead of asking why there is something rather than nothing, we attend to the amazing—what may seem miraculous—presentation of any thing and every thing. Even if it arises out of a prior nothingness—whatever that may be—each occurrence offers itself as an ontological marvel. Though it may have been caused in every detail, the patterns of causation will themselves be experienced as gratuitous and resplendent. All reality will then appear to be what Santayana calls "free entertainment."

We feel this most keenly when goods are showered upon us beyond our expectations—serendipities or unforeseen joys, and above all the gift of a newly created life with which we can identify. When we first experience parenthood, or vicariously share it with someone else, we sense the grandeur in this augmentation of living energy. When we make something with which we have mixed our labor and into which we have poured our imagination, we feel magically renewed and revitalized. Even as hunters and fishermen, we often have mixed feelings about "the one that got away"—regret that our efforts have failed but also a sense of awe and somber gladness that this fellow participant in life can have a further chance to go on living.

Our feeling of mystery tinged with delight need not be restricted to special occasions or gratifying events. On the contrary, we may feel joyful exhilaration just in being alive, and in the immediacy with which we experience our own existence. At the end of his tormented life, Jean-Jacques Rousseau claimed to have finally discovered the sweet pleasure that comes from savoring "le sentiment de l'existence." Mysticism is a means by which some people cultivate this capacity in themselves. For most of us it is hard to reconcile the implied passivity of mysticism with the need to act dynamically in order to survive. We may nevertheless approximate the mystical attitude by enjoying, and contributing to, the development and efflorescence of life. As the baby grows, its simplest

---

* According to Wittgenstein, "this astonishment cannot be expressed in the form of a question and there is no answer to it. Anything we can say must, a priori, be only nonsense. Nevertheless we thrust against the limits of language."[5]

attainments strike the doting mother as uniquely wonderful. Though she is responding to her child as someone she loves in a special way, she also knows that others feel something similar when they appreciate the vivid spontaneity of life wherever it occurs. We can sense the mystery of mere existence by looking in the eyes of a domestic animal as well as in those of a human being, and in both cases we may express our enjoyment through action for the welfare of the creature to which we are attending.

To have this experience it is not essential that we love the individual whose identity we intuit. Though love is one of the means by which we acknowledge the gratuitous splendor in anything being what it is—whatever it may happen to be—we can experience a similar wonderment even without love. We then see the object as a something that could just as easily be nothing. We immerse ourselves in the unfathomable mystery of its having the being it does have. We respond to its sheer reality, to its given but ontologically fortuitous presence in the universe. Our feeling is related to what Stendhal called an awareness of "l'imprévu" (the unforeseen) in all events. He thought that without such awareness one could not act spontaneously, or ever find the joy of living.

The state I am describing does not occur at every moment of human consciousness. For some people it is only a rare phenomenon. Even so, this feeling provides an access to meaningfulness. As long as one has such feelings, life is fraught with meaning. If we intuit the wonder in something existing and being as it is, we sense the importance of concerning ourselves with this particular entity. If we do not love the object, we may not care to preserve it. If it threatens us, we may even have to destroy it. Whatever our attitude may be, it will respond to the identity of this unique and individual being. Our life will become meaningful in relation to it.

This is not the only type of meaningfulness, and like all meaningfulness it is created by reactions that nothing can force upon us. If you are not astonished by mere existence, you cannot be coerced to have that feeling. I think of this condition as the "beginning" of meaning because it exists at such a fundamental level. Since it may not rise to consciousness in everyone, however, and since its occurrence may be infrequent in those who do have the experience, we should treat it as only one of the sources of meaning.

Among thinkers who speculate about intellectual development, wonder has often been extolled as a fertile component of human nature. In the *Metaphysics* Aristotle says it is the origin of philosophy; and Einstein remarked that a man who has no wonder about the universe is "as good as dead: his eyes are closed."[6] In Plato's *Euthyphro* Socrates shows how philosophy serves to arrest routine activities, thereby causing us to confront what is both puzzling and amazing in our actual experience. Religions have generally made a comparable attempt, and at their best they help us to celebrate the mysteries of life. When they enclose these mysteries in others of their own pseudo-scientific conception, they betray their primary mission. With innocence and purity of heart, each generation must find its own way to reinstate the initial wonderment.

The arts often exploit this experience as an aesthetic resource. Visual arts are especially suited to reveal the wonderful. A Chardin still-life presents us with apples and oranges that are very different from any real fruit we may have seen inasmuch as these are not three-dimensional and cannot be eaten. Still they express and vibrantly show forth the astounding fact that such objects, which we ordinarily take for granted, exist in a world that might just as well have had nothing like them. There they are, on the canvas as reminders of the originals that were on a plate in the artist's studio, marvels to behold just in being themselves. Music has greater difficulty in conveying this particular effect, but it readily communicates a sense of mystery. Though music can hardly represent or even get us to imagine objects existing in their individual and often mute condition, it can arouse feelings of awe, as in the opening chords of Bach's B-minor Mass, or astonishment, as in Haydn's *Creation*, or even the intuition that life is an "unanswered question," as in the tone poem by Charles Ives.

In poetry and prose we find a panoply of possible illustrations. Imagistic poems regularly encourage us, with almost simple-minded devotion, to revel in the plethora of things that appear to our senses. I choose one example from my own experience. Many years ago my wife and I attended an evening of poetry reading in a Parisian theater. It was an informal occasion and somewhat impromptu. Anyone in the audience could go up on stage and read his own poetry, or someone else's, whether published or not. One young lady, using the gestures of an actress, recited a poem that consisted of only two lines: "Il pleut,/C'est merveilleux." My wife and I both laughed. "It is raining,/That's marvellous"—this did not seem to us like much of a poem. Yet these lines have stayed with me through the years. Their diminutive structure, briefer than a haiku, the rapid rhyme signifying both immediacy and completion, expresses a feeling of wonder about mere existence. We are not told whether it is a warm and balmy rain, a cathartic cloudburst, or an exciting thunderstorm in the midst of summer. For all we know, it could be a freezing downpour. The poem merely says that rain is falling. But that is enough if one sees the common event as a marvel in itself. The force of this minimal art work would have been lessened if we had been informed about the rain's effect upon our comfort.

I find a similar instance in the second act of *Hamlet*. Telling his friend Horatio that of late he has lost all mirth, Hamlet enumerates aspects of the world that are nevertheless worthy of delight—"this goodly frame the earth," "this brave o'erhanging firmament." In the midst of his account Hamlet mentions "this most excellent canopy, the air, look you." I see him suddenly raising his eyes and acknowledging something in our ordinary experience that we normally ignore. He speaks of the *air*; he says nothing about a cooling breeze or the goodness of fresh, unpolluted oxygen. He realizes that just to live and breathe can make life worth living, if only we appreciate the wonderment in everything. In his demoralized condition, he himself is unable to do so.

Once we attain the relevant ability, we find that we can take an interest in the world apart from its utility. But, of course, wonderment does not preclude other kinds of response. Indeed, if we had no other attitude, we could not live. We are able to survive in nature only by using persons and things for our own benefit. Like it or not, we are and must be commodities for each other. If we treat another person as nothing *but* a commodity, we no longer experience him as a unique and wonderful manifestation of reality. But there is nothing to prevent us from accepting someone as he is, as a particular something that will eventually be nothing, while also profiting from his utility. Though these are very different attitudes, they may certainly coexist.

To the extent that others are commodities to us, we generally treat them as exchangeable units whose individuality has little or no significance. That is how we think about replaceable parts of a machine, for example spark plugs or transistors. One is as good as another if they all function alike. But when we cultivate our sense of mystery, the individuality in everything takes on a new importance. This importance is a value we bestow, and that is why the attitude approximates and to some extent duplicates love as I have described it in *The Nature of Love*. Life cannot be meaningless to anyone who loves. No one in love has ever asked whether anything matters. To the lover the beloved matters supremely, even if nothing else does.

But though love is related to meaningfulness, we should not assume that either is a subset of the other. Through love we make another person important to ourselves by means of our bestowal of value upon him. This may contribute to the meaningfulness of our own life, but meaning can arise in other ways as well. These other sources may also involve a kind of love—what I will call the love of life. I leave that issue for later. At the moment we do better to consider meaningfulness on its own. Similarly, we should not emphasize the role of wonderment to the exclusion of everything else. Ontological anxiety is not the only category that is basic in human experience. We are also constituted by "vital instincts," as William James calls them. These can make their own contribution to a meaningful life.

✳

The essay in which James employs this term has the title "Is Life Worth Living?" Characteristically, James begins with a jocular answer: "It depends on the liver." Does he mean the liver as the organ of digestion that so greatly controls our moods? Or is he referring to the liver as the living person who asks such questions, hoping to get an objective and all-inclusive reply but inevitably thrown back upon his own particular case?

When James examines the problem more closely, his discussion is anything but jocular. He documents the terrible sufferings human beings have undergone, the unspeakable cruelties they have inflicted on one another, and the great obstacles that attend every effort to improve their condition on earth. Far from wishing to encourage quietism or inhibit action, James thinks his horrifying account shows how meaning issues from the ever-present challenge to take up arms against a sea of troubles. If you find your existence meaningless, he says to the young man or woman in his audience, you need only recognize how abysmal life would be unless well-intentioned people like yourself accepted their responsibilities. Faced with an urgent crisis that demands moral commitment, James asserts, the ordinary person will respond. Vital instincts take over and they propel us into action that itself makes life meaningful: "A challenge of this sort, with proper designation of detail, is one that need only be made to be accepted by men whose normal instincts are not decayed."[7]

James obviously assumes that the moral imperatives with which he was reared are instinctual, or at least universal. Leaving aside this difficulty, we may also be dismayed by his implied belief that anyone who hesitates or lacks zealous dedication exemplifies the decay of "normal" instincts. We at the end of the twentieth century are likely to ask how anyone can know that such instincts exist. And if they *are* decayed, how will the Jamesian prescription be of help? The person who is floundering because his vital impulses have deteriorated will not be moved by appeals to his morality. Despite all exhortations to alleviate the sufferings of others, he will still find life meaningless. On the other hand, those who appreciate the urgency in acting as James suggests will have no need of such incentives. They will already feel that life is worth living.

One might reply that a sensitive adolescent, for instance, poised at the borderline between despair and wholesome immersion in a social cause, may benefit from the rousing appeal of Jamesian activism. This is true, and the benign character of James' preaching need not be doubted. But its actual utility is probably much less than James may have hoped.

Had he been more radical, or less eager to restore depressed humanity to health and hearty involvement, James might have raised doubts about the question with which he began. If we ask whether life is worth living, we put it in the scale with other possibilities in order to see which has greatest value. But what are those possibilities? Are we back to the absurdities of the Jewish joke about non-existence? Even someone contemplating suicide does not engage in that kind of deliberation. He thinks about killing himself because he fears that his experience will be no better in the future than it has been in the past and present. He is not evaluating life in general, only trying to decide whether he wants his share of it to continue.

In the next chapter I shall return to questions such as those that James discusses. I mentioned them here as a way of showing that an appeal to "vital instincts" requires much more analysis before it can explain how human beings create a life that is meaningful. A life of mere self-preservation, for which we may well have instincts, would be for most of us a life without meaning. We want something beyond the routine of a boring and aimless existence. We want to satisfy standards of value to which we consciously adhere. To some extent, and with tremendous variation in their level of awareness, all living things may be similar in this respect. Whether or not we believe in instincts as an underlying system of determinants, we must recognize that creatures make their own insistent demand on life: every organism acts self-righteously, as if its need to live is both obvious and inherently justifiable although dependent on other parts of nature. In its specific context, each entity asserts a claim to what is best for its own interests.

Life would seem to operate as a concatenation of discrete nodules, each manifesting its vitality from within. Something comparable may also be true of being as a whole. That was what Spinoza maintained. He held that everything always seeks to preserve, and to perpetuate, its pattern or mode of existence— "The endeavour wherewith each thing endeavours to persist in its own being is nothing more than the actual essence of the thing itself."[8] Nietzsche's notion of a universal "will to power" is also based on this conception.

I need not go that far to make my point. What strikes me as most remarkable is the fact that life expresses itself through creatures that act as if they were the center and focus of importance for all of life, as if the world "owes" them a living—as we say—and the meaning both *in* and *of* life resides in what they individually desire. I assume, moreover, that each can make this claim with as much legitimacy from its own point of view as we do from ours. I find it utterly impossible to observe another animal without seeing it as a kindred being, a bearer and representative of life just as I am, and in this respect wholly equal to myself. Everyone who enjoys the company of a cat or dog or any other pet will have had a similar experience. Though I differ in many ways from other living entities, I cannot feel that there is any ontological superiority in my being human. Life is *there* as much as *here* within me. As my own vital ends are valuable to me, I must believe the same is true for all the other myriad forms in which life occurs.

From this I derive an axiom about valuation that may help us to understand the nature of meaning. Not only do active creatures behave as if their immediate concerns are valuable, but also words like "good" and "bad," "right" and "wrong," "beautiful" and "ugly"—the terminology of value in general—must ultimately refer back to the needs, the drives, the impulses, the feelings and motives that arise from an organism's struggle to exist and promote its own particular being. From that attempt there issues a relevant type of meaning. Life has meaning for creatures that engage in the active preservation of their mode of existence.

The idea that value originates in vital demands, whether or not they are all instinctual, belongs to the naturalistic approach in Western philosophy. Thinkers as diverse as Hobbes, Hume, John Stuart Mill, Comte, James, Dewey, and Santayana have all constructed ethical systems based on this naturalistic premise. I shall not reproduce their arguments. I need only apply them to the analysis of meaning. At every moment each appearance of life makes an equal claim—though only from its own perspective—to goodness, to value, and to meaning. To see all living things this way may also increase our sense of wonder. As long as we empathize with another creature as something that is trying to secure its purchase upon life with the same self-affirmation that we ourselves feel, we cannot treat it merely as a thing, as nothing but a commodity for us to use. Even if we have to sacrifice its necessities to ours, or to the demands of a supervening morality that may require the sacrifice of our necessities as well, we will do so with humility and even reverence for the life that it contains.

I am not suggesting that this reverential attitude occurs automatically, or frequently. For though we may believe that each organism is valuable to itself, we may have little or no concern for its welfare. And regardless of our good will, we may have no compunction in subordinating its interests whenever they conflict with ours. In the order of nature there is little to suggest that animate beings often identify themselves with alien species. The lion that pounces on the antelope would seem to have no sense of unity with this other exemplification of life.

The man who slaughters an animal he wants to eat, or an enemy he wishes to destroy, will normally respond to the being of his victim much as the lion does. He acts from his own perspective. But human beings also have a deeply rooted capacity, at once conceptual and intuitive, to see the other creature as a comparable nexus of vitality, a manifestation of energy that is equivalent to what exists in them as well. When that capacity is realized, we accept the premise that our values are not uniquely justifiable, and like primitive people who worship the spirit of the animals they devour, we stand in awe before the fact that all forms of life assert themselves as an end and final embodiment of value. We are not the same as they, but we are alike in this regard.

❋

From the duality in our attitude toward life there result two modes of meaning. One of these pertains to a person's consecutive attempts to satisfy his own needs and desires. The second is a meaning that results from identification with other animate things. For our present purposes, we may put in abeyance questions about the total separability between these two types of meaning. One might plausibly argue that our ability to identify with life in others results from relevant needs and desires in ourselves. It is also possible that our conception of our self partly depends on our sense of unity with the life that others have, especially other human beings.

We shall have to return to problems of this sort. But first we should realize that each type of response contributes to meaning in life only by virtue of an intervening variable—our propensity to formulate ideals. More than any other animal, human beings are programmed to pursue distant and even unattainable goals that often serve as motives for their conduct. All organisms act in systematic and possibly agreeable ways that are needed for survival. That is why one can say that they normally have meaningful lives. The bird that builds its nest seems to care about the suitability of its building materials; the worker bees that provide food for their colony seem to act in a purposive fashion that matters greatly to them. The meaningfulness of human life is not entirely different. But unlike the bird or bee, and to a degree that is unequaled in lower primates, Homo sapiens uses his intellect and imagination to cultivate behavior that goes beyond what is needed for the preservation of either himself or others. Idealization is a notable example of this process.

To pursue ideals as human beings do is to direct one's striving toward remote achievements that are often subsumed under some imagined perfection. This goal orientation is not always prudential, for biological survival does not depend on it. Human beings do not require the works of Bach or Beethoven in order to adapt successfully to their environment. They may need the consolations of music, and in general the benefits that accrue from harmonious melody and rhythm. But lesser composers can satisfy such needs to the extent that they are merely biological. What happens throughout the ages is that human intelligence, having doubtless evolved as a device that enables our species to master its physical environment, creates infinitely varied systems of extended purposiveness. These systems become important to mankind; they acquire special value and often stimulate a further search for values. They may even cause some members of the species to believe that life is not worth living unless certain extraordinary standards are satisfied. Nevertheless, human beings could surely survive without many of the preferred ideals or valuational tropes to which they become accustomed.

Because they lie beyond our actual but meager capacities, ideals make our interests meaningful by placing them in a larger context fashioned by imagination. A feeling, an act, a momentary attitude seems meaningless to us when it occurs as an unrelated event. We need to see its ramifications within a complex of further desires and possible achievements. That is why a man who succumbs to a sexual urge for some beautiful stranger may honestly say to his wife that his infidelity meant nothing to him. Unlike Don Juan, for whom sexual conquest embodies the principal meaning in life, he may have been pursuing no erotic ideal. He experienced strong libidinal drive, perhaps, and he may have engaged in intimacies that his wife might have hoped or expected him to reserve for her alone. But in claiming that his dalliance was meaningless, he is saying that nothing really important occurred. Ideals can enrich meaning by bestowing great importance upon virtually anything we do or feel. If the wayward husband protests that his sexual fling was "just one of those things," an escapade that meant nothing at all, he treats it as a trivial event that is not related to any affective or marital ideal. If his wife is unpersuaded, it is because she sees his conduct as a threat to the network of shared ideals that define the meaning of their life together.

Similar considerations apply in other areas of our existence. People who devote themselves to a worthy but stultifying career toward which their upbringing has steered them may suddenly feel that everything they do is meaningless. This can happen to virtually anyone. In our generation it has become quite frequent, and not merely among those who have been favored in the way that Tolstoy was. A crisis of this sort occurs when men and women lose faith in the sustaining ideals with which they were raised, either because their society no longer cares about these goals or else because they themselves find them unrewarding. A man may have liked the idea of making money, for instance, but he may end up feeling that it contributes to nothing else he values. If it engages no other aspirations or attainments that matter to him, it will have lost all meaning.

For most people there is virtually no experience—not even a highly pleasurable one—that will seem meaningful unless it can be justified in terms of an ideal one has chosen. Even psychopaths have difficulty believing that whatever they happen to like is sufficient unto itself. Compulsive behavior on the part of an inveterate gambler or workaholic, or anyone else who enslaves himself to an overriding obsession, illustrates how powerful can be our need to find meaning through self-imposed ideals. The compulsiveness satisfies this need insofar as it enables an individual to pursue particular goals in a systematic and intensified manner. Betting with mystical fervor on number 7, or filling every minute with relentless toil, or diligently avoiding cracks in the sidewalk becomes supremely meaningful for such persons. They often believe that *only* these idiosyncratic ideals can give meaning to their lives.

People who are more healthy-minded, or more fortunate, idealize on a broader scale. They seek meaning through ideals that cannot be limited to isolating activities. The obsessive individual's search for meaning curtails his ability to explore. His attitude is diseased because it excludes further prospects that are available to human beings generally. When they are beneficial, ideals awaken the spirit to burgeoning possibilities for self-realization. Different ideals will be geared to different consummations, and even in the healthiest person ideals can always conflict with one another. But such constraints belong to a dynamic process that does not throttle human nature. On the contrary, it affords the maximum opportunity for creating new and more satisfying patterns of meaning.

Some thinkers, including Freud when he portrays civilization as an imposition upon biological impulses, seem to consider ideals extraneous to what is natural in us. Yet man would not be man unless he idealized, unless he constructed ideals of a deliberate and imperative character that guide his life and give it a feeling of urgency as well as direction. We might also assert that human beings would die of boredom if they somehow lost the capacity to create new standards of achievement. For an organism such as ours, idealization could thus have survival value after all. Whether or not this is true, we have evolved as a species composed of individuals who feel a constant need to pursue goals that are sometimes arbitrary and often infinitely remote.

This propensity may be uniquely human. If we can say that birds and bees act meaningfully in doing what they usually do, we may also assume that they "know" the difference between good and bad. It is good to get twigs that are solid rather than rotten, to fetch fresh rather than stale nectar. And perhaps all birds and bees have an innate sense of better or worse with respect to those elements of the environment that interest them. But we have no reason to think that *perfection* means anything to them. Or that they suffer—as human beings do—from assumed inadequacy if their efforts fail to satisfy criteria of excellence that are self-imposed and possibly a matter of individual taste.

My distinction can be illustrated by an experimental finding that at first may seem to weaken it. Ethologists have shown that in artificial conditions many species favor a pattern of behavior that is not beneficial and may even be antithetical to survival. For instance, the chicks of certain gulls are programmed to peck at a red dot on the parent's beak in order to get food. If a piece of wood is substituted for the parental beak, the chicks will peck at it provided that it too has a red dot. The bigger one makes the dot, the greater is the chick's attraction to it. In this mode of response, which can obviously be counterproductive as far as survival is concerned, we might see a parallel to the human propensity for creating ideals, establishing a gradation of values, and passionately devoting oneself to goals that make life meaningful regardless of their utility. The gulls would seem to be obsessed by the appearance of bigger and better red dots, just as some people expend their energy in the adoration of one or another type of perfectibility.

Seductive as it is, this reasoning fails in one important detail. The analogy between gull-obsessiveness and human dedication to ideals ignores the fact that in their *natural* state gulls do not show an interest in the biggest of all possible red dots. The opposite is true of men and women. Some of them, those who belong to preagricultural societies, for instance, may not care about ideals that matter to civilized people, but all human beings have a tendency to act like the manipulated gulls seeking the best red dot wherever it is to be found. What is contrived for the gulls by the experimenting scientist is natural for us. We constantly invent new ideals and yearn for unlimited possibilities. Even primitive, or unreflective humans create circumstances under which they can search for their equivalent of a perfect dot.

This does not mean that idealization is inherently directed toward perfection itself, perfection as a determinate and clearly definable entity. That concept belongs to idealist philosophies, of which Platonism is the most spectacular example. All such approaches falsify the nature of idealization. They assume that the making of ideals presupposes an ability to contemplate a purified essence which captivates us through the beauty and completeness of its form. To think in these terms is to give undue importance either to sensory acuities (above all, visual) or else to our logical faculties: the first because the philosopher interprets the pursuit of an ideal as if it were the search for a goal one observes in the mind's eye much as one directly perceives objects in a visual field; the second because the enticing perfection is generally seen as an abstract entity, like a number, as opposed to anything concrete in material experience.

We liberate ourselves from these theories of idealization by studying the search for perfection more empirically. Some people do hold aloft the image of a final, unimprovable though possibly unachievable, goal that ideally they would like to reach. The mind's eye, when it is located in the head of a particular kind of artist, does occasionally operate in this manner. For the most part, however, it does not—even for the greatest and most ambitious artists. Aesthetic creativity, like creativity in general, usually involves an endless quest toward new and ever-changing values. The artist may say that he is pursuing "the ideal," but rarely will he define it as a particular culmination that would be the absolute fulfillment of his labors if only he could attain it. Whatever he does accomplish becomes a springboard for further acts of creativity. The idea of perfection serves as a perennial incentive, but there is nothing that could be called a determinate perfection that guides his striving. Idealization functions in him, as in all of us, like a jet that propels the engine forward without any clear and distinct idea of where its trajectory must end. We are by nature internal guidance systems that maneuver ourselves through life but without any fixed or final targets.

The Platonic conception of ideals is ultimately defeatist. Despite its attempt to escape the dross of our mundane existence, despite its longing for elevated goals that reveal an infinity of aesthetic and moral goodness, despite its refusal to tolerate partial or imperfect achievements, Platonism yearns for unchanging ideals that forever float above and beyond human capabilities. They are said to motivate all our searching and yet, like the delectable fruit in the myth of Tantalus, they afford no satisfaction apart from the imaginative pleasure we get in contemplating them. The Platonist may insist that he is merely depicting the structure of reality. If frustration is inherent in all human aspiration, the fault is not of his making. He is just the messenger, he will say, bearing painful truths to mankind in the hope that we will learn how to profit from the shining essences revealed by his philosophy. Having shared his insight, will we not pursue these superior goods with greater understanding of our own limitations?

I do not dismiss this type of defense. Much of the best poetry in the Western world was written under the influence of the Platonic outlook, and without it one could hardly explain the flowering of religious mysticism in the Judaeo-Christian-Moslem tradition. All the same, this way of interpreting the nature of ideals belongs to a demoralized, and even pathological approach to human possibilities. It instills an alluring vision of goods that lie beyond each present experience, and it encourages us to take purposive action in the attempt to snare them. But then it systemically dashes every hope by asserting that nothing in the actual world, nothing in nature or the environment, is really valuable since none of it can possibly satisfy our craving for the absolute. From that remarkable assumption, this kind of theorizing concludes there must be another world or realm of being in which our losses will be restored and oneness with perfection finally consummated.

This, however, is a leap into the dark. Instead of positing an unverifiable domain in which perfectionist ideals predominate, we do better to reject all such dogmas about the nature of idealization. That faculty has an important function in human life, and we should thank the Platonists for alerting us to its pervasiveness throughout our experience. But it does not operate in the manner they envisage. As part of our life in nature, ideals provide rewards that often sustain us. We enjoy the limited degree to which we reach our goals despite their elusiveness, and we flourish through the acts of imagination and behavior that are involved in pursuing them. Though our actual achievements are not perfect, we realize that perfection is mainly a device for extrapolating beyond the status quo and that only rarely—if ever—can we hope to experience a pure example of it.

There is no inherent calamity in this aspect of the human condition, just as there is no failure in the fact that we cannot veto the laws of nature. The Platonist may be unwilling to accept the lack of perfection in the world, but to that extent he is out of touch with our reality. Those who are not will find ways to delight in the process of living for ideals that change direction as one or another proximate end is reached. Each experience of goodness serves to justify our ability to idealize. The organism is recompensed by what it has gained while also being spurred to continued action by the knowledge that ideally much more can always be imagined. A meaningful life results from this intermeshing of means and ends, purposeful efforts to satisfy ideals leading to gratifications that matter not only in themselves but also in their ability to awaken new desires and new pursuits. We do not create meaning by fluctuating between the manic-depressive extremes of Platonist metaphysics.[9]

＊

Some of the shortcomings in Plato's type of idealism were rectified by Hegel's variations on it. Hegel tries to overcome Plato's difficulties by erasing the distinction between the two realms of being. For Hegel the "other world" is simply this one seen from the point of view of its striving for greater goods. His philosophy is optimistic, not only in predicting that some day the perfect absolute will come into being, but also in claiming that every moment is a step in that direction and therefore contributes to the existence of immanent goodness. Thus ideals are always operating in nature and we need not despair even though everything we do or feel must be destroyed for the sake of some future development. If only we understood the rightness of it all, we would be grateful for our place in a world that is moving ever closer to perfection.

In effect Hegelian philosophy glorifies idealization in man while minimizing the brute materiality of the universe as a whole. To this extent it may well be guilty of what Santayana calls philosophical egotism. It is man extolling his own ability to idealize, bestowing infinite value upon this part of himself by assigning ontological hegemony to it throughout the cosmos. But even within human nature we have every reason to deny that idealization is the ultimate determinant. It is but one of many vectors interacting in our field of vital forces. Its ability to prevail is never guaranteed. And in the universe at large, there is no reason to think it has a major role to play. Ideals have great value for our species, and without them we would have difficulty explaining why many of the things that matter to us should mean as much as they do. But to extend the ontological status of ideals beyond these limits can only transmute healthy-minded self-assertion into perverse self-adulation.

Though idealist philosophies like Plato's and Hegel's may be scarcely creditable when taken at face value, or as the promulgation of literal truth, they exemplify one of our deepest attitudes. They manifest and proudly promulgate the *love* of ideals. The pervasive importance of such love should not be disregarded. When Hegel said that nothing great was ever achieved without passion, he was referring to our passionate need to serve one or another ideal. Not all men and women feel this love with the fervor and the desperate craving that belong to passion. But love occurs at various temperatures, sometimes hot and sometimes tepid. If we admit this differentiation into our thinking about the quality of love, we can readily see that the love of ideals performs a crucial function even in activities that do not lead to greatness. The idealists are therefore right in stressing, and celebrating, man's devotion to ideals. Their mistake consists in naively assuming that this type of love is necessarily preferable to all others.

To the lover, every love that is powerful seems to speak with absolute and objective authority. That is why love always runs the risk of self-delusion, as cynics have often observed (though they draw the wrong inferences). The love of ideals as felt by idealist philosophers is oblivious to the fact that some other love—for example, the love of persons—may be equally grounded in reality. Loving another person means experiencing him or her as more than just the embodiment or representation of an ideal. It means accepting this person as he is, bestowing value upon him while also appraising him in relation to one or another standard. That kind of love is different from a love of ideals, which involves dedication to them as abstractions regardless of how they may or may not pertain to actual persons.

Not only do the idealists mislead us when they ascribe ontological superiority to the love of ideals, but also they fail to admit that—for all practical purposes—their love reduces to a fascination with some ideal they personally favor. Warfare among human beings is often caused by conflict between particular ideals, each espoused with the same lofty devotion to ideals in general and the same assurance that the enemy is merely falsifying them. Passionate love can always have disastrous consequences, and the love of ideals is possibly the most dangerous. The sense of rectitude and heroic aspiration that it generates may shield our sight from the holocausts to which well-intentioned idealism can often lead.

Nevertheless, the love of ideals need not itself be impugned. I am not questioning its capacity to create a life worth living, but only its excessive glorification by an influential school of philosophers. By loving ideals we become participants in purposive behavior that expresses moral commitment and engagement in a cause beyond ourselves. Life then takes on a meaning that derives from this special kind of love. Such meaning is proof against the slings and emotional arrows that accompany the love of persons. No human being is perfect and many will not be able to reciprocate our interest. But the ideal burns brightly, like a perpetual beacon that lights our path into a terrain of ever-increasing goodness or beauty. It is Cyrano's white plume or Henry V's banner fluttering over the battlefield in Olivier's film. Though our hearts must beat responsively, and our imagination must teach us how to pursue the glittering prospect, none of this would be meaningful unless we were guided by ideals that have elicited our love—ideals of courage, truth, beauty, creativity, justice, honesty, freedom, happiness, self-fulfillment, compassion, rectitude, and even the perfection of life itself.

These ideals and others considered less noble—fame, reputation, family honor, efficiency, wealth, pleasure, comfort, social standing, eminence in a profession or sport—provide their own types of meaning. They are all created by humanity in the course of its natural and historical evolution. But as there is no prior essence that can define humanity, neither is there a preordained harmony among the ideals that different individuals or cultures must seek in their quest for meaning. The making of a unified and meaningful whole is necessary if one hopes to have a good life. But can there be a single pattern that is best for all human beings? I do not think so.

In examining this kind of problem in the following chapter, we shall have to address questions about meaning that we have thus far deferred, questions about what makes a life significant or worth living. If anything matters, how can we determine what *truly* matters? And how can these reflections help us to solve the practical problems of day-by-day existence?

4.
LIVES OF MEANING AND SIGNIFICANCE

Think of a life that has ended: a person lived, and now is dead. Imagine that someone asks whether this person had a meaningful existence. What kind of question is that? Note that we are not being asked whether the man or woman was *happy*. Despite the relation between happiness and meaning, they are not the same. We may say that happiness requires a harmonious adjustment between oneself and one's surroundings; but an individual who finds himself *out* of harmony, his experience largely consisting in a struggle against a hostile environment, might nevertheless have a meaningful life. The meaning in his life may even result from his refusal to accept the dictates of his surroundings. Given the opportunity to have a happy life if only he conforms to circumstances he considers morally repugnant, he may renounce happiness and choose uncomfortable resistance.

The hero and, to some extent, the saint are people who often feel the need to make this kind of choice. They may experience happiness, but they are prepared to sacrifice it for the sake of some goal that has greater importance for them. Though their lives are not the only ones that are meaningful, they reveal that meaning and happiness are not identical. A life without much happiness can be a meaningful one, even if—as I shall argue—a meaningful life provides its own measure of happiness.

The relationship between happiness and meaning is a dominant theme in John Stuart Mill's autobiography. Describing his life as a young man, he documents his dedication to the principles of utilitarian philosophy he had inherited from his father and Jeremy Bentham:

> I had what might truly be called an object in life; to be a reformer of the world. My conception of my own happiness was entirely identified with this object. . . . As a serious and permanent personal satisfaction to rest upon, my whole reliance was placed on this; and I was accustomed to felicitate myself on the certainty of a happy life which I enjoyed, through placing my happiness in something durable and distant, in which some progress might be always making, while it could never be exhausted by complete attainment.[1]

One could infer from this account that Mill's life at the time was both meaningful and happy. But at the age of twenty he had what he calls "a crisis in my mental development." That phrase, which he uses as the title of a chapter, is interesting in itself. For what he experienced was more than just an intellectual crisis. It was also depression or affective exhaustion. His suffering, which lasted for a period of years, taught him the difference between a meaningful and a happy life. Mill's breakdown occurred when he asked himself whether his reformist activities, his strenuous and by now habitual attempts to bring about the greatest happiness of the greatest number of human beings, would add to his own happiness if these efforts ever succeeded. He concluded that he had been deceiving himself, and that even if he did change society in ways conducive to general happiness it would not make *him* any happier.

Throughout its duration, and despite the misery it entailed,

Mill's dejected state does not seem to have undermined his pursuit of utilitarian ideals. In some respects the condition may actually have strengthened his commitment. He tells us that his pathological experience taught him that people can be happy only if they "have their minds fixed on some object other than their own happiness: on the happiness of others, on the improvement of mankind, even on some art or pursuit, followed not as a means, but as itself an ideal end."[2]

Writing many years later, Mill says that he still thinks this to be the best maxim for most people. But it does not explain the onset of his psychological crisis. All along he had been acting for the happiness of others, which he treated as his "ideal end." Yet this moral concern of his did not lead to happiness for him. It gave him something to live for, but it could not alleviate his personal distress.

Mill accurately diagnoses his problem when he says that his education had been too greatly oriented toward the acquisition of cerebral skills. Even in the midst of his crisis, he recognized that his upbringing had rendered him overly analytic and deficient in the capacity to commiserate with others. He sensed a lack of sympathetic feelings in himself. He also felt that he had attained inadequate cultivation in "passive susceptibilities" that need to be fostered as much as active and intellectual faculties. Mill associates the susceptibilities he considers passive with the imaginative pleasures that poetry, music, and the fine arts in general are able to produce. In other words, it was aesthetic responsiveness and the experience of sympathy or compassion that had been neglected in his early education. He saw now that in order to maximize the chances for happiness this area of life had to be put in balance with one's ethical and cognitive development.

Later in the autobiography, Mill shows how his enjoyment of Romantic poetry, and his love for Harriet Taylor, helped him to outgrow his previous difficulties. He does not discuss the relationship between happiness and meaning, but in other books he touches on this issue at various points. In *Utilitarianism*, for instance, it enters into his attempt to prove that there are different qualities of happiness as well as different quantities. Having asserted that no action can be morally justified if it militates against the happiness of the greatest number, Mill defends this maxim by claiming that only happiness is desirable as an end of life. At the same time, however, he insists that some kinds of happiness are "more desirable and more valuable" than others: "It is better to be a human being dissatisfied than a pig satisfied; better to be Socrates dissatisfied than a fool satisfied. And if the fool, or the pig, is of a different opinion, it is because they only know their own side of the question. The other party to the comparison knows both sides."[3]

Apart from doubts that we may have about human beings really knowing what it is like to be a pig, we may question the arguments Mill adduces to support his belief that some kinds of happiness are higher than others. He says that a "superior being" will prefer the higher kinds even though they involve a way of life that is liable to greater dissatisfaction. To explain this paradox, Mill reverts to criteria that go beyond the concept of happiness itself. He speaks of "a sense of dignity" which prevents us from exalting the happiness that would satisfy other creatures but would lessen our human capacity for intellectual and aesthetic achievement. Details about the condition Mill is advocating need not concern us. What matters here is the fact that the sense of dignity and refinement he considers paramount involves more than just happiness. Whatever the amount or type of happiness it can yield, it consists in making life meaningful by giving precedence to some of our goals at the expense of others. The "competent judges" to whom Mill appeals in determining which happiness is higher inevitably reflect their own conception of a meaningful life. People who have different ends or aspirations, and therefore create different meanings for themselves, will not agree with their judgments about the relative quality of different kinds of happiness.

We must therefore move beyond Mill's analysis. A meaningful life, whether Socrates' or a fool's, is a continuous process that includes purposive goals as well as consummations related to them. A person's behavior becomes meaningful by virtue of the ends that matter to him, whatever they may be. The world around him is then intelligible as a pattern to which his activities contribute. When these afford satisfaction, either in themselves or in their consequences, human beings are happy to some degree; and unless they have at least a modicum of happiness, it may be impossible for them to pursue most of the projects they care about. The concepts of meaning and happiness are thus interwoven. They are nevertheless distinct. We cannot explain the nature of meaningfulness merely by discovering what makes people happy.[4]

❄

How then can we determine what makes a life meaningful? The two senses of the word "meaning" that I previously mentioned—one involving cognitive clarification, the other ascribing value or purpose—can easily lead to unstable conclusions. For instance, when we survey someone's life in its totality, we may find that it lacked any outstanding purposes or controlling values that the person himself recognized and consecutively pursued. A man who has a dull and somewhat dreary existence, doing mainly what he must to keep alive, may not be aware of having any dominating purpose. Is his life therefore meaningless? He cannot avoid having values of his own; nor will he fail to act in accordance with drives that nature has generated in him. Does this prove his life is meaningful? An outsider might find a meaning in the man's life in the sense that it reveals and even typifies how people are manipulated by contemporary society, or by economic and psychological forces in the modern world, etc. But this is extraneous. It is not the kind of meaning we are trying to elucidate.

For that matter, one's own beliefs about the inner constitution of one's life may also be misleading. A man's interpretation of what his life has been does not necessarily tell us much about its meaning. He may believe that he is nothing but a trivial and disposable element within the enormous machinery of nature. Can we conclude from this opinion that his life is devoid of meaning? Certainly not. We still must find out how he actually lives despite these ideas about his meager role in the scheme of things. Regardless of how he or anyone else feels about his life, and whether or not it includes much happiness, its meaning depends on the purposes and values that make it what it is.

Our purposes are directed toward the fulfillment of our desires and the acquisition of what we value. Though satisfaction can sometimes occur gratuitously, it usually results from behavior that is deliberately carried to completion. A meaningful life consists of purposive activities that are satisfying either in themselves or in their culminating consummations, which are then followed by new purposes with new consummations relevant to them, and so forth throughout one's existence. In some areas of life—love, for instance—the purposive and the consummatory are so tightly conjoined that we disentangle them only with great difficulty. In my trilogy *The Nature of Love* I attempt to do so by analyzing appraisal and bestowal: the former as a way of searching for benefits that people get from one another, and the latter as a focusing of attention upon someone or something which thereby gives that person or thing a special value. A unique, but highly characteristic meaning results from the successful integration between appraisal and bestowal, and from their quasi-rhythmic cooperation, each dynamically feeding the other.

In the dogmas of most religions, it is assumed that a meaningful life must adhere to a single grand and all-encompassing purpose that fills one's whole existence. If the plan or prior purposiveness of some deity reveals the meaning of life, it seems plausible to think that human beings can hope to attain meaning by accommodating their individual purposes and values to that providential scheme. But why limit meaningfulness in so partial a manner? Could one not give meaning to one's life by *rejecting* the divine plan? This is what Lucifer does. We can imagine him defending his rebellion by arguing that though he could have attained happiness through always saying "yea," such total and eternal acquiescence would have prevented him from creating a meaningful life of his own. We may even read God's willingness to tolerate Lucifer's rebellion as divine recognition that creatures have to make their lives meaningful by themselves, regardless of any prior meaning imposed upon them.

By discarding the usual preoccupation with a predetermined meaning of life, we also free ourselves from the Aristotelian idea that only a comprehensive "plan of life" can make a life meaningful. Aristotle thought the good life depends on rational dedication to some goal that structures one's entire being. But his view is unrealistic. At different times and at different ages a person rightly pursues different purposes. What is appropriate for a child acting out the demands of a growing consciousness that seeks knowledge and emotional expression will vary greatly from the interests he or she finds meaningful in later years. Nor should we expect all who are young or all who are old to have the same kind of goals. A life without compelling purposes, or one in which they are systematically thwarted and consummations totally denied, would not be a meaningful existence. But the fabric of meaning may vary from person to person, none of whom need have an overarching aim or super-purpose in order to make life meaningful.[5]

By insisting on this diversity, we build into our conception a pluralism that is essential for the problem of meaning as much as for other regions of philosophy. It is soothing to believe that there can be a single solution to anything, that if we train our ears properly we shall hear the legitimate voice that tells us: "This and this alone is what you must do in order to be saved." That is an enticing fantasy, but we must eschew it. The world—the actual world as opposed to a wish-fulfilling one that many people prefer—cannot sustain our yearning for such moral reassurance.

❄

I can show some of the ramifications of the pluralist approach by examining ideas about meaning that the philosopher Richard Taylor has recently offered. Taylor proposes the following as the components of a meaningful life:

> It would be a life that has a purpose—not just any sort of purpose that we happen to find satisfying, but one that is truly noble and good. And it must be one that is in fact achieved and not just endlessly pursued; and it must be lasting; and finally, it must be our *own* rather

than just something imbibed. In short, the only genuinely meaningful existence is one that is *creative*.[6]

Taylor's definition has much to recommend it. Without invoking any supernatural sanction, it describes what might be called a "high road" to meaningfulness. Mankind has always revered creativity, and people who thought themselves creative have frequently insisted that this justifies their existence. Taylor does not limit creativity to artistic production or acts of genius. He broadens the concept to include all behavior and experience that have an innovative aspect. I interpret him as acknowledging the life-sustaining character of imagination itself. And surely we may agree that human existence cannot be meaningful unless it is imaginative—which is to say, unless it surmounts the routine, repetitive, mechanical elements in life by using them for purposive activity that stimulates our thought with new perspectives, sharpens our sensations while also gratifying them, awakens our emotions to fresh possibilities of expression, and in general encourages the onward flow of consciousness to explore unknown capacities of our being. A life that is boring or without novelty is not meaningful for us.

The situation may be different in creatures that are endowed with less imaginative capacity than human beings. In one place Taylor cites the behavior of ground moles to illustrate "the meaninglessness of animal life."[7] Virtually blind, constantly burrowing underground, incessantly seeking worms or tuberous roots, forever defecating on one another, these rodents live a life that Taylor considers "pointless." It has no meaning, he says: "It is all for nothing, it just goes on and on, to no end whatever."[8] But, of course, Taylor is a human being with human interests and ideals. While using them to understand human meaningfulness, he apparently assumes that they can also explain what would be meaningful for other animals.

But why make this assumption? Though a mole does not have an imagination that is comparable to ours, either in scope or (presumably) in vividness, we have no reason to think that its mode of existence—which certainly would be meaningless for us—is meaningless for it. What Theseus in *A Midsummer Night's Dream* says of the lunatic, the lover, and the poet applies to human beings as a whole: we are "of imagination all compact." Ground moles are not. We make our lives meaningful by accepting the recurrent drudgery in them for the sake of complex and relatively cerebral goals that the imagination has made attractive to us. Other animals have other ways of living, but we need not doubt that their purposive and satisfying behavior is equally meaningful from their own point of view.

Even if Taylor allowed this modification, however, his kind of approach would still be unacceptable. When he speaks of meaningful life having "a purpose," he seems to single out one that matters uniquely in it. Perhaps he means a single network of purposes, but that also is too much to expect. Looking back at a meaningful life in its entirety, we may not be able to discover any grandiose design. The meandering trajectory may include only a broad variety of unrelated purposes. In a sense, they attain a unity in belonging to a particular life. This, however, is a trivial sense.

Furthermore, Taylor insists that meaning depends on doing what is "truly noble and good" rather than having experiences that are merely pleasant or engaging. He argues that even if an activity is meaningful to someone, it does not necessarily become meaningful *in itself*. For a man may devote his life to the mere amassing of money or, in one of Taylor's examples, the digging of a big hole. If this person believes such goals are valuable, he may think he has a meaningful existence; and Taylor agrees that his existence will be meaningful *to him*. But he denies that this kind of life will be meaningful in itself. It will not be objectively meaningful, he says, since it is not directed toward good and noble ends.

But why is this criterion essential or even relevant? Leaving aside any question of how we can *know* what is noble and good, how could such considerations apply to all meaningful lives?

One might reply that what runs counter to the truly noble or good inevitably impairs our ability to have a purposeful and rewarding life. Plato develops this argument at great length in the

Republic, and even non-Platonists have often accepted his belief that all instances of a life worth living would have to give prominence to certain preferential aspects of human nature. But having allowed this much of Plato's philosophy, the most we could infer is that some meaningful lives are not as good as others. It seems foolish to tell a man that an activity he finds engrossing is not really meaningful simply because there are other activities that are inherently better or that he would find more meaningful if only he decided to live differently. It may be true that the life we are recommending would be chosen by this particular man, and he might eventually inform us that he is now sorry to have pursued the goals that previously had meaning for him. But the fact remains that the person's life was meaningful at that time, and therefore no distinction can be made between what is meaningful to him and what is meaningful in itself.

In this respect, meaning is like pleasure. Pleasures may be delusory or short-lived or even conducive to suffering, as they may also be of a sort that we would consider disgusting or vicious, but it makes no sense to doubt that what someone experiences as a pleasure really is one. The same holds for the patterns of action or experience that constitute meaningfulness. If someone has a purposeful life that he finds satisfying, or as Taylor would say, that he "happens" to find satisfying, then that *is* a meaningful life. At least, for as long as he continues the same pursuits and finds them satisfying.

Some meaningful activities are crude or unworthy; others are harmful, either to the individual or to society; still others may be immoral. These judgments pertain to desirability, not to meaning per se. They do not enable us to distinguish between "objective" and "subjective" meaning.

Taylor also errs when he asserts that the purpose that defines a meaningful existence must lead to some lasting achievement. He gives this criterion as a contrast to the punishment of Sisyphus. Endlessly pushing his boulder up the mountain, only to see it roll back again as he reaches the top, Sisyphus is thought by Taylor (as he was by Camus) to typify the experience of meaninglessness.

Taylor argues that for the life of Sisyphus to become meaningful, he would have to achieve something—build a house or possibly a temple—instead of rolling boulders that are never put to use. This may be true, but only in the sense that a meaningful life must include consummatory experiences. Each of them is an achievement in itself. It makes no sense, however, to limit meaningfulness to any particular consummation, be it permanent or ephemeral. Constructing a lasting product is not the only way that Sisyphus can remedy his meaningless life.

Taylor claims that even if, for some obscure reason, Sisyphus enjoyed pushing rocks up a mountain while knowing they would immediately roll down again, his delighting in this process would not render it meaningful. But why not? The pleasure he derives from that activity should be recognized as an accomplishment whose value need not be disprized. It is not a "lasting" achievement, but only because no one enjoyment can last for very long. And even something that does—for example, a beautiful edifice that Sisyphus might build—is not likely to last for more than a few centuries. I shall return to the relationship between time and meaning. Here I need only remark that it is odd to think that nothing but enduring achievements are worth pursuing, or that some forms of consummation disqualify us from having a meaningful life.

Taylor's remaining criterion, possibly the most valid of them all, specifies that a meaningful existence is one that we recognize as *our own*. If a man feels bound to a routine he has not and would not freely choose—if he is a prisoner forced to do slave labor or an addict in the power of foreign substances he cannot control—he can hardly be expected to find meaning in his life of subjugation or insatiable craving. But here too we should maintain a pluralistic stance. The man whose waking hours are dominated by a compulsive need to work, as in my previous example, or to seduce beautiful women, may insist that this gives meaning to his life. Are we prepared to say that it does not? What seems to one person like meaningless enslavement may well appear to another as the creative giving of himself. Parents of devotees to some cult may feel that their children have imbibed a mind-destroying doctrine, a system of beliefs that delude and coerce in the manner of a hallucinogenic drug. But if the children claim to have found a life that is more meaningful, they may welcome their submissiveness as an expression of what they really are and really want. Even if they are mistaken, one need not doubt that any way of life can be meaningful to some extent if it has indeed been chosen as one's own.

This is not a sufficient condition for meaning; and its utility as a criterion may be more circumscribed than one might initially think. As Sartre and others have argued, human beings always retain an ultimate layer of freedom in the lives they lead. Even the prisoner and the addict can alter their existence by one means or another—through suicide, if necessary, or through an inward refusal to acquiesce in their present circumstance. In this respect, one's life is one's "own" on all occasions; and if we wish to admit some exceptions as limiting cases, they will not affect our generalization very much. But even the inalienable freedom that human beings have cannot assure them of a meaningful life. When Sisyphus—in Camus' version of the myth—casts off his meaningless state by submitting to his punishment with defiance and self-affirmation, he does more than manifest the freedom of his will. He is also asserting it in the manner of a hero. He knows what he is and what he must do. In bravely accepting his role in life, he overcomes anything the gods could have forced upon him. His meaningfulness is a function of that creative gesture, that bestowal of greatness upon himself, which he achieves by thinking and acting heroically.

✳

The pluralism I have been proposing may seem equivocal and overly relativistic to some people. They will feel perturbed at the suggestion that two men may have equally meaningful lives even though one of them acts for the good of others while the second cares only about his own selfish pleasures and is even immoral. Should we not distinguish between behavior that merely *seems* to be meaningful and behavior that really is? Should we not insist that being meaningful to oneself must somehow be contrasted with being objectively meaningful? If a person is devoted to the collecting of bottle tops or antique tobacco tins, we may agree that his quest for the biggest and best collection—worthy, perhaps, of inclusion in the *Guinness Book of World Records*—will provide a source of meaning in his life. But do we want to say that he therefore leads a life that is *really* meaningful? Or that it can be just as meaningful as the life of someone who struggles year after year to conquer terrible diseases, or spends decades perfecting an art, or dedicates himself to fighting injustice and ignorance? Traditional wisdom has always maintained that saintly and heroic lives are not only more desirable but also more meaningful than others.

This challenge seems formidable and must give us pause. Correctly understood, however, it involves something more than just meaningfulness. If we were to rank the hero and the bottle-top collector on a scale of greater meaning, we might sometimes give a higher rating to the latter. Beset by doubts, distractions, or a sense of personal inadequacy, the hero may have a more chaotic and less meaningful life than the one who allows nothing to deter him from his clearly demarcated goal and well-coordinated action. And yet, the traditional view is also right. For there is a kind of meaningfulness—let us call it *significance*—in which the hero's life excels.

It would appear that we now need a distinction between significance and meaningfulness in general. In ordinary language the two words are often used interchangeably. I separate them here in the hope that this bit of technical refinement will accommodate our intuition that some meaningful lives can be superior to others. Though a life may be entirely meaningful within its own dimensions, this does not guarantee that it will have much importance beyond itself.

What, then, makes a life "significant"? In his essay on that question, William James lists two principal characteristics. First, he says, there must be an ideal that is "intellectually conceived" and able to convey a sense of novelty that prevents an action from being wholly routine. Second, there must be a willingness to work in pursuit of that ideal, to labor and make concentrated efforts to realize it to the best of one's ability. According to James, what makes a life significant "is always the same eternal thing,—the marriage, namely, of some unhabitual ideal, however special, with some fidelity, courage, and endurance; with some man's or woman's pains."[9]

We may applaud these suggestions as far as they go, but they do not go far enough. The humble bottle-top collector who suddenly discovers the delights of collecting baseball cards has enriched his consciousness with a novel ideal that may possibly elicit sustained dedication. But if his interest has merely changed from bottle tops to baseball cards, if nothing else is involved in the meaning the man has now created for himself, we are not likely to believe that the new obsession makes his life any more significant than it previously was. He may find joy in moving from one ideal to the other; and given the limitations of human nature—its restlessness, its propensity to become sated with current pleasures while always hungering for greener pastures, and above all its usual inability to persevere for very long in any effort—the achievement of happiness may indeed require some such periodic alternation of ideals. They can scarcely add to the significance of our lives, however, if they are directed toward personal benefits for ourselves but not for anyone else.

This may be what James has in mind when he says that an intellectually conceived ideal provides an "uplift" and enlarges our horizons. He speaks of education as "a means of multiplying our ideals."[10] But he tells us very little about the content of these uplifting and enlarging ideals, and to me it seems crucial to emphasize that narrow or self-indulgent ideals do not make a life significant.

To some readers this remark may sound platitudinous. Particularly in the Western world, we have always been inundated with edifying proclamations designed to encourage people to sacrifice their own interests for the sake of the family, the nation, or the human race. We have seen that, despite his own experience, John

Stuart Mill was convinced that the best way to achieve well-being consists in working for the happiness of others. In human beings generally, we may wonder how often the empirical data bear out these moral prescriptions. If it is only a question of happiness or meaningful behavior, one could probably find many instances of people who lead good and wholesome lives that benefit themselves much more than others. It is true that even selfish men or women are gregarious and have feelings of affability that they may cultivate for reasons of self-interest; and like everyone else, they can expect society to make their lives miserable unless they conform to its many demands. But these are secondary considerations, since the requisite adjustments to the needs and values of other persons serve as payment for the pleasures one hopes to attain by means of them. The ideals that govern one's life may always remain in an orbit that primarily centers about gratifications for oneself.

I am not saying that everyone can find happiness and a life that is meaningful merely by acting selfishly. But I think it would be difficult to prove that no one can. That is why I introduced the further concept of significance: to show that additional conditions must be met if we are to believe that our lives amount to something. A significant life—one that is more than just happy or meaningful —requires dedication to ends that we choose *because* they exceed the goal of personal well-being. We attain and feel our significance in the world when we create, and act for, ideals that may originate in self-interest but ultimately benefit others. This mode of life comes naturally to us. It employs intelligence and imagination of a sort that is highly evolved in human beings.

The situation for most other species is quite different. As I have suggested, many animals have lives that appear to be meaningful and even happy in varying degrees. One might also say that their existence normally contributes to a biological system or ecological harmony that goes beyond their individual welfare. But this does not mean that they pursue impersonal goals for the sake of ideals that they have consciously created. Though the behavior of a queen bee may have great importance for her colony, all her activities being directed toward its survival, she is uncreative and relatively insignificant in herself. She does not formulate new types of meaning or initiate new modes of happiness. She is just the transmitter of a genetic code which she does not alter through determined efforts of her own. Any other functional queen bee would serve as well as she, and the whole life of her society is predicated upon this fundamental fact. Even if she is a mutant that introduces a novel strain within the species, she is still a conduit for material forces she cannot modify. The kind of significance that human beings recognize and care about requires more creativity than that.

As a more plausible guide to what we would consider significant, we might study the lives of dominant baboons or wolves or even sheep. Among the mammals, numerous species have a social order that reaches its apex in a leader who makes decisions for the group and possibly changes the direction of its future existence. Though he enjoys great advantages, including principal access to food and fertile females, his importance for the colony consists in behavior that is not entirely geared toward his own well-being. He must fight off invaders as well as rivals who wish to displace him. In order to retain his dominance he may have to jeopardize, and even sacrifice his own happiness to a greater extent than others in the group. As Shakespeare says, "Uneasy lies the head that wears a crown."[11]

The character in Shakespeare was talking about our own species, of course, and it is among human beings that the quest for significance becomes most interesting. Every young male baboon may want to become the dominant leader some day, and many will compete for that position throughout their lives. But so much of baboon life is regulated by laws of instinct that even those who succeed in the struggle for dominance will have little capacity to create new kinds of meaning. Moreover, there will be only one type of preeminence that makes an individual significant. For a baboon it largely consists in political power based on cunning and physical strength. Human beings can hope to obtain a significant life in many other ways as well.

Throughout the varied pursuits that make a life significant, what remains constant is the growth of meaning when this involves creation of values in the service of transpersonal ideals. The bottle-top collector may have a happy life within the special realm of meaning he has fashioned for himself, but his existence takes on greater significance when his collection attracts the attention of other collectors, when it is cited as a record-breaking achievement, when it becomes a model that strangers seek to equal or exceed. How can these peripheral reactions make one's own life more significant? By manifesting the idealist and perfectionist aspects of human nature which link a particular life with goals that matter to many others.

For one reason or another, most people do not share the interest in collecting bottle caps. We tend to place a higher value on pursuits of a different sort. But whatever the activities we may prefer, we can recognize that the significance of any life will always be a function of its ability to affect other lives. And not that alone, since our perfectionism involves a longing to create the greatest possible good or beauty to which our imagination gives us access. When asked what they would like to be remembered for, most people mention something beneficial to humanity. Beethoven's music and Mill's humanitarian philosophy are expressions of that sentiment. The greater the benefit to the greater number of lives, the greater the significance of our own. In this respect, significance does not depend on fame, power, wealth, or social standing. It depends on the value one provides—directly or indirectly—to those who can thereby make their lives happier or more meaningful or even more significant.

I realize that words like "benefit" or "value" are very vague. Partly this results from the fact that what is beneficial for one person may be harmful to another. Moreover, different people or societies create different ideals and therefore different notions of well-being. Whether we opt for a relativism that considers such disparity unavoidable or seek objective standards that reveal what is truly beneficial, a particular life can have significance only insofar as it augments the meaning and happiness of life as a whole, regardless of any effect upon one's own desires.

✳

Schopenhauer claimed that someone's life is real and important only as an enlightened manifestation of the unitary life-force which is Being itself. That was why he considered the sense of individuality to be an illusion as well as the cause of human suffering. Our ordinary experience is futile, Schopenhauer thought, because this fundamental fallacy encourages us to pursue selfish goals predicated upon the belief that we are each a separate substance. He extolled the faculty of compassion because he thought that it alone enables us to perceive our oneness with all other living creatures, recognizing them as fellow victims within the single reality of life. Though we are insignificant as mere units of vitality that foolishly think ourselves unique and independent, we become significant once we identify with, and act to benefit, every other manifestation of life.

This part of Schopenhauer's philosophy is tempered by his unrelenting pessimism, which insists that human efforts cannot do much to alter the universal misery in animate existence. But if that is true, one cannot believe that even a significant life adds up to very much. Though he builds his moral philosophy on an identification with all living things, Schopenhauer would seem to denigrate life from every point of view. In human beings the general degradation appears as either an illusory sense of individuality or else as compassionate feeling that can have virtually no effect upon the world one wants to change. We might very well infer that no form of life can ever be really significant.

We escape this baleful conclusion not only by avoiding metaphysical assumptions such as Schopenhauer's but also by advancing a different view of nature. Humans—and possibly some other animals as well—have a double being: we are conscious of ourselves both as individuals and as manifestations of life. Neither self-conception is illusory. As individuals, we act to preserve our own existence as well as the existence of anything that can help us survive. When we succeed in this endeavor and enjoy the process, the reward is happiness; the penalty for failure is depression, disease, and premature decay. As persons who are happy, or hope for happiness, each of us wants to go on forever and we are saddened by the realization that this will not happen and may even be impossible. We may want to prolong our lives indefinitely, but we suspect that everything in nature disintegrates and finally disappears. Though we may cling to theories about life in another world after death, we also—and often simultaneously—fear that they are all implausible. To some extent, everyone who thinks about the matter feels that his existence must be finite.

If we had nothing else in consciousness, our fixation on our approaching doom would make life an unalloyed horror—as it often is for inmates in a concentration camp or prisoners on death row. Instead, we mitigate the sentiment of dread by fulfilling our nature not merely as persons who live or die within our separate being but also as expressions and embodiments of a life that includes more than just its particular manifestation in ourselves.

In cultivating this further attitude, we move beyond our individuality and diminish our concern about its finitude. We expand our own selves by creating additional selves that issue from us: children who can live on when we are gone. We make material objects that will enter into the experience of others whether or not we are still alive. We create institutions and engage in pursuits, as in science or technology or the humanities, whose accomplishments endure long after we have died. Much of human imagination is activated by goals that have only a tenuous or indirect relation to our own personal existence. Fame may be the spur, as Milton said, but also part of our being—in varying degrees, no doubt—identifies with life as it exists in other creatures. Though our efforts are often thwarted, we try to put ourselves in their position, to see the world from their perspective, to imagine what life in them is like. All poetry and fiction arise from this inclination. We also learn about ourselves by analogy to others, and through their immediate or eventual conception of us. Since we depend extensively on other people, our sympathetic awareness of them readily turns into concern about their welfare.

When this element in our nature combines with our faculty of idealization, there results the kind of behavior that seeks to preserve and to improve life beyond ourselves. This mode of response, reinforced by explicit achievements that enable us to believe the enterprise is succeeding, makes our life significant. For life is then propelling itself into new approaches to perfectibility, transcending the littleness of any individual. In view of what we are, where else could we hope to find significance in our lives?

Thus significance is more than just the attaining of meaning or happiness in one's own life. It derives from an imaginative struggle for meaning and happiness in other lives, even when the effect upon ourselves is not to our advantage. Under ideal conditions, we would increase our happiness and find ever greater meaning through acts that augment the quality of life wherever it occurs. But that is an impossible dream: the world is not ideal. Life as it appears in the AIDS virus is inimical to life in human beings. We cannot hope to preserve and perfect both simultaneously. But then, one might ask, what does it mean to preserve and perfect life in general?

The argument seems to have reached an impasse. One could easily cut the knot by saying that concern about life as such is just an illusion, a cunning device of self-love. That, however, goes against all observation. The mother who carries a child within her will often have no perception of it as a benefit to herself. On the contrary, she may feel that she is merely the source and fertile receptacle out of which this new existence will come forth. If she wants the child, she wants it for reasons that neither she nor anyone else may fully understand. She has an impulse to create life, an instinct to propagate a living entity that continues her being but also exists apart from her own individuality. In the mythology of many peoples, women are regularly represented as the bearers of life, the vehicles that it has chosen in its unrelenting self-assertion. Such myths are primitive, but they are primitive in us all. And they become persuasive when we recognize that, in their own way, men also convey life. They bear not only the seeds from which it grows, but also the social constructs—created by members of both sexes—in which it shows itself as surely as in its material embodiments.

If the ideal of protecting and perfecting life had no influence on human behavior, we could hardly understand the great preoccupation that many people have about the world as it will be after they are dead. One might say that wills and testaments, endowments, plans for some remote future are simply imaginative devices by which we try to perpetuate our own values, and thus pretend that we are prolonging our existence beyond the grave. Though we know we may not live to see our great grandchildren, we bestow a fictive longevity upon ourselves by participating vicariously in the world that they will have. This explanation is partly correct. But our interest in the future also reveals a concern about the preservation and improvement of life, at least as it occurs in manifestations that we care about. The ideal of leaving the world a better place than when we entered it has been a motive force in the lives of many people. It may often be reduced to little more than a desire to improve the lot of one's own children (or of one's gene pool, as the sociobiologists would say) but this alone does not account for the efforts that are often made on behalf of other animals and unrelated human beings.

In these final years of the twentieth century, we have a striking example of the attitude I am trying to describe in mankind's fascination with space travel. No one has suggested that life on earth will disappear or become untenable for centuries to come. Neither can anyone believe that the material and technological pay-off in the proximate future will balance the huge expenditures that extra-terrestrial exploration involves. What fires our imagination and justifies the heroic deeds of our astronauts is the feeling that life as we know it, which may be the only life there is in the universe, must find some way of continuing even after the extinction of our planet. Though *we* cannot go on, we feel that life must do so. Our individual death will have lost some of its bitterness if in living as we did we contributed to the furtherance of life beyond ourselves.

I am not suggesting that the ideal of preserving and perfecting life takes precedence over all others as a matter of objective necessity. We need not agree with those metaphysical idealists who say that everything is motivated by a longing for greater and better life throughout the universe. No ideal is ontologically supreme. Like all ideals, this one must struggle as a partial vector within the field of forces that nature is forever germinating. It has no inherent priority, and its relative importance is always subject to circumstances that are constantly in flux.

If this is what we believe, however, why *should* anyone pay much attention to what does or does not improve other lives—to say nothing of life as a whole? We have been studying the nature of ideals, above all the devotion to life itself, as a way of explaining what can make our existence not only meaningful but also significant. But if significance arises from pursuing an ideal that is itself variable and haphazard, or at least lacking in objective authority as far as the cosmos is concerned, why would anyone risk an iota of well-being in order to have a significant life? Why think that this aspect of our nature really matters? Indeed, why should we think that anything does?

✳

In Camus' novel *The Stranger* a depressed and somewhat psychopathic young man commits a senseless murder. Dazzled by the sun and acting on an impulse he himself cannot understand, he kills someone on the beach who happens to annoy him. The murderer is arrested and condemned to death. When a priest entreats him to confess, he reacts violently and shouts: "Nothing matters."

Analyzing the character's use of language, R. M. Hare argues that it should not be taken as referring to any objective state of affairs. Hare suggests that when we say something does or does not matter we are merely expressing our own concern about it, or else the concern some other person has (in which case we would say that it does or does not matter "to him"). Hare means that the word "matter" in this context cannot apply directly to any thing or condition in the world but only to someone's feelings about it. Asserting that nothing matters is just the character's way of informing us that nothing has importance for him; and therefore his statement should not be treated as a comment upon the universe at large. According to Hare, it only reveals the man's dejected and defeated state of mind on this particular occasion. The language would not be appropriate in a different situation or for most other people, since they are obviously concerned about many things— the quality of their breakfast, their continued good health, etc.[12]

Hare's analysis does an injustice to Camus and to his protagonist, each of whom may surely be interpreted as making claims about the universe. Both are insisting that, regardless of what matters to them or to other human beings, nothing is *really* important. In other words, no interests and concerns that define our values can be justified or even corroborated by independent facts. Various things matter to one or another person, but nothing matters in any further context and therefore nothing truly matters.

If this is what Camus does intend, one might immediately offer two responses diametrically opposite to each other. For many people, it will suffice to reply that if something matters to someone it really does matter and that's that. What other criterion is needed? What other validation would count for very much? Isn't Camus assuming, naively but falsely, that individual mattering is somehow insufficient, as if we might possibly hope to discover a higher standard or authority which he himself does not believe in? The other kind of answer is typified by the *reductio ad absurdum* I mentioned earlier: If nothing really matters, then neither does it matter that nothing matters.

Both responses are entirely legitimate, and each helps to protect us from the demoralization that often accompanies the belief that nothing matters. The first does so by emphasizing that however trivial our interests may be in a different frame of reference—in relation, let us say, to superior beings who inhabit another galaxy—there can be no justification for denying that they really matter to *us*. The second answer serves to quiet the uneasiness that we may feel in questioning the actual importance of what we care about. For if nothing does matter, we need not allow this fact, unimportant like all others, to affect our behavior or emotions very much.

Though these replies can be reassuring, they will not satisfy everyone. Hidden as it may be, a desire lurks in human beings to get beyond their glassy essence and smug contentment with what is merely of value to themselves. Moreover, a person who is upset by the idea that nothing matters apart from someone's interest may be further troubled by the suggestion that this advance in his ability to think has no greater importance than anything else. In concluding that nothing matters, he had hoped to reach a level of insight that would afford him a secure understanding of himself in relation to the world. If this cognitive achievement also does not matter, he might well feel even more demoralized than before.

In trying to resolve this problem, we should begin by recognizing how comforting it can be to think that nothing matters. Dr. Johnson, the eighteenth-century moralist, advised those who suffer from the belief that they have committed a social faux pas to imagine how miniscule the event will seem twelve months later. Having made a fool of yourself in public, you may feel anguish that certainly matters to you at present. But in time it will diminish and probably disappear. Even if you do not forget the experience, others will: it will be smothered by all the subsequent happenings that eventually push it into oblivion. Something similar can be said about most of our failures. If we see them from the vantage of some future epoch or remote corner of the universe, we are likely to free ourselves from acute remorse and "agenbite of inwit," as James Joyce calls it. We are tranquillized by the idea that "this too will pass."

By extension, this kind of remedy may be applied to everything that matters to human beings. Idealist philosophies have often encouraged us to assume a cosmic perspective on all things temporal and merely natural. We are told to envisage them from God's point of view or in terms of absolute spirit. The concept of "the eternal" was constructed with that in mind. Seeing all things under the aspect of eternity implied a recognition that, despite its apparent or current importance to oneself, nothing could possibly matter in comparison to the ideal reality which is the foundation of being. If we truly subscribed to this article of faith, would we not be bolstered by the assurance that our daily and inescapable struggle for existence, for happiness, for rectitude, and even for the preservation of those we love does not really matter? At the very least, we would no longer be tormented by our knowledge that sooner or later our works and efforts will all be buried in the sands of time.

This anodyne in idealist philosophy is nevertheless hurtful. It lessens the painfulness of seeking endlessly for the goods of this world, but only by denying their inherent goodness. Moreover, it increases our sense of failure, instead of counteracting it. Though our merely natural shortcomings will not matter to us as they might have previously, neither will anything else that belongs to our condition. Striving for transcendental goals that can never be satisfied by our existence in nature, we shall be laden with a feeling of inadequacy more total and more devastating than before. The darker side of all religions—the part that issues into asceticism or assurance of original and ineradicable sin—shows how frightening the consequences of idealism can be.

As opposed to these gross distortions of the human spirit, how much saner and more benign is the deflationary idea that really nothing matters! Like a mother who tells her child that he can do no wrong, the nihilist approach may bring its own kind of blessed peace. Without terrifying us by a contrast between the meager, ephemeral lives that we lead and the infinitely greater importance of absolute ideals and underlying realities, the belief that nothing matters can make us tolerant of each other. By ridding us of pomposity and autocratic self-righteousness, it may even help us to become more compassionate. What it cannot do is to provide a motivation for living, an energy to keep on going despite all impediments, an élan or vital impetus that declares the value and imperative necessity in doing one thing rather than another.

To discover these aspects of a viable solution, we need a different approach. We have considered, and found wanting, the notion that some thing or principle beyond the empirical world might reveal what really matters. In searching for an alternative, we should ask why it is that human beings raise these questions in the first place. Other animals, with their inferior intellects, are not prone to such dilemmas. Unless they are imprisoned by our species or poisoned by noxious elements in the environment, for which humans are also usually responsible, they live meaningful lives and that is what matters to them. When someone asks whether anything *really* matters, the intellect has created a gulf between that individual and his origins in nature. The intellect does not operate in isolation, of course. It is basically a tool that vital interests use for purposes of survival and mastery. If those interests have been crushed or weakened, as happens in states of despair and pathological disorientation, the intellect readily becomes subservient to these new conditions and—like the sorcerer's apprentice—it multiplies the difficulties of life without being able to control them.

The person who convinces himself that nothing matters has lost contact either with the instincts that would normally direct him toward his own well-being or else with those that bind him to other creatures. To act as if nothing matters is to thwart the innate program of life itself. It is in their nature for all living things to find something (and usually a great deal) that matters to them. Human beings are able to minimize this aspect of themselves as they may also commit suicide or even destroy all life on the planet. This does not mean that ultimately nothing matters, but only that we are free—if we so choose—to bring about an end of mattering.

Once we ask whether anything matters we thus entangle ourselves in logical problems about the concept of life. The question is asked on the assumption that living creatures exist and that something might or might not matter to them. But part of what we mean by life or being alive includes the idea that various things do matter to some organism. If we assert, on a particular occasion, that what matters to one or another person does not *really* matter, we mean that greater importance is, or should be, ascribed to something else. Even when there is no way of adjudicating among these different claims, what we call life requires us to make them.

It might seem that I am merely reminding the skeptic that many things matter to individuals and therefore that one cannot say that nothing does. But I wish to go beyond that. For we are constantly changing our ideas about what matters; and it is always proper to ask whether something in particular really matters. If someone replies "It does to *me*," that ends the problem. It is not that we believe the other person has an infallible authority or will not renounce his statement at some later date. It is just that we see in him, and in his remark, a demonstration of what it is to be alive. By its very nature, all life manifests active choice and selectivity. In creatures like ourselves this means having a preference for one or another possibility and therefore wanting it to exist. That is what makes something matter.

But we often say that one thing matters more than another, don't we? Yes. And we also know that what matters to one person does not always matter to anyone else. How then can we tell what *truly* matters? And if someone denies that anything does, is he not asserting that no sanction exists for choosing one particular system of values rather than another? How have we strengthened the argument by saying the nature of life requires that something matters to whatever lives? This might be of interest if there were a single goal or principle that matters most to everything, but otherwise how does our probing help us determine that anything really matters?

The discussion can be useful by directing attention to what might be called the "ontological biogrammar" of each living thing. It is not by chance that something matters in the universe, for this is part of the definition of life once it comes into existence. Our conception also serves to elucidate the double being of man to which I previously referred. Insofar as man experiences himself as a separate individual, what matters to him is anything that brings about his own happiness and sustains the meaningful life he has chosen. Insofar as he is one among other manifestations of life, however, and perceives himself as such, he becomes aware that what matters to other creatures matters equally and really does matter. This growth of consciousness is not automatic. It is gratuitous, like all spiritual development: it harkens freely to a pervasive but ignorable fact about life and is not motivated by an exclusive desire to promote our own material interests. In its own way, it enlarges our capacity for self-fulfillment. It expands our pattern of meaningfulness, giving increased value to what matters for others as well as what matters for ourselves. In beings such as we, that is what really matters.[13]

✳

I propose this way of thinking in order to use what is best in Schopenhauer's ideas about identification with other embodiments of life while avoiding his vitalistic dogmas. Compassion does not require an intuition of underlying unity, as Schopenhauer thought, but rather the active recognition that life in others—as in ourselves—includes a concern about something that matters. What matters to the other may not matter to us, but in feeling compassion we show that we care about this different exemplification of the life we have in common. Out of this there arises (though not ineluctably) an interest in preserving, extending, and improving life in general. And that, I have suggested, is what enables human beings to have lives that are truly significant, not merely meaningful or conducive to happiness.

But what exactly does it mean to preserve, extend, and improve life? Each species acts as if its own survival fulfills the content of these demands. And within our species, there is endless diversity among the notions of perfectibility that guide behavior. Even Nazi ideology, which almost everyone abhors nowadays, claimed that it sought to purify the human race by eliminating soft and sentimental attitudes that run counter to the deepest stirrings of nature. Though different in many respects, this dreadful delusion is on a par with Spinoza's idea that the excellence of human reason justifies our subjugating less rational creatures; and both may derive from the biblical belief that man is uniquely the child of God and therefore entitled to dominion over all other forms of life. These doctrines would seem to satisfy my criteria for significance as fully as Albert Schweitzer's "reverence for life." Is this a consequence we are willing to accept?

To some extent, we must. The Nazi philosophy was able to beguile as much of humanity as it did precisely because it promised a significant life to those who were willing to sacrifice everything to it. Evil as it was behind its idealistic veneer, it satisfied the heroic imagination of many people who saw no other possibility of achieving a meaningful life. It pacified their doubts about whether life is worth living by providing a cause for which they were even willing to die. Having subdued this particular nightmare of the twentieth century—though new ones keep occurring—we must try to invent healthier and more desirable ways of making life significant.

CONCLUSION

The Love of Life

In Ingmar Bergman's film *The Seventh Seal* Death agrees to play a game of chess with a knight who is returning from the wars. The knight can go on living as long as the match continues. In one scene Death, posing as a father confessor, tricks him into disclosing his strategy on the chessboard. The knight's first reaction is a surge of indignation at this treachery. But suddenly he feels his own importance as one who has survived thus far and is playing the game, which is life itself. "This is my hand," he says, "I can move it, feel the blood pulsing through it. The sun is still high in the sky, and I, Antonius Block, am playing chess with Death!" In the background we hear celestial voices intoning the goodness in this moment of self-realization.

The knight has experienced what Joseph Campbell calls "the rapture of being alive." It is an exhilaration that everyone desires. Nevertheless, it alone cannot tell us how to cope with our reality as human beings. Problems of life and death cannot be resolved by any feeling, however rapturous. The knight intuits that he must go beyond his momentary exaltation by enacting "one meaningful deed" that will complete his mission on earth. In doing so, he preserves life and defeats death, though he himself dies in the process.

But is a single deed capable of providing an adequate solution? If so, what kind of deed must it be? If not, how should we characterize the multiple deeds that may be needed? My argument has been gradual throughout this book, and one can wonder about its practical implications as well as its direction. The reader may possibly have turned to this concluding chapter in the hope of finding an inspirational bottom line. I will try to satisfy this demand but I fear that the cat I let out of the bag may only be a scrawny kitten.

I have sought to lead attention away from questions about the meaning of life, as if there were only one and as if it were a prior reality that can be discovered. I have emphasized that human beings *give* meaning to their existence, and that they do so by creative and increasingly imaginative acts that reveal what matters to them as living entities in nature. I distinguished between happiness and meaningfulness as a way of suggesting that a life filled with meaning may not always be an especially happy one. Though a meaningful life provides many gratifications, and though happiness requires a certain degree of meaningfulness, the two conditions are not necessarily proportionate to one another. I argued that philosophers who use happiness as the sole or supreme criterion of the good life are neglecting a quest for meaning that may be more important in human nature.[1] And I also recognized that we characteristically seek experiences that are more than just meaningful for us as separate individuals. I claimed that a truly significant life would be an innovative one that is devoted to the preservation and perfecting of life itself. This idea is, however, vague and unsettling. How can we make sense of it?

From the outset, I have resisted the seductive assurances of optimists who tell us that in life all is for the best and that beyond (or even within) our vale of tears an ultimate, though possibly unknowable reality sustains and justifies man's finest aspirations. There is something in the phenomenology of experience that makes me distrust such theories about our predicament. Our mere existence in time, as creatures whose immersion in past and future prevents us from adequately *realizing* the present, convinces me that the optimists are deluding themselves.

What I am referring to appears in the final act of Thornton Wilder's play *Our Town*. Having died in childbirth and taken her place in the local cemetery, Emily returns to the world as a spectator of her own previous existence. On the advice of others among the dead, she has chosen to observe a happy but relatively uneventful day in her life. It is her twelfth birthday, and she watches the day as it unfolded for herself and for her family. She is astonished to see how young and beautiful everyone looks, as we often feel when we come across old photographs. But what brings tears to her eyes, and to ours, is her sudden awareness that we never really savor or consummate our being in time. It is as if time, as we live it, is something we cannot fully experience. It is always escaping us. We always seem to be out of phase, unable to synchronize our feelings and our needs with time's uncontrollable movement. "I can't go on," Emily says, ready now to accept her burial in the earth: "It goes so fast. We don't have time to look at one another. [She breaks down sobbing.] I didn't realize. So all that was going on and we never noticed. Take me back—up the hill—to my grave." Before leaving, she asks the Stage Manager: "Do any human beings ever realize life while they live it?—every, every minute?" No, he replies, but then adds: "The saints and poets, maybe—they do some."[2]

The Stage Manager's answer is ambiguous. Does he mean that some saints and poets may possibly realize life at every minute? Or else that they do so but only on some occasions and to some degree? In either event, one might say that the playwright himself helps us toward the realizing of life merely by portraying our usual inability to do so. This is part of the aesthetic value in art, and I am not questioning its life-enhancing goodness. But like Emily and the Stage Manager, I feel the unredeemable sadness out of which artistic effort arises.

In the history of philosophy a long line of thinkers—from Plato to Alfred North Whitehead, Paul Tillich, and others in our century—have developed concepts of "eternal objects" that are different from the content of temporal experience.[3] We get "out" of time, they say, when we liberate ourselves from the headlong plunge of past-present-future. By stepping back from the temporal, by contemplating its given qualities without considering what precedes or follows them, what causes or results from them, we realize that which is timeless and therefore eternal in every moment. But beautiful as this vision may be, it is, I believe, simply untrue to reality. The qualities or formal properties to which these thinkers refer are just abstractions—like mathematical truths or logical tautologies. They do not acquaint us with the full concreteness of experience, with life as it is actually lived not only from moment to moment but also in every single moment. Eternal objects are snapshots of reality, and therefore static. Life is not.

This does not mean that we must eschew the artificial definition of the eternal that philosophers have offered us. We may sometimes meet their criteria for "living in eternity," if we so desire and have received an adequate training. But while we are enjoying this aesthetic experience, we still belong to life as it flows on; we remain participants in the temporality from which we tried to emancipate ourselves. And if that flux is tragic because of its basic unrealizability, it is doubly so when we allow our intellect to fabricate glamorous language that merely disguises the inescapable. Nor can we learn to love life by seeking means of denying or ignoring its dismaying reality.

What follows from all this? Shall we spend our days gnashing our teeth and agreeing with the character in Euripides who claims that "all of human life is filled with anguish,/Nor is there remission from its sorrow"?[4] Many people have thought that the belief in immortality offers an avenue of joyful expectation. If our present condition is melancholy, they say, can we not hope for goodness in some life after death that continues for a non-finite duration? But why think that time will be any different then? If we cannot realize temporal existence in this world, why think that we would be able to do so in one that goes on for very much longer? In the *Tractatus* Wittgenstein remarks: "This assumption [immortality] completely fails to accomplish the purpose for which it has always been intended. Or is some riddle solved by my surviving forever? Is not this eternal life itself as much of a riddle as our present life?"[5]

Elsewhere Wittgenstein states that "a man lives eternally if he lives in the present."[6] Possibly he means a man who takes each moment as it comes and neither dwells upon the past nor worries about the future. That kind of life may be blissful but it would not free us from the limitations of temporality. Whatever our life in the present may be, and however long it might last, we are still bound by the constraints of our existence in time.

The Hindu concept of karma may seem preferable to Western ideas about an immortality that cures the malady of man's temporal being. In the twentieth century, at least, we are likely to share the sentiments of the character in John Mortimer's play *Voyage Round My Father* who says he cannot imagine anything worse than "living for an infinity in some great transcendental hotel with nothing to do in the evening." If our immortality follows the pattern of karma, however, there is always something to do. Each life a person undergoes has a mission: to purify the eternal soul that recurrently dips into materiality, like a pebble skipping across the waters of time. This alone would serve as a meaning to life in general. But karma cannot explain why the purification of a soul should matter, or even its existence. And unless the totality of successive incarnations is worthwhile in itself, one cannot infer that a single segment within the trajectory—for instance, the life we are now living—has any value.

We have thus returned to our earlier questions: Is life worthwhile? Is life worth living? Though closely related, these are in fact two different questions. The former pertains to the value of life in its entirety. It is the kind of question that the Judaeo-Christian God, who is presumably beyond life though also alive in some sense, might have asked himself when he first contemplated creating a universe. Is it better, he may have wondered, to have laws of nature that produce animate as well as inanimate beings? Since life abounds on our planet, we may think that this deity saw some value in having both living and non-living substance. But whether or not we believe in any such creator, we must give some thought to the original question: Is a cosmos that has life in it more valuable than one that does not? In other words, is life itself worthwhile?

This is quite different from inquiring whether life is worth living. For that is what an individual may ask about his own participation in life, or the participation of others. Even if life is worthwhile in itself, its occurrence in us may not be such as to warrant the struggle to stay alive as long as possible.

The first question is very puzzling. It is one of the facts about the universe that life exists in it. We observe life in other creatures and we experience it in ourselves. Can we ever attain a vantage point from which to decide whether the universe is better or worse because it does include life? It is even problematic whether we can say it is better for *us* that there should be life. For what we mean by "us" already presupposes that we are alive. Possibly the question lingers as a vestige of beliefs in another type of being, that spirit-world in which disembodied souls survive their natural demise. But that is not our world, and whatever may define their being can represent life only in an obliquely symbolic manner.

Even so, one might say that there is nothing illogical in asserting that animate nature—including our own—either does or does not have value. One could then go on to claim that the universe is better because it has life in it, or else that it would be better without life. But using language this way, how could we explain the meaning of the valuational terms? Words like "worse" or "better" refer to what matters to living creatures. In a world without them, how would anything be more or less worthwhile, or valuable in any sense? Possibly one might say that life is so painful or pernicious that even from the point of view of its own values it is not worthwhile. In effect, this reduces the first question to the second one: it implies that, in all animate beings alike, life is not worth living.

That suggestion appears in the joke I cited in an earlier chapter about the two old friends who discuss the lives they have had. Though he has a good life, one of them asserts that he would prefer not to have been born at all. In a similar vein, Byron tells us that "whatever thou hast been,/'Tis something better not to be"; and a Chorus in Sophocles expresses the idea that "never to be born is far best."[7] A contrary view is held by those who believe that life is *always* worth living, regardless of how wretched or absurd it may be. This assertion has been made by Camus, but it was already present in Homer's *Odyssey*. Though he is now a king among the shades, Achilles insists that any condition of life—however lowly or miserable—is preferable to being dead. An extension of this idea occurs in a seminal article by Thomas Nagel. Attempting to prove that death must always be an evil, Nagel claims that life is inherently worth living. Over and above the elements in experience that make life better or worse, he argues, there remains something that has positive value. This is "experience itself, rather than . . . any of its contents." According to Nagel, that additional factor makes life "worth living even when the bad elements of experience are plentiful and the good ones too meager to outweigh the bad ones on their own."[8]

But can the experience of life be evaluated in isolation from all its contents? Apart from its good and bad elements, there is no human experience. There is no substratum of experience to which good or bad elements may be added but which remains "emphatically positive," as Nagel says, whether or not they are added. Experience is always good or bad in some respect, satisfying or unsatisfying, rewarding or unrewarding. It is always hedonically and affectively charged. As a result there cannot be a residue that provides an underlying value capable of outweighing bad elements. If we eliminate all positive and negative contents, we eliminate experience itself and reduce human life to the level of a plant or vegetable.

Is there an inherent good in being a vegetable? If they could speak, some vegetables would surely say there is. But the life of a vegetable must also consist of good and bad elements, healthy and diseased components. By extending the argument to their condition, we have done nothing to demonstrate that life either is or is not worth living.[9]

As a possible solution, I suggest that life is worth living when its good elements outweigh the bad but that life is not worth living when the bad greatly predominate and there is hardly any goodness left. In making such judgments, one must always factor in predictions about the future and hopes about events whose outcome is still unknown. The meaning of "good" and "bad" will have to be determined by the speaker's standards of value, and these can obviously differ from person to person. But what matters most is the fact that no life carries with it a prior assurance of its own permanent worth.

We may also say that those who feel that life is worth living are manifesting the goodness in their own experience, and their buoyant confidence that in the future some semblance of this goodness will continue. This projection may be accurate to some extent, and in any event I have no desire to undermine whatever sustenance such belief may bring. It can be a life-preserver and therefore self-fulfilling as a prediction. It is part of how we make life worth living, assuming a virtue in experience—to reformulate what Hamlet says to Gertrude—even if it has none independently. This feat of the imagination is often benign and beneficial. It need only be understood for what it is.

My approach has implications for practical moral issues. If life is not worth living when the bad elements vastly outweigh the good, we have less reason to prolong the existence of those who are terminally ill and incapable of experiencing more than pain or unbearable misery. We may have other grounds for opposing euthanasia or suicide, and each patient must be encouraged to consider the possibility that his suffering may someday be alleviated. We shall also have to gauge the consequences to others if this individual's life is either extended or curtailed, to say nothing of the danger in making such decisions at all. But the premise about life being *inherently and necessarily* worth living, which is sometimes assumed in these deliberations, will no longer apply.

❄

Having come this far, however, we may still wonder where our exploration has led us. In order to determine what truly matters and contributes to a significant existence, I suggested that the preserving and perfecting of life—unclarified as this conception may still be—affords an outstanding kind of meaning. But if I say that life is not always worth living, am I not negating the importance of that vital principle in the service of which we were supposed to attain our own significance? Must I now revert to the comfortable relativism of those who claim that nothing matters objectively and that what does matter varies in accordance with the particular meanings each person individually creates?

This solution is unpalatable because it neglects the character of our striving for perfection. Human beings seek for unlimited goodness not only in projects that benefit them as separate individuals, but also in relation to life beyond themselves. The baseball player who pitches a no-hitter will have accomplished something meaningful, but it is a significant achievement only to the extent that his skill warrants the approbation of people who know the game and delight in seeing it played perfectly. The pitcher does not merely wish to trounce his opponents. He wants to do so in the context of an activity, the sport of baseball, that enriches life for all its fans and players. The more that an art form or communal enterprise fulfills such ideals, the more significant it becomes. Its significance consists in the wealth of meaning that it makes available to human beings and thus, in that degree, to life itself. By adding to this fund of meaningfulness, individuals attain their own significance.

What is significant in life, and what makes us feel our own lives are significant, involves participation in creative acts that lead to greater meaning in the cosmos. This is the message, albeit crammed with distressful metaphysics, that Hegel and the nineteenth-century Romantics conveyed to us in the modern world. But also, I suggest, these creative acts are morally justified only in relation to utilitarian principles about the greatest happiness of the greatest number of human beings and—wherever possible—all other forms of life. Though their benevolence was normally limited to mere humanity, the utilitarians who attacked Hegel from the bastion of their empiricism were more reliable moralists than he.

My statement skirts many difficult problems in ethical theory. But that is not the subject of the present book, and in any case these reflections about meaning can be transplanted into the soil of various other normative standards. I mention the utilitarian philosophy because I wish to modify it by proposing that neither happiness nor meaningfulness alone is adequate for defining the good life. An existence that combines the two is preferable to one in which they conflict. And though there is little reason to believe that achieving happiness or meaning in one's own life necessarily depends upon a dedication to happiness and meaning in life as a whole, living in accordance with this composite ideal can serve as an example of human existence at its best and most significant.

George Bernard Shaw advocates a similar ideal in a passage that is worthy of being memorized. Just a few years after he rejected the interviewer's request for a meaning of the "world-comedy," as quoted earlier, he proclaimed one magnificently in the following words:

> This is the true joy in life, the being used for a purpose recognized by yourself as a mighty one; the being thoroughly worn out before you are thrown on the scrap heap; the being a force of Nature instead of a feverish selfish little clod of ailments and grievances complaining that the world will not devote itself to making you happy. And also the only real tragedy in life is the being used by personally minded men for purposes which you recognize to be base. All the rest is at worst mere misfortune and mortality; this alone is misery, slavery, hell on earth; and the revolt against it is the only force that offers a

man's work to the poor artist, whom our personally minded rich people would so willingly employ as pander, buffoon, beauty monger, sentimentalizer, and the like.[10]

Inspiring as it is, this message nevertheless fails to satisfy in several respects. For one thing, Shaw does not tell us where to find the all-engulfing purpose that instils such joy. Does he think that any humanitarian effort will do? Or does he assume that everyone has the capacity to determine which are truly worthy and which are specious or even base? Many of us in the twentieth century shudder at the succession of massive purposes that have squandered human energies for the ends of bigotry, oppression, and unnecessary suffering. At the same time, Shaw understands the benefits of having a mission in life. Except during wartime, democracies devoted to "life, liberty and the pursuit of happiness" have generally ignored the motivational goods that derive from joint commitment to a mighty cause.

Authoritarian regimes have often made a greater effort to impart a single purpose that would make life meaningful for millions of their citizens. When the totalitarian governments fail, as they usually do, it is because they neglect the equally essential demands for freedom and personal happiness. The ideal integration between meaning and happiness has eluded contemporary society in ways that Shaw could not have foreseen when he wrote at the turn of the century.

Moreover, Shaw does not explain what it is to be "a force of Nature." As human beings, we all incorporate divergent and frequently conflicting elements of what is natural. Making ourselves into a force, rather than a selfish clod, means accentuating one or another of these elements—be it aggressiveness or compassion, self-determination or conformity, hatred or love. These and other tendencies in our nature normally interact as vectors that prevent any one of them from dominating exclusively. Does Shaw believe that the true joy in life, the attaining of what is really important, entails a preferential hierarchy among them? If so, how can it be known and used to order our behavior? If not, should we indiscriminately give free rein to all or any instincts, doing whatever bursts forth, regardless of the consequences?

To answer such questions we would have to formulate a complete and unified theory of human nature. Much of recent anthropology and primatology, piecemeal though this research may as yet be, is devoted to constructing that kind of theory. There is no need for me to summarize the scientific data. Nonetheless, two aspects of our natural being should be mentioned as clues for understanding what it means to preserve and perfect life.

I have introduced this expression in an attempt to find some attitude or way of living that we could accept as that which makes a life significant. The effort will be groundless unless we see ourselves as parts of nature. This in turn implies we *have* a nature—both as examplars of an evolutionary species and as diverse but similar individuals within that species. These two aspects bear further analysis.

Nowadays it has become fashionable among philosophers to deny that there is a human nature. Existentialists who reject the idea that man has any definable essence do well to insist that he is always free to change his condition and thus to modify his being extensively. But these modifications occur within limits established by realities that are given to us and not merely chosen—physical laws, biological determinants of life on this planet, social, histori-cal, and cultural realities to which we are born and through which we must fashion our generic as well as our individual nature.[11]

Coordinates such as these, the facts of our condition as human beings together with our personal modes of responding to them, create a dual nature that each of us possesses. To a large degree, success in life requires having the talent and the courage to be true to one's own nature as it has developed throughout the years. We are not endowed with infinite capacities, and we cannot annihilate the lingering presence of the past. To think otherwise is to live in fantasy. We are able to realize what is in us at any moment only to the extent that we harness forces—often too deep or remote in origin for us to perceive them clearly—that have made us what we are. The first requirement for preserving and perfecting life involves allegiance to the potentialities within us that constitute our nature as individuals. We cannot truly be ourselves if we merely drift with the times, passively submit to other people's desires, or refuse to face up to the implications of what we want and what we do. The *acceptance* of our nature—which does not mean compliant acquiescence in faults that we can remedy—is essential for living a meaningful life, and therefore one that is significant as well. It is because we accept our nature that we can improve it. We show respect for what it is even while we alter it in pursuing ideals to which we commit ourselves.

The acceptance of our individual nature is sometimes called "self-love." Traditional religions have often condemned it as a variant of arrogance or hunger for aggrandizement at the expense of others. This assumes that all self-love reduces to selfishness. But that is not the case. On the contrary, self-love can strengthen our capacity to love someone else; and, in general, we cannot love another unless we love ourselves.

Even when it originates as vanity, self-love can become a healthy and commendable attitude. This happens to Mr. Darcy in Jane Austen's novel *Pride and Prejudice*. Though the vain man may seem smug and wholly pleased with his own attributes, he observes himself through the eyes of other people. He tries to gratify his need for self-love through his appearance to them regardless of what he really is or does. If he comes to recognize that self-love cannot be satisfied in a relationship of this sort, he may possibly learn how to make himself *worthy* of approbation. One way of doing this is to act for others in a manner that exceeds his own selfish benefit. To that extent they become separate persons for him rather than mirrors reflecting only himself. He may eventually appreciate the fact that they are autonomous realities and most of what they care about has nothing to do with him. When vanity is transmuted into this greater awareness, self-love remains but now increases, not diminishes, the ability to accept the nature in other people.

Some philosophers have argued that we love others in the same way that we love ourselves. I think they are mistaken. Despite the biblical injunction, we cannot love our neighbor *as* ourselves— for that he is not: we are necessarily different. Through love we accept and bestow value upon whatever it is that makes the neighbor different. And if we managed to love the entire universe, as the nineteenth-century mystic Margaret Fuller said she did, we would love all the myriad properties that distinguish its many components from one another. But are we really able to do this? Much of the world lies beyond our acquaintance and most of it defeats our efforts to appreciate or even understand its inner workings.

For similar reasons we may doubt whether human beings are able to love all of life. And if not, how can they want to preserve and perfect it? Love requires a bestowal of value that unites imagination, intellect, and feeling. But our powers of bestowal are highly circumscribed, and the reach of imagination, intellect, or feeling is always delimited by our cultural and genetic inheritance. Even the saints are bound to some creed that others have manufactured for them, as a kind of uniform that clothes their subtlest intuitions and can always misrepresent the spiritual import of their lives. In wishing to love God by loving all that he has created, we end up loving whatever our conceptual system denotes as "the universe." And in all of us, our willingness to love is often impeded by negative feelings beyond our control. Can anyone love, in the sense that he might love himself or another human being, the virus that has invaded his body and will now proceed to kill him?

If we cannot love all living things as the specific reality that each of them is, we can nevertheless treat them as possible *candidates* for love. We thereby experience every life as something that may be seen within its natural context and from its own point of view. Without being able to speak, the murderous virus affirms its need to live with the same urgency that we feel in wanting to destroy it. We have no reason to love this much of animate existence, but in realizing that we attack it merely because we want to stay alive, and not because of any supreme legitimacy on our part, we recognize its equivalent claim, accept it as a kindred being, and thus identify ourselves with it to some degree.

By extension to the cosmos as a whole, this may be what Nietzsche meant by amor fati. But possibly not. What I have in mind is an ability, as Santayana and perhaps Spinoza would say, "to love the love in [everything]."[12] I interpret this notion to imply that all things that live love themselves inasmuch as they do what they do as a means of preserving and perfecting their own being. We may not, and in fact we cannot, share or even fathom their varied and conflicting interests, many of which are actually self-defeating. But we are capable of imagining that there is in them something comparable to what we experience, even if it is only self-love. And why should one deny that we can accept that aspect of reality?

In making this act of acceptance, we recognize the ontological indefeasibility of other creatures, bestowing value upon it even when we try to annihilate them. We assert an a priori good will toward life in all its variations. What we affirm is nature seeking to preserve and possibly improve itself in each occurrence. To love the love in everything is to acknowledge this as a trope that may be universal in life and to treat it as something we value. That bestowal need not happen; on most occasions it does not happen. But to that extent, I wish to say, we all neglect a potentiality in our being and lose out on opportunities to create a more significant life for ourselves.

I do not speak as one who has succeeded in this endeavor. Love of the love in everything capable of love, acceptance of the striving nature of all things that are alive, is an achievement that few human beings can honestly hope to attain. It is nevertheless an ideal that has mattered to many people—most obviously to the saints and mystics, but also to persons who feel no need for doctrinal affiliations. In pursuing this ideal, we add a dimension to our experience that supplements our practical or material necessities. We thereby enlarge our being as self-regarding animals and align ourselves with that much of nature that seeks to protect and perfect life. Small and isolated as we may be, we thereby establish our place within the universe.

Pantheistic religions have often described this love of love as attunement to a divinity that pervades nature and is present in us even if we repudiate it. Those who feel the force in such religions will understand why I say that accepting one's own nature as well as the nature in everything else contributes to a significant life. But for many others, this idea may seem outrageous. For one thing, they will insist, it implies no particular course of action. It prescribes no deeds that are specifically good in themselves or necessarily beneficial to others. The two types of acceptance to which I have referred would seem to be nothing but attitudes toward life, feelings that may not lead to any detailed effort that changes the world and possibly makes it better. How then can they illuminate what is significant in life? How can we claim to have found a means of exploiting imaginative and creative capabilities that really matter?

This line of criticism is apt and wholly appropriate. All the same, it is short-sighted: it forgets that our strongest attitudes will normally appear in our behavior. Love is emotion that issues into action and often employs the greatest powers of creativity. Directing itself to life in general, it will engender whatever purposiveness is needed under the circumstances. If we love the love in everything, we recognize that all of life is searching for its own meaning and we act accordingly. By enabling others to make their lives more meaningful, we make our own significant. To the degree that we realize this faculty in ourselves, our lives and our experiences truly matter, as much as anything can.

Being a pluralist, I have no desire to specify which conduct is always and uniquely commendable. Nor is there any need to do so. The calamities that human beings have inflicted on themselves are not ordinarily caused by those who have the reverence for life that I am describing. On the other hand, this attitude's importance in the universe should not be overestimated. Nothing in heaven or earth will totally free us from our dependence on the material fate that governs all existence. Once we digest this truth, however, we may learn how to live with our limitations and to cultivate a love that fulfills our nature. To that extent, we not only endure our precarious condition: we complete and partly surmount it.

I previously mentioned Tolstoy's assertion that he learned how to live by observing the simple faith of Russian peasants. Without swallowing the various theses that Tolstoy uses to package his kind of faith, we may agree that even people who have become alienated from their "consciousness of life" can learn how to live. It is not something we learn in the way that we learn how to do mathematics or master a computer program. It would not be a suitable subject for earning credits at a university, and the usual how-to book will not help us very much.

Tolstoy was therefore right when he sought to emulate the attitude of ordinary people working on the land. Philosophy may help to cleanse our thinking, but only in experience itself, in stumbling through life and reflecting about our moments of joy and despair, can we learn how to live. It is something that we all do imperfectly, and the man who concludes that nothing matters has failed in it completely. To help him, we must strengthen his self-love and his love of others. Many things will then be meaningful to him that were not otherwise. If he can identify with the love in everything, including himself, his life will seem significant to him. And indeed it will be.

But what if someone is only interested in "having a good time," pursuing mindless pleasures or the honeyed delights of *la douceur de vivre?* What if he wishes to refine a talent or technique that will never benefit others? What if he merely wants to purify his soul and attain esoteric insights that cannot be communicated to anyone else? These are exotic islands in the ocean of life, and they may sometimes be very beautiful. They can certainly be meaningful, and they can even illustrate how some individuals may approach perfection within a limited compartment of their being. But otherwise, their significance will be virtually nil. They do not reveal how to fulfill one's nature. As Socrates says about the good man in a bad society who withdraws and takes "the shelter of a wall," this partial response may be all he can do under the circumstances and yet he is not functioning fully or reaching his ultimate potentiality.

But surely, one might say, a person could very well insist that he does not want to realize his potential or live what I call a significant life. Like all achievements, it demands sacrifices, and he may be unwilling to make them. A man or woman may prefer the commonplace goods of a selfish but happy existence, or even one that is merely contented, given over to bodily comforts and so undistinguished that most of us might consider it meaningless. If we are faithful to our own pluralism, we cannot maintain that such people have necessarily made a wrong decision. Though our ideals are rooted in human nature, they cannot command allegiance. Those who spurn them are always free to choose their own destiny. A good society will tolerate all ways of life, and all deviations from someone else's, as long as the rights of others are respected.

❊

In attempting to determine what might constitute a life that is both meaningful and significant, I have left unanswered many questions about "the meaning of life." I saw no direct way of handling them. Nevertheless, these questions cannot be dismissed entirely. They linger as a permanent striving to move beyond the barriers of our intellect. Even at the risk of talking nonsense, human beings will always speculate about the universe in its totality. I have no desire to impede that endeavor. I only ask that all proposed solutions about the meaning of life remain coherent with our knowledge of what it is to have a meaningful life. For in that area of exploration we can make definite progress, and perhaps the meaning of life is the life of meaning, the attaining and augmenting of meaningful life in ourselves and in life as a whole.

If I am right in this surmise, we fulfill our basic humanity whenever we live a life that has significance in terms of life itself. Those who love the love in everything, who care about this bestowal and devote themselves to it, experience an authentic love of life. It is a love that yields its own kind of happiness and affords many opportunities for joyfulness. Can anything in nature or reality be better than that?

NOTES

INTRODUCTION

1. Bernard Shaw, *Sixteen Self Sketches* (London: Constable, 1949), pp. 90–91.

2. Quoted in Ernest Jones, M.D., *The Life and Work of Sigmund Freud* (New York: Basic Books, 1953–57), 3:465.

3. Leo Tolstoy, *Confession*, trans. David Patterson (New York: W. W. Norton, 1983), p. 26.

4. Ibid., pp. 27–28.

5. Ibid., pp. 28–29.

6. Ibid., p. 51.

7. Ibid.

8. Ibid., p. 52.

9. Ibid., p. 55.

10. On this, see the chapter on Tolstoy in Karl Stern, *The Flight from Woman* (New York: Paragon House, 1985), pp. 173–97. For an analysis of Tolstoy's *Confession*, see Antony Flew, "What Does It Mean to Ask: 'What is the Meaning of Life?'" in his *The Presumption of Atheism and Other Philosophical Essays on God, Freedom and Immortality* (New York: Barnes & Noble, 1976), pp. 155–67.

11. Thomas Hobbes, *Leviathan*, part I, chap. 13.

12. Ludwig Wittgenstein, *Notebooks 1914–1916*, 2d ed., ed. G. H. von Wright and G. E. M. Anscombe, trans. G. E. M. Anscombe (Chicago: The

University of Chicago Press, 1979), pp. 73e–74e; see also his *Tractatus Logico-Philosophicus*, trans. D. F. Pears and B. F. McGuinness (London: Routledge & Kegan Paul, 1961), pp. 149–51. For a commentary that detects an implied reference to Tolstoy in the relevant passage, see G. E. M. Anscombe, *An Introduction to Wittgenstein's Tractatus* (London: Hutchinson University Library, 1963), p. 170.

13. Douglas Adams, *The Hitchhiker's Guide to the Galaxy* (New York: Pocket Books, 1981), p. 181.

CHAPTER 1. THE MEANING OF LIFE

1. Friedrich Nietzsche, *Ecce Homo,* in his *On the Genealogy of Morals and Ecce Homo,* trans. Walter Kaufmann and R. J. Hollingdale (New York: Vintage Books, 1967), p. 258.

2. There are lengthier analyses of the relationship among these three philosophers in my trilogy *The Nature of Love* (Chicago: The University of Chicago Press, 1984–87). See volume 2, *The Nature of Love: Courtly and Romantic,* pp. 393–411, 443–68; and volume 3, *The Nature of Love: The Modern World,* pp. 65–94.

3. See Paul Edwards, "Why?" in *The Meaning of Life,* ed. E. D. Klemke (New York: Oxford University Press, 1981), pp. 227–40.

4. William James, *Pragmatism: A New Name for Some Old Ways of Thinking* (New York: Longmans, Green, 1910), pp. 106–7.

5. *The Dialogues of Plato,* trans. B. Jowett (New York: Random House, 1937), 2:14.

6. On this, see A. J. Ayer, "The Claims of Philosophy," in *Philosophy of the Social Sciences,* ed. Maurice Natanson (New York: Random House, 1963), pp. 475–79; and Robert Nozick, *Philosophical Explanations* (Cambridge: Harvard University Press, 1981), pp. 588ff. For a contrasting view, see Reinhold Niebuhr, "The Self and Its Search for Ultimate Meaning," in *The Meaning of Life,* ed. Klemke, pp. 41–45.

7. On this, see the following essays in *The Meaning of Life: Questions, Answers and Analysis,* ed. Steven Sanders and David R. Cheney (Englewood Cliffs, N.J.: Prentice-Hall, 1980): Kurt Baier, "The Meaning of Life," pp. 47–63; R. W. Hepburn, "Questions about the Meaning of Life," pp. 113–28. See also Ilham Dilman, "Professor Hepburn on Meaning in Life," *Religious Studies* 3 (Apr. 1968): 547–54; and his essay "Life and Meaning," in Ilham Dilman and D. Z. Phillips, *Sense and Delusion* (New York: Humanities Press, 1971), pp. 1–39.

8. Cf. John Wisdom, "The Meanings of the Questions of Life," in his *Paradox and Discovery* (Oxford: Basil Blackwell, 1965), pp. 38–42.

9. Albert Camus, "An Absurd Reasoning," in his *The Myth of Sisyphus and Other Essays,* trans. Justin O'Brien (New York: Vintage Books, 1955), p. 21.

10. Thomas Nagel, "The Absurd," in his *Mortal Questions* (Cambridge: Cambridge University Press, 1979), p. 21.

11. Ibid., p. 23.

12. Thomas Nagel, *The View from Nowhere* (New York: Oxford University Press, 1986), p. 223.

13. Simone de Beauvoir, *The Ethics of Ambiguity*, trans. Bernard Frechtman (New York: Philosophical Library, 1948), p. 129.

14. *Leaves of Grass* (1891–92), 32.

CHAPTER 2. THE MEANING OF DEATH

1. George Santayana, "A Long Way Round to Nirvana; or Much Ado about Dying," in his *Some Turns of Thought in Modern Philosophy: Five Essays* (New York: Charles Scribner's Sons, 1933), pp. 98–101.

2. See Martin Heidegger, *Being and Time*, sections 50–53.

3. For Heidegger on death, see E. F. Kaelin, *Being and Time: A Reading for Readers* (Tallahassee: Florida State University, 1988), pp. 154–65; Michael Gelven, *A Commentary on Heidegger's Being and Time* (New York: Harper and Row, 1970), pp. 137–58. See also Paul Edwards, *Heidegger on Death: A Critical Evaluation* (La Salle, Ill.: The Hegeler Institute, 1979). For Heidegger on "authentic existence," see Gelven, *Commentary*, pp. 159–72.

4. Jean-Paul Sartre, *Being and Nothingness*, trans. Hazel E. Barnes (New York: Washington Square Press, 1966), pp. 682–83. For Sartre's views on death as well as Heidegger's, see Jacques Choron, *Death and Western Thought* (New York: Collier Books, 1963), pp. 230–54.

5. Sartre, *Being and Nothingness*, p. 678. Italics deleted.

6. Ibid., p. 690.

7. Quoted in Simone de Beauvoir, *Adieux: A Farewell to Sartre*, trans. Patrick O'Brian (New York: Pantheon, 1984), p. 432.

8. Nagel, *The View from Nowhere*, p. 228.

9. Richard Wilbur, "The Genie in the Bottle," in *Mid-Century American Poets*, ed. John Ciardi (New York: Twayne, 1950), p. 7.

10. "Do Not Go Gentle into That Good Night," in *The Collected Poems of Dylan Thomas, 1934–1952* (New York: New Directions, 1971), p. 128.

11. On the acceptance of death, see also Richard Wollheim, *The Thread of Life* (Cambridge: Harvard University Press, 1984), pp. 281–83.

12. For a different, though complementary analysis, see Derek Parfit, *Reasons and Persons* (Oxford: Oxford University Press, 1986), pp. 174–77.

13. *As You Like It*, Act IV, scene i.

14. Quoted in Choron, *Death and Western Thought*, p. 258.

15. T. S. Eliot, "A Dedication to My Wife," in his *Collected Poems 1909–1962* (New York: Harcourt, Brace & World, 1963), p. 221.

CHAPTER 3. THE CREATION OF MEANING

1. George Santayana, "A Brief History of My Opinions," in *The Philosophy of Santayana*, ed. Irwin Edman (New York: Modern Library, 1936), p. 8.

2. See Rudolf Carnap, "The Overcoming of Metaphysics through Logical

Analysis of Language," in *Heidegger and Modern Philosophy: Critical Essays*, ed. Michael Murray (New Haven: Yale University Press, 1978), pp. 23–24. For a more sympathetic analysis of Heidegger's views, see, in the same volume, Stanley Rosen, "Thinking about Nothing," pp. 116–37.

3. See Martin Heidegger, "What Is Metaphysics?" in *Basic Writings from Being and Time (1927) to The Task of Thinking (1964)*, ed. David Farrell Krell (New York: Harper and Row, 1977), pp. 71–112.

4. Tom Stoppard, *Rosencrantz and Guildenstern Are Dead* (New York: Grove Press, 1968), p. 128. The two sets of three ellipsis points are in the original text.

5. "Notes on Talks with Wittgenstein," appended to Ludwig Wittgenstein, "A Lecture on Ethics," trans. Max Black, *The Philosophical Review* 74, No. 1 (Jan. 1965): 12. See also Michael Murray, "Wittgenstein on Heidegger on Being and Dread," in *Heidegger and Modern Philosophy*, pp. 80–83.

6. Albert Einstein, in *Living Philosophies* (New York: Simon & Schuster, 1931), p. 6.

7. William James, "Is Life Worth Living?" in his *Essays on Faith and Morals* (New York: New American Library, 1974), p. 19.

8. Baruch de Spinoza, *Ethics*, in *The Collected Works of Spinoza*, ed. and trans. Edwin Curley (Princeton: Princeton University Press, 1985), vol. 1, pt. 3, prop. 7.

9. For recent discussions about the nature of ideals, see John Kekes, *The Examined Life* (Lewisburg, Pa.: Bucknell University Press, 1988), pp. 77–94; and Robert Nozick, *The Examined Life: Philosophical Meditations* (New York: Simon & Schuster, 1989), pp. 279–85.

CHAPTER 4. LIVES OF MEANING AND SIGNIFICANCE

1. John Stuart Mill, *Autobiography*, in *John Stuart Mill: A Selection of His Works*, ed. John M. Robson (New York: Odyssey Press, 1966), p. 279.

2. Ibid., p. 286.

3. John Stuart Mill, *Utilitarianism*, in *John Stuart Mill: A Selection of His Works*, ed. Robson, p. 161.

4. On Mill's ideas about happiness, see Fred R. Berger, *Happiness, Justice and Freedom: The Moral and Political Philosophy of John Stuart Mill* (Berkeley: University of California Press, 1984), pp. 30–120, 281–89. On the nature of happiness, see Elizabeth Telfer, *Happiness* (London: Macmillan, 1980); Paul W. Taylor, *Principles of Ethics: An Introduction* (Belmont, Calif.: Wadsworth, 1975), pp. 129–43; and Kekes, *The Examined Life*, pp. 161–73.

5. For different ideas about an overall "plan of life," see *Aristotle's Eudemian Ethics: Books I, II, and VIII*, trans. Michael Woods (Oxford: Clarendon Press, 1982), book I, chap. 2 and pp. 52–53; Robert Nozick, *Anarchy, State, and Utopia* (New York: Basic Books, 1974), pp. 50–51; John Rawls, *A Theory of Justice* (Cambridge: Harvard University Press, 1971), pp. 407ff; and Josiah Royce, *The Philosophy of Loyalty*, in *The Basic Writings of Josiah Royce*, ed. John J. McDermott (Chicago: The University of Chicago Press, 1969), 2:920–23.

6. Richard Taylor, "The Meaning of Human Existence," in *Values in Conflict: Life, Liberty, and the Rule of Law*, ed. Burton M. Leiser (New York: Macmillan, 1981), p. 24. See also Richard Taylor, "Time and Life's Meaning," in *Reflective Wisdom: Richard Taylor on Issues That Matter*, ed. John Donnelly (Buffalo: Prometheus, 1989), pp. 38–47; and Richard Taylor, *Good and Evil: A New Direction* (Buffalo: Prometheus, 1984), pp. 256–68.

7. Taylor, "The Meaning of Human Existence," p. 9.

8. Ibid., p. 10.

9. William James, "What Makes a Life Significant?" in his *Essays on Faith and Morals*, pp. 308–9.

10. Ibid., p. 304.

11. *Henry IV*, Pt. 2, Act III, scene i.

12. See R. M. Hare, " 'Nothing Matters,' " in *The Meaning of Life: Questions, Answers and Analysis*, ed. Sanders and Cheney, pp. 97–103.

13. For further discussion of self-fulfillment in relation to meaning in life, see Joel Feinberg, "Absurd Self-Fulfillment," in *Philosophy and the Human Condition*, 2d ed., ed. Tom L. Beauchamp, Joel Feinberg, James M. Smith (Englewood Cliffs: Prentice-Hall, 1989), pp. 586–605.

CONCLUSION

1. On this, see David Wiggins, "Truth, Invention and the Meaning of Life," in his *Needs, Values, Truth: Essays in the Philosophy of Value* (Oxford: Basil Blackwell, 1987), pp. 88ff; and Marvin Kohl, "Meaning of Life and Happiness: A Preliminary Outline," *Dialectics and Humanism* 4 (1981): 39–43.

2. Thornton Wilder, *Our Town* (New York: Avon Books, 1975), pp. 138–39.

3. See Paul Tillich, "The Eternal Now," in *The Meaning of Death*, ed. Herman Feifel (New York: McGraw-Hill, 1959), pp. 30–38.

4. *Hippolytus*, 189.

5. Wittgenstein, *Tractatus Logico-Philosophicus*, p. 149; see also Warren Shibles, "Wittgenstein," in his *Death: An Interdisciplinary Analysis* (Whitewater, Wis.: The Language Press, 1974), pp. 69–80. For doubts about the superior goodness of a future life, see A. J. Ayer, *The Meaning of Life and Other Essays* (London: Weidenfeld & Nicolson, 1990), pp. 203–4.

6. Wittgenstein, *Notebooks 1914–1916*, p. 75e; see also his *Tractatus Logico-Philosophicus*, p. 147.

7. Byron, *Euthanasia*; Sophocles, *Oedipus at Colonus*, 1225—both quoted approvingly in Arthur Schopenhauer, *The World as Will and Representation*, trans. E. F. J. Payne (New York: Dover, 1966), 2:587–88.

8. Nagel, "Death," in his *Mortal Questions*, p. 2.

9. For further discussions of Nagel's position, see Mary Mothersill, "Death," in *Life and Meaning: A Reader*, ed. Oswald Hanfling (Oxford: Basil Blackwell, 1987), pp. 83–92; and Bernard Williams, "The Makropulos Case: Reflections on the Tedium of Immortality," in *Problems of the Self: Philosophical*

Papers 1956–1972 (Cambridge: Cambridge University Press, 1973), pp. 87–89ff.

10. Bernard Shaw, "Epistle Dedicatory to Arthur Bingham Walkley," in *Man and Superman: A Comedy and a Philosophy* (New York: Brentano's, 1905), pp. xxxi–xxxii.

11. On the concept of human nature, see Oswald Hanfling, *The Quest for Meaning* (New York: Basil Blackwell, 1988), pp. 109–64; and Kekes, *The Examined Life*, pp. 31–44.

12. George Santayana, "Ultimate Religion," in *The Philosophy of Santayana*, ed. Edman, p. 581.

INDEX